RELIGIOUS PLURALISM IN CHRISTIAN AND ISLAMIC PHILOSOPHY

The Thought of John Hick and Seyyed Hossein Nasr

RELIGIOUS PLURALISM IN CHRISTIAN AND ISLAMIC PHILOSOPHY

The Thought of John Hick and Seyyed Hossein Nasr

Adnan Aslan

CURZON

BRITAIN & JAPAN: BIOGRAPHICAL PORTRAITS

First published 1994 by
JAPAN LIBRARY
Knoll House, 35 The Crescent, Sandgate
Folkestone, Kent, CT20 3EE

Japan Library is an imprint of Curzon Press Ltd
Richmond, Surrey, United Kingdom
www.curzonpress.co.uk

ISBN   1-873410-27-1

British Library Cataloguing in Publication Data
A CIP entry for this book is available
from the British Library

Produced by Bookchase UK Ltd

Contents

Contents

Acknowledgements

This book originated as a thesis written during my time at the Department of Religious Studies, Lancaster University, and was submitted in the autumn of 1995.

During this period of research I have received much support from my family and friends which, together with the thoughtful guidance and encouragement of Prof. Oliver Leaman and Prof. John Clayton, have made these challenging years exciting and worthwhile. I should also like to thank John Hick and Seyyed Hossein Nasr for their guidance and providing me with the opportunity to interview them.

This undertaking would not have been possible if The Centre for Islamic Studies in Istanbul had not sponsored me during my postgraduate studies in England. I would like to extend my thanks to all my colleagues in The Centre.

Introduction

Disciplines such as philosophy of religion and theology are, to a certain extent, related to the culture in which they have developed. Such fields of study provide a source of values and vision to the culture of which they are a part while at the same time being delimited and defined by their culture. With this in mind, we should expect that the predominantly secular and partly liberal Western culture would stamp its norms and values on the disciplines it has produced. Herein lies a problem for those whose mind has been constructed according to the norms and values of non-Western culture and who want to undertake research in the West. One is inevitably confronted with linguistic, methodological and 'ideological' problems that would not appear to be problematic to a Westerner.

Central to this enquiry is the theme of religious pluralism. This subject risks being overlooked because it is located in the no-man's land that lies between theology and the philosophy of religion. In theology, the question of religious pluralism is generally introduced under the subject of theology of religions in which religions are viewed from the perspective of the paradigms of inclusivism or exclusivism. Generally, religious pluralism is more at home in philosophy of religion than theology, although it seems less inherently philosophical when compared with the main subjects of philosophy of religion such as the arguments for and against the existence of God and the problem of evil.

It was only with the emergence of modernism, the concomitant marginalisation of confessional language in theology and religious studies, and the advances in communication technology that religious pluralism could become an important area of philosophy of religion. This trend has been greatly enhanced by the work of John Hick. As one writing from a position of religious commitment, I am of the view that the problem of religious pluralism is a more serious one for religious people than is, for example, the question of the existence of God or the problem of evil. I would argue that for the believer, the question of the existence of God does not pose a major threat to his or her devotional life; if the believer engages with such a question it is not generally because he or she doubts the existence of God, but because the question functions as a useful tool in rationalising the faith that has already been accepted. One could argue that, whereas the question of God's existence is theoretical and speculative, the problem of religious pluralism is a practical and unavoidable problem.

Since our enquiry places itself within the boundaries of the philosophy of religion, it is normative and critical and does not pretend to be a value free enquiry.[1] It makes its own value-judgements and endeavours to justify them.

On the other hand, this study compares the ideas of two contemporary philosophers, John Hick and Seyyed Hossein Nasr on the issue of religion, religions, the concept of Ultimate Reality and the notion of sacred knowledge. But, on a broader level, it compares two worldviews; it considers the worldview formed by Western culture, which is religious in its intention but secular in its essence, against the worldview which is formed through the assimilation of traditional wisdom, which is against the norms of secular culture and therefore religious in its intention as well as in its essence. Although the topics that I am dealing with are limited in scope, the principles behind the topics are broad. They can be regarded as a Muslim response to the questions with which the book deals.

What are the main reasons which led me to study the issue of religious pluralism in the writings of John Hick and Seyyed Hossein Nasr? This question somehow related to my own personal experience. As a person who was brought up and educated in a traditional Muslim society and who feels strongly about the truth of Islam, I have always considered the question of salvation as one of the vital existential questions in my own life. When I came to England to carry out postgraduate study in Religious Studies, and consequently met several people from different traditions, the question which came immediately to my mind was whether or not they would be saved. If they are excluded from salvation simply because they were not born to the society to which I was born, then how could I justify the soteriological claims of my religion? In other words, if in the majority of cases, we simply inherit religious 'truth' from our parents and community, how can we reasonably justify the good and bad consequences of holding such a belief?

The question of salvation has always been a vital one for me because it poses a threat to my religious identity. In this area, John Hick was the first person that was drawn to my attention. When I first read Hick, I was impressed and more or less accepted almost everything that he said. However, the more I read and considered his ideas the more I felt uncertain about those aspects of Hick's thought which conflict with the traditional view that I hold. Over time I have become gradually convinced that there should be a viable answer from an Islamic perspective to those issues that Hick is dealing with, including the issue of religious pluralism. I also believe that a Muslim contribution to the discussion would be useful for those who are interested in building a peaceful world community. What is the best way of making such a contribution? I came to conclude that the best way to bring out the potential of Islamic culture, was to find a contemporary Muslim thinker and compare him with Hick.

It is hard to find a Muslim thinker who writes in English and deals with contemporary issues of philosophy of religion. When I first started to read Nasr, I became convinced that he would be an interesting thinker to compare with Hick.

Now let me point out how some of the difficulties involved in considering the issue of pluralism according to Hick and Nasr affected this study. At first sight, Hick and Nasr appear intellectually too far apart to enable one to produce a reasonable comparison between them. This is not because they belong to different traditions, but because their central concern is different. While Hick focuses on the issue of religious pluralism, Nasr deals with the perennial philosophy, and its notion of tradition. But in the course of time it became apparent that Nasr's notion of tradition is in fact a form of 'religious pluralism'. When I discovered this, everything fell into place.

The diversity of Hick's and Nasr's writings, nevertheless compelled me to carry out a general rather than detailed comparison. I will consider major themes such as religion, the concept of Ultimate Reality and knowledge, and address those issues as they are dealt with by Hick and Nasr. In order to do this, I will divide each chapter into two parts: the first will deal with Hick's views, the second with Nasr's. If appropriate I will offer a comparison of the particular solutions offered by them.

Although Nasr and Hick are contemporary, they have hardly written anything about, or made any comment on, each other's work. This has on occasion put me in the position of having to speculate on what Nasr's opinion would be about Hick's thought, or Hick's opinion about Nasr's thought.

When I say 'from the traditional point of view' with regard to any ideas, I mean from the perspective of the perennial philosophy in general, and from Nasr's point of view in particular. When I make some comments on Nasr's views from the perspective of Hick I present those comments under the term 'the modern outlook'.

The quest to find a satisfactory answer to the question of the plurality of religions has functioned as a driving force in this book. But I shall not make attempt to address the issue directly in order to produce an answer independent of Hick and Nasr. Rather I prefer to present their views in a way that implicitly conforms to the answer that I have in mind.

In considering the truth claims of religions three paradigms have emerged in contemporary religious studies: pluralism, exclusivism and inclusivism. There are, of course many forms of pluralism. I am interested in a pluralism that aims to encompass all religions within a plausible framework while maintaining belief in the existence of a Transcendent Reality. In this sense, the pluralist paradigm has been characterised as one that claims that different religions provide an equally salvific path to one God. Exclusivism, on the other hand, claims the authenticity of one religion as the salvific path to God, while inclusivism sees one religion as the fulfilment of other paths. Now let me offer a brief account of these paradigms with regard to Christianity.

Christianity has historically been exclusivist. An important representative of this approach from the Protestant side is Hendrik Kraemer, a Dutch missionary. He presented his views on this issue in his two influential books, *The Christian Message in a Non-Christian World* (1938) and *Religion and Christian Faith* (1956). In the Catholic world, however, the majority of the theologians have maintained a Thomist line, categorising non-Christians as infidels. '*Extra ecclesiam nulla salus*' (there is no salvation outside the Church) was the official line, and was maintained until Vatican II.[2]

Inclusivism, has mainly developed as a response from Christian orthodoxy to the pressure posed by the pluralist paradigm. During the first half of this century, the Scottish Protestant missionary in India John Farquhar, in his *The Crown of Hinduism* (1913) defended inclusivism. In Catholicism an attempt was made to interpret the Thomist line as allowing for inclusivism, as exemplified by Philippe Glorieux. Later John Robinson and Paul Tillich defended a liberal form of Christian inclusivism. The process-theologian philosopher, John Cobb maintained a tangible form of inclusivism examining Buddhism from the perspective of Christianity in his *Beyond Dialogue: Towards a Mutual Transformation of Christianity and Buddhism* (1982). The prominent representative of this paradigm, and the author of the term 'anonymous Christians' is of course Karl Rahner. His main writings on this topic are found in his *Theological Investigations*, published in twenty volumes between 1961 and 1984.[3]

The paradigm with which this inquiry is concerned is pluralism. A form of pluralism in the first part of this century is defended by Ernst Troeltsch in his essay, 'The Place of Christianity Among the World Religions' (1923). Later the American philosopher William Hocking in his *Re-thinking Missions* spoke about the historical and cultural relativism of Christianity. The English historian Arnold Toynbee in his *Christianity Among the Religions of the World* (1957) followed Troeltsch's form of pluralism. The Canadian historian of religion, Wilfred Cantwell Smith, a predecessor of Hick, argued for a world theology as a form of diverse, yet in certain respects unified, living religiosity. The prominent representative of this paradigm is John Hick. Unlike others Hick puts this issue at the centre of his intellectual enterprise.[4]

These three paradigms do not cover the entire theological spectrum. To categorise from the perspective of these three paradigms is often misleading. Nasr would be a case in point. He sounds pluralist in that he endorses the validity of every revealed religion as a path to salvation; and yet he also refuses to endorse certain ideological aspects of pluralism. For Hick, pluralism is 'truth' and therefore religions must modify their truth to the truth of pluralism by making substantial revisions of their theological tenets. For Nasr, the truth is the 'truths' of revealed religions; what we must do is to be humble before such 'truth' and accept it without seeking to change it. Our duty, Nasr would say, is not to invent truth but to be transparent before truth and reflect it as it is.

Holding such ideas inevitably affects their methods and the intellectual contribution which they make to the field of religious studies. Hick trusts reason and science and human ability to produce good; he is quite clear and articulate and operates within the framework of the Western philosophical tradition. Nasr, on the other hand, believes reason to be limited, and considers secular science as irrelevant in one's quest for the Real. He believes that it is not reason but intellect (mystical vision) which plays a significant part in one's perception of Reality. He does not operate within the framework of the Western philosophical tradition.

To understand Nasr's ideas we need to be aware of his distinction between philosophy and metaphysics. By defining metaphysics or *scientia sacra* as 'the science of Ultimate Reality', Nasr aims not only to distinguish it from metaphysics in its conventional sense, but also to present it as the only 'discipline' or 'science' through which one can attain Ultimate Reality. According to Nasr, philosophy is based on reason and sense experience, whereas metaphysics, although drawing upon reason, is fundamentally based on the intellect (mystical vision). Philosophy aims to convince people, while metaphysics aims to illuminate and sanctify those who are prepared to undergo such transformation. In Nasr's thought Kant's *Critique of Pure Reason* would represent philosophy, whereas 'Arabi's *Bezels of Wisdom* would represent metaphysics.

If this thesis sounds less critical with regard to the ideas of Nasr, it is because of the 'metaphysical' nature of his writings. When I read Nasr as saying that religions develop according to their celestial archetypes, I am in a certain respect compelled either to endorse it or to dismiss it altogether. He does not present an argument for his opinion in such a way that one could produce a counter argument. What he does is to cite a proposition or belief as if it is revealed from heaven. Such a way of presenting the issues leaves little room for proper philosophical discussion. Hick, on the other hand, is articulate and clear and, offers his point of view through a philosophical discussion in a thought provoking manner.[5] If this study appears less critical and more appreciative with regard to Nasr's ideas, and more critical and less appreciative with regard to Hick's ideas, that is because I, as an insider, am naturally more able to delve into the depth of Nasr's ideas and therefore to present Nasr in a manner that exhibits my ability as such. On the other hand, in spite of a considerable effort on my part to engage with Hick's thought, I remain an outsider with regard to Hick's ideas. Hence, it has been difficult for me to operate through the same norms as Hick. I believe the same thing would be the case for a British student of religion studying Nasr.

It might seem that too much attention has been given to the background of Hick and Nasr. I believe that such a presentation is necessary to place the two philosophers in the cultural atmosphere in which they are writing. Wilfred Cantwell Smith will be referred to in order illuminate the background of Hick's hypothesis of religious pluralism. An account of the perennial philosophy, on the other hand, will be offered in order to indicate Nasr's background and the cultural norms through which he has developed his ideas. Several meetings with Hick and Nasr during the writing of this work provided me with a further dimension in my attempt to comprehend their ideas. During this time, I have discovered that religion is not the subject of scholarship. It is the most effective thing in shaping one's existential life.

'The first meeting with the writings of Seyyed Hossein Nasr may often leave one either pleasantly surprised or disconcerted and annoyed,' writes William Chittick. It is true that Nasr may sound annoying to those who see Western rationality as the only criterion for truth. In this study, however, I have made no effort to make Nasr's ideas more 'pleasing' since I felt that this would be a total misrepresentation of him. Rather I have preferred to develop Nasr's ideas along the same line as he sought to develop them without considering the implication with regard to the norms of modern thought.

By presenting comprehensive intellectual biographies of Hick and Nasr, this study aims to create an affinity between the reader and the life and thought of the two philosophers. Reading and contemplating their life stories will once again remind us of the fact that the ideas which we come across in books can always make more sense when they are considered within the context of the life experience of the authors. Chapter two will seek further to illuminate the background or the sources of their opinion by depicting the characteristics of the intellectual and spiritual abode in which they and their ideas evolved. Attention will be drawn to the distinct characteristics of their ideas in such a manner that Hick's ideas may be labelled as 'secular', and Nasr's 'religious'. Chapter three will simply seek to present the role of knowledge, sacred and otherwise, in relating human beings and the universe to the Ultimate, or the Ultimate to human beings and the universe. In the remaining three chapters the focus will be shifted towards the issue of religious pluralism. Chapter four will explore the factors that indicate the need for a pluralistic approach in religion. Chapter five, on the other hand, examines the plausibility of holding a genuinely pluralistic attitude while believing in one Transcendent Reality and being committed to the norms and values of one religion. At the end, chapter six will investigate the possibility of settling the question through the mainstream 'theological' body of Islam and Christianity by exploring the potential of these revealed religions in this respect.

Chapter One

Intellectual Biographies

In this opening chapter I would like to present comprehensive intellectual biographies of both John Hick and Seyyed Hossein Nasr. I consider such an account to be of value since there is an interesting correlation between their life experiences and their thought. As will be pointed out, Hick's 'Birmingham experience' and Nasr's education in America have played an important part in their intellectual outlook.

In Hick's biography, I shall highlight certain events which influenced Hick's intellectual development. I will also mention some of the prominent thinkers from whom Hick derived his ideas and inspiration. The major publications of Hick and Nasr will be referred to as important landmarks in their life. I will conclude the first part of this chapter by citing a long paragraph through which Hick himself eloquently summarises his attitude toward the major traditions of humanity.

As far as Nasr is concerned, this chapter will draw attention to the impact his traditional as well as 'modern' education has had upon his thought. There were three major events which marked Nasr's career. The first was his move to America when he was thirteen. This provided him with an opportunity to acquaint himself with Western thought. The second is Nasr's return to Iran from America after gaining a Ph.D. at Harvard. This event helped him to realise his intellectual potential which he acquired in America. The third is the political turmoil in Iran in 1979, which forced Nasr to leave his home country. This event, strangely enough, played a significant part in establishing Nasr's international reputation as a philosopher. I will conclude this chapter by citing a long passage that summarises his quest for the eternal *sophia*.

★ ★ ★

JOHN HICK

John Harwood Hick was born in Scarborough, Yorkshire on 20 January 1922. As a child, he was taken to the local Anglican parish church. He was not impressed by his early religious education; the services, as he remembers, were 'a matter of infinite boredom'.[1] Although dissatisfied with what the Church offered him in his spiritual quest, Hick always maintained the belief in a 'rather strong sense of the reality of God as the personal and loving lord of the universe'.[2]

When he was eighteen years old, he had already started pursuing a more meaningful spirituality outside Christianity. When he read *The Principles of Theosophy* – a book about a Western version of the Hindu vedantic philosophy – he thought that he had encountered the first comprehensive and coherent interpretation of life. Although initially impressed, Hick later, rejected the book on the ground that it was 'too tidy and impersonal'.[3]

Hick was in his late teens when he realised that he was in a 'state of spiritual searching' which led him to conclude: 'The eastern religious world, in the form of theosophy, was attractive, but not sufficiently so for me to enter it. The western religious world of Christianity was all around me but seemed utterly lifeless and uninteresting'.[4]

From his early youth Hick began to realise the value of possessing 'an independent and questioning mind'. It was this ability that set Hick off on an intellectual journey to find a more satisfying and spiritually accommodating religious outlook in which he would feel at home.[5]

Hick began his university education as a law student at the University of Hull where his intellectual life was marked by a very important event, a religious conversion by which 'the whole world of Christian belief and experience came vividly to life', making him a 'Christian of a strong evangelical and indeed fundamentalist kind'.[6] He describes his conversion experience (which took place on the top deck of a bus) as follows:

> As everyone will be conscious who can themselves remember such a moment, all descriptions are inadequate. But it was as though the skies opened up and light poured down and filled me with a sense of overflowing joy in response to an immense transcendent goodness and love. I remember that I couldn't help smiling broadly – smiling back, as it were, at God – though

if any of the other passengers were looking they must have thought that I was a lunatic, grinning at nothing.[7]

Hick's conversion experience which occurred through the power of 'the New Testament picture of Jesus Christ' was not a sudden and easy one. It was, rather, a result of a 'period of several days of intense inner turmoil'.[8] This disturbing demand became a liberating invitation leading him to the world of Christian faith with great joy. As a result of this, he accepted 'as a whole without question the entire evangelical package of theology – the verbal inspiration of the Bible; creation and fall; Jesus as God the Son incarnate, born of a virgin, conscious of his divine nature and performing miracles of divine power; redemption by his blood from sin and guilt; his bodily resurrection and ascension and future return in glory; heaven and hell'.[9]

By instinct 'conservative, cautious and timid'[10] but intellectually liberal, high-spirited and daring, Hick was eventually to reach the conclusion that this package of evangelical theology required reinterpretation and needed to be modified to a certain degree.[11]

In 1942, Hick joined the Presbyterian Church of England with the intention of entering the Christian ministry. In the same year, Hick's quest for truth and a more comprehensive and coherent *Weltanschauung* convinced him to pursue a degree course in philosophy.[12] For this purpose he enrolled at Edinburgh University where he came to know Norman Kemp Smith, an idealist Kantian scholar who made the best contemporary translation of Kant's *Critique of Pure Reason* into English. Smith's impact upon Hick's thought is quite remarkable. As Hick also acknowledges, the main ideas of his D.Phil. thesis were inspired by the philosophical teachings of Kemp Smith.[13]

From then on, Hick established a Kantian attitude in his philosophy of religion, reading Kant through Kemp Smith. Kant has always remained one of the most important sources of his ideas. The substantial Kantian ingredients can be first seen in his theory of faith, in which faith is defined as an interpretative element within religious experience, which is the major theme of *Faith and Knowledge*. Kantian influence has also played a major role in constituting his hypothesis of religious pluralism.

At Edinburgh University, Hick was a keen member of the Christian Union 'attending virtually all its Bible studies, prayer meetings and talks, and engaging in such evangelistic activities'.[14] But unfortunately, his education was interrupted by the Second World

War,[15] which forced him to leave Edinburgh. During the war, he went to the Middle East, Italy and Greece to serve in the Friends' Ambulance Unit.[16] In 1944, during a calm winter in Italy, Hick started to fill a note book with the outline of his theory of religious cognition, which was the first sketch of his D.Phil. thesis.[17] This was published as his first book, *Faith and Knowledge*.

Although Hick spent many months in Muslim Egypt, Syria and Lebanon, and a short time in Palestine during the war, he 'had no appreciation whatever of Islam or Judaism as religions'.[18] After the war, Hick returned to Edinburgh to continue his education. Although he was 'as emphatically a Christian as before',[19] he did not rejoin the Christian Union.

With the help of his training in philosophy and his fresh experience of the war, Hick came to notice that there was little sympathy for the questioning mind in the circle of Christian fellowship. He began to feel some discomfort in such an environment and instead looked for a place where he would feel more intellectually at home. However, his evangelical background helped him to enter imaginatively into the mind of the evangelical Christians:

> ... I believe that anyone who is either born or 'born again' into the conservative evangelical thought world, and who has a questioning mind, will find that he has to face challenges to the belief system within which his Christian faith was first made available to him, and will almost certainly be led by rational or moral considerations to modify or discard many of its elements. His response to Jesus Christ as his lord, and as his saviour from alienation from God, may remain the same; but the body of theological theories associated with it in his mind will usually change, and surely ought to change, in the light of further living, learning and thinking.[20]

In 1948, having graduated from Edinburgh University with first class honours, Hick began a research programme at Oriel College, Oxford, with the help of a Campell Fraser scholarship under 'the benign but penetrating critical supervision of H. H. Price',[21] whose implicit influence on Hick can be discerned in his writings.

In 1950, Hick completed his doctoral thesis, and then went on to Westminster Theological College, Cambridge. There he undertook his first formal study of theology. This comprised courses of Old and New Testament studies, Christian Doctrine and Church History.[22] In 1953, after qualifying as a minister, Hick moved to Belford

Presbyterian Church, Northumberland, to take up his only parish appointment which he held until 1956. There he wrote the manuscript for his first book, *Faith and Knowledge*.[23]

In 1956, Hick moved to America to take up the post of Assistant Professor of Philosophy at Cornell University, where he worked until 1959. After being appointed to the Stuart Professorship of Christian Philosophy at Princeton Theological Seminary (1959–1964), two major events which affected Hick's intellectual development took place.

The first was the publication of his book *Faith and Knowledge* in 1957 by Cornell University Press.[24] The book has played an important role in Hick's philosophy of religion.[25] In it, Hick introduced his revolutionary theory of faith as a total interpretation of the universe which functions as the interpretative element within religious experience. This theory is revolutionary because it asserts that faith is not an affirmation of certain 'revealed' propositions, but is a way of looking at or interpreting the things that we encounter.[26] However, when faith is defined as a total interpretation of the universe, the emphasis upon believing the revealed propositions of a particular religion is minimised. Hence it opens the way by which one can acknowledge the value of other religions. In *Faith and Knowledge*, although Hick makes no explicit reference to other traditions such as Islam, Buddhism and Hinduism as alternative ways of seeing things, his view of faith is a basis for a kind of extrapolation which can embrace the great religions of humankind.

Two terms, 'interpretative element' and 'religious experience', employed in his view of faith, give us a clue about the source from which Hick derived this theory. The term 'interpretative element' connotes Kant; 'religious experience', William James. As Hick himself acknowledges, a Kantian notion that the mind plays an active role in experience is reformulated within the religious context, and therefore faith is recognised as the interpretative element within religious experience.[27] Kant's impact upon Hick has prevailed as one of the essential features of his intellectual development. In this respect, however, one thing must be pointed out whenever Hick borrows ideas or concepts from Kant. What he does is extrapolate from them in order to use them for his purpose, which often goes beyond what Kant meant by those concepts. For example, contrary to Hick, Kant would not have sanctioned any attempt to account for experience of God, because Kant did not think it was possible. Hick's application of the noumena and phenomena distinction to the experience of the Real and its manifestations is also meaningless as far as Kant's philosophy is concerned.[28]

In *The Varieties of Religious Experience*, William James, dividing religion into the institutional and the personal,[29] successfully shifted the focus of religious thought from theology and ecclesiastical organisation to the relevance of religion for a human life. However, James concedes that those who hope to cultivate some goodness out of religion should appropriately value religious experiences rather than celebrating theological doctrines. After James, this approach has been widely adopted by scholars of modern religious studies. Hick, having been inspired by James, adopted the attitude which values the productive power of religion. Therefore, the concept of religious experience has played a very significant part in Hick's interpretation of religion.[30]

After Kant and James, John Oman[31] should be added to the list of the thinkers who contributed to the development of Hick's thought. If the term 'interpretative element' relates to Kant, and 'religious experience' to William James, then the idea that faith is a total interpretation of the universe in the light of the supernatural brings John Oman to mind. As Hick acknowledges, however, his *Faith and Knowledge* can be seen as an exposition of Oman's main ideas in a different context.[32]

The second significant event which took place while Hick was at Princeton Seminary was his dispute with the United Presbyterian Church concerning the doctrine of the virgin birth. When Hick was asked by Synod about his position with regard to the doctrine, he said that he would neither deny nor positively affirm it. This agnostic position was sufficient for the Synod of New Jersey to abolish his ministerial membership to the Presbytery of New Brunswick in March 1962.[33] When the Synod decision was announced, in response to the call for comment from various newspapers, Hick offered this statement:

> The theological question at issue is whether every Presbyterian minister must affirm a biological miracle in connection with the birth of Christ, or whether this is a secondary matter about which it is possible for some of us to be uncertain. I distinguish between the central Christian faith in the Incarnation, and the theologically peripheral story of the Virgin Birth, and following St Paul, St John, St Mark and most of the other New Testament writers, I do not found my belief in the Incarnation upon the

Virgin Birth tradition. I would therefore not exclude from the Presbyterian ministry those who decline to make the Christian Gospel stand or fall on something inessential, and I anticipate that when this matter is finally decided by the General Assembly of our church, the broader view will prevail.[34]

Having published *Faith and Knowledge* in 1957, with the intention that this would be his only book, Hick increasingly became occupied with 'the theodicy issue, the question whether the reality of suffering and wickedness are compatible with the reality of a loving God'.[35] It took Hick almost four years (1962–1966) to compile such a well-documented and quite influential book, namely *Evil and the God of Love*, which contains Hick's sound response to the problem of evil. As Badham points out, this book, together with *Faith and Knowledge*, have become almost classics in contemporary philosophy of religion, thereby establishing Hick's reputation in the field.[36]

In 1963, Hick moved to Cambridge, taking up firstly the S. A. Cook Bye-Fellowship at Gonville and Caius College and later the post of lecturer in the philosophy of religion in the Divinity School at Cambridge University (1964–1967). During this period, he published three important books, namely, *Philosophy of Religion* (1963), *Classical and Contemporary Readings in the Philosophy of Religion* (1964) and *Evil and the God of Love* (1966). At that time, the philosophy of religion meant for him the philosophy of the 'Judeo-Christian tradition'.[37]

During this period, Hick's writings, books and articles were still written to support and defend the orthodox Christian faith. For instance, in one of his first published articles[38] he criticised a conclusion which he himself eventually reached. However, there were some implicit signs of a paradigm shift from the Christ-centred point of view to the Real-centred one in his writings at that time. But he did not fully realise the magnitude of the problem of religious pluralism. He reviews that period as follows:

During this period I had virtually no contact with other religious traditions – neither Judaism or Islam, nor the faiths of Indian and Chinese origin. In spite of having spent many months in Muslim Egypt, Syria and Lebanon, and a short time in Palestine (as it then was), I had no appreciation whatever of Islam or Judaism as religions. Nor, except for one short course, was I introduced during my theological training to the history or

7

theology of religions; and during my subsequent pastorate in rural Northumberland such matters were for beyond the horizon alike of my congregation and of myself... Further, I long shared the common ecclesiastical assumption that the whole human race ought to be converted to Christianity. I remember being indignant at Reinhold Niebuhr's statement that the mission to the Jews was a mistake – though I can now see that he was entirely right.[39]

In 1967, Hick moved from Cambridge to Birmingham to occupy the H. G. Wood Professorship in the Theology Department in Birmingham University. As Hick himself observes this was a turning point in his life as far as the issue of religious pluralism was concerned.[40]

In Birmingham, Hick became involved in the work of 'race and community relations'. He made several friends and colleagues from non-Christian religious communities such as Muslims, Hindus and Sikhs, and hence became a 'practitioner of multi-faiths', attending the worships in a mosque, synagogue, temple and gurdwara. When Hick observed non-Christian believers at the moment when they were worshipping, he discovered that 'essentially the same kind of thing is taking place in them as in a Christian church – namely, human beings opening their minds to a higher divine Reality, known as personal and good and as demanding righteousness and love between man and man'.[41]

In Birmingham, Hick was one of the founders and first chairman of a voluntary liberal group called All Faiths for One Race, (AFFOR). Working together with some radicals and humanists, Hick fought against racism and racist organisations such as the National Front and the British National Party.[42]

Hick's religious experience in Birmingham marked a significant stage in the development of his philosophy of religion:

> ... [I]t was not so much new thoughts as new experiences that drew me, as a philosopher, into the issue of religious pluralism, and as a Christian into inter-faith dialogue. (Subsequent visits to Hindu India, the Sikh Punjab, Buddhist Sri Lanka and multi-faith Japan were prompted by the initial impact of the Birmingham experience.) Encounters with remarkable individuals of several faiths, people whom I cannot but deeply respect, and in some cases even regard as saints, have reinforced the realisation that our very different religious traditions

8

constitute alternative human contexts of response to the one ultimate transcendent divine Reality.[43]

Hick taught at Birmingham University until 1982. During this period he engaged with two major themes, the critique of traditional Christology, and the problem of religious pluralism, in such a way that the former would aid the promotion of the latter. These two major themes have eventually become the focus of his life-time intellectual endeavours. In this period he published three important books, namely, *God and the Universe of Faiths* (1973), *Death and Eternal Life* (1976), and *The Myth of God Incarnate* (1977).

God and the Universe of Faiths is composed of a number of important articles, some of which were delivered as public lectures in Birmingham. The book itself covers the major themes of Hick's philosophy of religion including such subjects as theodicy, religious pluralism and Christology. When one glances at Hick's overall writings, one might state that *God and the Universe of Faiths* can be regarded as a brief summary of Hick's entire philosophy. But it was articles such as 'The Copernican Revolution in Theology', 'Christ and Incarnation' together with 'Incarnation and Mythology' that made an indelible impact not only upon contemporary philosophy of religion but also upon modern Christian Theology.

In *God and the Universe of Faiths*, Hick wanted to establish a viable theology of religions suggesting a Copernican Revolution in theology.[44] To illustrate the point, Hick uses an astronomical analogy: Ptolemaic astronomers saw the earth as the centre of the universe and explained the movements of the planets by postulating epicycles. The Copernican revolution replaced Ptolemaic theory by offering a simple alternative explanation – that the sun, rather than the earth, was at the centre of the universe. Hick claimed that the old Ptolemaic theology envisaged an implausible system in which Christ is located at the centre of the universe of faiths. Instead, a Copernican revolution in theology aims at a 'shift from the dogma that Christianity is at the centre to the realisation that it is *God* who is at the centre, and that all the religions of mankind, including our own, serve and revolve around him.'[45]

Three years after the publication of *God and the Universe of Faiths*, Hick produced his eschatological *magnum opus*, *Death and Eternal Life* which was published in 1976. This book was the result of six years work and lectures delivered in places such as the University of Virginia, St Stephen's College, Delhi, Christian College, Madras and

Bishops College, Calcutta. Hick's travel to India (1974 and 1975 – 1976) and to Sri Lanka (1974) gave him an opportunity to learn about Hinduism and Buddhism. In *Death and Eternal Life*, Hick for the first time included Hinduism and Buddhism in his interpretation of religion.[46]

While he was at Birmingham University Hick edited a book which not only caused a controversy over the issue of the Incarnation but also triggered a process which has resulted in a significant body of literature on the issue. *The Myth of God Incarnate* published in 1977, comprises the contributions of several respected scholars of modern religious studies such as Maurice Wiles, Don Cupitt, Leslie Houlden, Frances Young, Michael Goulder and Dennis Nineham. The book sought to promote three major theses, namely: (1) Jesus did not teach that he was in any sense God incarnate; (2) it is not possible to trace the development of the incarnational doctrine which was finally established at the Council of Nicaea and Chalcedon in the fourth and fifth centuries; (3) the language of divine incarnation is metaphorical, or mythic, rather than literal – this latter issue being Hick's own individual concern.[47]

As soon as the book was published, there was furious reaction[48] from conservative Christian organisations in Britain:

> It was widely reported, and discussed in the national newspapers. The religious press was full of it for several weeks. The *Church Times* ran the headline 'Seven against Christ?'. The word 'heresy' was freely used. The Sunday after publication a preacher in St Paul's Cathedral declared that the *Myth* authors should consider whether they are still Christians. In the Synod of the Church of England, which happened to be in session when the book was published, we were likened, by the person appointed to lead the prayers, to the German Christians who supported Hitler! The *Sunday Telegraph* published a picture of Christ on the cross, with a copy of our book nailed above his head.[49]

During his stay in Birmingham, there were two further aims which Hick wanted to achieve. The first, which was intellectual, was to establish religious pluralism as one of the major subjects in the philosophy of religion as well as creating an awareness with regard to a new understanding of traditional Christology among scholars. The second, which was practical, was to create toleration and understanding between the adherents of major religions. He believed that he could achieve this by reformulating those aspects of Christian theology which are the cause of its exclusivist attitude and also by inviting scholars from other traditions to do the same in their own traditions. *The Myth of God Incarnate* is the book which, in my opinion can deliver such a result and according to Hick it has partly done so.

In the 1980s, Hick devoted his life and energy to reformulating and revising his idea of religious pluralism in a more philosophical fashion. In 1982 he moved to California to occupy the Danforth Chair in the Philosophy of Religion at Claremont Graduate School where he had already been working part-time since 1979. Hick's second period of stay in America was eventful. While teaching at Claremont Graduate School, Hick took every opportunity to promote his hypothesis of religious pluralism and his other opinions about Christology. Here, Hick was the director of the annual 'Philosophy of Religion Conference' which has addressed a wide range of topics related to the philosophy of religion.[50] In Claremont Graduate School, Hick often gathered together with celebrated scholars to discuss some of the fundamental issues in the philosophy of religion .[51]

In this period (1982–1992), another significant event which marked a remarkable step in Hick's thought was his delivery of the prestigious Gifford Lectures (1986–1987). This eventually contributed to another significant book in the field of religious studies: *An Interpretation of Religion: Human Responses to the Transcendent*. This book is devoted to a philosophical exposition of his hypothesis of religious pluralism.

The impact of Wilfred Cantwell Smith upon the development of Hick's idea of religious pluralism is evident.[52] W. C. Smith's works, as Hick himself observes,[53] gave him an important insight into the understanding of world religions. Through him and his works, Hick realised that world religions could be seen not as immutable theological systems[54] but rather as a dynamic interactive process. Hick seems to have become familiar with Islam through Smith's writings. Hick's hypothesis of religious pluralism is rather similar to Smith's conception of a 'world theology'.[55]

An Interpretation of Religion, upon which a significant part of this book is based, is Hick's most important contribution to the discussion of religious pluralism. Hick aims to achieve a religious interpretation of religion by reconstructing all his already cited arguments in order to constitute a hypothesis of religious pluralism.

After *Interpretation*, Hick published two further books, *The Metaphor of God Incarnate* and *Disputed Questions in Theology and the Philosophy of Religion*. In both, Hick once again returned to the issue of Christology, thereby reformulating the doctrines of incarnation, the resurrection and the divinity of Christ.

The significance of Hick's contribution to religious studies can best be realised when one looks at the amount of references to Hick in any serious contemporary work. More than one hundred articles have been written by others about his work, together with over sixty book chapters and over eighteen doctoral dissertations, and six full length books. In 1991 Hick was awarded the Grawemeyer Award in Religion for *An Interpretation of Religion*.[56]

In 1993, Arvind Sharma compiled essays in honour of Hick which were published under the title of *God, Truth and Reality*. In this *Festschrift*, several celebrated scholars from various traditions, including W. P. Alston, W. L. Rowe, M. Arkoun, J. Bowker, J. B. Cobb Jr., T. Penelhum, N. Smart, N. Solomon, S. Sutherland, K. Ward, M. Wiles and Y. Sei'ichi expressed their appreciation by contributing articles.

Hick retired in 1992, and is currently writing a book which will probably be entitled *The Rainbow of Faiths: Critical Dialogues on Religious Pluralism*. This book will be a response, mostly in dialogue form, to the published criticisms of his version of religious pluralism.

Hick's spiritual pilgrimage,[57] or his quest for truth, which started with a conversion experience in Hull, went through various stages and ended with the following verbal celebration:

> From a pluralist point of view, then, I do not, in inter-faith dialogue, have politely to conceal an assumption of the religious superiority of my own tradition. I am not set in judgement over the other great world faiths, but can explore, often with great fascination and profit, other ways in which other human beings know the one ultimate divine Reality. Because our traditions represent different limited ways of conceiving, experiencing and responding to that Reality, I sometimes come to see through others' eyes what are to me exciting new glimpses of the Transcendent as reflected in the meaning and possibilities of our human existence. I rejoice in the moving beauty of the Jewish way of life, with its ancient symbols through which God's presence has been felt during so many centuries; I rejoice in the impressive voice of the Qur'an, in the Muslim awareness of God as awesome and yet always gracious and merciful, and in the ordered

structure of life which it makes possible; I rejoice in the marvellous openness and mystical fervour of Guru Nanak and the communal dedication of the Sikh tradition which he founded; I rejoice in the consciously mythological way of thinking symbolized in Hindu temples, in their ecstatic moments, in the orderly shape of human life within the Hindu world of meaning; and I rejoice in the transcendence of ego that occurs in Buddhist awakening to *nirvana* and the outgoing compassion that it releases. But I have myself been formed by the Christian vision of God as revealed in the life and teaching of Jesus as reflected in the Gospels, and continue to be most at home in this, despite family disputes with more conservative fellow Christians. And yet looking out towards my friends of other faiths I recognise, with Jalaluddin Rumi that 'The lamps are different, but the Light is the same: it comes from Beyond'.[58]

★ ★ ★

SEYYED HOSSEIN NASR

Seyyed[59] Hossein Nasr was born on 7 April 1933 in Tehran, 'in a family of religious scholars and traditional physicians'.[60] As was common in traditional societies, as a child he started his education rather informally, at an early age, at home. His father,[61] was 'at once a practitioner of medicine, well versed in both traditional and modern medicine, and one of Persia's outstanding literary scholars and educators'.[62] He was also Nasr's first teacher, training him in a traditional manner which included reading and memorising chapters from the Quran and from the famous Persian poets. The impact of Nasr's early traditional education upon his intellectual development is very significant[63]:

A classical and traditional Persian education in my early years left an indelible mark upon my mind as stories from the *Holy Quran* and the poems of Sa'di and Hafiz became engraved upon the deepest layers of my soul during this period. At the same time, even these early years brought me face to face with the presence of another world view, that of the modern West, which appeared at that time at once enticing and threatening.[64]

In 1945, at the close of World War II, when he was 12 years old, Nasr was sent abroad to continue his education. A family tragedy, the death of his father, was the cause of his travel to America earlier than was usual for a young student. Alone, the young Nasr travelled by single-engine plane, train and bus to Egypt, where he waited two months for a ship with enough space to take him across the Atlantic.[65] For this traditional boy the West meant a domain of science and technology in which success and progress lay. He started his education in the Peddie School in Hightstown, New Jersey, in 1946, where he finished eighth grade, which he had begun in Tehran. He then continued his secondary education until he graduated from the Peddie with honours and as valedictorian of his class in 1950. It was also in 1950 that Nasr started a degree education in physics and mathematics at one of the most prestigious universities of America, M.I.T., where he became a notable student, displaying a gift for the study of science. He chose to study science, and particularly physics, because he thought it would serve his purpose. Nasr himself writes:

> I have been interested in science ever since I was a young boy. *I thought that through science I would discover the nature of things*; that was really what was at the back of my mind...
>
> I went to M.I.T. to pursue my scientific studies; I thought that there I could get the best scientific education. While I was a sophomore, as a result of contact with leading physicists, with the late Giorgio De Santillana, the great philosopher and historian of science, and through hearing lectures by such famous people as Bertrand Russell about the nature of modern science, I became aware that the most important proponents of the scientific world view believed that, in fact, *it was not the role of modern science to reach the nature of reality at all.*
>
> I felt that somehow this was not what I was looking for, that I was not going to understand the why of things, which was outside of the domain of modern science, or even the how of things [my italics].[66]

In 1951, the eighteen-year-old Nasr became interested in searching for some other way to study the nature of things and the world of nature. This metaphysical urge, which led him very far afield, drew him more and more into the study of philosophy and the history of science, though formally he was still studying physics and mathematics at M.I.T.

During this time, Nasr enjoyed following the debates between E. Meyerson and H. Poincare'. However, it was the late Giorgio Di

Santillana who made a notable impact upon his intellectual development, introducing him into the world of the inner struggle between science, philosophy and religion in the West. In the light of this, it is interesting to note that he persuaded Di Santillana to teach a course on Hinduism, long before the discipline of comparative religion was formally established in the Western universities.[67] Di Santillana introduced Nasr not only to Galileo but also to Dante, whose *Divine Comedy* opened up to Nasr the profoundest aspects of the Western tradition, and which brought the notion of 'traditional wisdom' to Nasr's attention.[68]

In the early fifties, Nasr joined a small group of students of physics, mathematics and chemistry who wanted to question the foundations of Western civilisation. He was a very active member of this group, which a decade later became identified by Theodore Roszak as the 'counter-culture'. Through being involved with this group, Nasr sought to go beyond the confines of Western thought and delve into Oriental teachings. It was again Di Santillana who pointed Nasr to the work of R. Guenon which marked a major turning point in Nasr's intellectual life,[69] converting him to the perennial philosophy.

After several years of a roundabout journey for the eternal *sophia*, he was eventually guided by a person of Western origin to the vast ocean of Oriental and especially Hindu metaphysics. He delved into the treasures of the Indian tradition through the writings of Sri Aurobindo, S. Radhakrishnan and S. Dasgupta. But it was eventually the writings of A. K. Coomaraswamy which introduced Nasr to Hinduism and Indian traditions, as well as to the perennial philosophy.[70]

Before going to Harvard to study for a Ph.D., Nasr was already familiar with the perennial philosophy which eventually became a lifetime commitment. Having received his B.S. at M.I.T. in 1954, Nasr entered Harvard. There, after a period of studying geology and geophysics and having completed an MA degree, he undertook a research project in the field of the history of science[71] under the supervision of Sir Hamilton Gibb, H. A. Wolfson and I. B. Cohen. Nasr was intellectually very active; he did not want to miss any opportunity which would broaden his horizons and deepen his knowledge. He met with the scholars D. Z. Suzuki and Sh. Hisamutsu, and he benefited enormously from the unique Coomaraswamy library which, for Nasr, was a route to Oriental wisdom.[72]

However, intellectually Nasr was still in India and seemed reluctant to move to *dar al-Islam* (the realm of Islam). It was the writings of Frithjof Schuon, and also to a great extent Titus Burckhardt, that eventually brought Nasr intellectually to the realm of Islam and made 'traditional wisdom a living reality'.[73] Islamic tradition for 'twice born' Nasr once again became meaningful both intellectually and existentially. Nasr himself describes the aftermath of his 'conversion' experience:

> The writings of Sufi masters and Islamic philosophers began to regain the profoundest meaning for me after this long journey through various schools of Western philosophy and science. But this newly gained meaning was no longer simple imitation or repetition of things inherited. It was based upon personal re-discovery after long search and one might add suffering. Islamic wisdom became a most intense living reality, not because I had happened to be born and educated as a Muslim but because *I had been guided by the grace of Heaven to the eternal sophia* of which Islamic wisdom is one of the most universal and vital embodiments. Henceforth, I was set upon the intellectual path which I have followed ever since, that is, during the past two decades, a period during which my quest has not been so much to discover an unknown beyond the boundaries of the known, but to deepen and realize the knowledge already given to me doctrinally and principally and to apply this knowledge to the world within which the hands of destiny have since placed me [my italics].[74]

Two outstanding personalities, F. Schuon and T. Burckhardt – the former is his spiritual master, the latter an intimate friend – have played a major role in Nasr's adoption of the perennial philosophy. The impact of Schuon, Swiss-born metaphysician and leading representative of the perennial philosophy, upon Nasr's thought is so great that his writings as a whole might even be seen as expositions of Schuon's ideas. For Nasr, Schuon's 'coming' in this modern time is not without significance. Schuon is 'like the cosmic intellect itself impregnated by the energy of divine grace surveying the whole of the reality surrounding man and elucidating all the concerns of human existence in the light of sacred knowledge'.[75] Schuon's works on the other hand can be considered as 'the final testament of pure gnosis reflecting both upon the object of knowledge and the subject or consciousness whose root is the Sacred as such'.[76] He 'speaks from the point of view of realised knowledge not theory, and his writings bear an "existential" impact[77] that can only come from realisation'.[78]

16

For Nasr, Schuon is a reliable master whose wisdom and spiritual initiation is important.

Nasr's deep appreciation of traditional Muslim masters, whether medieval or contemporary, and his uncritical acquiescence to the authority of tradition, has led him to become a 'mirror' for traditional wisdom, or (as he himself calls it) 'transparent before the ray of Truth'.[79] He prefers a mediating role, this in itself prevents him from being totally original.[80]

Burckhardt is another intellectual from whom Nasr has drawn his inspiration. Burckhardt wrote extensively about Islamic esoterism, sacred art and especially Islamic art as a prominent representative of the school of the *sophia perennis*. Nasr corresponded with Burckhardt and met him several times. In the fall of 1966, he met Burckhardt in Beirut, Lebanon, for the occasion of the 100th anniversary of the founding of the American University of Beirut. In that year, they travelled together to Damascus to visit the tomb of the Ibn 'Arabi[81] and several years later together circumambulated the Ka'bah.[82]

Nasr was also influenced by other perennialists including Marco Pallis, Martin Lings, Huston Smith, and also Louis Massignon who is one of the great scholars of Sufism, and Henry Corbin. Nasr met with Massignon in his student days and he continued his contact until his death. Nasr also met with Corbin while he was returning to Tehran from America in 1958, and collaborated with him closely for twenty years, teaching and producing various works.[83]

In 1958, when he was just twenty-five years old, Nasr completed his Ph.D. thesis on the subject of Islamic Cosmology, which was published as a book under the title, *An Introduction to Islamic Cosmological Doctrines: Conceptions of Nature and Methods Used for Its Study by the Ikhwan al-Safa, al-Biruni and Ibn Sina* (1964).

In the same year after spending thirteen years in America, Nasr returned to Iran with a Ph.D. from Harvard as well as a 'new appreciation of the still living Islamic tradition and also a complete awareness of those errors and deviations which comprise the modern world and which in fact have become much more evident during the past two decades'.[84]

Despite his scholarly intensity, Nasr is also a man of action. During twenty-one year period, in Iran, Nasr lived a very active professional life. He was Professor of Science and Philosophy at Tehran University. He participated in nearly every educational council in the country. He was also a Dean and Vice-Chancellor of Tehran University and President of Aryamehr University. Alongside his many activities he also played a major role in building a huge university campus in the city of Isfahan in Iran. In 1974, he established the Iranian Academy of Philosophy[85] and served as its first Director.[86]

Upon returning home, Nasr started teaching but never gave up learning. Iran is among the very few Islamic countries where traditional teaching of Islamic philosophy is still operating today. For almost ten years, Nasr attended classes in traditional *madrasah* and, in private homes, was taught traditional Islamic philosophy by a number of Persia's religious authorities, including three of the leading philosopher-sages of Iran: Sayyid Muhammad Kazim Assar, Allamah Sayyid Muhammad Husayn Tabataba'i and Sayyid Abu'l-Hasan Rafi'i.[87] It was interesting for him to view a classic figure of Islamic philosophy such as Ibn Sina through their eyes, after having already seen him through the eyes of Wolfson and Gilson. Through collaboration with Corbin, Nasr sought to introduce and make known this traditional perspective on Islamic philosophy to the Western academic community.[88] Nasr himself reveals the incentive behind his returning to Iran:

> Within Persia, my most important task was to revive the authentic intellectual traditions of our own land and to provide keys for a penetrating analysis and criticism of Western thought, which has paralysed so many Westernised Orientals during the past century. This task was to take me to many other Muslim countries, so that my writings, lectures and debates in this domain have not been limited to Persia alone. In fact, some of my philosophical works in this area have had a small role to play in causing a certain amount of internal debate among the Muslim intelligentsia and a new appreciation of their own intellectual tradition, helping to begin a process which is now speeding ahead in many areas of the Islamic world.[89]

In 1961–1962, Nasr was a visiting lecturer at the Centre for the Study of World Religions at Harvard, where he delivered open lectures on Ibn Sina, Suhrawardi and Ibn 'Arabi which were later published as a book under the title of *Three Muslim Sages*. The book was translated into all major Islamic languages.

In 1964–1965, Nasr was invited to the American University of Beirut to be the first occupant of the Aga Khan Chair of Islamic Studies in Lebanon. He undertook a series of fifteen public lectures[90] entitled 'Dimensions of Islam', from which the first six lectures were published under the title of *Ideals and Realities of Islam*. In this book Nasr dealt with several issues such as Islam as religion, the Quran, the Prophet, the *Shariah*, the *Tariqah*, Sunnism and Shi'ism from the perspective of the perennial philosophy. The book itself was written with a strong awareness of the reality of the plurality of religion;[91] in it Nasr indirectly addresses the question of how Islam and Muslims can accommodate the existing reality of other religions.

During this period of his life in Iran (1958–1979), Nasr produced a sizeable collection of books, articles and other works. He published over twenty books and two hundred articles (including prefaces and book reviews) in English, Persian and French. The books written in this period can be divided into two major groups. The first is those related to Islamic Science including *An Introduction to Islamic Cosmological Science, Science and Civilisation in Islam* and *Islamic Science – An Illustrated Study*. The second comprises those related to the perennial philosophy including books on Sufism and Islamic Philosophy, such as, *Ideals and Realities of Islam, Man and Nature, Islam and the Plight of Modern Man, Three Muslim Sages* and *Sufi Essays*.

Nasr sought to resuscitate Islamic cosmology and the sciences. He sees Islamic science as not 'simply a bridge between the Graeco-Roman antiquity and the high Middle Ages in the West; or as merely a stage in historical development of Western Science, but as an alternative way of viewing things'.[92] The most important book in this domain is *An Introduction to Islamic Cosmological Science* (1964), which is a revised and elaborated version of his Ph.D. thesis.[93]

Another book of his in this area is *Science and Civilisation in Islam* (1968), prefaced by Giorgio Di Santillana. In it Nasr speaks of the Islamic traditional teaching system and educational institutions. He presents an historical account of the sciences in Islamic culture, namely, Cosmology, Cosmography, Geography, Natural History, Physics, Mathematics, Astronomy, Medicine and Alchemy. Nasr through his study of science at M.I.T., had developed a consistent criticism of modern science. He argued that in traditional civilisation, science was part and parcel of the existing sacred world. The Enlightenment has wrongly separated science from religion or from the sacred principles, thereby causing the emergence of secularisation. Hence, desacralised science, by declaring its independence from religion, has become an unbridled power, causing unprecedented problems threatening the whole existence of humankind. Nasr, however, opposes blind repetition and imitation of modern science by

Muslims without considering the consequences of such an act to Islam and Muslims' lives.[94]

Three books which were written from the perspective of the perennial philosophy are also worth mentioning. These are: *Man and Nature* (1868), *Sufi Essays* (1972), and *Islam and the Plight of Modern Man* (1975).

Man and Nature, which is based on four lectures delivered at the University of Chicago during May 1966, is a brilliant response of the perennial philosophy to the environmental crises of our age, offering a viable alternative route which can lead humanity out of this crisis. The aim of this book, states Nasr, is 'to investigate in the broadest sense the problems posed for peace and human life itself by the various applications of modern science'.[95] Nasr brings our attention to the fact that the demand for technological and economic development is totally incompatible with the desire for a peaceful and unpolluted environment. He goes on to say that the environmental and social crisis with which the modern person is faced is the result of 'disequiblirum' between man and God.

Sufi Essays is a collection of articles which explicates a perennialist's account of Sufism. In an article 'Islam and the Encounter of Religions', Nasr deals with the problem of religious pluralism. The solution to this problem, according to Nasr, lies within Sufism for Muslims and within the context of the perennial philosophy for the adherents of other faiths.

In *Islam and the Plight of Modern Man*, Nasr draws our attention to the spiritual crisis of the modern person, arguing that the causes of such problems derive from the norms of modernity and the solution lies in the message of Sufism. Intellectual problems of present-day Muslims can be surmounted by the revival of the intellectual and spiritual heritage of Islam.

Nasr's many professional activities and scholarly intensity were extremely fruitful while he was living in Iran:

> Since I have been living in Persia as an active member of its intellectual community, my philosophical activities have naturally gravitated around that world and its needs. One of my primary tasks has been the resuscitation of the traditions of Islamic philosophy for the younger generation of Persians themselves. Through nearly twenty years of teaching at Tehran University, during which many students, both Persian and non-Persian, have been trained, the editing and analyzing of the

works of such masters as Avicenna, Biruni, Suhrawardi and Mulla Sadra and finally being able to play a role in the establishment of the Imperial Iranian Academy of Philosophy, I have had a humble share in the major revival of Islamic thought that is to be seen today in Persia and even in certain other Islamic countries.[96]

In 1979, the political situation in Iran forced Nasr to leave his home country. He took with him a small amount of money and several suitcases and began to rebuild his life in America.

Nasr was first appointed as Professor of Islamic Studies at Temple University in Philadelphia where he worked until 1984. In 1981, he was invited to the University of Edinburgh to deliver the prestigious Gifford Lectures. Nasr was not only the first Muslim but also the only person from the Orient to deliver the Gifford lectures in their history. These lectures, which resulted in a brilliant book, *Knowledge and the Sacred* (1981), aimed at 'the resuscitation of the sacred quality of knowledge and the revival of the veritable intellectual tradition of the West with the aid of the still living traditions of the Orient where knowledge has never become divorced from the sacred.'[97] His task is 'to deal first of all with an aspect of the truth as such which resides at the very nature of intelligence and secondarily with the revival of the sapiential perspective in the West, without which no civilisation worthy of the name can survive'.[98]

Knowledge and the Sacred, upon which a substantial part of the present study is based, can be regarded as a comprehensive summary of the perennial philosophy. This *magnum opus* when properly understood and assimilated, is indeed able to evoke an intellectual transformation. It means more than it says directly: it is written in a fashion which communicates not only the domain of reason but also of 'spirit'. Hence it is not surprising to see that those who are not accustomed to communicate at such a level often fail to grasp the message of the book.[99]

Knowledge and the Sacred speaks of three important subjects: the secularisation process, tradition, and the characteristics and qualities of sacred knowledge in the context of the perennial philosophy. It claims that sacred knowledge transcends rational knowledge, because it possesses a transforming quality. Secondly, it claims that the *sophia perennis*, will reassert its saving power by resuscitating tradition, that tradition being a web of principles of divine origin which have been crystallised within the forms of religions, arts and traditional sciences.

Thus, it attempts to solve the problem of religious pluralism by suggesting that all religions are forms of the everlasting truth which has been revealed by God to humankind through various agencies. No wonder that upon the publication of *Knowledge and the Sacred*, Huston Smith, could write these words:

> As for the book at hand, if its author is a phenomenon, this latest book is an event... The 1981 Gifford Lectures are unique in this series in being the first to be delivered by an Oriental. If we are looking for clear signs of a new day, one in which the West is seriously trying to globalize its outlook, here is one that can be pinpointed. Looking back on *Knowledge and the Sacred*, intellectual historians may one day rank it with William of Moerbeke's Latin translations of Aristotle in the thirteenth century, Marsiglio Ficino's of Plato in the fifteenth, or D. T. Suziki's 1927 *Essays in Zen Buddhism* as a landmark showing that a new stage in cross-cultural understanding has been achieved.[100]

In 1984, Nasr became University Professor of Islamic Studies at the George Washington University. He has developed a core curriculum in Islamic studies, covering history, theology and philosophy, and art.[101]

Between 1979 and 1995 Nasr added to his already massive body of publications more than ten books and several articles.[102] In addition to his intensive scholarly work he has devoted a good deal of effort to translation, both from Persian to English and from English and French to Persian and Arabic.[103]

Four particular books written in this period, namely *Knowledge and the Sacred* (1981), *Traditional Islam in the Modern World* (1987), *Islamic Art and Spirituality* (1987) and *The Need for Sacred Science* (1993) deserve a brief description.

In *Traditional Islam in the Modern World*, Nasr considers his traditional view as one of the popular types of Islam, along with modernism and 'fundamentalism'. For Nasr traditional Islam is quite distinctive from its counterparts. He argues that both traditionalists and 'fundamentalists' agree in accepting the Quran and *sunnah* of the Prophet and the *Shariah*, but there are profound differences. For instance, according to Nasr 'fundamentalists' reject the sapiential dimension of Islam, that is, Sufism, Islamic philosophy and Islamic art, whereas traditionalists reject nothing of Islam.[104]

A brief examination of *Islamic Art and Spirituality* (1987) is sufficient to appreciate the richness and profundity of Nasr's thought.

In the book, Nasr has shown that he has a remarkable concern for and a tremendous insight into traditional art.

The Need For A Sacred Science is an attempt to establish the perennial philosophy as a sacred science, a universal metaphysics which is entitled to speak of Reality as such. Like *Knowledge and the Sacred, The Need for a Sacred Science* stems substantially not only from sound scholarship but also from a spiritual vision. It speaks about God as Reality which manifests itself in various levels and consciousnessesw. It illustrates that Reality as like a cascade gushing forth from a central point and descending down to the world of senses; it can be perceived as unity within 'the Divine Stratosphere' whence the rays of the Origin are traced. It can also be perceived as the diversity within 'the human atmosphere', when it is seen from a vantage point of human conditions on earth.

In 1994, Nasr delivered yet another important series of lectures, the Cadbury Lectures at the University of Birmingham. These lectures, which explore the sacred principles and their manifestations in nature, will result in yet another *magnum opus, Religion and the Order of Nature*. In eight talks, over the course of about three weeks, Nasr dealt with the issue of environmental crises from the perspective of the perennial philosophy. The lectures themselves are the result of Nasr's thirty years of study of Islam and other religions, as well as science. The frequent references to the Quran, Upanishads, and Confucian and Taoist texts are sufficient to show Nasr's wide range of interests.

In the lectures, Nasr touched upon the issue of religious pluralism, seeing the reality of religions as different manifestations of the 'immutable and everlasting truth' within the context of the perennial philosophy. He also spoke of the order of nature, misdeeds of philosophy and science, and the scientific revolution. The most important contribution in these lectures is in his analysis of the environmental crisis and its relation to humanism and science. The solution is, of course, sought in the wisdom of tradition and resacralisation of Nature.

Seyyed Hossein Nasr is the right person to make such a presentation of the value of tradition and essentially of religious principles. He is a devout Muslim, a Shi'ite, a philosopher,[105] a scientist, an artist, and one well acquainted with the Sufi path. He occasionally writes poetry and other literary texts in addition to his scholarly, metaphysical or philosophical writings.[106] W. Chittick characterises Nasr's works as follows:

... [W]hat is truly unusual and even extraordinary in Nasr's works is this invisible force which integrates and harmonizes diverse elements and focuses them in one direction. Some authors may have his background in the various disciplines of the modern West – although few are so well versed in both the sciences and the humanities – and others may have his background in the traditional sciences, even if they are rarely able to express these teachings in a manner that seems logical and consistent to the modern reader. Probably no other living thinker unites all of these fields through a spiritual discipline which transcends them, at least not while writing in a felicitous English prose which somehow captures the magic of the classical Persian of a Sa'di or Hafiz.[107]

Alongside his traditional and classical education, and cross-cultural experience, Nasr is also well versed in Western physical and social sciences, history and philosophy, and classical and modern Christian doctrines and theologies. As J. I. Smith rightly observes, Nasr's Persian Shi'ite identity, although evident in some of his explications, does not excessively colour his writings.[108]

Nasr's linguistic abilities are impressive. He is fluent in Farsi, Arabic and English, competent in French and German. He possesses some competence in Italian, Latin and Greek. No wonder that Huston Smith could write about him in his review of *Knowledge and the Sacred* in such a manner:

Let me right off tip my hand and say that I consider Hossein Nasr a phenomenon. He makes mistakes as we all do, and most readers of this journal will know that he has a well-defined perspective from which he sees things. But who else in our time bridges East and West as substantially as he does? Who works as effortlessly in as many languages, is as prolific with writings that also have substance, and combines range of information with genuine metaphysical depth? Many possess one or several of these virtues, but all four is remarkable. I have heard him criticized for sounding dogmatic, but that can be expected of those whose words have the ring of certitude. So, in our relativistic age, add that, too, to the credits I have listed.[109]

Nasr, a follower of the *sophia perennis* summarises his journey for 'quest of the eternal sophia'[110] with these words:

My own intellectual activity has been not only to immerse myself in this wisdom and to seek to become 'no one' through the removal of the self before the Truth, to know this wisdom and to make it known, but also to apply its principles to the conditions of our times and to the problems posed for contemporary man. I have found the greatest joy of creativity not in fabricating a 'truth from my own mind and experience, which in fact would be absurd from a traditional point of view, but in trying to become transparent before the ray of Truth which shines whenever and wherever the veil before it is lifted or rent asunder (the *kashf al-mahjub* of the Sufis). Once that process is achieved, the understanding, 'observation' and explication of the manner in which that light shines upon problems of contemporary man constitutes for me philosophical creativity in the deepest sense of the term. Otherwise, philosophy becomes sheer mental acrobatics and reason cut off from both the Intellect and revelation, nothing but a luciferian instrument leading to dispersion and ultimately dissolution. It must never be forgotten that according to teachings of the *sophia perennis* itself, the discovery of the Truth is essentially the discovery of oneself and ultimately of the Self, and that is none other than what the father of philosophy in the West, namely Plato, defined as the role of philosophy, for he said, 'philosophy is the practice of death' (Phaedo 66). And the self cannot be discovered except through the death of the self and that re-birth which is the goal and entelechy of human life and the aim of *sophia* in all its multiple manifestations within the traditions of the East and the West.[111]

This brief biographical account of Hick and Nasr provides a significant insight which helps us understand their approaches to religion. In their personal lives, there are certain similarities as well as dissimilarities. For instance, in his childhood, Hick was uninterested in Christianity, while Nasr was brought up in a traditional and religious environment. Hence, he was conscious of the role of Islam in his life. When they were in their late teens they displayed different attitudes toward their traditions. Hick became an evangelical Christian, whereas Nasr became less interested in his tradition. After their university education, both became intellectually and existentially engaged with religion. It is interesting to note that during their academic careers, Hick has leaned toward liberalism while Nasr has inclined toward Islamic orthodoxy.

Through examining their biographies we see that both are alert to the spiritual and intellectual problems of our time and have therefore devoted their lives to the search for answers to these problems. Hick has been concerned with the evil nature of religious as well as secular wars, while Nasr has become concerned with the environmental crisis. One of the distinct qualities of these two thinkers is that both strongly believe in their cause. Hick believes that his hypothesis of religious pluralism can contribute immensely to building a peaceful religious world community. Nasr, on the other hand, believes that the salvation of humanity is only possible when the values of tradition are rediscovered.

Chapter Two

Religion and Tradition

The Origin of Religion

In the late nineteenth and early twentieth century, it was fashionable to write about the origin of religion. Such scholarship gave rise to a massive body of literature written under the shadow of 'positivist-scientism', which tended to consider traditional religious belief as primitive and superstitious. In spite of their tremendous confidence, the social scientists who dealt with the study of the origin of religion have failed to produce a convincing theory which can settle the issue. Although the study of the origin of religion has more or less disappeared from the field of religious studies, the massive body of writing which it has produced has always provided a source of important historical material and played a major role in modern religious studies. Further, in spite of a widespread belief that the quest for the origin of religion was dead, attempts have been made to revive this enterprise in the light of post-modernism.[1]

The second half of the nineteenth century witnessed a rapid development in the field of religious studies.[2] An important milestone in this process was Charles Darwin's *Origin of Species* which sought to explain the origin of humankind. His writings have left a legacy in which everything was seen and examined from the perspective of 'evolution', a concept which functions as a paradigm in almost all modern disciplines, including religious studies.

Herbert Spencer (1820–1904), was perhaps the first person to view religion from a Darwinian perspective. In his *First Principles*, he applied evolution not only to the development of the earth and life but also to the development of law, society and language. Within such a framework, religion was seen as reminiscent of primitive life and beliefs. Partly thanks to Spencer, evolution was transformed from a

27

theory to an 'atmosphere' functioning as one of the most fundamental paradigms in the mind of the intellectuals at that time.[3] Friedrich Max Müller (1794–1827) dealt with the question of the origin of religion in a scholarly fashion for the first time. He defines religion as '... the perception of the infinite under such manifestations as are able to influence the moral character of man'.[4] Max Müller who is 'a true son of the Enlightenment, and a genuine disciple of Kant',[5] popularised the science of religion giving it a terminology and set of ideas.

It was Emile Durkheim (1858–1917) and his sociological theory of religion that made a particular impact on the modern field of religious studies. According to Durkheim, religion originates in collective states of mind and can be defined as:

... a unified system of beliefs and practices relative to sacred things, that is to say, things set apart and forbidden – beliefs and practices which unite into one single moral community called a Church, all those who adhere to them.[6]

Although widely read and inspiring many followers, Durkheim's theories were confined within a perspective which did not accept humankind's belief in the actual existence of the unseen supernatural order. This secular theory of religion might be significant from a sociological point of view, but it did little to explain religious traditions as belief systems which for many function as the ground for morality and the meaning of life.

At the beginning of the twentieth century there was a shift of interest from seeing religion as belonging to the 'peculiar' life and beliefs of primitive people to the recognition of it as the 'data' of religious experiences. Perhaps the first person who effectively made this kind of point was Rudolf Otto (1869–1937). In his *The Idea of the Holy*, Otto coined the word 'numinous', derived from the Latin *numen*, a supernatural entity. For him, to experience the numinous was to experience the presence of a *numen*, which manifests itself as a *mysterium tremendum*, communicating a sense of otherness, awefulness, majesty and energy.[7] Ordinary language does not have the means with which to speak of the qualities and attributes of *numen*. That is to say, *numen* is ineffable.[8]

With the publication of *Totem and Taboo*, Sigmund Freud also returned to the age-old problem of the origin of religion. He followed the path of Frazer and Tylor, rather than that of Otto and James. According to Freud, 'the beginnings of religion, ethics, society and art meet in the Oedipus complex'[9] – which can be defined as the repressed sexual desire for the mother on the part of a male child, with consequent rivalry and jealousy of the father's sexual rights and privileges.

The real question which has to be considered is why Freud's extreme and questionable theory of religion has become almost a common belief to three successive generations of Western intelligentsia. The reasons for this should be sought in the scientific transformation of the West during this time. In the heyday of science, people tended to believe that science was able to solve all the old mysteries, including religion. Freud's theory of religion gained popularity in the West, firstly, because the secularisation process has made a lasting impact on the mind set of the Western intelligentsia, creating a cultural atmosphere where these kinds of theories can be accommodated, and, secondly, because Freud's theory of psychoanalysis won the battle against other forms of human science and became a cultural fashion.

There was, however, a more genuine and pragmatic interest in religion which aimed to draw attention to the value of religion for society as well as the individual. This endeavour was led by William James. James, whose impact upon Hick's thought is notable, defined religion as 'the feelings, acts and experiences of individual men in their solitude, so far as they apprehend themselves to stand in relation to whatever they consider the divine.'[10] James adopted three subjective criteria for estimating the value of religious experience. These he identified as 'immediate luminousness', 'philosophical reasonableness' and 'moral helpfulness'. James' psychological approach to religion was a big step forward in the realisation of the 'true' nature of religion but, his concentration on cases of religious pathology and the association of religion with some kinds of psychological illnesses have shadowed his success. Nevertheless his *The Varieties of Religious Experience* has become a classic which has continued to serve as a major text in the field.

It is my view that such attempts to explain the nature and the origin of religion have simply created a body of theories which are diverse and, in some cases, conflicting.[11] Firstly, the project of discovering the origins of, and inventing definitions for, religion has left a legacy of speculation which has imposed its secular content on generations to come. That is why it is not surprising to see why, even a hundred years after Müller, a thinker like Hick was still very interested in establishing a theory of religion which is concerned with the origin and definition of religion.[12] The second and more important concern is that, if our understanding of religion has to reflect the fashion of the time in question, and if it is culturally conditioned, as this project clearly intends to show, then all attempts to discover the 'true' nature of religion including 'meta-traditional' theses like Hick's hypothesis of religious pluralism, will always remain questionable.

To define religion, as Hick himself is aware, is always problematic. In the introduction to one of his first editions of *Philosophy of Religion*, he wrote, '[t]here is ... no universally accepted definition of religion, and quite possibly there never will be'.[13] Although he held this position with regard to a phenomenological description of religion for practical purposes, he nevertheless could not refrain from considering a working definition of religion in order to make his religious interpretation of religion credible.

However, as will be discussed in the coming chapter, one of the fundamental features of Hick's hypothesis of religious pluralism, is that human beings stand in an 'epistemic distance' before the Transcendent. In other words, the universe is religiously ambiguous, thereby making both the religious and naturalistic interpretations equally valid. Hence, these two distinctive interpretations have led to the emergence of two different blocks of definitions, namely the naturalistic and the religious. The naturalistic definitions, which see religion as 'a purely human activity or state of mind'[14], and branch into the phenomenological, psychological and sociological,[15] are not within the scope of Hick's interest. Although acknowledging that it is plausible to propose a naturalistic definition of religion, Hick is, in fact, searching for a religious interpretation of religion. Thus, he proposes 'a working definition of religion' as 'an understanding of the universe, together with an appropriate way of living within it, which involves reference beyond the natural world to God or gods or to the Absolute or to a transcendent order or process'[16] In another context, he suggests that religion can be defined as 'an awareness of and response to a reality that transcends ourselves and our world, whether the 'direction' of transcendence be beyond or within or both'.[17]

Hick's definition of religion obviously encompasses the major traditions, namely Judaism, Christianity, Islam, Hinduism and Buddhism, but excludes naturalistic systems of beliefs such as Marxism. He intentionally narrows his definition further by insisting that the genuine encounter with the Real is likely to occur in religion which 'has come out of a great revolutionary religious experience and has been tested through a long tradition of worship, and has sustained human faith over centuries of time and in millions of lives.'[18] This definition does not consider new religious movements and archaic religions to be as significant as the major religions. However, this does not mean that Hick rules out the possibility of salvation or transformation in new religious movements.[19]

As has been pointed out, there are certain affinities between Hick's conception of religion and those of Frazer and Müller insofar as they all are intended to explain religious phenomena by applying scientific methods available at the time in question. But one striking difference between them and Hick is that Hick shifts the emphasis from definition and explanation to description and to interpretation. This change has in fact, functioned as the key factor directing Hick to the intention to value each tradition according to its fruits in human life.

Hick believes that the 'family resemblance model'[20] can establish a ground on which religion, like the term 'game' can accommodate various forms and patterns of religious phenomena.[21] Analogous to the concept of 'game', which is applicable to all kinds of games, solitary or competitive, religion covers a set of traditions, movements, and ideologies which might not exemplify the common essence but which form a complex continuum of resemblance and differences similar to those found within the family.[22]

From the traditional perspective, Hick's attempt to value all religions, including new religious movements, has led him to a position in which he is unable to establish criteria which can distinguish those religions which transmit the sacred qualities of the Ultimate, from new religious movements which are regarded as parodies of the 'authentic' traditions.

The early twentieth century paradigm, the quest for the origin of things, including the origin of humankind, the origin of the universe and the origin of species, has left a legacy of the so-called scientific method for intellectual generations to come. This paradigm is evident in Hick's conception of religion.[23] Throughout his analysis of the concept of religion, Hick advocates that religions, as empirical dynamic entities, originated from the existence of a Divine presence through 'revelation' at the moment of an intense spiritual experience.

In this context, I would like to examine further the question of the origin of religion in Hick's thought. He believes that the universal presence of the Real, which is capable of (directly or indirectly) influencing the human psyche,[24] 'generates within certain exception-ally open and sensitive individuals an unconscious awareness of an aspect or aspects of its meaning for our human existence.'[25] Hick maintains:

> In cybernetic terms this is 'information' about the significance of the Real for our lives. In order to be consciously received and responded to this information is transformed into inner or outer visions or voices, the psychological machinery which transforms the transcendent information into such experiences consisting of the mystic's own mind-set and creative imagination.[26]

Hick identifies two kinds of such experience. In one kind, the information is mediated through our material environment. In this respect, the ordinary objects and events are imbued with religious character or meaning. For instance, in Christian history healing is experienced as a divine miracle. In the other kind, often distinguished as 'mystical', the information is received by a direct influence, analogous to telepathy, between two human minds.[27] Such mystical experiences, according to Hick, are themselves of two main kinds: unitive and communitive. The former are unmediated mystical experiences by which the mystic exceeds duality and hence is able to enjoy a unitive intuition of Ultimate Reality. The latter are moments in which the mystic encounters a divine being through visions, or auditory experiences.[28]

Whatever the type of religious experience, the information is transferred into a conscious mode through which the mystic regulates his or her religious environment. The outcome of such mystical experiences is significant. Hick believes that not only the main characteristics of the Real, such as goodness, love and mercy, but also the religions together with their doctrines themselves, religious rites and distinctive characteristics, have been constituted through such religious experiences.

However, Hick rejects the possibility of unmediated mystical experience because he believes that it neglects the 'human-cultural' contributions to the constitution of religion. In addition to this, unmediated mystical experience poses a threat to Hick's hypothesis that the 'information' received through such a moment possesses an absolute value. Here suffice it to say that according to Hick, unitive mystical experience is not possible because mystics within the different traditions 'do not float their cultural conditioning', and 'they are still embodied minds, rooted in their time and place.'[29]

In short, Hick claims that the 'seeds' of religions were planted at the moment of divine-mystic encounter. This received information is transferred into a conscious mode and dressed in the cultural concepts available to at that moment so that the mystic's community can make use of the information in question.[30]

Before proceeding any further a number of points must be made. To see religion as the product of the impact of the Real upon the mystic's own mind-set is a plausible supposition, but requires a thorough explanation. The best way to analyse such an idea is to apply it to a specific religion. In order to substantiate this point, then, Hick could have examined the process that constituted Christianity or a new religion in the new religious movements. Yet he has not done so, preferring to make more general points on this crucial issue.

According to Hick, Islam came into being through the Real's encounter with Muhammad in an intense religious experience. Yet such a statement requires more explanation. The first thing to be explained is the manner in which the supposed encounter took place and the nature or mechanisms of the encounter. One cannot help asking: Is the Real-human encounter a natural i.e. simultaneous phenomenon which can occur at any time and in any place? And does accepting the plausibility of such an encounter mean that the Real possesses a capability of affecting some individuals without having an *intention* to affect them? If the Real *does* have the capacity of (intentionally) relating itself to human beings, then how can Hick defend his notion that the Real is totally ineffable, and therefore cannot have any qualities which contradict its nature?

In the case of Islam, extrapolating from Hick, the 'information', namely the Quran which resulted from this meeting, has to be the product of both the Real and the mind of Muhammad. Such a statement, however, mystifies rather than illuminates the phenomenon of revelation. Hick's claim is only valid if he is able to substantiate it with a more detailed explanation, i.e., the nature of the mechanism through which this information was generated. But he has not done so.

However, what I am more interested in is the religious, i.e. Islamic, impact of this account, rather than the nature of the mechanism of the transmission of such information. From a Muslim point of view, to seek the answers to these questions is not only appropriate but crucial. Hick's main ideas entail asking such questions as: How much of the Quran is the product of the Real and how much is the product of Muhammad's mind? Or to put it another way: how do they, namely, Muhammad and the Real, share out the information? Are the ideas of the Quran from the Divine and the words from the human, i.e. from Muhammad? The answer to these questions is very important, because the Muslim, naturally, wants to dismiss those religious concepts, rules and rites which are the product of the cultural norms of seventh century Arabia, and to observe only those which come directly from the Real.[31] Can Hick recommend, for instance, the norms of modernity as the criterion by which Muslims can distinguish the divine contribution from the human one?

However, all these questions are left unanswered. Hick endorses the view, although he does not explicitly state it, that the cultural norms of our age are the 'invisible' criteria by which traditional dogma, whether Christian or Islamic, have to be demystified. Hick seems to be saying that the concept of the Divine as infinite and absolute in Islamic tradition, and also the ethical principles of Islam, such as the 'Golden Rule', must come from the Real. But the *Shariah* law, such as capital punishment, and, 'events' such as Allah's favour to the Muslims in the battle of Badr, must come from the imagination of the Prophet. The traditional Islamic reply to such enquiries is as follows:

> If today we disown what we take to be factually erroneous, perhaps tomorrow we will reject apparent moral anachronisms – such as scriptural claims about the relatively low status of women or the impropriety of 'deviant' sexual behaviour, not to speak of the occasional questionable doctrine about the nature or activity of the Deity. We surely need a principled account of the limits of this sacrifice at the altar of secularism; we need grounds rather than motives for establishing a coincidence between the essence of a faith and just exactly those scandals to the intellect which today's worldly folk will tolerate.[32]

However, in practical terms the major religions were founded by people 'eligible' to mediate between the Ultimate and ordinary people.[33] These spiritual masters, outstanding individuals who have been extraordinarily open and responsive to the higher reality can be seen as the great primary mediators. The founders of the religions, says Hick, such as Gautama, Confucius, Jesus and Muhammad, are such mediators, who have initiated streams of religious life that have lasted for many centuries. There are also lesser founders of new traditions and subtraditions such as such as Guru Nanak, Joseph Smith, Mary Baker Eddy, Baha'ullah, Kimbangu, Mokichi Okada and many others. Now, the question is this: how does one know that they are the genuine mediators of the transcendent Reality?

Hick considers three criteria through which one can distinguish genuine mediators from the rest. The first is a moral criterion. Although the moral codes of humanity differ from society to society, there seems to be a universal awareness of the need to distinguish between good and bad. In this context, the founders of religions have emerged as examples of moral quality, which has often been interpreted as a sign of their genuineness.[34] The second criterion is 'that he opens up a new, exciting and commanding vision of reality in terms of which people feel called to live'.[35] Hick also realises that in addition to the novel features of the message, there should be common ground between the new message and the basic foundations of the culture in which the mediator lives. The third criterion is the power of the mediator and his or her message which should be able to win the approval and hearts and minds of the people who encountered it so that the new perception of reality can come into light in the life of that community.[36]

In addition to all these, there are also social, economic and geographical factors.[37] Social crisis, major disturbances and turmoil 'urge' the Real to respond to a given situation. Such turmoil originates in 'the great creative moments' in which religion is born.

The secular characteristics of Hick's account of religion are in fact more visible when he attempts to trace historically the origin of the major traditions. There are two main regions of the earth in which religions first emerged. These are Mesopotamia in the Near East and the Indus Valley of the northern India where the early developments of religions took place, which Hick describes as 'the growth of natural religion, prior to any special intrusions of divine revelation or illumination'.[38] Hick maintains:

> Primitive spirit-worship expressed man's fears of unknown forces; his reverence for nature deities expressed his sense of dependence upon realities greater than himself; and his tribal gods expressed the unity and continuity of his group over against other groups. One can in fact discern all sorts of causal connections between the forms which early religion took and the material circumstances of man's life, indicating the large part played by human element within the history of religion.'[39]

In Mesopotamia, the nomadic herd-keeping people imagining the divine as 'the desert dwelling herdsmen' established the male concept of God as the King, and the Father; whereas in the Indus Valley, agricultural people aware of the importance of fertility and making use of the mother principles constituted their image of deities as God the Mother, the more specialised female deities.[40] In other words, two pieces of the land, Mesopotamia and the Indus Valley, provided their inhabitants not only with food and nourishment, but also with images of God and goddesses.[41]

What I am suggesting is the possibility that Hick's account of the origin of religion is in fact secular and embodies the same merits and demerits as those of Frazer, Müller and Durkheim. As has been pointed out, Hick endeavours to explain religion with reference to Enlightenment rationality as well as the products of such rationality, in particular science. This attitude makes Hick's account secular. Furthermore, Hick's interpretation of religion is not able to bring substantial insights which offer a lasting and sound explanation of the phenomenon of religion. To substantiate this claim I will draw on Eliade's well-known article, 'The Quest for the "Origins" of Religion'.

One of the important points which Eliade illustrates in this paper is that through the translation of the *Corpus Hermeticum* by Ficino, the concept of *primordial revelation*, which could encompass not only Moses but also Plato and the ancient religions of Egypt and Persia, became viable, thereby creating a significant concern in the Renaissance.[42] But later the search for a pre-Mosaic revelation diminished. After a series of crises, Western Christendom headed towards the naturalistic and positivistic ideologies of the nineteenth century. In this century, Christianity and all the other religions were considered 'not only groundless but culturally dangerous because they usually obstructed the progress of science.'[43] Eliade states that Western man's quest for the 'origins' of religion forced him into an encounter with history,[44] and the historian of religion knows now that 'he is unable to reach the "origin" of religion'.[45]

However, he states that after a century of struggle and untiring scholarly work, scholars were forced to give up 'the old dream of grasping the origin of religion with the help of historical tools'.[46] He maintains:

... [T]he historicity of a religious experience does not tell us what a religious experience ultimately *is*. We know that we can grasp the sacred only through manifestations which are always historically conditioned. But the study of these historically conditioned expressions does not give us the answer to the question: what is the sacred? What does a religious experience actually mean?[47]

In this paper, Eliade has argued for two conclusions: the first is that a human being is not capable of penetrating history and seeing the real characteristics and the nature of religious experience. What one can do is to interpret and make sense of historical religious occurrences according to the norms and values rendered by a specific culture in which one lives. In other words, we are always conditioned by history. But this does not mean that human beings are passive and do not respond to historical and cosmic conditioning. Secondly, Eliade points out that we cannot have an account of a 'bare religious experience', because we are always obliged to confront a religious experience through history.

What are the implications of these conclusions for Hick's account of religion? In the light of Eliade's argument, one can claim that any theory of religion, whether religious or naturalistic, is and has to be relative because it is always generated out of the human creative response to historical conditioning. Hick's account of religion, although he claims otherwise, is another relativist theory which will fade away like its counterparts with the passage of time.[48]

Religion and Change

How does religion cope with change? This is one of the topics in which the difference of opinion between Hick and Nasr is salient and very interesting. As has been pointed out, for Hick, religions have been constituted in the divine human-encounter. They are historical entities which can be historically traced and geographically mapped as a human phenomenon. They are like a living organism evolving throughout centuries. Although in their experiential roots they are all in contact with the same ultimate reality, historical and cultural experiences have caused observable differentiation resulting in the creation of many different religious worlds.[49] Hick states:

> ... [N]ow that the religious traditions are consciously interacting with each other in the 'one world' of today, in mutual observation and dialogue, it is possible that their future developments may be on gradually converging courses. For during the next few centuries they will no doubt continue to change, and it may be that they will grow closer together, and even that one day such names as 'Christianity', 'Buddhism', 'Islam', 'Hinduism', will no longer describe the then current configurations of men's religious experience and belief.[50]

37

This on-going transformation, says Hick, can be characterised within three distinguished blocks of events and creativity which feature the three major eras of religious history: pre-axial, axial and post-axial. In the pre-axial age[51], which will cover 'the religions of stone-age humanity' religion functioned as 'a defence against chaos, meaninglessness and the breakdown of social cohesion'.[52] The gods or even the higher God of this period acted as creator and protector but not saviour or liberator.[53]

The axial-age starting from sometime after 1000 BC. and ending with the rise of Islam, is not a block of time but rather a concentration of events.[54] In this period of time, humanity witnessed the rise of the major traditions. For instance, in China we see the rise of Confucianism and Taoism, while in India, there is the emergence of Gautama, the Buddha and Mahavira, the founder of Jainism. The Upanishads and the Bhagavad Gita also appeared in this particular period. As did Zoroaster in Persia, the great Hebrew prophets, in Israel, Pythagoras, Socrates, Plato and Aristotle in Greece. Then, after a gap of three hundred years, we see the coming of Jesus of Nazareth; and, then, after another gap, the Prophet Muhammad and the rise of Islam.[55]

However in this unique and significant stretch of time, observes Hick, all major religious traditions exhibited the some soteriological characteristics. The gods of all these religions are not only creators and preservers, but also saviours. After the axial age no comparatively novel events occurred in religious history.

In the post-axial age Hick allocates new roles for religions. In this new age, the aim of religion is not to protect society from chaos, nor to offer people salvation in the hereafter, but to lead the believer to a human transformation, from ego-centredness to reality-centredness.[56]

As has been mentioned before, one of the main theses of this work is that Hick's account of religious pluralism as a 'supra-traditional' theory is not religiously convincing because it is implicitly Christian and explicitly 'modern-secular'. His notion of history is an instance of this point. Hick sees history like a 'power' which does not just govern humanity, but also leads people to certain goals. We have seen how these goals changed in terms of the period; the goal of history in the pre-axial age is entirely different from the goal of the post-axial age. This can be seen as a form of interpretation inspired by the Christian conception of redemption. From the perspective of Hick's cosmic optimism, history has been seen as the means of transformation bringing us to the phase of transformation from self-centredness to reality-centredness.

The major source of Hick's idea that religions are dynamic entities subject to constant change and transformation is surely Wilfred Cantwell Smith. In his influential book *The Meaning and End of Religion*, Smith successfully argues that the vocabulary and concepts generated in the Western cultural environment often misrepresent not only its own 'religious background,' namely, Christianity, but also traditions of other cultures. Take, for instance, the term 'religion'. The conceptualisation of the religious life of the believer with the aid of these terms such as 'religion', functions as an obstacle in comprehending the religious life of believers. In fact, for Smith, the notion of religion can become an enemy to piety.[57] He maintains that the employment of terms like 'Christianity', 'Buddhism' and 'Hinduism'[58] to characterise the religious life of believers is quite a recent phenomenon.[59]

I believe W. Cantwell Smith's notion of the cumulative tradition is quite helpful because it wants to shift the interest of the student of religious studies from religion as a system of theological propositions to religion as living reality actualised in the religious life of believers. On the other hand, the concept of the cumulative tradition is not able to fulfil the requirements of a pluralistic vision as long as it ignores 'the truths' of religions which have always functioned as driving forces behind the dynamic religious life. Furthermore, as is implicit in Smith's exposition, this term is not equally applicable to all the major traditions. Since this concept of the cumulative tradition was formed through a consideration of the Hindu tradition, it might be appropriate to use it to characterise that tradition alone. The term is not able to characterise Islam as it does Hinduism. As Smith is aware, Islam poses a real challenge to his notion of cumulative tradition.

It is now time to address the problem of the change in religion from the traditional perspective. As far as the issue of religion and change is concerned, there is a difference of emphasis between the traditional point of view and the current modern one. Although the traditional point of view does not ignore changes in religion, it sees changes in religion as processes through which the immutable principles have been unfolded. It does this because it is concerned with truth in religion. The modern point of view, in contrast, sees religion through variations or ever-changing flows of religious life, because it is concerned with practical usefulness or function of religion. In this context, the traditional point of view does not seem attractive, since it is prepared to accommodate the ever-changing norms of modernity:

> With the same proviso it is also not progressive, for truth is neither the one nor the other, being wholly independent of human attitudes. Truth does not change because it is expressed in a different way, nor because opinions change, nor because it may not fit in with individual or collective likes and dislikes. It remains what it is and was and always will be, whether man remembers it or not.[60]

Religions, notes Nasr, have been sent down from God to the world of becoming. That is why their teachings speak of the relation between the Eternal Order and its terrestrial manifestations. However, Nasr believes that the reality of religion cannot be identified only with its historical unfolding. Each religion possesses its 'seed', that is, its principles or possibilities in its celestial archetypes in the Divine Intellect. What has been sent down to this terrestrial domain, as far as religion is concerned is just its pre-determined manifestations. Through such a way the possibility of religion within the Divine domain is realised or becomes unfolded in a historical period and 'within humanity according to cultural and temporal conditions.[61]

Nasr does not deny that there have been changes in the religions. But these changes are seen through the perspective that views religions as materialisation of already existing 'ideas' (in the Platonic sense) in the Divine realms. The earthly expansions of religions are none other than their actualisation of the possibilities which exist in the celestial realm.

The concepts of change and development are two working paradigms in the current configuration of the Western cultural enterprise. The impact of such a paradigm is visible in almost every modern discipline. It is true that Christianity has been subject to immense change as a result of the pressures of Enlightenment values, to the extent that it makes sense to speak about 'an atheist Christianity' today.[62] It is not surprising to see that thinkers such as Hick and W. C. Smith, who view religion through a Christian background in the post-Enlightenment West, are biased in favour of the idea that religion is the product of human creativity and naturally subject to change. Therefore, religion is seen as 'the cumulative tradition' or 'growing organism'.

When one looks at the issue from an Islamic point of view, however, the picture is different. Islam, as a religion based on the unchanged sacred text, the Quran, which contains the Sacred Law, the *Shariah*, poses a real threat to the conception that religion is the product of human creativity. As W. C. Smith acknowledges, Muslims today believe that Islam is a transcendent truth, stable, permanent and free from vicissitudes and contingencies. The concept of permanence is central to Islam.

According to Hick, the reason why Islam has failed to fulfil the requirements of the modern age by changing itself is that an 'Enlightenment' has not occurred in Muslim intellectual history. But Hick is optimistic about the future of Islam, maintaining that Islam will possibly go through the same Christian trauma and eventually come to terms with modern knowledge and the new ecumenical outlook: 'the Muslim world will eventually find its own Quranic way of combining modern knowledge with its faith in the Transcendent and its commitment to a morality of human community'.[63]

W. C. Smith concedes that the reason why the conception of permanence appears as the central theme in Islam is due to the Muslims' strong commitment and belief in the *Shariah*. By 'deconstructing' the development and codification of the Muslim sacred law, Smith thinks that he will be able to make the concept of the cumulative tradition applicable to Muslims. He states that Islam as a historical phenomenon can be seen to have developed from a point where the *Shariah* as an elaborate legal system did not exist. 'Islam' at that time was used to refer to a religious system in which there was not the *Shariah*. For Smith, Islam as a system of religious ideas has been constituted by the contribution of several outstanding intellectuals such as al-Shafi'i, al-Ghazzali, al-Ash'ari and Ibn Sina.[64] He claims that 'if al-Shafi'i had not lived, or someone whose work would have been curiously like his (. . .) then, a historian must assert, the Islamic complex that exists today would have been different from what it is'.[65] In other words, what he is saying is that Islam cannot be an unchanging, stable religious system if the contributions of great intellectuals make changes in the overall picture of Islam. Therefore, Islamic tradition has reached its present shape through a gradual and complex historical process.[66] Consequently, 'to be a Muslim today is something different from being a Muslim in the first or sixth century'.[67]

However, the problem does not stem from the historical codification of the *Shariah*, as Smith assumes, but from the Quran

41

itself. If Islam as a religious system seems to have possessed some qualities which appear to be functioning as resistance to ongoing changes, that is not solely because of the codification of the *Shariah*, but because of the uniformed text of the Quran.[68]

On the other hand, as Nasr observes, such an understanding of Islam comes not from the conception of Islam as it is, as it is accepted by its followers, but from the attitude 'we wish it were so'. Nasr illustrates the point:

> For Islam, the crushing evidence is of permanence, that which comprises Islam's central reality. The Ka'ba is still the Ka'ba, the pilgrimage is what the Prophet performed, the daily prayers are what he did, the shariah as codified on the basis of the Qur'an and prophetic Sunnah still defines the reality of the Muslim's religious life... I do not say that there is a monolithic Islam, but what I want to say is that the idea of permanence in Islam permeates the whole of Islamic consciousness about itself despite this diversity of interpretations.[69]

It seems to be unreasonable to claim that Islam as a living tradition is immune to change. There has been change in Islam throughout the centuries. From an Islamic point of view it is equally unreasonable to believe that such a historical process or ever-changing intellectual contributions will eventually transform Islam into some kind of religious system that satisfies the expectations and norms of modernity. An account generally acceptable to the Muslim point of view on this issue is that there are changing aspects of Islam as well as unchanging aspects. For instance, those theological propositions formed by the Quran itself, and religious rites and acts of worship performed in a certain manner, do not change because the Quran has not changed through time. But what has been subject to change in Islam is the particular understanding of theological propositions as such. The Quranic description of God as an all-powerful and all-knowing being does not change. But what changes is the particular understanding or interpretation of those propositions by certain individuals in a certain time and place. That is why Ghazzali's interpretation of the doctrine of God's knowledge can be different from those of Ibn Sina or Fazlur Rahman. Of course, Islam as a historical living tradition has always been changing. Such a change can be seen as a 'growth' or 'unfolding' of the celestial archetypes. From a Muslim point of view, to assume that one day Islam, in going through the same traumatic experience as Christianity, will come to terms with the secular and non-religious powers of modernity, thereby producing some kind of Islamic non-realism, does not seem likely.[70]

The Sophia Perennis

During the last two decades, the impact of post-modernist philosophy and the New Age movement have shifted the interest in religious studies from religion as a systematic authoritative and external entity (i.e. institutionalised religion) to 'tradition' as the compound of local and therefore diverse beliefs, practices and customs (i.e. personalised religion). I shall deal later with the issue of the definition of tradition. However, some people, who give the term 'tradition' a different meaning from its conventional sense, identify it with the perennial wisdom, or the Sophia, which is said to be comprised in the wisdom of the East and the West. This eternal wisdom is named by this group as the *sophia perennis*, which the Hindus know as the *sanatana dharma* and the Muslims *al-hikmat al-khalidah*.

The term 'perennial philosophy' has acquired some recognition in the West as a result of Aldous Huxley's book *The Perennial Philosophy* published in 1946.[71] However, it is due to the work of three outstanding thinkers of this century, Rene Guenon, Ananda Coomaraswamy and Frithjof Schuon, that the perennial philosophy has been recognised as not only a branch in the study of mysticism, but also as a philosophy, or *Weltanschauung*, that is able to provide an overview of the whole intellectual enterprise, as well as of life itself.

The *sophia perennis* is neither a discipline nor an 'ism' but rather a world view which not only provides a perspective on intellectual disciplines, but also contributes to everyday life itself. Aldous Huxley defines the perennial philosophy[72] as 'the metaphysic that recognises a divine Reality substantial to the worlds of things and lives and minds; the psychology that finds in the soul something similar to, or even identical with, divine Reality; the ethic that places man's final end in the knowledge of the immanent and transcendent Ground of all being – the thing is immemorial and universal'.[73]

Traditionalists believe that the perennial philosophy, far from being a recent innovation, is everlasting wisdom, which changes in form but not in essence:

Rudiments of the Perennial Philosophy may be found among the traditionary lore of primitive peoples in every region of the

43

world, and in its fully developed forms it has a place in every one of the higher religions. A version of this Highest Common Factor in all preceding and subsequent theologies was first committed to writing more than twenty-five centuries ago, and since that time the inexhaustible theme has been treated again and again, from the standpoint of every religious tradition and in all principle languages of Asia and Europe.[74]

There are indeed many merits to the perennial philosophy. First of all, the perennialist claims that it can potentially be a proper ground for the study of religions, because it is able to give full consideration and appreciation of each religion's sacred qualities, since it believes the sacred is the highest value. In this respect, the perennial philosophy seems more appropriate than any other approach, whether phenomenological, ecumenical or scientific, that has been developed in the secular atmosphere of the post-Enlightenment West. Secondly, the traditionalist claims that the perennial philosophy possesses a unique quality in that it speaks of knowledge that is able to transform. It is also claimed that contrary to the knowledge that is understood in a conventional sense, the sacred knowledge of the perennial philosophy demands 'a sacred quality' in the knower and therefore aims at making an impact upon the existential life of the person in question. Thirdly, and more importantly, the traditionalist claims that the perennial philosophy is unique in its claim that it possesses an alternative culture which is able to provide a proper solution to the problems created by modernity. It is this claim that I want to examine briefly here.

As S. R. Isenberg and G. R. Thursby argue, the modern world has come into being through a process which has, at least on the surface, eliminated some of the sacred characteristics of traditional culture. The eighteenth-century Enlightenment managed to shift the interest from traditional values to scientific values which concentrated on autonomous reason and technical progress. The historical and cultural experience of the twentieth century, especially of two world wars and the destruction of the community values, accompanied by the unseen consequences of unbridled technology, has made people start to question the very foundation of modern values.[75] As has been rightly observed, neither anti-intellectualism nor a sentimental traditionalism has been able to produce 'the means of integration necessary to take us beyond the contradictions that threaten to destroy us'.[76]

The traditionalist argues that in such cultural and spiritual turmoil the perennial philosophy has presented itself as a branch of thought which claims to go beyond the paradigm of modernity by transcending rather than by simply opposing it. According to the perennial philosophy, modernity has reduced human images in one dimension, having managed to destroy their heavenly images. In traditional societies, God is not only the outer authority but also the ground of transformation or realisation of the higher levels of being.

As has been pointed out, the traditionalist argues that the attempts of modern philosophy and psychology to limit human faculties of apprehension to the body level, mind level or body-mind level with a scientifically approved consensus, have implicitly severed the possibility of knowing and acknowledging the hierarchical dimensions of Reality. Therefore, modern philosophy is forced to prove the 'extra-ordinary' Reality from the basis of the ordinary. Such a philosophy is seen as not only mistaken in its vision of Ultimate Reality or God, but also in its image of 'ordinary reality' or the world, because, in essence, the world is inseparable from God. The perennial philosophy claims that only from a perspective which transcends physical and mental domains, can we speak of Ultimate Reality as such.[77]

The claim of the perennial philosophy to be an alternative culture which potentially embodies an answer to the problems of modernity can best be understood when one seriously considers its potential to integrate individuals into society as well as into the higher levels of Reality. It can do so because it believes that all existence is a manifestation or point on a continuum of hierarchically ordered Reality. In such a vision, there is no room for dualism of a psychological and cosmological kind which has been the real source of alienation. Hence, individuals, according to their level in communication with the Higher Consciousness as the source of reality, can move towards the more sustained awareness of unity. This unity is all-encompassing: unity within society as well as with humanity, unity with all creatures, eventually aiming at the final unity, that is, unity with Ultimate Reality.[78] The intellect, which is both divine and human, and revelations that actualise the intellect, are both indispensable on the path of unity. However, in this respect, the perennial philosophy is a language which still makes sense to the secularised mentality. That is to say, the perennial philosophy will have a say in the future when the search for an answer to the crises of modernity becomes desperate.

The Sacred, that is, the source of unity, stability and certitude, no longer regulates power in modern societies. Entire segments of culture and life, including religion, art and science, have been desacralised in modern societies. Individuals are born into environments already socially and culturally constructed which make the higher levels of reality inaccessible for them. They are left spiritually impoverished and limited in an attempt to apprehend Ultimate Reality, because secularisation has created a cultural atmosphere that does not tolerate the existence of the notion of 'revealed truth' let alone accept it.

What is Tradition?

A Tibetan saying states that 'when a pickpocket sees a saint all he sees are his pockets'. St. Thomas Aquinas says, 'The thing known is in the knower according to the mode of the knower.' It is true that we think and perceive according to the concepts and paradigms given us by the culture we live in.[79] After the Enlightenment concepts such as 'progress', 'development', 'evolution', 'change', 'novelty' and 'invention' have become a working paradigm which has coloured almost the entire intellectual enterprise of the modern age. Now we tend to look at any cultural phenomenon through these working paradigms. The study of religion and tradition takes place in the shadow of this tendency.

Tradition is clearly in steady decline in Western societies. The loss of faith in long-standing values, especially religious values, is a common phenomenon. The number of adult church goers has dramatically decreased in England over the last century. In 1851, church attendance was about 40% of the population; in 1979 adult church attendance stood at 11%; in 1989 it was 10% of the adult population.[80] The family as an institution has also been passing through the most difficult time in its entire history in the West: it is a common fact that single people now make up a quarter of all British households. The political system has also lost its credibility.[81] From these statistical data, however, it would be naive to jump to the conclusion that 'de-traditionalisation' or the decline of tradition is a universal phenomenon in the West. There is another side to the coin. In America, there is evidence of the vitality of religious organisations and the continuing commitment of individuals to religion. Church adherence rates displayed a remarkable increase during the nineteenth century and show considerable stability throughout the twentieth century.[82] Such a trend has convinced some thinkers that the current model of secularisation is not applicable to America and therefore has to be reconsidered.[83] 'Islamic resurgence' or religiosity throughout the Muslim world is a strong social phenomenon demanding explanation. To illustrate the point one can mention such events in the Islamic world, for instance, as the sermons of a blind Egyptian, Sheikh Kishk, which still attract enough people to halt the Friday traffic outside ancient Cairo's overflowing Sunni mosques. The Muslim population in Europe and in America is on the steady increase. In 1989, it was estimated that there were 2.5 million Muslims in France. Between 1976 and 1985, 941 Muslim places of worship were founded in France. In Germany, the total number of Muslims registered in May 1987 was around 2 million. In Great Britain, the 1986 census estimated there to be one million Muslims.[84] In the 1980s, there were 500 registered mosques in Great Britain.[85] Such figures are sufficient to show that the Muslim population in Europe is steadily on the increase through immigration, birth and conversion.

From the traditional point of view, one can argue that the low level of religiosity in continental Europe is no reason to predict the future demise of tradition and traditional values. Religion is still alive. And there are certain indications that religion will permeate the events of the next century.[86] To substantiate this, the traditionalist would maintain that, since God is the source of all reality, He in his infinite goodness and justice cannot tolerate the disappearance of religion, a necessary 'device' for the manifestation of truth. History, they say, has not asserted its final say. Rather, they argue, the problems of modernity have been functioning as an incentive for the quest for spirituality creating a need for the rediscovery of the sacred principles of tradition. The formulation of the traditional point of view during the last five decades can be seen as a response of the Sacred to the impoverished spiritual condition of the modern person.[87] Hence:

'The First who comes Last,' the reassertion at this late hour of human history of tradition which itself is both of a primordial character and possesses continuity over the ages, made possible once again access to that Truth by which human beings have lived during most – or rather nearly all – of their terrestrial history. This Truth had to be stated anew and reformulated in the name of tradition precisely because of the nearly total eclipse and loss of that reality which has constituted the matrix of life of normal humanity over the ages.[88]

The word tradition comes from the Latin *traditio* which means handing over. In Christian tradition this term is commonly used to designate the body of teachings transmitted by the Church.[89] This term is generally used to refer to something static, left over from the past subject to the pressure of innovation. But it is ultimately used to signify the process of 'handing over' or 'transmission'. In the sense of religious tradition, some writers argue that to define tradition is to reshape it. In other words, to define tradition is to interpret it; interpretation by definition cannot be unique and implies the possibility of other forms of interpretation. Hence, as with religion, it is not plausible to produce one single definition of tradition.

Although, the perennialist's notion of tradition probably includes the meaning of the term used in the conventional sense, it is essentially different from it. What Nasr finds peculiar is that although works of a traditional character have continued to appear in the West during the last sixty or seventy years, the concept of tradition is still identified with customs, habits and inherited patterns of thought. The concept of tradition that Nasr speaks of is the compound of the sacred principles and their application to whole segments of life including religion, art, science and philosophy.[90] Nasr however, offers a comprehensive perennialist definition of tradition. He defines tradition as:

> ... [T]ruths and principles of a divine origin revealed or unveiled to mankind and, in fact, a whole cosmic sector through various figures envisaged as messengers, prophets, *avatars*, the Logos or other transmitting agencies, along with all the ramifications and applications of these principles in different realms including law and social structure, art, symbolism, the sciences, and embracing of course Supreme Knowledge along with the means for its attainment.[91]

Broadly speaking, tradition, in this sense, comprises all the distinctive characteristics and principles or norms that are hereditary and contribute substantially to the main ingredients of civilisation. The notion of tradition is not an arbitrary or invented one, because, according to the perennialist, it is related to the very root of our existence. From another perspective, the perennialist can also define tradition as the composite of everything that links us to the Beginning in order to make us aware of the End since the Beginning and the End are the same.[92] Religion in this sense is a more direct and essential way for the individual to serve God.[93]

One of the problems of such notions of tradition, as Nasr realises, is that traditional languages in premodern times did not use a term corresponding exactly to tradition, although there are some fundamental terms like the Hindu and Buddhist *dharma*, the Islamic *al-din* and the Taoist *Tao* which can be related to the term tradition. The absence of an equivalent term in traditional societies does not indicate the irrelevance of the concept of tradition as such, but, on the contrary, the overwhelming presence of it. Premodern people, according to Nasr, were too deeply immersed in the environment which was created by tradition to have an external sense of tradition.[94] It is secularisation that necessitates an awareness or sense of tradition.[95]

The profane point of view, seeing things from the perspective of celebrated paradigms such as change, progress and invention, is only able to deal with 'the accidentals' shaped by the flow of events and thoughts. On the other hand, the traditional point of view sees things in principle and deals with the essentials. It speaks of truth and therefore error. It is not willing to compromise between truth and 'acceptability' for the sake of being 'normal'.

Tradition as understood here is like a living entity which appears in every activity of traditional people:

> In a civilisation characterized as traditional, nothing lies outside the realm of tradition. There is no domain of reality which has a right to existence outside the traditional principles and their applications. Tradition therefore concerns not only knowledge but also love and works. It is the source of the law which governs society even in cases where the law is not derived directly from the revelation. It is the foundation of ethics. In fact, ethics has no meaning outside the cadre established by the tradition. It also sets the principles and norms for the political aspect of the life of society, and political authority is related to that of the spiritual although the relation between the two is far from being uniform in different traditions. Likewise, tradition determines the structure of society applying immutable principles to the social order, resulting in structures outwardly as different as the Hindu caste system and the Islamic 'democracy of married monks' as some have characterized theocratic Islamic society, in which there is nevertheless an equality before God and the Divine Law, but of course not in the quantitative modern sense.[96]

In addition to tradition and religions there is also the Primordial Tradition, or the *sophia perennis*, everlasting truth which contains all truths of all religions. From the traditional point of view, the plurality of religions does not negate the existence of the Primordial Tradition. On the contrary, when one sees religions from an esoteric dimension, such plurality confirms the presence of the underlying truth in all religions. All traditions, says Nasr:

> [A]re earthly manifestations of celestial archetypes[97] of the Primordial Tradition in the same way that all revelations are related to the Logos or the Word which was at the beginning and which is at once an aspect of the Universal Logos and the Universal Logos as such.[98]

But Nasr reminds us that each tradition is based on a direct message from Heaven and cannot be seen simply as the historical continuation of the Primordial Tradition. To accept it does not mean rejecting the celestial origin of any of the revealed religions. It is rather to endorse the 'presence' which is inseparable from the sacred.[99] The notion of the Primordial Tradition, which Nasr relates to an Islamic concept of *al-din al-hanif*, the religion of the prophet Abraham, can be seen as a block of principles which were often revitalised through revelation. In other words, since all religions stem from the same origin, they share a substance, that is, the Primordial Tradition, which binds religions not only to the Source but also to each other.

Tradition possesses two basic dimensions: exoteric and esoteric. The exoteric aspect appears mostly in its rites and rituals as well as in law. The theological articulation, or the doctrines of a religion which render its particularity and individuality are also included within the exoteric aspect, that is, the forms of the tradition in question. The esoteric dimension, that is, the inward dimension of tradition, contains not only its spiritual substance, but also its intellectual qualities. For instance, in Islam the *Shariah* is the exoteric dimension, whereas the *Tariqah* is its esoteric aspect. In Judaism, the Talmudic interpretation is exoteric, whereas the Kabbalah is the esoteric. The esoteric dimension of tradition, which is the essence and the core of tradition itself, is not accessible to everyone, but only to those who are able to appreciate the inward dimension of tradition.[100]

To explain further the meaning of tradition in the sense employed in the perennial philosophy it is necessary to discuss somewhat more fully its relation with religion and the ethnological roots of these words, namely, religion signifies the 'binding', while tradition means

50

'transmission', which gives us a clue to their function and overall meaning. Religion is regarded as a means of binding man to God, whereas tradition transmits from generation to generation what religion contains. In this sense, religion is the origin of tradition. Conversely, tradition compasses religion and its ramifications as well its application to every aspect of life. Tradition can thus be used in this more general sense to include religion and its historical unfoldings.[101]

However, if one applies this distinction to Islam, one sees that Islam as a religion contains both the theological propositions articulated by the Quran and rituals and obligation set up by both the Quran and *sunnah*. As a tradition, Islam contains not only the main body of beliefs and practices but also the whole historical and current application and unfolding of those beliefs and practices. One might even say that while Islam as a religion comprises the unchanging aspects of the whole of Islam, Islam as a tradition includes both its unchanging and changing aspects. Islam as a religion is static and stagnant, whereas Islam as a tradition is dynamic and live.[102]

Tradition, as defined in the perennial philosophy, is the collection of shared truths of all revealed religions. It is concerned with the Sacred as well as being present in all 'authentic' religions, which are the sole sources of earthly transformation and eschatological salvation. But what is important for Nasr is that the religious point of view should not be confused with the traditional point of view. The religious point of view does not necessarily represent the traditional point of view, since secularism and modernism have intruded into the realm of religion since the Enlightenment.[103]

Before 'the fall', when the celestial realm was close to the terrestrial, more precisely when human beings were in *divinis*, they were embodied with all perfection. After 'the fall', in our terrestrial dwelling religions as manifestations of the Ultimate were ordained in order to guide humanity towards the unity, thereby making us remember our 'origin' and regain our celestial beatitude. In this respect, religion, says Nasr, is the Divine guide which is established to rescue human beings from duality, from 'the prison of senses'.[104]

As far as the origin of religion is concerned, Nasr defends the thesis that religion is ordained by God:

Religion in its earthly manifestation comes from the wedding between a Divine Norm and a human collectivity destined

51

providentially to receive the imprint of that Norm. From this wedding is born religion as seen in this world among different peoples and cultures. The differences in the recipient are certainly important and constitute one of the causes for the multiplicity of religious forms and phenomena, but religion itself cannot be reduced to its terrestrial embodiment. If a day would come when not a single Muslim or Christian were to be left on the surface of the earth, Islam or Christianity would not cease to exist nor lose their reality in the ultimate sense.[105]

Religion is composed of three fundamental elements: the doctrinal, the ritual and the ethical, which are inseparable. From the traditional point of view, the modern tendency to emphasise the ethical core of religion while disregarding its doctrinal tenets believing that they are irrelevant in the modern age does harm rather than good because without the firm affirmation of the doctrine in question, it is really impossible to sustain the ethical commitment derived from that particular religion.

From another perspective, says Nasr, at the heart of every religion there is *religio perennis*,[106] which contains a doctrine regarding the nature of reality and a method which prescribes the attainment of Reality as such. Although doctrinal languages and the prescriptions of the method vary from religion to religion, the essence and the goal of the doctrine and method remain universal within every religion.[107]

Modernism has brought about massive problems ranging from the social to the environmental. Criticisms of modernism offered by intellectuals of a post-modernist outlook or a New Age spirituality are inadequate, because they derive from the results or 'accidentals' that are created by modernity. For instance, the post-modernist outlook cannot propound any substantial solution to the problems of modernity, since it believes that a 'solution-offering-attitude' is the source of the problems of modernity. As Nasr observes, such a criticism of the traditional outlook of modernism is total and is concerned with principles. It deals rather with the causes that have generated the illnesses. Tradition disapproves of modernism because, it believes, the premises upon which modernism is based are false, since they are constituted through the employment of reason that rebels against the sacred and revelation.[108] The traditional point of view believes that to maintain social stability and real peace among people it is necessary to maintain the commitment that establishes the immutable principles that on the surface may go against reason and the personal interest of the individual. These principles or traditions, without which social stability becomes hard to sustain, function as focal points in the constitution of a society.[109]

From the traditional point of view, the invention of tradition only by human endeavour is senseless. In *The Invention of Tradition* Eric Hobsbawm identifies tradition with rituals or institutions known as 'traditional' in contemporary Britain societies such as the monarchy, the Queen's Christmas broadcast and the Cup Final. He relates traditions to national festivals, the display of flags, gun-salutes, toasts and oratory. The invention of such practices is related to the functions of that particular tradition in that particular society.[110] This has nothing to do with the conception of tradition that the perennialist speak of. From the traditional point of view, Hobsbawm is confusing tradition with habits or customs, some of which might be related to revealed principles whereas others might not be. In the sense in which he is using the word, it is possible to invent a tradition. In the traditional sense, however, to invent a tradition relying on human endeavour alone is no more possible than to invent a body of beliefs which give rise to a civilisation.

Thomas Dean claims that Nasr is absolutising one particular metaphysics or esoterism. He also criticises Nasr as defining tradition in an exclusive manner, thereby putting it in a position of being another 'ism', an ideology which naturally discriminates and necessarily excludes some other outlook.[111] In his reply, Nasr insists that the traditional point of view cannot simply be reduced to another 'ism' or one philosophical school among many in the modern world. Nor can traditional doctrine, says Nasr, enter into dialogue with the anti-traditional world in order to reach the intermediate compromise any more than the sacred can compromise with the secular without ceasing to be sacred.[112] Tradition, states Nasr, can present itself as 'an alternative to the modern world while using the contemporary medium to present its eternal message in a language which the present-day world can comprehend'.[113]

In this chapter, I have sought to argue that Hick's religious interpretation of religion can be characterised as secular when it is viewed from the perspective of the traditional religious perspective. I make this claim because Hick, like Müller and Durkheim, believes that religion can be explained as well as interpreted with reference to Enlightenment rationality together with the products of such a rationality, particularly modern science. Hick's account of the origin of religion is a case in point. Applying this account to Islam, I drew attention to the kinds of problem that Hick would raise about the religiosity of religious people. I also sought to point out that the dissimilarities between Hick and Nasr can be clearly discerned when their distinctive views on religion and change are put forward. As Nasr indicates, the emphasis on change and temporality in religion in recent religious studies has overshadowed the permanent aspects of religion. To substantiate this, I pointed out the changing and unchanging aspects of Islam.

A brief account of the perennial philosophy was presented in order to shed light on Nasr's philosophical background. I emphasised that the traditionalist regards the perennial philosophy as not only a discipline or approach in contemporary religious studies, but also a world-view which is able to cause a religious transformation in one's existential life. I specifically drew attention to the all-encompassing characteristics of the perennialist's concept of tradition, and argued that the tradition in this sense is able to accommodate not only all revealed religions but also their sacred quality, in contrast to other modern approaches in religious studies, such as the scientific, phenomenological and historical.

Chapter Three

Knowledge and the Ultimate

A brief examination of modern works on epistemology, such as A. J. Ayer's *The Problem of Knowledge* or Karl Popper's *Objective Knowledge*, reveals the enormous gap between the epistemology of modern philosophy and that of the perennial philosophy. In contemporary philosophy, epistemological theories generally speak of sense perception, reasoning, induction and experience as the means to knowledge, while the epistemology of the perennial philosophy, speaks of intellection and revelation, along with reasoning and induction as the means to achieve sacred knowledge. Modern philosophy deals with such questions as whether the physical world is real or what it means to be conscious. By contrast, perennialist epistemology deals not with the question of the existence of God, but of how to attain a knowledge of God. It attempts to elucidate the role of the intellect, and of revelation and reason, in the process of knowing. For the perennialist, knowledge is concerned with truth or reality and the exposition of that reality through intellection and revelation.

The Religious 'Neutrality' of the Universe

John Hick's main contributions to the areas of contemporary philosophy of religion are represented by the following three statements: the universe is religiously ambiguous, that is, both naturalistic and theistic interpretations of the universe are equally possible; faith is a total interpretation of the universe; and the plural religious life of humanity necessitates the existence of a reality which goes beyond any religiously imagined deities.[1]

The idea that the universe is religiously ambiguous plays a significant role in determining Hick's attitude toward the arguments for and against the existence of God.[2]

Hick believes that human beings are situated not at a spatial but at an 'epistemic distance' from the Transcendent, a state of affairs which, for him, is a precondition of the human response to the Ultimate. Without such an epistemic distance human beings can no longer possess freedom in their responses to the Ultimate.[3]

Although the philosophical arguments for and against the existence of God have been among philosophy of religion's proudest achievements, they have not been able to offer decisive proof for or against the existence of a transcendent religious reality. As Hick points out, these philosophical arguments have entered into religious thought in order to support and confirm an already existent religious faith, not to form a faith.[4] Philosophical reasoning plays only a small part in the formation of religious belief.[5]

Now let us see how Hick evaluates the major arguments for the existence of God from the position that the universe is religiously ambiguous. As far as the ontological argument[6] is concerned, having endorsed Kant's criticism that existence cannot be a predicate, Hick concludes that this argument does not provide a firm ground for belief in the reality of God.[7] As for the cosmological argument, Hick believes that, although it expresses some truth with regard to our cognitive situation, it does not compel us to believe that there is a God. Therefore this argument proves nothing for a person who takes the physical universe itself to be the ultimate unexplained reality.[8]

In Hick's eyes, argument from design or teleological argument – which has gained some support from contemporary scientific developments – deserves more credit than the others. According to Hick, although the argument from design is formulated in order to demonstrate the existence of God to non-religious as well as to religious people, it in fact only enables already religious people to see the universe religiously, and does not disturb the basic 'neutrality' of the universe.[9]

Hick concludes that among these various arguments and theories, some support the theistic conclusion and some the naturalistic. But neither side is able to reach a firm conclusion with regard to a religious or naturalistic interpretation of the universe. In other words, Hick claims that since the universe is religiously ambiguous, the theistic evidence can be interpreted naturalistically while equally the naturalistic evidence can be interpreted theistically.[10]

In this context, one might argue that Hick's realist stand becomes difficult to sustain. Is the notion of the religious ambiguity of the universe reconcilable with religious realism? Hick's response to this question is affirmative. He would say there is no contradiction in believing that the universe is religiously ambiguous and, at the same time, holding the view of religious realism. The proposition in question is reminiscent of his belief in liberal-secular values and naturally conflicts with his religious position. So much so that it can threaten his commitment to religious realism. Furthermore, one can claim, like D'Costa[11] that Hick's present position with regard to religious reality can be truly justifiable from an agnostic point of view. Let me develop the point further. Hick states:

> And in this post-Enlightenment age of doubt we have realised that the universe is religiously ambiguous. It evokes and sustains non-religious as well as religious responses. The culture within which modern science first arose was theistic; and accordingly the prevailing form of modern scepticism has been atheistic.[12]

As is clear from this passage, the postulate of the religious ambiguity of the Universe is presented as a culture-specific interpretation of the universe, rather than a statement of fact that attempts to describe the universe objectively. Against such a presentation it might be argued that the whole of reality, including the physical universe, can be seen as part and parcel of the Transcendent Reality, as has been argued in the metaphysics of the perennial philosophy. But this post-Enlightenment thought, because of its secular attitude, can present the universe as something which lacks religious significance. This does not mean that the universe is really religiously ambiguous.

Hick's faith in empiricism encroaches into his epistemology. He appears to be aligning himself more with the empiricist position than with analytical reasoning.[13] For instance, in his hypothesis of religious pluralism, 'the gods' of the various religions are presented as phenomenal manifestations of the divine noumenon, not because this religious reality is ontologically accountable, but because the existence of a plurality of religions leads *solely* to such a hypothesis. However, one can argue against Hick's assumption by stating that his hypothesis is only one among many possible interpretations of the fact that there is a plurality of religions. It is conceivable that the plurality of religions could lead to other conclusions; it might suggest a different picture of religious reality from the one which Hick envisages.

The same methodological problem, in fact, can be observed in his postulate that the universe is religiously ambiguous. Hick presents his argument as if he is saying that the universe is religiously ambiguous not because this is the objective and actual state of the universe, but because there is so much empirical evidence to defend such a belief, in particular the post-Enlightenment scientific exposition of the universe.

Let me return to Hick's view that the proposition in question is compatible with a realist-theist view. Hick would say that, like Pascal,[14] he can be a realist and at the same time believe that the universe is religiously ambiguous. But Hick's account of this issue stems from his assumption that the voluntariness of faith is interdependent with the religiously ambiguous character of the universe. In other words, if there were only one interpretation of the universe, i.e. religious or naturalistic, there would be no choice and therefore no freedom of faith. These two propositions, namely that faith in God is voluntary and that the universe is religiously ambiguous, though being subtly related, are not interdependent. For instance, it is possible to believe that faith in God is voluntary while rejecting the religious ambiguity of the universe without contradicting oneself.

Beyond all these, the primary reason for defending this position is that the notion of the religious ambiguity of the universe *allows* Hick to hold the view that faith in God is a voluntary 'action'. In other words, if the religious interpretation of the universe, or the arguments for and against the existence of God, were religiously compelling, then voluntary belief in God would not be possible. That is why the universe must be religiously ambiguous. Let me examine this notion in detail to see whether the religious ambiguity of the universe does really secure the voluntariness of faith.

Before proceeding any further we need to state that Hick's belief that religious faith, is voluntary is the natural result of his theory of faith and differs in essence from the traditional doctrines of freedom and predestination. In his theory of faith, Hick argues that we live in a faith-centred three-dimensional existence. The first is the physical dimension, then comes the human, that is, the moral dimension of our existence. The third dimension is the religious one interpenetrating both the physical and the moral. In the physical environment, we do not possess the freedom of interpretation; we are coerced to experience accurately;[15] we have to interpret aright in order to survive. In our religious environment, however, we do have the freedom of interpretation. We can interpret it religiously or naturalistically by depending upon the concepts that we have in our mind. Hence, Hick asserts:

If man is to be personal, God must be *deus absconditus*. He must, so to speak, stand back, hiding himself behind his creation, and leaving to us the freedom to recognize or fail to recognize his dealings with us. Therefore, God does not manipulate our minds or override our wills, but seeks our unforced recognition of his presence and our free allegiance to his purposes.[16]

Hick's defence of the thesis of voluntariness of religious faith has not passed without notice. Donald Henze criticised Hick's defence by arguing that his usage of the terms such as 'coerced' and 'compelled' is not appropriate. Henze claims that Hick is mistaken in saying that sense perception is coercive and 'religious experience' non-coercive and therefore we have freedom to have religious faith.[17] Hick responds to this criticism stating that his main point is to contrast the involuntariness of sense perception and the voluntariness of religious experience in order to expose the cognitive freedom of humankind in relation to God.[18] However, the more important point in Hick's thesis is that lack of sufficient evidence for the existence of God or God's disclosure of himself is not only necessary to preserve human freedom but also required if faith is not to lose its significance.[19]

In the Islamic tradition, this issue has always been considered within the subject of predestination and human freedom, a debate which consumed the entire energy of early and medieval Islamic thought. It was this issue that played the major role in bringing about the theological schools such as the Mu'tazila, Ash'ariya and Maturidiya.[20]

To decide whether faith is voluntary, one has to explain whether or not belief is a matter of will. If it is a matter of will, it must be possible to *decide* to believe or not to believe in God. This is a very interesting notion and requires some explanation. For instance, I can decide to go to London, a decision which and I might or might not carry out. I can decide to go shopping this afternoon and in normal circumstances I could and would. But it seems quite odd to *decide* to believe in God. It is like deciding to fall in love with somebody. I could consciously involve myself in some series of events which eventually *might* lead me to fall in love with somebody. But it is equally possible that the series of events I entered consciously would not end up with my falling in love. In the same way, one can consciously decide to involve oneself in a series of events with the intention of developing a faith; it is quite possible that one might develop a faith, but it is equally possible that one might not develop a faith. That is because the course of events that leads us in one direction rather than another is not entirely within our control. At the end of the day, we will find ourselves either believing or not believing in God. It seems to me that belief is something that happens to people, not something they do, like going shopping. In other words, I assume that we do contribute to the process of forming a faith, but the result is not totally within our control. We possess a considerable degree of freedom to involve ourselves in a faith-formation process, but we do not have the same 'freedom' to secure the result we want. Since we are not able (or do not have freedom) to secure the result that we want, unlike the act of shopping, then the capacity to have freedom to develop a faith is not the same as the capacity to have the freedom to go shopping. My point here is this: If, (as I assume) the analysis of faith-formation reveals that our capacity to secure the result we wanted in the case of religious belief is naturally limited as compared with ordinary activities like shopping, then God's setting up the world in a manner through which we can exercise our freedom to have a religious faith is not so significant. In other words, God contradicts himself if he, on the one hand, deliberately sets up the world in a religiously ambiguous way in order to enable humankind to choose to have faith and, on the other hand, creates humans in such a way that they are unable to exercise fully their freedom of faith.

There are, however, some critics of Hick such as Roy Perret, who argues that since believing in something is not a matter of will (if it were, he says, it would make sense to talk of *ordering* someone to believe something), it is not possible for any type of evidence or argument to be coercive. Hence, there is no need to insist on the thesis that in order to preserve the voluntariness of faith, God has to create the world as religiously ambiguous.[21]

The implication of the postulate of the religious ambiguity of the universe for the focal question of this chapter – whether knowledge can play a mediating role between God and humankind – is of crucial importance. As has become clear in the course of our discussion, Hick believes that the exposition and interpretation of the universe through certain philosophical arguments, and also through the natural sciences, have to be religiously neutral in order to preserve the human freedom of religious faith. Therefore, the arguments from the universe, such as the cosmological and design arguments, as well as the ontological arguments, do not resolve the religious ambiguity of the universe. They rather confirm existing religious belief.

According to Hick, knowledge derived from the world of things through science, whether arguments for or against the existence of God, and knowledge derived from religious experience, cannot play an intermediary role between God and human beings in any decisive manner, because God 'created' human beings in an epistemic distance to himself.

Religious Experience

One of the important contributions of this dissertation, as far as Hick's account of religion is concerned, is its claim that the religious vocabulary of today, most of which has been produced within the atmosphere of the secular liberal values of post-Enlightenment West, is the prime cause of any misunderstanding and misrepresentation of religious terminologies, beliefs and practices. Of this vocabulary, 'religion' itself is the most obviously problematic term. In his celebrated book, *The Meaning and End of Religion*, W. Cantwell Smith has urged Western scholars to drop this word completely from religious studies. Such terms as 'spirituality', 'revelation' and 'religious experience' are also potentially problematic especially when they are used to describe the life and culture of people who have not yet experienced anything similar to the European Enlightenment.[22]

The concept that concerns us here in this respect is that of religious experience. The concept of religious experience has been constructed in the context of Enlightenment philosophy, and it therefore bears the mark of Enlightenment values.

As Proudfoot rightly observes in his *Religious Experience*, the common usage of the term 'religious experience' and the focus on personal religious life were motivated on the whole by an interest in divorcing religious doctrines and practices from the dominance of metaphysical beliefs and ecclesiastical institutions in order to ground them in personal experience.[23]

Schleiermacher, who is the earliest and most systematic proponent of the concept of religious experience, employed this concept in order to save religion from the dominance of science and ethics. His book *On Religion* was a defence of religion against Kant who wanted to identify religion with morality. After Schleiermacher, R. Otto and later William James – whose *Varieties of Religious Experience* has made this concept widely known – were the thinkers who applauded individualistic religious life and religious feelings in preference to doctrinal religions.

61

When William James delivered his Gifford Lectures in 1902, fifty years after the publication of Auguste Comte's *Course of Positive Philosophy*, he felt he had to defend religion not by appealing to metaphysical doctrines – which at that time seemed to have lost their credibility in the face of the advance of science – but by appealing to the religious experiences of individuals, because empiricism was considered scientifically more credible. James' *Varieties of Religious Experience* can be seen as a book whose primary aim is to vindicate religion before the scientifically-minded intellectuals who had already invested so much hope in science. As Proudfoot points out, in the late nineteenth and early twentieth centuries, interest in the concept of religious experience was motivated by the search for a basic definition of religion.[24]

In the modern West, however, at least since the eighteenth century, the concept of religious experience has been available so that Western writers have taken this term for granted and have started to identify and correlate religious practices, doctrines and concepts with terminologies available in their culture. As Proudfoot observes, James' *Varieties* could only be written in a culture in which religious experience means something. He states:

> The concept of a religious experience, as distinct from Christian conversion, Buddhist meditation, or Jewish study or prayer, is a recent one. Were we to explicate our concept of religious experience as an experience that the subject identifies as religious, we would be forced to admit that religious experiences have been confined to the modern West. A good case could be made for this conclusion. The criteria that have been proposed by Schleiermacher, Otto, and others for the identification of the religious moment in experience are criteria that have *a history and that employ concepts that are recent and culture specific.* If only experiences that are apprehended by their subjects in those terms are to be counted as religious experiences, then the phenomenon is a very recent one. If, however, we want to accommodate in our expatiation of the concept its use to refer to experiences of persons to whom the term *religious* or its counterparts are not available, we must revise our account. The explication, to be useful, ought to capture some of our intuitions about the concept, and one of those is that it should be applicable to experiences outside the modern West [my italics].[25]

The danger of applying this concept to other religious cultures does not derive simply from the difficulty of identifying the meaning of the words 'religious' or 'experience' but also often from its 'handiness' or 'availability' for correlating some religious phenomenon in another religious tradition with something that exists in Western religious culture.

An experience, according to Hick, can be defined as 'a modification of the concept of consciousness', and religious experiences as 'those in the formation of which distinctively religious concepts are employed'.[26] From the point of view of his 'religious' interpretation of religion, religious experience can be defined as 'a transformation of the "information" generated at the interface between the Real and the human psyche'.[27]

As has been pointed out in the previous chapter, mystical experience generated at the moment of divine-human encounter is classified as unitive and communicative. The unitive mystical experiences, according to Hick, are 'experiences of oneness with God or with the absolute reality of Brahman or the eternal Buddha-nature'.[28] The communicative mystical experiences, on the other hand, are 'moments in which a divine being seems to encounter the mystic through visions, auditions'.[29]

Hick believes that in different traditions mystical visions and auditory experiences are shaped according to the cultural content of the tradition in question. For example, Hick argues that Isaiah's vision of Yahweh was different from Lady Julian's seeing a crucifix, and from Sri Ramakrishna's vision of Kali; and Samuel's experience of hearing the voice of Yahweh was different from Muhammad's hearing of Gabriel. For Hick, this diversity strongly suggests that 'the distinctive ideas and images, the historical and mythological themes, and the range of expectation made available by the mystic's tradition have provided the material out of which the experience is constructed'.[30]

Communicative mystical experiences occur as the result of the impact of the Real upon the mystic and this eventually generates information that can be assimilated by the mode of consciousness of the mystics and their community. Here the mystic's mind plays a distinctive role in transforming the information into meaningful human experience. Hick notes that such experiences are analogous to dream experiences or 'crisis apparitions'.[31]

What is important with regard to the main points of this work is that Hick, without questioning whether or not scientific explanation is relevant to the so-called 'religious experience', applies 'science' to the reports of religious experience. He believes that just as modern psychology can explain dream experiences and 'crisis apparitions', so mystical experiences can also be scientifically explained. Contrary to what Hick assumes, modern science including psychology is not able to comprehend the nature of mystical experience let alone to explain it, for the following reasons:

1 Scientific methods such as observation and experiment are not applicable to mystical experience because mystical experience is not repeatable.

2 The existence of the object of mystical experience is not scientifically provable. Hence, to what extent is it sensible for science to analyse an 'experience' whose source, or more specifically the existence of whose source, is not scientifically provable?

3 A scientific explanation of something, let us say the nature of water, must depend on the examination of the thing itself (water in this case), not a report or picture of the thing (writing about water or a picture of it). In the case of mystical experience we are always dependent upon the reports of such experiences, not the experiences themselves.

4 If some mystics claim that the nature of mystical experience is really ineffable, then there is no room left for a scientific explanation.[32]

One of the major problems with regard to the study of mystical experience is the relation between the mystic and the object of the experience, and the impact of cultural diversity upon the nature of experience.[33]

The claim that there can be unmediated mystical experience obviously conflicts with Hick's postulate that religion is the joint product of the Divine-human encounter. If there were found to be a process that enabled the human mind to transcend our dual consciousness, so that it could attain awareness of the Real as it is beyond all human conceptions, then it would become imperative for Hick to amend his conception of the Real.

The concept of religious experience is culturally specific and therefore is not able to provide an adequate means of understanding other religions outside the modern Christianity.

With regard to this, I suggest that to represent the Islamic terms *wahy* (revelation), *kashf* (vision), *jazba* (ecstasy) and *zuhd* (piety) with the term 'religious experience' is a mistake, not only because the term 'religious experience' is inadequate to convey the significance of these phenomena, but also because this concept actually misrepresents the meaning of some of these Islamic terms. This can be seen if we try to apply the concept of religious experience to the concept of *wahy*.[34]

Religious experience can simply be defined as apprehension or experience of the Divine.[35] But such a statement is quite vague and requires more detailed explanation. What does it mean to experience or apprehend God, given the fact that God is not a material being and therefore not subject to any kind of observation and measurement? If an experience is 'a roughly datable mental event'[36] and if religious experience is a roughly datable mental event whose subject is religious, how can such solely private experience be grounds for something that is mainly public, that is religion?

The concept of 'religious experience' explicitly conflicts with the theistic qualification of God. If God, as accepted by the theistic monotheistic religions such as Judaism, Christianity and Islam, is infinite, transcendent, eternal, all-powerful and all-knowing then the meaning of the experience of God is senseless, because finite and mortal human beings cannot experience a being that is infinite and transcendent.[37] If the concept of religious experience were essential for the description and understanding of religion, why did the great thinkers such as St. Thomas Aquinas, St. Anselm, Ibn 'Arabi, al-Ghazzali and al-Ash'ari not use this concept in their exposition of religious thought?

If the concept of religious experience is defined as experience or apprehension of God by *human mental endeavour*, then it seems that such a definition conflicts with the mainstream Islamic concept of God[38] The 'experience of God' sounds quite odd to the Muslim ear.[39] Rather Islam proposes that the knowledge of God-with-attributes (*sifat*), not of Godhead (*al-dhat*), is possible not through religious experience, that is, voluntary human mental endeavour, but through *wahy* (revelation).

The indiscriminate usage of the term 'religious experience' confuses the prophetic revelation (*wahy*) with mystical experience. The differences between mystical experience and prophetic revelation are too immense to ignore. What are these basic differences?[40]

Firstly, mystical experience is voluntary[41] and the mind of the mystic is active at the moment of experience. The mystic can choose to have a mystical experience. The knowledge resulting from mystical experience is the outcome of the active human mind. That is the reason why Ibn 'Arabi, al-Ghazzali and Eckhart, although acknowledging a Divine inspiration, were always claiming the possession of the knowledge they produced.

The prophetic revelation, on the other hand is involuntary,[42] and the mind of the prophet at the moment of such experience is passive. No one has become a prophet by virtue of training and hard work. The information received through prophetic experience is always attributed to God not to a prophet; the prophets are mere messengers in the real sense of the term. Ibn Khaldun illustrates the point:

> The knowledge that God gave them [prophets], and the wonders He manifested through their statements, indicated that there exist things beyond the reach of man that can be learned only from God through the mediation of such individuals, and that these individuals themselves cannot know unless God instructs them. Muhammed said: 'Indeed, I know only what God taught me.' It should be known that the information they gave is intrinsically and necessarily true...[43]

Hick, however, rejects the traditional Thomist Catholic notion of prepositional revelation which to a certain extent corresponds to the Islamic notion of revelation. Rather, he prefers an alternative view of revelation according to which:

> ... revelation consists, not in the divine communication of religious truth; but in the self-revealing actions of God within human history which Christianity sees as *Heilsgeschichte* holy history: beginning with the calling out of the Hebrews as a people in covenant with their God; continuing through their stormy career, during which God was seeking through events and circumstances, as interpreted to them by the prophets, to lead his people into a fuller knowledge of himself; culminating in the Christ event, in which God's love for mankind was seen directly at work on earth in the actions of Jesus.[44]

Secondly, the information brought about by prophetic revelation creates new religions. It speaks of the doctrines concerning the nature of reality as well as religious rituals. It constitutes the divine law, establishes 'do's and 'don't's. It lays a foundation for a body of ethics.

On the other hand, mythical experience often does not bring about new religions. It does not establish the Divine law, does not speak about 'do's and 'don'ts' in the manner of prophetic revelation. Mystics often consolidate the moral norms of the society in which they were brought up rather than laying down the foundation of new ethical norms. They do not form new religious rituals alongside already existing ones. They are generally aware of the limits of their message and do not consider it as universal.[45]

Thirdly, prophets often rebel against the religious norms of their society. The mystics, on the other hand, consolidate the religious norms of their society.

The term 'religious experience' should be dropped altogether, or at least must be restricted to describing 'mystical experience',[46] not prophetic revelation.

To substantiate my claim, I want to introduce the Islamic concept of *wahy* in order to see whether the concept of religious experience can convey the meaning of this term as it has been understood by Muslims.

In Islamic tradition *wahy* is, in fact, the primary source of all that is Islamic. Strangely enough, a phenomenon with such importance has been almost completely overlooked by most Muslim intellectuals, and it is quite difficult to find books devoted solely to the subject. With the exception of the philosophers, orthodox Muslim intellectuals have not analysed the nature or process of *wahy*. The reason for this is to be found in the 'political' power of orthodoxy: mainstream Islamic scholars from Sunnism as well as Shi'ism have often thought that it would be dangerous to initiate a process that questions the nature of *wahy*, the fundamental source of their faith. The other reason for this might be that in their eyes such theoretical speculation has not been as religiously valuable as those Islamic sciences.[47] Akhtar echoes such feelings:

> In Muslim interpretation, the Qur'an is the unadulterated Word of God. Who cares about the exact mechanism whereby it was revealed – if our interest is merely to understand its message? To be sure, one can understand someone's interest in the mechanics of *wahy*, but that interest would typically be motivated by some variety of scepticism or reserve about the authority. There can be no doubt that the question of mechanics of the revelation of the Qur'an is most likely to be interesting to those who reject its authority as divine. Unless the question of the genesis of the Qur'an – whether in the divine mind or Muhammadan psyche – is an open one, there is little motivation for being interested in the nature of the prophetic experience.[48]

On the other hand, Hick states:

> We become conscious of the existence of other objects in the universe, whether things or persons, either by experiencing them for ourselves or by inferring their existence from evidences within our experience. The awareness of God reported by the ordinary religious believer is of the former kind.[49]

For the purpose of this discussion, I would like to suggest an alternative account of knowing other objects and propose that we come to know things by experience, inference and intuition (revelation). I suggest that the knowledge of God reported by prophets comes to us through revelation. That is to say, we are aware of the existence of God and thus we believe in him not because we ourselves 'experience' God, but because we trust in the information that we receive through prophets.[50]

As has been indicated, it is difficult to speak of the nature of *wahy*, because it is involuntary and occurs quite rarely. Nevertheless, there seems to be some correspondence between intuition (*ilham*), which is the lower level of *wahy*, and prophetic revelation.[51] *Wahy* in the Islamic tradition is seen as information (*naba'*) from the unseen world (*'alam al-ghayb*). That is why the messenger is also named as *nabiy* 'informer'.[52]

In Islamic thought however, revelation (*wahy*) is regarded as an act by which God discloses himself to humankind through messengers. The precise nature of *wahy* is necessarily closed to non-participants. Such a revelatory process is fundamentally unobservable, but it can be known through its fruits. Mystical experience can also be acknowledged through its fruits. But there is an immense qualitative difference between the products of prophetic revelation and of mystical experience. Ibn Khaldun describes prophetic experience as 'an immersion in and encounter with the spiritual kingdom, the result of perception is congenial to them [prophets] but entirely foreign to the ordinary perceptions of men'.[53]

There are certain theories which attempt to explain the nature of *wahy* in the Islamic tradition. In Muslim intellectual history, to understand the nature of *wahy* has appeared not as a religious problem but as a rational problem. The scholars of Islamic sciences such as *fiqh* (Islamic jurisprudence), *hadith*, and *tafsir* (exegesis of the Quran), generally believe that this is a matter of belief (*iman*); hence it would be dangerous to speculate over it. On the other hand, Muslim philosophers – since they believed that they could rationalise every aspect of religion – developed a rational doctrine of *wahy* depending upon the Greek theories of the soul and its power of cognition. For instance Farabi and Ibn Sina developed their doctrine of prophetic revelation relying on Aristotle's doctrine of intellectual cognition exposed in his third book of *De Anima*. As Rahman points out, they see the prophet as 'a person of extraordinary intellectual endowment such that, by means of it, he is able to know all things by himself without the help of instruction by an external source.'[54] To explain the prophetic revelation Farabi insists on three important points which distinguish the prophet from the ordinary mind. Firstly, he claims that the prophet, unlike the ordinary person, is gifted with an extraordinary intellectual power. Secondly, the prophet's intellect differs from the philosopher's and mystic's intellect on the basis that it does not need an external instructor but develops by itself with the aid of divine power. Thirdly, at the end of the development, the prophetic intellect makes contact with the Active Intelligence which is considered to be the source of *wahy*. On the other hand, Ibn Sina, although he develops this doctrine further, objects to Farabi's third point maintaining that the prophetic revelation is not the result of a noetic development but something sudden, starting with a *coup*. He maintains that prophets differ from ordinary people in their power of intuition. They actually receive a truth without consciously turning it over it in their mind.[55] Ibn Sina states that the Active Intellect (*al-'aql al-fa'al*) is part and parcel of the prophet and is identical with him as far as prophetic revelation is concerned.[56] He also makes clear that an ordinary mystic does not possess an ability to receive prophetic revelation whereby a verbal revelation is received and a religious law is instituted. When the prophet receives a particular image from the heavenly bodies or when he receives intellectual and spiritual truth, he presents them with symbols since it is not possible to introduce the 'naked truth' to the realm whose categories are not applicable to it.[57] As Rahman points out, contrary to what Islamic orthodoxy assumed, the Muslim philosophers did not endorse the view that any human being, whether a philosopher or a mystic, can be a prophet.[58]

The Muslim philosophers' doctrine of *wahy* is consistent with my main point that there is an insurmountable difference between mystical experience and prophetic revelation. Therefore, I object to an indiscriminate usage of the term 'religious experience' on the basis that it confuses mystical experience with prophetic revelation. But the Muslim philosophers' doctrine of *wahy* does not seem convincing because, as Ibn Taymiyya points out,[59] they regard the Greek doctrine of intellectual perception as the precondition or the basis for explaining of the Islamic concept of *wahy* without questioning. Their doctrines of *wahy* in essence sound Greek rather than Islamic, and that is the reason why they have always remained marginal as far as mainstream Islamic thought is concerned.

In this context Ibn Khaldun is more convincing in his exposition of *wahy* than the Muslim philosophers. He believes that human beings are located at the threshold between the spiritual kingdom and the world of things. They are connected with the world of things through their bodies, the spiritual kingdom through their souls. He states:

> Above the soul there must exist something else that gives the soul the power of perception and motion, and that is also connected with it. Its essence should be pure perception and absolute intellection. This is the world of the angels. The soul, consequently, must be prepared to exchange humanity for angelicality, in order actually to become part of the angelic species at certain times in the flash of a moment. This happens after the spiritual essence of the soul has become perfect in actuality. . .[60]

He maintains that the soul is connected both upwards and downwards. Downwards, it is connected to the body from which it derives sense perception and the means to think. Upwards, it is connected with the level of the angels from which it receives its supernatural perceptions.[61]

For Ibn Khaldun, human souls are of three kinds. One is by nature too weak to arrive at spiritual perception. Therefore, it is happy to move downwards toward the perceptions of the senses and imagination. It can formulate ideas with the help of the power of the memory and 'the estimative power'. In this way, he says, people acquire 'perceptive and appreciative knowledge, which is the product of thinking in the body.'[62] It gains knowledge through the power of imagination. From its starting point, it can reach the 'primary' (*intelligibilia*) but cannot go beyond it. This is the goal of the perception of the scholars.

The second kind of soul is that which, through thinking, moves in the direction of spiritual intellection. It can perceive without using the body. In such perception the soul can go beyond the primary (*intelligibilia*) thereby covering 'the ground of inward observations, which are all intuitive.'[63] This is the perception of the saints.

The third kind of soul is that which can exchange humanity, both corporeal and spiritual humanity, for angelicality. In such a state, 'it may actually become an angel in the flash of a moment, glimpse the highest group within their own stage, and listen to essential speech and divine address during that moment.'[64] Ibn Khaldun writes:

(Individuals possessing this kind of soul) are prophets. God implanted and formed in them the natural ability to slough off humanity in that moment which is the state of revelation. God freed them from the lets and hindrances of the body, by which they were afflicted as human beings. He did this by means of *'ismah* (infallibility) and the straightforwardness, which He implanted in them and which gave them that particular outlook, and by means of a desire for divine worship which He centred in them and which converges from all sides toward that goal. They thus move toward the angelic, sloughing off humanity at will, by virtue of their natural constitution, and not with the help of any acquired faculty or craft.[65]

Ibn Khaldun's presentation of the doctrine of *wahy* can be located between Muslim philosophers and Muslim orthodox scholars such as Ibn Taymiyya and Shahrastani. As Rahman points out, he certainly differs in one crucial point from the philosophers and leans toward orthodoxy with regard to the actual verbal revelation. The philosophers believe that although verbal revelation cannot present pure truth, it nevertheless presents truth through symbolic representations; Ibn Khaldun, on the other hand, claims that the recorded revelation, the Quran, is the human form of the purely spiritual divine logos. For him there is no gap between word and spiritual message; the word is not the interpretation of the message that is received.[66]

Islam, however, discriminates between various categories of revelation in the technical sense, starting with the most concrete written revelation that is the sacred text of the Muslims, and proceeding down to the lower category of intuition (*ilham*). The most obvious revelation in Islam is the Quran through which God addresses humankind directly using the first person plural. After the Quran comes *al-hadith al-qudsi* (divine sayings) in which God also speaks in the first person. Then comes the *hadith* which is more akin to inspiration.[67] The authority of a specific revelation for a Muslim depends upon where it is situated in this hierarchical structure. Muslims believe that the Quran has absolute authority as the word of God, followed by *al-hadith al-qudsi*, then the *hadith*. In this context, the distinction between the Quran and the *hadith* has important theological implications. In the Islamic tradition it is believed that the Quran is immutable and the absolute word of God; some Muslim theologians have claimed that it was uncreated, and existed eternally as the divine attribute of speech (*kalam Allah*). On the other hand, the *hadith* as the channel of the prophetic *sunnah* is historically contingent; it is believed that the ideas of the *hadith* are from God, whereas its words are not.[68]

As Zaki observes, the concept of *wahy* in Islam is seen essentially as the disclosure of things which would otherwise be unknown. The source of *wahy* is regarded as being the 'supersensible' or unseen world. The Quran speaks of itself as being 'information from the Unseen' (*al-ghayb*). It is also regarded as the transcript of a celestial archetype. The Quranic term *al-lawh al-mahfuz* (the Preserved Tablet) refers to such an archetype. In the Quran the process of revelation is expressed by the term *inzal* (sending down), which comes from a transitive verb, *anzala*, which signifies 'sending down' something which is already in existence. It is possible to argue that this notion of 'descent' affirms not only the transcendence of God – since the Quran could only descend to things that it transcends – but also the hierarchical existence of unseen worlds.[69] In the Quran the Prophet is commanded to adhere strictly to the text of what is revealed to him (43:43) when his critics suggested that he made some alteration or change it. He replied by saying 'it is not for me of my own accord to change it. I follow not but what is revealed unto me. If I were to disobey my Lord, I should myself fear the Penalty of a Great Day (to come)' (10:15).

Very little is known about the manner in which the revelation of the Quran took place. The Quran itself speaks of the ways by which God disclosed himself: 'And it was never given to any mortal that God should speak to him but by revelation or behind a veil or by sending an envoy to reveal whatever he wills' (45:51).

The companions of the Prophet observed a physical change in him at the moment when he was receiving the revelation. Ibn Khaldun interprets this physical change as the sign of transformation from one stage to another:

> It should be known that, in general, the state of revelation presents difficulties and pains throughout. Revelation means leaving one's humanity, in order to attain angelic perceptions and to hear the speech of the soul. This causes pain, since it

means that an essence leaves its own essence and exchanges its own stage for the ultimate stage. This is the meaning of the choking feeling which Muhammad referred to in connection with the beginning of the revelation in his statement: 'And he (Gabriel) choked me until it became too much for me; then he released me. . .'[70]

Ibn Khaldun maintains that a person who receives revelations initially finds the experience a difficult and even alien one. This is the reason why the earliest passages and verses of the Quran revealed to Muhammad in Mecca, are shorter than those revealed to him in Medina.[71]

There are some passages in the *hadith* collection which describe how the revelation to the Prophet took place. For instance, Bukhari refers to the ringing of bells[72] and Tirmidhi mentions a sound like the humming of bees. Apart from these passages, very little has been said concerning the 'psychology' of revelation.

This brief presentation of the Islamic conception of *wahy* is sufficient to show that Hick's attempt to encapsulate *wahy* vaguely under the heading of religious experience is misleading: not only does his account of religious experience confuse the prophetic revelation with mystical revelation, but also his concept of religious experience is not able to discriminate between the religious experience of Julian of Norwich and that of Shirley MacLaine. Again it might be argued that Hick's conception of religious experience does not acknowledge any difference between revelation as the source of religions and *ilham* (inspiration) as the source of intuitive knowledge and poetry, which do not seem to have any significant theological implications.

Religious Language

One of the concerns of the present study is to analyse Hick's notion of religious language in relation to his belief in religious realism. To hold the view, as Hick does, that religious language truly refers to a transcendent reality characterises one as realist rather than non-realist. The realist, says Hick, understands religious language 'as referring to an object of discourse that is 'there' to be referred to'.[73] Hence, according to Hick, in 'the Judeo-Christian-Islamic talk about God', the realist belief is that God exists as an unlimited personal being. Hick reminds us that his notion of religious realism[74] should not of course be equated with a straightforward literal affirmation of

73

religious discourse, because he believes that religious concepts, such as the concepts of God and the Absolute, are constructed according to the conceptual systems embodied in the language of a particular society. His critical realism[75] differs from the kind of religious 'naive realism' which takes the scriptural and traditional religious teachings literally.[76] Rather, it affirms that 'the realm of religious experience is not *in toto* a human projection and illusion but constitutes a range of cognitive responses, varying from culture to culture, to the presence of a transcendent reality or realities'.[77]

Hick's critical realism should not be confused with the non-realism which has been exemplified by such thinkers as L. Feuerbach, R. B. Braithwaite, J. H. Randall, D. Z. Phillips and D. Cupitt. The core of their understanding of religion is that religious language, despite its empirical and historical bearings, is non-cognitive. For Feuerbach, for instance, the objects of religious faith are human projections; while for R. B. Braithwaite religious statements are moral statements dressed in the symbols, metaphors and myths of religion. D. Z. Phillips, whose main inspiration comes from Wittgenstein, sees religious language as coded language about our present spiritual state. According to him, 'it would be foolish to speak of eternal life as some kind of appendage to human existence, something which happens *after* human life on earth is over.'[78] Rather, he believes, eternal life is not more life but this life seen under certain moral and religious modes of thought.[79] Don Cupitt, who believes that the importance of religious life and belief can be maintained if religious language is construed in a non-realist way, claims that religious belief is none other than believing in 'various supernatural beings, powers and events'.[80]

In Hick's view, although contemporary non-realists are right on penultimate issues, that is in their emphasis on the fruits of faith in ordinary human life as well as in moral and spiritual life, they are mistaken in their understanding of religious language with regard to the ultimate issue of the nature of the universe and the place of humanity within it. Hick considers that they are mistaken in believing that the physical universe, including consciousness, is itself the only reality. The implication of such thinking for the concept of God is that God would then be considered to exist only as an idea in our mind.[81]

Hick believes the non-realist interpretation of religious language is basically a misinterpretation and misrepresentation of what the believer understands from religious language.[82] On this particular point, there is the observation that the moral and spiritual fruits of faith with which the non-realists are supposedly so concerned, are only possible if the believer interprets religious language realistically. In no circumstances could a serious believer, let us say, a saint believe that God is a human projection in the modern sense and at the same time carry on fulfilling his or her religious and spiritual obligations with vigour.

Hick's main criticism of the non-realists is that they are essentially pessimistic with regard to the future of humankind, while his own critical realism is not:

> There is, however, a fundamental anomaly in this non-realist position: namely that whereas the central core of religious discourse interpreted in a realist way constitutes, if true, good news to all humankind, on a non-realist interpretation it constitutes bad news for all except a fortunate minority. This is a major and disturbing anomaly, for the non-realist interpretation professes to express the permanently valuable meaning of our traditional religious language. That language presents a picture which, whilst often grimly pessimistic in the short run -acknowledging fully the structural inevitability of suffering and the universality of moral wickedness – is nevertheless on the long view profoundly optimistic. For it looks beyond death to resurrection, beyond sin and suffering to an eternal heavenly life, beyond the pain-ridden wheel of Samsara through the gateway of enlightenment to Moksha or to the 'further shore' of Nirvana.[83]

A number of comments must be made on this point. There seems to be a problem in holding that our traditional religious languages promote a profound optimism. If, let us say, each of five traditions A, B, C, D, E claims that only its own believers, who are always a minority of the whole world population, can be saved, this does not mean that the totality of believers, irrespective of their tradition, can be saved. In other words, if salvation beyond earthly transformation is a tradition-specific doctrine and therefore cannot embrace the members of other traditions, then it seems to me implausible to derive a sense of universal optimism from such particularity.

As has been pointed out, Hick's critical realism differs substantially from naive religious realism inasmuch as it interprets religious language as the means of conveying mythological religious truth. Hick believes that if religious language, such as 'God created the world', clashes with our conventional and scientific understanding of the universe, it has to be regarded as mythological language speaking about a religious truth in its own manner.

According to Hick, mythological truth can be defined as follows: 'a statement or set of statements about X is mythologically true if it is not literally true but nevertheless tends to evoke an appropriate dispositional attitude to X.'[84] Mythological truth as compared with literal truth, is 'practical' and existential. For instance, according to Hick, the fall, or the story of the Buddha's flight through the sky to Sri Lanka, or the belief that the *suras* of the Quran were dictated by Gabriel, are all mythologically expressed 'truths'. Again, the Christian ceremony of the Eucharist can be seen as a mythological way of expressing openness to God through Christ, the doctrine of reincarnation and is a mythological way of making the moral claim that our actions here have inevitable future consequences.[85] Hick concludes that a mythological truth is 'one which rightly relates us to a reality about which we cannot speak in non-mythological terms'.[86]

As can be inferred from Hick's realist commitment, he does not consider the discourse of religious language to be totally mythological. Some religious statements are factual statements expressing meaning literally about reality.

A number of comments must be made on this point. If there are (using Hick's own term) 'fact asserting' statements alongside the 'myth asserting' ones, there surely has to be some criterion according to which one would be able to distinguish the fact asserting religious statements from the myth asserting ones. Without such a distinction it would be extremely difficult for a believer to maintain his or her religious commitment. Hick overlooks the importance of identifying such a criterion. But the criterion Hick seems to identify is the 'inexpressibility' of religious propositions in literal ways. In other words, Hick believes that a statement is mythological if it is not possible to express its meaning literally.

As has been pointed out, although it is of crucial importance, Hick does not explain clearly the difference between of the mythological and non-mythological. To clarify Hick's standpoint, let me apply his notion 'mythological truth' to a specific religious statement. I would like to analyse the statement 'the Quran is the word of God'. Is this statement mythological or non-mythological? For Hick it is mythological because it is not possible to read this statement literally, since the Real cannot speak and has not spoken with people and hence the notion of 'the word of God' sounds senseless. This means that Hick's view on this issue is determined by his prior belief that the Real cannot communicate with people. In the same manner, those Muslims who understand this statement literally do so because of their prior belief that God can communicate and has communicated with people.

I believe that beyond such an account lies Hick's implicit affirmation of liberal values and his trust in science. For him it is, ultimately, the conventional modern understanding of religion and science which can function as the criteria for distinguishing factual religious statements from mythological ones. Hick's endeavour to demythologise religious language cannot be effective until he has dealt clearly with this problem. In fact, to relate the issue of religious language to our main discussion, I would argue that religious language understood in such a manner could not, even in principle, be a source of knowledge conveying the message of the Divine.

Knowledge as Vision

It is certainly a problematical task to compare Hick, whose philosophy of religion bears the stamp of the idealism of Kant and the empiricism of Hume, with Nasr, whom it is hard to situate within any mainstream philosophical orientation of the West, with the possible exception of Neoplatonism. The two thinkers differ entirely in their conceptions of knowledge: Hick's concept is basically constituted from elements of post-Enlightenment philosophy, while Nasr's is constituted by the principles of Islamic faith and the perennial philosophy. One point on which they seem to come together is that they both see a unity behind the diversity of religions, but even that unity they understand differently. The unity that Nasr envisages is an all-encompassing unity: it is unity with all existence, with the universe, humanity and the Unseen. On the other hand, the unity that Hick sees is in the One i.e. the Real *an sich* that is the basis of religious experience as well as all religious transformations. Hick, however, sees no concrete correlation between the universe and the Real *an sich*. Since we cannot find a direct relationship between them, we are obliged to consider Hick's critique of the infallibilist theory of knowledge as an indirect criticism of Nasr's conception of knowledge, while regarding Nasr's critique of rational and empirical knowledge as an indirect critique of Hick's account of knowledge.

In *Faith and Knowledge* Hick examines the Platonist view that knowledge is a direct and infallible acquaintance with reality. He notes that, according to this view, knowing is a generalised form of seeing construed as simple intuition; it is the result of intellectual vision.[87] Hick believes that in contemporary philosophy, knowledge is concerned with the truth of propositions, but has nothing to do with the 'acquaintance with reality'. For him the central tenet of Platonist theory is that knowing is self-authenticating and infallible: to 'know' in this sense means to 'be confronted by fact or truth'. Knowledge, although by definition infallible, is not of course exhaustive.[88]

For Hick, the infallibilist theory of knowledge, although coherent in its own terms, represents a misleading approach as far as our field of inquiry is concerned. He states:

Instead of sitting down before the facts and treating our cognitive experiences as data to be described, compared and classified, the infallibilist philosophers have defined a priori an ideal concept of knowledge and have assumed that this must be exemplified in our experience. They have constructed an epistemological model, instead of scrutinising human knowledge in the sense in which we actually possess it and seeking to determine precisely what that sense is. They have, in effect, in the spirit of 'high priorism', sought to view human knowledge from a vantage point outside human nature and thus to play the part of an angelic or godlike intelligence.[89]

The traditional idealisation of the concept of knowledge, according to Hick, is self-defeating, because when it elevates knowledge to a metaphysical domain it cuts off all contact with common human experience and therefore ignores all concrete instances of cognition. Hick thinks that this is a paradox inasmuch as the infallibilist theory of knowledge adopts a procedure whose aim is to exalt human cognition but ends with a general deflation of it. Hick believes that the claim to knowledge in this sense, that is, the infallibilist acquaintance with truth, is not plausible, because there is no state of mind which could grant to the knowing process an absolute guarantee of freedom from error. If to know is the equivalent of to see 'or to be acquainted with truth', it should not be possible for one to think mistakenly that one knows, since the truth of knowledge is guaranteed by the knowing process itself.[90]

The application of this theory to the case of religious knowledge is interesting. Having rejected the view that knowledge is the infallible acquaintance with truth, Hick does not accept the view that, for instance, the prophets' or saints' knowledge of God is self-authenticating. Rather, Hick tends to shift from an idealised intellectual vision to ordinary religious experience as being the source of religious knowledge. The certainty that religious people have had concerning the reality of God, according to Hick, comes from their own religious experience.

As has been pointed out, I mainly object to the indiscriminate use of the term 'religious experience', and claim that believers in most cases do not construct their religious belief or knowledge of God *through their own religious experience*. If they had formed their own concept of God through their own experience, then religion would be something solely personal whose characteristics would differ from individual to individual. As a matter of fact, what believers do is simply trust the beliefs they received from their parents. They then accept or reject the given faith according to their socio-political and religious circumstances[91].

Hick believes that the infallibilist theory of knowledge is defective since it belittles the power of our cognitive experience. My reply to such a criticism on behalf on the infallibilist would be as follows: Our ordinary cognitive experience, as it has been presented in modern epistemology, is legitimate insofar as it deals with the domain that falls within the scope of the senses and reason. In other words, I believe that our cognitive experience, as it is envisaged in the epistemology of modern philosophy, has principally to do with knowledge of physical reality and is legitimate within that domain. But knowledge of the Ultimate does not occur through the religious experience of ordinary people, but through the intellectual vision which can be available only to the chosen few. Such intellectual vision does not contradict our sense perception with regard to the experience of the physical world. This experience cannot be denied by the knowledge that is supposed to be attained by intellectual vision. On the contrary, intellectual vision transcends sense perception and reason. It is not opposed to, but goes beyond our ordinary faculties of knowledge.[92]

Contrary to Hick's view, it is not the state or activity of mind called 'knowing' that ensures the authenticity of the results of that process. Rather, it is the *nature* of the knowledge received in such an extraordinary state that ensures the sense of authenticity. Such knowledge possesses a supernatural quality through which it speaks of the nature of reality and human responsibility, i.e. ethics as well as the end, salvation such unequivocal and poetic fashions. It addresses humankind with authority as if it comes from somewhere beyond human reach. It differs from rational knowledge inasmuch as it has not generally been bounded within the historical circumstances of a specific culture. It is not confined to the particular individual who conveys such knowledge.

One of the most important characteristics of such knowledge of the Ultimate is that it aims not only to inform or persuade the people it addresses, but also to guide them to salvation. The knowledge itself has the quality of being able to transform those who know it. Then it is certainly conceivable that such knowledge could sound infallible for those who are already prepared for such a transformation. From this standpoint, the perennialist can dismiss Hick's critique of infallibilist theory by saying that he could have realised the power of such self-authenticating knowledge if his existential being had been ready to receive an appropriately illuminating intellectual revelation.

Having answered the question whether knowledge of the Ultimate is available according to Hick's writings, it is now time to pose the same question to Nasr. The answer to this question is crucial to one of the main themes of this thesis, namely, religious pluralism.

'Given Knowledge' or 'Gained Knowledge'; Intellect or Reason

> It was we who created man, and we know what dark suggestion his soul makes to him: for we are nearer to him than (his) jugular vein. (The Quran 50:16)

> God is nearer to me than I am to myself: He is just as nearer to wood and stone, but they do not know it. (Meister Eckhart)

> Now, if anyone should put the questions, whether I admit any view at all, he should be answered thus: The Perfect One is free from any theory, for the Perfect One has understood what the body is, and how it arises and passes away. He has understood what the mental functions are, and how they arise and pass away. He had understood what consciousness is, and how it arises and passes away. Therefore, I say, the Perfect One has won complete deliverance through the extinction, fading away, disappearance, rejection, and getting rid of all opinions and conjectures, of all inclination to the vainglory of 'I' and 'mine'. (The Buddha)

Why do such statements tend to sound peculiar to those who are touched by the secular norms of modernity? The answer to this question lies in the perennialist claim that the sacred quality of the human being has been impoverished by the desacralization of culture. Thus, a modern person has gradually become unaware of his or her inner spirituality. However, if the secularisation process is the main cause preventing the modern person from having religious and spiritual awareness, then the perennialist has a point in claiming that to acknowledge the message of the Sacred requires awareness of a spiritual and esoteric dimension. In other words, according to such a traditional perspective, the modern person has limited himself or herself in the attempt to apprehend the sacred message.[93]

One way of introducing Nasr's notion of knowledge to the Western academy is perhaps to compare it with some of the disciplines which possess a certain similarity to the perennial philosophy. Neoplatonism and mysticism are two such disciplines.

Although in his major works, such as *Knowledge and the Sacred* and *The Need For Sacred Science*, there are a number of references to Plato, Plotinus, Proclus and Pythagoras, Nasr is not in fact a Neoplatonist, because his entire thought and his existential and intellectual concerns are primarily religious rather than philosophical.

The epistemology of the perennial philosophy in general and Nasr's understanding of knowledge in particular differ substantially from the epistemology of Neoplatonism. The perennialist and the Neoplatonist are in accord in their claim that there is a hierarchical chain of being corresponding to the hierarchical chain of knowing. But Nasr differs in his theory of knowledge from the epistemology of Neoplatonism inasmuch as he puts the emphasis on revelation – understood in a religious rather than philosophical context – and on the intellect, which is regarded as somehow divine.

Neoplatonist epistemology speaks of the soul's gradual procession starting with 'reception' and 'judgement of sense perception', proceeding through the collection of 'intelligible objects' or universals, and finally reaching tranquillity, when it attains a unity with its origin. It talks about particulars and universals. It is also concerned with intellect and grades of intellect in a familiar philosophical fashion. Its main emphasis, however, focuses on the procession or emanation of all creation from the One.[94]

Although both Neoplatonism and Nasr speak of unity, Nasr differs from Neoplatonism by introducing unity with more religious colour. He believes that there is underlying unity within all diversity, diversity in religions, diversity in the cosmos. One of the tasks of the perennial philosophy is to exhibit 'unifying truth' using whatever means are available, whether Neoplatonist concepts or Hindu or Christian or Jewish or Islamic. In other words, the perennialist claims that there is an immutable, the *sophia perennis*, which is the essence of all religions and traditions and does not change with changes of time and place. What changes is the form or theological expression of this *sophia perennis*. Hence, at the present time, the perennialist would say, the *sophia perennis* has reformulated itself by employing a kind of modern language in order to express the Truth.

As for mysticism, Nasr claims that it should not be equated with the perennial philosophy, though he does maintain that if mysticism retains its positive meaning as something speaking about 'Divine Mysteries', then the sapiential perspective can itself be regarded as mystical.[95]

There are a number of different approaches to the classification of the studies of mysticism. For instance, W. T. Stace classifies mysticism as extrovertive and introvertive,[96] while R. C. Zaehner prefers to make a distinction between panenthetic, monistic and theistic mysticism.[97] In contemporary religious studies two approaches introduced by S. T. Katz have been widely recognised in classifying mystical experiences.[98] These are known as constructivist and essentialist views of mysticism.

There are a number of different constructivist views, but they are united in their claim that all mystical experiences are determined by the mystic's conceptual framework. The mystic's own inherited conceptual structure, they believe, not only colours the interpretations of mystical experience, but actually affects the nature of the experience itself. That is to say, according to the constructivist, there are no pure (i.e. unmediated) mystical experiences. The chief representatives of this group are S. T. Katz, Robert M. Gimello,[99] Michael Stoeber[100] and John Hick.[101]

In contrast to the constructivist stance, the essentialist view claims that in spite of cultural diversity and conceptual differences, all mystical experiences are essentially the same. Although the essentialists are united in making this claim they differ in the emphasis they place on the role of the mystic's conceptual framework in characterising the nature of mystical experience. As Katz notes, there are three different forms of the essentialist view:

i) One group believes that mystical experiences are the same and are caused by the same unique reality, although they differ 'formally' in their 'descriptions' of that reality. They claim that mystical experiences ultimately express the unique underlying truth which transcends cultural and religious diversity. This thesis has been defended by perennialist philosophers like Frithjof Schuon, Rene Gue'non, Ananda Coomaraswamy, Aldous Huxley and S. H. Nasr.[102]

ii) A second thesis holds that all mystical experiences are the same but that mystics' reports of their experiences are culturally bound. This view is expressed by R. Otto,[103] E. Underhill[104] and D. T. Suzuki.

iii) The third thesis argues that, although the language used by the mystics to describe their experiences is culturally bound, their experiences are not. Among the representative of this thesis are R. C. Zaehner, W. T. Stance and N. Smart.[105]

Smart[106] and Katz[107] see the perennial philosophy as an approach within contemporary religious thought. But, I believe, the perennialists themselves would object to such a classification; they do not want to circumscribe their ideas within the domain of the study of mysticism. For them the *sophia perennis* is not only an approach, but also a *Weltanschauung*, which possesses a potential that can offer guidelines not only to religious studies, but also to life itself.

What makes the perennial philosophy quite distinct from any modern knowledge is the kind of discrimination it imposes within the field of knowledge. It aims to distinguish metaphysical knowledge, or the *scientia sacra*, from ordinary or discursive knowledge. It believes that while the former is primarily concerned with knowledge of the Ultimate, the latter is mainly involved with knowledge of the universe and with us as conscious beings.

Before examining the nature of sacred knowledge, something should be said about this division of knowledge into sacred and 'non-sacred'. From the perspective of the contemporary philosophy of religion, it might be argued that such a distinction is unjustifiable, in that human beings, who are equipped with senses and reason, are thereby endowed with an ability to know whatever becomes subject to their knowledge.

However, the perennialist's division of knowledge is in fact warranted, since it is by no means unreasonable to assume that the means of knowing the Ultimate should be different from the means of knowing the physical universe. On the contrary, since the nature of the Ultimate is completely different from the nature of the Universe, the means that are appointed to attain the knowledge of the Ultimate should necessarily be different from the means that are assigned to know the physical universe. Our human faculties of knowledge include reason, and our senses are qualified to know the subjects that fall into the domain of such faculties. The Transcendent being by definition transcends the realm of senses and reason. Although human faculties can be helpful in rationalising the given knowledge of the Ultimate, they alone are not able to attain the Ultimate.[108]

On the other hand, it might also be argued that the history of rational philosophy since Descartes has at least proved that knowledge which is produced through inductive reasoning and argumentation, always generates antithetical forms of reasoning and counter-argumentation, thus creating in the thought of modern people the prevailing situation of uncertainty. Moreover, one might argue that the perennialist's distinction with regard to knowledge may be justifiable because, in addition to what modern philosophy envisages as the characteristics of that knowledge, the perennial philosophy considers virtue and morality to be additional aspects, with the implication that knowledge is capable of making an impact on the moral behaviour of the knower.

Nevertheless, the perennial philosophy can be related to current philosophy through its claim that it deals with metaphysics, which is defined as an attempt to characterise existence and reality as a whole or an attempt to explore the realm of the 'suprasensible'.[109] In this context, Nasr defines metaphysics as 'the science of the Real or, more specifically, the knowledge by means of which man is able to distinguish between the Real and the illusory and to know things in their essence or as they are, which means ultimately to know them *in divinis*'.[110]

In a very speculative manner, and availing oneself of Kantian vocabulary, one might say that for Nasr, metaphysics, which is viable through intellectual intuition, can be regarded as the knowledge of the noumenon:[111]

The knowledge of the Principle which is at once the absolute and infinite Reality is the heart of metaphysics while the distinction between the levels of universal and cosmic existence, including both the macrocosm and the microcosm, are like its limbs. Metaphysics concerns not only the Principle in Itself and its manifestations but also the principles of the various sciences of a cosmological order. At the heart of the traditional sciences of the cosmos, as well as the traditional anthropology, psychology, and aesthetics stands the *scientia sacra* which contains the principles of these sciences while being primarily concerned with the knowledge of the Principle which is both sacred knowledge and knowledge of the sacred par excellence, since the Sacred as such is none other than the Principle.[112]

However, our interest here is not to argue for the superiority of sacred knowledge over other forms of knowledge, but to bring the main features of such knowledge to light in order to make a comparison possible.

Before proceeding any further, one has to acknowledge that Nasr's implicit classification of knowledge as sacred or otherwise is anomalous and sounds odd from the perspective of modern epistemology.[113] But this must not deter us from pursuing the implication of Nasr's ideas, which are potentially more appropriate than Hick's when it comes to the description of religion.

It is possible to speak of the different characteristics of sacred knowledge in the following manner. The *scientia sacra* differs from discursive knowledge in its identification of the source of knowledge. The sources of 'ordinary knowledge', as they are identified by contemporary epistemology, are sense perception and inductive reasoning, whereas the sources of sacred knowledge, according to Nasr, are revelation and intellectual intuition in addition to reason and sense perception. It is claimed that, while reasoning stems from the mind, intellection issues from the heart, illuminating the mind of the person in question. What distinguishes the *scientia sacra* from other forms of knowledge is the fact that while other kinds of knowledge are the product of speculating on or reasoning about the subject matter, sacred knowledge is a knowledge acquired through intuition in which human speculation plays no part. However, this does not mean that it is unintelligible. What is received through intellectual intuition is itself intelligible. But 'the human intelligence which perceives this message and receives this truth does not impose upon it the *intellectual nature or content of a spiritual experience* of a sapiential character.[114] (my italics). In the constitution of such knowledge human intelligence functions not as a source but as a participant:

The truth descends upon the mind like an eagle landing upon a mountain top or it gushes forth and inundates the mind like a deep well which has suddenly burst forth into a spring. In either case, the sapiential nature of what the human being receives through spiritual experience is not the result of man's mental faculty but issues from the nature of that experience itself. Man can know through intuition and revelation not because he is a thinking being who imposes the categories of his thought upon what he perceives but because knowledge is being. The nature of reality is none other than consciousness, which, needless to say, cannot be limited to only its individual human mode.[115]

Needless to say, such a conception of knowledge stands completely opposed to modern epistemology, let alone Hick's theory of knowledge, since Hick believes that the person who undergoes such spiritual experience is still an embodied mind and therefore imposes his or her conceptual framework upon the results of that experience.

It is not feasible within the scope of the present work, to try and resolve the question of whether unmediated mystical (revealed) knowledge is possible. Suffice it to say that what mystics report of their spiritual experience, employing a particular language, is unlikely to be a complete description of what they have encountered.[116] Intense spiritual experience, which is analogous perhaps to certain forms of drug induced experience, must itself be ineffable. For mystics, religious language and concepts are only an inadequate means, available at that particular moment to express the message which has been conveyed.

In order to clarify the nature of sacred knowledge as compared to ordinary knowledge, something must be said about the relation between both reason and the intellect, and the intellect and revelation. Firstly, what is the intellect? The concept of intellect, which already existed in Neoplatonism and also in medieval Islamic philosophy, has been resurrected by the perennial philosophy through bestowing on it a new role to play in the modern era. It is this emphasis upon the divinely guided intellect that separates the perennialists from modernist thinkers.

According to Nasr, intelligence is a divine gift which is able to penetrate veils of cosmic existence and know the Ultimate as it is. The intellect, Nasr believes, is itself divine. But it can be human to the extent that one can participate in it. Therefore, the intellect is divine and human both in substance and function, while reason is a 'reflection of the Intellect upon the human plane'.[117] That is to say, through reasoning one can only apprehend reality partially, and often discursively, while through intellection or intellectual intuition one can transcend reason and attain what cannot be apprehended through reason. Intellection, according to Nasr, is nothing other than 'joining our consciousness to the Divine consciousness':

> The metacosmic principle which is the Intellect is the source of both knowledge and being, of the subjective conscience which knows and the objective order which is known. It is also the source of revelation which creates a nexus between man and the cosmos and of course the metacosmic Reality. The Logos or *Buddhi* or *aql*, as the Intellect is called in various traditions, is the luminous centre which is the generating agent of the world – for 'it was by the Word that all things were made' – of man, and of religion. It is God's knowledge of Himself and the first in His creation.[118]

According to Nasr, the objection that is raised by the rationalistic argument against the viability of such sacred knowledge does not hold, because intellection transcending reason does not arrive at the truth as a result of profane thought, but 'through a priori direct intuition of the truth'. Although reasoning may act as the occasion of intellection, it cannot be the actual cause of intellection. That is why, for Nasr, results arrived at through intellection cannot be nullified by reasoning. While reasoning unavoidably involves the limitations of the person who reasons and is therefore often subject to error, intellection goes beyond reasoning and so captures reality without 'disturbing' it.[119]

As far as the relation between the intellect and revelation is concerned, Nasr believes that, since human beings became separated from their primordial nature, that is, from their celestial essence, they have not been able to make use of the intellect without aid from heaven. Revelation, according to Nasr, is this aid from heaven and it alone can bring about the actualisation of the potential of the intellect that exists in human nature. As regards the kind of external revelation exemplified in sacred scripture, the intellect functions as a key to unlock the door to the treasures of wisdom stored up in the sacred books of the traditions. According to Nasr, the revealed books can only open up their inner dimension to those who are able to use their intellection, and remain veiled to those who are cut off from this inner sacrament.[120]

However, to say the intellect transcends reason is not to say that intellection nullifies reasoning, but rather to affirm the intellect as the cause or root of reason. That is to say, the intelligence of the heart incorporates the results of reasoning. In this respect, as Nasr notes, the perennial philosophy does not oppose the use of reason, or activity of the mind. What it objects to is the divorce of reason from its root, that is, from the intellect or heart. Therefore, the attempt of modern rationality to discover the intellect is misguided since:

'... the object which the rational faculty is trying to perceive is actually the subject which makes the very act of perception by the rational faculty possible. A mind which is cut off from the light of the intelligence of the heart and which seeks to find God is unaware that the light with which it is seeking to discover God is itself a ray of the Light of God. Such a mind cannot but be like a person wandering in the desert in the brightness of day with a lamp in his hand looking for the sun. Blindness does not issue from reason but from reason being cut off from the intellect and then trying to play the role of the intellect in the attainment of knowledge'.[121]

One of the problems in maintaining the viability of sacred knowledge is, I suspect, that there is no agreed criterion according to which one could distinguish the *scientia sacra* from so-called ordinary knowledge. For rational knowledge the common sense understanding of 'reasonableness' or reason itself functions as the criterion. In the case of scientific knowledge, for instance, we have laboratories to further test the findings of scientific research and therefore we are able to see 'verified scientific knowledge', whence the remarkable scientific achievements which are the outcome of such precise and meticulous questioning.[122] But for sacred knowledge, we are told, the questioning mind is inadequate because such knowledge functions on a different plane. If reason falls short in its enquiry into the results of intellection, then there must be something else which replaces reason. There appears to be no plausible ground on which one could distinguish a genuine intellectual intuition from an illusory one. Hence, Nasr would not be able to give a convincing answer to a practitioner of New Age religion who claimed to have had a spiritual experience by which, let us say, he or she has come upon knowledge that nullifies the main proposition of the perennial philosophy.[123]

Is God Knowable?

Before replying to the above question, Hick would immediately object to its construction and would wish to be told to what kind of question is being asked. Is the question about knowledge of the 'gods' of religions or about knowledge of the Real *an sich*? If the former, Hick would reply that knowledge of the Real *an sich* on a phenomenological level is always possible, not as knowledge of the Real itself but of its manifestations; for him, one could easily have access to knowledge of Allah through Islamic tradition, that of Adonai through the Jewish tradition, that of the Heavenly Father through the Christian tradition, that of Vishnu or Shiva through the Hindu tradition, and so on. However, if one were inquiring whether it is possible to have knowledge of the Real *an sich* as the noumenal ground of these phenomenal deities, Hick's answer would be in the negative. The Real *an sich* cannot be knowable because the person who experiences transcendent Reality always imposes his or her own conceptual framework upon the knowledge which he or she receives. In other words, since Hick believes that unmediated knowledge of the Ultimate is impossible, it follows that any knowledge of the transcendent Reality has to be culturally relative.

If there is 'unmediated metaphysical knowledge', that is, knowledge through revelation, then it is possible to hold the view that objective knowledge of the Ultimate is viable. In other words, from such a perspective it is possible to divide knowledge into 'metaphysical knowledge' that is available through a divinely illuminated intellect, and 'rational knowledge', which is available through *ratio*. The latter, which is argumentative in character, seems very 'human' and appeals to the mind of the person who examines it. The arguments for the existence of God, whether they be modern (such as R. Swinburne's probability arguments[124] or Alvin Plantinga's version of the ontological argument[125]) or medieval (such as Anselm's ontological argument) can be regarded as rational knowledge. Since they all possess forms of argumentation, they always generate counter-arguments and criticisms of themselves. The history of the philosophy of religion can be seen as the unfolding of this enterprise.

The *scientia sacra*, on the other hand, which is sapiential and 'poetic', seems very much a 'given knowledge' and appeals to the heart of the knower. In contrast to rational knowledge, the *scientia sacra* can only be acknowledged by those who have activated their intellect with the help of revelation. The prime and most obvious exemplification of such knowledge occurs in the sacred scriptures of the traditions, and secondarily it is found in the books written by outstanding metaphysicians such as Meister Eckhart and Ibn 'Arabi. Again, it can be noted that, as opposed to rational knowledge, metaphysical knowledge is said to possess a power which religiously transforms those who attain it. It is also possible to state, using Pascal's distinction, that while rational knowledge speaks of the God of philosophers, metaphysical knowledge reflects the God of prophets and mystics.

As has been pointed out already, Nasr's position on the metaphysical knowability of God is positive. For him, God as Reality is knowable not only because human beings are equipped with intellect but also because the cosmos, religion and human beings are embodied with a sacred substance manifesting the Ultimate to those who have prepared themselves for the reception of such knowledge.[126]

Inspired by the Islamic concept of *'ilm* (knowledge) as one of the divine qualities of Allah, Nasr considers knowledge as an 'entity' that exists as a being alongside the Divine. Therefore, for Nasr, knowledge, whether manifested through the macrocosm or microcosm, continues to be inseparable from the Ultimate since 'the very substance of knowledge is the knowledge of that reality which is the Supreme Substance, the Sacred as such, compared to which all levels of existence and all forms of the manifold are but accidents'.[127] Intelligence, maintains Nasr, is 'like a ray which emanates from and returns to the Absolute' and therefore is imbued with the possibility of knowing Ultimate Reality. Since this sacred faculty continues to reside at the centre of the human being, one is always able to transcend duality and journey on the path towards union with the Sacred:

> Man is endowed with the precious gift of intelligence which allows him to know the Ultimate Reality as the Transcendent, the Beyond, and the objective world as a distinct reality on its own level, and the Ultimate Reality as the Immanent, as the Supreme Self underlying all the veils of subjectivity and the many 'selves' or layers of consciousness within him. Knowledge can attain the Sacred both beyond the subject which knows and at the heart of this very subject, for finally the Ultimate Reality which *is* the Sacred as such is both the knower and the known, inner consciousness and outer reality, the pure immanent Subject and the Transcendent Object, the Infinite Self and Absolute Being which does not exclude Beyond Being.[128]

Nasr claims that metaphysical knowledge, which primarily deals with Reality and its diversity and unity, comprehends theological knowledge, but theological knowledge does not comprehend metaphysical knowledge. He would say that theological knowledge is exoteric in its characteristics and often makes sense to those who are interested in it, while 'metaphysical knowledge' is esoteric and makes sense only to those who are prepared for it.

However, according to Nasr, traditional metaphysics distinguishes not only between 'the Real and apparent and Being and becoming but also between grades of existence'.[129] Although Nasr does not state how the hierarchic levels of reality are structured, it can be inferred from his presentation of the *sophia perennis* that at the highest, metaphysical level, there is God as Ultimate Reality or the Absolute which can only be attained through intellectual intuition.[130] Knowledge of this realm, which is said to be esoteric in its nature, is only 'given' to those who are chosen. Beneath this highest level there exists a theological level on which God is responded to through faith and revelation. The articulation of God's nature at this level is prepositional and exoteric. At the third level, the philosophical level, there exist phenomena which are conceived by the faculty of *ratio*. At the lowest level, that is the scientific level, there exists the physical world which is perceived by the senses and scientific observation. In this scheme the hierarchical structure of Being corresponds to a hierarchical structure of knowing. Different forms of knowing are envisaged, depending upon the level at which the knower is operating. An each level, it is said that the means of knowledge alters. On the lowest level, the physical world is known by sense data analysis, while at the highest level the Absolute is attained through intellectual intuition. In this hierarchical structure, it is claimed that 'only the higher can comprehend the lower'; 'only that which stands on a higher level of existence can encompass that which lies below it', while the reverse is not true.[131] In other words, this hierarchy of levels of Being is structured in a manner such that every lower level points to the one that is above it.[132]

The claim that there is a *scientia sacra*, a knowledge through which the Ultimate can be attainable, is not something totally new. Nasr claims that natural theology as 'sapientia' and as understood by Plato in the *Republic* and *Laws* is a form of sacred knowledge and has been available throughout the centuries. However, he believes the basic teachings of religion distinctively contain a sapiential perspective which speaks solely of Ultimate Reality. According to Nasr, the entirety of ancient and medieval religious texts can be seen and read from the perspective of the perennial philosophy. Although modern interpretations of Christianity and Judaism tend to neglect or pass over the sapiential dimension of these religions, the emphasis upon

hokhmah and *Eyn Sof* in Judaism and upon Sophia in Medieval and
ancient Christianity is sufficient to show the importance of sapiential
knowledge. The Pythagorean-Platonic school and Hermeticism in
Greek traditions and the writings of such figures as Saint Gregory of
Nyssa, Clement of Alexandria, Origen, Saint Augustine, Scotus
Erigena, Saint Bonaventura, Duns Scotus, Meister Eckhart, Nicholas
of Cusa and Jacob Boehme can, according to Nasr, be seen as prime
representatives of the *sophia perennis*.

As regards Islam, Nasr notes, the testimony of faith *La ilaha
illa'Llah* ('there is no divinity but the Divine') and the names for the
sacred scripture of Islam, such as *al-quran* (recitation), *al-furqan*
(discernment), and *umm al-kitab* (the mother of the book), are some
of the pointers which indicate how sapiential knowledge is significant
in traditional Islam. For Nasr, the Quranic emphasis upon the
importance of intellection and knowledge; and *fiqh* (Islamic
jurisprudence) – which actually means intellection and knowing –
are sufficient to show how the Quran and the Islamic sciences have
intermingled with sapiential knowledge.[133]

One issue that helps to delineate the difference between Hick and
Nasr is the role of science in relation to religious matters. In his
introduction to *The Centre of Christianity*, Hick clearly states that the
development of modern science has brought the history of
Christianity to a turning point by rendering incredible much of the
content of traditional Christian belief such as the origin of the
universe, the fall, miracles, the incarnation of Jesus and the
infallibility of the Bible.[134] He also argues that in the seventeenth
and eighteenth centuries science undermined the 'dogmatic and
superstitious mentality' of medieval Europe by introducing a more
open and critical outlook.[135]

Nasr, however, states that traditional authors like himself do not
deny the validity of scientific discovery, if only it is taken for what it is.
Scientific knowledge is legitimate as knowledge of one of the orders of
reality. What is wrong, according to Nasr, is that modern science has
refused to accept any authority which might limit the extent to which
it could be applied. That is why, says Nasr 'modern science does
transgress beyond the realm which is properly its own and serves as
background for monstrous philosophical generalisations ...'.[136] He
maintains:

Moreover, by token of the same fact, the metaphysical
significance of scientific discoveries remains totally neglected

by the supposedly scientifically minded public which usually knows very little about science but is mesmerised by it. And here again, despite the loud protests of some reputable scientists, instead of the metascientific significance of what science has actually discovered becoming revealed, the reverse process takes place whereby, through wild interpolations and usually well-hidden assumptions, metaphysical truths become rejected in the name of scientific knowledge. What tradition opposes in modern science is not that it knows so much about the social habits of ants and the spins of the electron but that it knows nothing of God while functioning in a world in which it alone is considered as science or objective knowledge.[137]

As far as the main theme of this chapter is concerned, it is possible to state that, for Hick, although science is not a means through which God is knowable, it can be regarded as a set of criteria according to which one can differentiate certain mythological religious statements from factual statements. For Nasr, on the other hand, although scientific discoveries could have significant implications for metaphysics, science itself, because of its method and content, is not actually qualified to speak of metaphysics. When it speaks of the metaphysical realm by extrapolation, it is liable to make mistakes. Therefore, for Nasr, science should be kept in its own domain and should not be used for testing metaphysical truths.

To Know is to be Saved

What makes sacred knowledge distinctive from other forms of knowledge is that, it transforms the person who acquires it; it is related to the ethical perfection of the person who wants to attain it. Nasr argues that since the Sacred is the Infinite and Eternal, knowledge of the Sacred leads to freedom and deliverance from all limitations and bondage. In his view, therefore, the role of the *scientia sacra* is not to illustrate how matter behaves differently in different conditions; nor is it to settle the argument about the existence of God, or to overcome philosophical dualism by reducing the One to a mental concept. The role of sacred knowledge is salvation and freedom from 'ignorance' and from the limits of human subjectivity. To know, for Nasr, means to be saved.[138]

In this sense, knowledge is not the result of inventing or 'discovering' or knowing something unknown, rather, it is the rediscovery of that which has always been known but has been forgotten. Such a concept of knowledge has no place in the epistemology of modern philosophy, religious or otherwise.[139]

As Nasr makes clear, ordinary knowledge, received by the senses and the rational analysis of empirical data, is legitimate on its own level but cannot lead to freedom and salvation. On the contrary, says Nasr, when such knowledge is accompanied by passion, it can lead people to a kind of excessive knowledge of detail which has no essential and substantial contribution to make as far as knowledge of Ultimate Reality is concerned. However, according to Nasr, there are certain conditions which must be followed before one can attain to the kind of sacred knowledge that transforms the knower. It is claimed that such knowledge can only save a person if it is realised by the whole being of that person. This knowledge, it is said, is not the source of perplexity and confusion but a source of illumination, peace and unity, since it is the highest knowledge of its kind. Even intellectual intuition and the truth received through intellectual intuition, although valuable are not realised knowledge. Realised knowledge involves not only intellection and other faculties of knowing, but also the will and psyche of the knower; it requires spiritual training and the acquisition of spiritual virtues. It is able to transform the person who is engaged with it, including his or her corporal being. While ordinary knowledge issues from the mind and body of the knower, realised knowledge emanates from the heart, though it is capable of transforming both the mind and body.[140]

As has already been pointed out, attaining 'salvific-knowledge' is very much related to acquiring virtues which can be defined as 'our way of participating in the truth'. Passion is considered an impediment by which the intelligence is prevented from functioning in its extra-ordinary fashion. In this context, evils and sins are not only considered from a moral point of view but from an 'ontological point of view related to being and knowledge'. To acquire intellectual humility, charity and truthfulness are essential for those who want to attain the knowledge which has the power to save. The association of this form of knowledge with spiritual virtues and love is sufficient to show how far such knowledge is from rational and empirical knowledge and their applications.[141]

It is this knowledge that ultimately brings the knower to the realisation of the One. It is through such knowledge that people can reach the truth 'and taste the actual experience of the One, which yet allows the servant to have the awareness of his own nothingness in the light of the One'.[142]

However, the question is this: How can one attain the knowledge that sanctifies and saves? The obvious answer that Nasr could give us is, of course, 'through tradition'. But tradition, says Nasr, though necessary, is not adequate for the attainment of realised knowledge. This is because, since sacred knowledge is essentially esoteric in its nature, it cannot be acquired by everyone even in a traditional context; it can be harmful for a person who is not prepared for its reception. Apart from this, the acquisition of sacred knowledge requires moral qualification and spiritual training at the hands of an authentic spiritual master. And even beyond that, Nasr says, there is need for 'a special power or grace which cannot but come from the source of tradition in question'.[143]

As has been pointed out, sacred knowledge ultimately functions as an indispensable means of peace and tranquillity:

> To gain such a knowledge is to gain certitude, to be saved from the doubt that causes aberration of the mind and destroys inner peace. Sacred knowledge is based upon and leads to certitude because it is not based on conjecture or mental concepts but involves the whole of man's being. Even when such a knowledge appears as theory, it is not in the modern meaning of theory, but in its etymological sense as vision. It imposes itself with blinding clarity upon the mind of the person who has been given the possibility of such a vision through intellectual intuition. Then as the process of realization of this knowledge unfolds, it begins to encompass the whole of man and to consume him, leaving no locus wherein doubt could linger.[144]

On the other hand, Nasr claims that knowledge which is devoid of qualitative content can be harmful, no matter how brilliantly it has led to scientific and technological development. The ecological and social crises that humanity has confronted in the present century are the result of such secularised knowledge which is divorced from its roots, that is, from metaphysical knowledge.

Nasr devoted his work *Man and Nature* to the issue of environmental crises and their relation to secularisation and sacred knowledge. He argues that the emergence of the environmental crises that threaten the existence of humankind on earth coincided with the emergence of the desacralization of nature and knowledge. There are good reasons for this. Human beings have lost their sense of the meaning of human existence and have been alienated from their environment because the realm of nature has become a 'thing' devoid of significance and meaning. The domination of nature without any clear goals has created problems such as overpopulation, over-consumption of natural resources, and the destruction of natural beauty.[145] Nasr believes that the harmony between humankind and nature has been destroyed as a consequence of the destruction of the harmony between God and human beings. Natural science, divorced from its metaphysical and theological roots, has become a harmful and aimless roaming around. The result of this, asserts Nasr, is the segregation of nature from other orders of reality, thereby making it spiritually meaningless.[146]

The destruction of the wholeness of human life and the increasing separation of the human mind and soul are two of the unfortunate results of the secularisation of knowledge. It can even be argued that the change in the dimensions and proportions of modern warfare with its dangerous consequences is closely related to the ethical implications of the use of technology and science.[147] The real solution to all these environmental and social crises lies in 'a discovery of metaphysical knowledge, and revitalisation of a theology and philosophy of nature that could set a limit upon the application of science and technology'.[148]

Is Nasr's or Hick's epistemology more appropriate as a description of religion and its accompanying experience?

The traditional view, in general, and Nasr's epistemology in particular constitute a suitable basis for the description of religion. This is because the traditional view is explicitly religious; it does not sacrifice the so-called 'outmoded' doctrine of religion for the sake of being recognised or becoming integrated into the present modern culture. Its objective is to create an atmosphere in which all traditional religions can be accommodated, whether they be Judaism, Christianity or the Native American religions together with all their 'unacceptable' features. Moreover, this account, unlike Hick's pluralism, wants to resist truncating the 'truth' of a particular religion in order to integrate the major religions within one system. Nor does it propagate exclusivism stating that 'mine is true and the rest is false' which ultimately denies the very concept of the goodness of God. Rather, it wants to provide a traditional-pluralistic atmo-sphere in which it is possible to hold one particular religion as one way alongside others which lead to the same summit. It can achieve this task by accomplishing an 'existential' transformation within those who sincerely want to understand religion, because it believes that understanding religion is closely related to the ability to acknowledge the sacred characteristics of religion. What makes Nasr's epistemology more suitable than Hick's for a description of religion is that it wants to resist the powerful forces of secularisation which are the prime factors which create the misunderstanding and misrepresentation of religion.

On the other hand, Hick's epistemology, although endorsing the existence of the ineffable Real, in fact seems to be more limited than Nasr's in describing religion for the following reasons: Firstly, Hick's epistemology is ambiguous and lacks a sound criterion for rejecting or accepting the particular doctrines of any given religion. Secondly, it does not recognize the secularisation process as a problem in understanding religion. In fact, the reason that leads Hick to ignore secularisation as an obstacle to understanding religion is the very effect of the secularisation process in his own thought. Thirdly, it is less in harmony with religion than the perennial philosophy, since it does not aim to create a sacred atmosphere in which the Sacred can be conveniently accommodated.

Chapter Four

The Need for a Pluralistic Approach in Religion

Globalization and Religion

Globalization and its relation to religion has become one of the central themes of the sociology of religion in recent years.[1] Globalization is principally the phenomenon brought about by rapid developments in communication technology and the concomitant rapid increase in the transmission of knowledge and information. Through the power of communication technology, it has become possible to observe or record any event in any part of the world, virtually bringing to an end the isolated community. An event taking place in one part of the world makes an impact on the life of a person who lives in another part of the world. The reactions from all over the Islamic world to the Salman Rushdie affair illustrate this point. Here, a single incident in the United Kingdom provoked responses in Istanbul, Islamabad and Bombay in an extremely short period of time.

The effects of globalization on people's life are diverse and complex. Globalization can in some cases undermine a culture's values and identity, and in other cases contribute to reviving its inherited values and religious identity.[2] Sometimes, depending on the circumstances, religion can play a part in resisting the domination of the global system.[3]

Three distinct effects of globalization on religion can be observed. Firstly, it brings about changes within a religion.[4] In this context, the responses of religions to this phenomenon differ according to their theological and doctrinal characteristics. Hick would confirm this claim by arguing that historical developments and globalization can bring about changes in the theological constitution of a given religion because 'the religious life of mankind is a continuous field of relationship to the divine Reality'.[5]

Nasr, however, would say that globalization or historical developments cannot bring about a change in the theological codes of a given religion since these are established by revelation. He would maintain that the development of communication technologies and cultural interactions can only set a context for a new interpretation of a doctrine of a given religion.

Secondly, globalization has brought about interaction between religions and religious communities. Through such interactions, some religions, such as Christianity and Hinduism, have started to redefine some of their traditional doctrines, whereas some others such as Islam and Judaism have taken globalization as the incentive through which they intend to review their historical identity.

Thirdly, globalization has created a new context for various 'theories' of religious pluralism. This is the result of the interaction between religions. For instance, Hick argues that through the impact of globalization, religions have come close to each other. In the future, he remarks, it might not be necessary to maintain the cultural-historical boundaries of religions. Therefore the theologians of our time have to prepare themselves for a 'global theology' suitable for the world community; exclusivist and inclusivist claims of religions have to be modified. He writes:

> Until recently the different religious traditions have run their separate courses, each more or less ignoring the others in the construction of its own beliefs. This was appropriate in the centuries before human history had begun to coalesce into a single global history. But now we are in a new situation created by the virtual unification of the world as a communicational system. And whereas it was hitherto reasonable to develop our theology in disregard of God's dealing with the non-christian world, it has now ceased to be reasonable to do that. We must be prepared to respond to the new situation by beginning the long-term task of forming a global or human theology.
>
> It should be noted that a global theology would be compatible with the continued existence of a plurality of religions as concrete forms of religious life.[6]

As someone interested in religious pluralism, Hick would claim that religions should not seek to resist globalization. On the contrary, they have indicated the possibility of a 'global theology' since they share not only common characteristics such as doctrines, rituals and ethical systems but also common objectives such as cosmic optimism and salvation, saintliness and ethical qualities. Religions in this sense have contributed to the on-going globalization process.

Is it really the case that globalization necessarily requires either a global theology or an ideological religious pluralism of the kind that Hick has in mind. Such a form of religious pluralism has its own drawbacks. On the contrary, it is possible to develop a religious response to the plurality of religions without the need to remove the cultural-religious boundaries of given religions.[7] It is also equally plausible to constitute a 'supra-traditional' approach such as that of Nasr without considering the modifications of the truth claims of religions.

Another problem with Hick's vision of a global theology is that there is, as Surin points out, an implicit correlation between the discourse of global theology and religious pluralism and the particular characteristics of European history. In the period of Western imperial expansion, Surin argues, Christian thinkers have propagated the discourse of the absoluteness of Christianity, Christian exclusivism and non-dialogue, while in the period of post-colonialism, they have started to speak of pluralism, non-absoluteness of Christianity and dialogue.[8] Hence, he concludes: 'The Cantwell Smiths and Hicks of this world are seemingly a new kind of subject, one that is "universal" or "global" in the way that McDonald's hamburger has become the "universal" or "global" food.'[9]

In support of this point, there is a noticeable correlation between the creation of certain forms of knowledge and the 'political intention' of a given culture. It is not unreasonable to envisage that 'ideological pluralisms' such as Hick's have been promoted by a global power in order to settle potential religious conflicts. But such a possible intention must not lead us to ignore the reality of problems posed by the plurality of religions and the need for a convincing solution.[10]

Hick's view of a global theology is very much rooted in his perception of the historical development of Christianity. Hick believes that Christianity has always responded to the requirements of the present age positively, developing in conjunction with of the culture within which it grows; it is not a static, well-defined single entity but a dynamic process of religious experience which is concentrated in one doctrinal system. Such an assumption, which is the result of Hick's experience of Christianity, has led him to believe that every religion can respond to globalization in more or less the same way as Christianity. Therefore, he believes that Islam's response to globalization should essentially be the same as Christianity's. But the signs we can gather from the cultural development in contemporary Islam indicate the contrary. If a theory of religious pluralism were going to be one of the results of the globalization process, Islam would respond in its own way, creating the form of 'pluralism' to which it can adapt.

Religious Identity and Fortuity of 'Birth'

To examine what constitutes personal identity is extremely complicated. My aim is not to examine the role of religion in the formation of one's identity. Rather I would like to consider how one's 'accidental birth' into a family or community can contribute to the formation of one's religious identity. It is worth trying to draw attention to the fact that there is a subtle relation between the formation of one's religious identity and the need for a pluralistic approach to religion.

It is true that one's affiliation to a particular religion, is mostly determined by the 'accidents of birth'. Hick argues:

> ... [I]t is a fact evident to ordinary people (even though not always taken into account by theologians) that in the great majority of the cases – say 98 or 99 per cent – the religion in which a person believes and to which he adheres depends upon where he was born. That is to say, if someone is born to Muslim parents in Egypt or Pakistan, that person is very likely to be a Muslim; if to Buddhist parents in Sri Lanka or Burma, that person is very likely to be a Buddhist; if to Hindu parents in India, that person is very likely to be a Hindu; if to Christian parents in Europe or the Americas, that person is very likely to be a Christian.[11]

There are some important conclusions which Hick aims to reach by repeating this passage several times in his various works, especially in those concerned with religious pluralism.[12] Hick sees 'the accidents of birth' as a universal phenomenon which may provide the basis of a hypothesis of religious pluralism. He would argue that if, in the majority of the cases, one's affiliation to a particular religion depends upon where or in which family one was born, one's 'exclusive' religious truth claims cannot be at all convincing. Let me elaborate this point further. A religious person, let us say, a Muslim claims that Islam is the only way to truth and salvation. The reason why he or she claims this is the case, is that he or she was born to a Muslim family. That is to say, a religious person's accidental birth into a family entitles him or her to claim possession of unique truth. That means, truth comes through 'the accidents of birth' which sounds absurd. The obvious conclusion of this argument is that the 'exclusive' truth claims of religions function as obstacles to a comprehensive theory of religious pluralism.[13]

One of the main aims of this chapter is to identify the factors which lead a religious person to form a religious identity. In addition to 'accident of birth', Hick identifies another factor, that is, an 'innate religious tendency or disposition'. For him, the human being can be defined as 'a worshipping animal, with an ingrained propensity to construe his world religiously'.[14] Hick claims that the evidence for such an 'innate religious tendency' lies in the universal occurrence of religions in every age. He also maintains that such a religious bias operates as an 'inclining cause' in the modern person and a 'determining cause'[15] in the primitive person in the formation of a religious identity.

It is interesting to note that Islam considers this 'innate religious tendency' (the Quran calls it *al-fitrah*) together with the role of the parent as the inclining cause of the acceptance of the Islamic faith. From an Islamic point of view, *fitrah* can be defined as an unqualified and pure primordial religiosity.[16] In *hadith* the Prophet said: 'Every child is born with *al-fitrah* (the primordial religiosity). Then it is his parents who make him Jewish, Christian and Magian'.[17] Interestingly enough, al-Bukhari mentions this *hadith* in the context of an interpretation of this verse: 'So set your face to the religion, a man of pure faith (*hanif*) – God's original (*fitrat* Allah) upon which he originated mankind. There is no change in God's creation. That is the well rooted religion (*al-din al-qayyim*); but most men know it not' (30:30).[18]

One might ask that what might be the relationship between humankind's 'innate religious disposition' and the problem of religious pluralism? The universal existence of religion in every age and in every place is the result of an innate religiosity. If every individual by nature possesses the same common religiosity, then the apparent diversity of religion is not something essential but accidental. In other words, the pluralistic approach to religions which promotes unity is subtly rooted in a common natural and religious disposition.

Absolute Truth Claims of Religions

Is the diversity of religions a problem? The multiple existence of religions does not seem a problem for those who are strongly convinced that it is their religion alone which is true and the rest are false. Nor is it a problem for those who see religions as various human projections or speculations about something mysterious which has been construed as God. The plurality of religions is a problem when a person believes there is one Transcendent Reality, and yet at the same time he or she is willing to consider the place of other religions in the human quest for truth and salvation.

Religious exclusivism is self contradictory. If the Christian feels entitled to adopt a position exclusivism, then it must be equally acceptable that a Muslim, by virtue of being Muslim, can adhere to an Islamic exclusivism. The reason why a Muslim believes in an Islamic exclusivism is that Islam makes such absolute truth claims and convinces its adherents to believe that is so. The same is true for Christians. That leads us to the acceptance of the proposition that a Muslim must endorse the same right for Christians to say that they have the right to profess a Christian exclusivism. There is a serious problem here. A religious exclusivism, let us say, an Islamic exclusivism, by definition must rule out the possibility of the occurrence of truth and salvation in other traditions. That is to say, an Islamic exclusivism, instead of endorsing that other religions can have the same right, by definition must invalidate any other religion's religious exclusivism. This is a self contradiction. A religious exclusivism must be formed in a manner that eventually nullifies its own existence. Therefore, the absolute truth claims of religions are not a solution to the problem but one of the main sources of it. Besides this, the absolute truth claims of religions are also a powerful incentive to lead us eventually to establish an all-accommodating pluralistic approach.

As a solution to the problem, there are two different approaches in the context of this work: religious and ideological. I shall be suggesting an Islamic 'solution' as one of the possible examples of religious solution in the chapter six.[19] In my opinion, Hick's hypothesis of religious pluralism offers an ideological rather than a religious solution. I would go further and even suggest that Hick, in order to make his hypothesis more plausible, in fact blocks the way to a religious solution by claiming that religious exclusivism is universal among religions.[20] He states:

Looking at the religions of the world then in the plural we are presented with competing claims to possess the saving truth. For each community believes that its own gospel is true and that other gospels are false in so far as they differ from it. Each believes that the way of salvation to which it witnesses is the authentic way, the only sure path to eternal blessedness.[21] ... The Jew claims that God has revealed himself through Hebrew history as interpreted by the faith of the prophets. The Muslim claims that God has, through his prophet Mohammed, revealed his truth in the Koran.[22]

Contrary to what Hick assumes, religious exclusivism is not a universal phenomenon. Every religion has a different attitude to different religions. For instance, Islam recognises Christianity, Judaism and Islam as religions that belong to the same Abrahamic family, while ignoring others such as Buddhism and Hinduism.[23]

Nevertheless, Hick is right in assuming that the exclusivist attitude of a given religion cannot go hand in hand with the notion of universal salvation. He illustrates his point as follows:

We say as Christians that God is the God of universal love, that he is the creator and Father of all mankind, that he wills the ultimate good and the salvation of all men. But we also say, traditionally, that the only way to salvation is the christian way. And yet we know, when we stop to think about it, that the large majority of the human race who have lived and died up to the present moment have lived either before Christ or outside the borders of Christendom. Can we then accept the conclusion that the God of love who seeks to save all mankind has nevertheless ordained that men must be saved in such a way that only a small minority can in fact receive this salvation?[24]

This passage expresses very clearly the deficiency of any religious exclusivism, whether Islamic or Christian.

Hick however, maintains that historically, religious exclusivism was the only approach as far as Christianity is concerned.[25] The Roman Catholic teachings on the issue can be summed up in the doctrinal statement, *extra ecclesiam nulla salus*, outside the church there is no salvation. There have been several attempts, including the Vatican II declaration and K. Rahner's notion of the 'anonymous Christian' which aim to modify this original dogma. But such attempts were unsuccessful. Hick claims that instead of seeking a solution from a traditional Christian perspective, they could have sought a solution by forming a theoretical framework like his hypothesis, which can offer a plausible alternative to religious exclusivism. Christian inclusivism cannot work. The solution, according to Hick, can only be sought in a 'Copernican revolution' in theology:

> Now the Copernican revolution in astronomy consisted in a transformation in the way in which men understood the universe and their own location within it. It involved a shift from the dogma that the earth is the centre of the revolving universe to the realisation that it is the sun that is at the centre, with all the planets, including our own earth, moving around it. And the needed Copernican revolution in theology involves an equally radical transformation in our conception of the universe of faiths and the place of our own religion within it. It involves a shift from the dogma that Christianity is at the centre to the realisation that it is *God* who is at the centre, and that all the religions of mankind, including our own, serve and revolve around him.[26]

Although the Copernican revolution in theology was an early form of his hypothesis of religious pluralism, it drew considerable attention from a number of thinkers.[27] Some were worried about its dangerous implications for mainstream Christology, while some saw it as a useful theological enterprise which would eventually help to re-establish a new framework for existing Christian theological thought.

One of the strongest criticisms came from Gavin D'Costa.[28] He sought to integrate Hick's Copernican revolution in a Christian theology of religions, offering a form of Christian inclusivism as an alternative. His main argument was that the fundamental premises of Hick's thesis, such as the assertion of an all-loving God who desires the salvation of all humankind, is an explicitly Christian doctrine. Therefore, D'Costa maintains that instead of putting God at the centre of the universe of faiths in order to achieve a fully realised revolution, Hick puts the God of Christianity at the centre of the universe of faiths, thereby making his 'revolution' another epicycle[29]. D'Costa writes:

> Although Hick is trying to sever an exclusive ontological linking of Jesus and God, I would submit that his mythological understanding still maintains (implicitly if not explicitly) a

normative ontological linking of Jesus and God which is in fact necessary to support his central axiom of a God of universal love. Without this premise, the Copernican enterprise will collapse. With this premise and its inevitable *Christological* implications, the Copernican revolution looks rather like yet another ingenious Ptolemaic epicycle![30]

D'Costa's claim that the premises of the Copernican revolution are exclusively Christian are dubious. Christianity, in Hick's premises of the Copernican revolution, is not an essential ingredient but accidental. Hick as a Christian thinker has naturally developed within the Christian culture. Hence, it is quite natural for him to employ Christianity in construction of his hypothesis. The same argument can be reconstructed outside the realm of Christianity, for example within a natural theology or Islam, or any other theistic religions.

We could reconstruct the same argument in a more philosophical fashion. God by definition is good[31] and just. If God is all-good, it is quite natural to think that such a good God must will 'ultimate-goodness', i.e. salvation of all people. If a good God desires the salvation of all people but locates the people in such a way that only the minority attains salvation, He cannot be just. Therefore, it is imperative for a just God to exhibit his justice, that is to provide an available means to salvation for every individual. The argument in this form can stand for any kind of theism, whether philosophical or religious.[32] Ultimately, the premises of Hick's argument are not entirely Christian and therefore they can stand independently of Christianity, with their own philosophical coherence.

Hick maintains that the exclusive truth claims of religion must be modified, not only because they contradict the notion of an all-loving God, but also because they stem from a human subjectivity. Hence, he is not entirely convinced that the notion of 'divinely revealed truth' is plausible in this modern age.[33] Hick maintains that the absolute truth claims of each religion do not originate from the Absolute but from each religion's self-validating development within its closed spheres; they stem from human subjectivity not 'divine objectivity'. In challenging Hick's view one might claim that if the absolute truth claims of each religion do not come from a self-validating process but from the Absolute itself, then Hick's hypothesis of religious pluralism requires a reformulation. The traditional point of view, however, considers that the fundamental doctrines of religions, including their truth, claim to be from God himself and therefore must be respected as sacred. As Schuon puts it so succinctly:

> [I]f the religions are true it is because each time it is God who has spoken, and, if they are different it is because God has spoken in different 'languages' in conformity with the diversity of the receptacles. ... If they are absolute and exclusive, it is because in each of them God has said 'I'.[34]

The traditional point of view would also claim that Hick is mistaken in his understanding of the Gospel's exclusive language. When Jesus says, 'Anyone who has seen me has seen the Father'[35] and 'I am the way, the truth, and the life: no man comes unto the Father except by me',[36] he aims to emphasise not solely the uniqueness of Christianity but Christ's role as Messiah. However, as Nasr points out,[37] 'no one comes to the Father except by me' means that I am the legitimate way to God. It means that if anyone tries any other way, in other words tries to reach God through his or her own endeavour without recognising me, that certainly is not acceptable. That is to say, such a warning was issued not to sever the authenticity of other religions but to state the invalidity of a personal, voluntary, human endeavour to attain Divine Reality. When such 'exclusive' language is being used in a traditional religion, it aims to stress not solely the uniqueness of that particular religion, but the necessity of divine revelation in one's quest for salvation.

The Diversity of Religions

One of the most important reasons for the need for a 'trans-traditional' view of religions is the plural existence of religions themselves. If there were only one religious tradition, or many which explicitly referred to the same reality without cancelling each other's legitimacy, then there would not be the need for any forms of pluralistic or exclusivistic considerations. But the reality is just the opposite. There are many religions and many claims to truth. Hence, a 'trans-traditional' consideration seems to be necessary.[38]

Hick, however, sees the plural religious life of humanity not only as an incentive for the formation of a hypothesis of religious pluralism, but also as a reason for postulating an ineffable Real:

> But if the Real in itself is not and cannot be humanly experienced, why postulate such an unknown and unknowable

Ding an sich? The answer is that the divine noumenon is a necessary postulate of the pluralistic religious life of humanity. For within each tradition we regard as real the object of our worship or contemplation. If . . . it is also proper to regard as real the objects of worship and contemplation within the other traditions, we are led to postulate the Real *an sich* as the presupposition of the veridical character of this range of forms of religious experience. Without this postulate we should be left with a plurality of *personae* and *impersonae* each of which is claimed to be the Ultimate, but no one of which alone can be. We should have either to regard all the reported experiences as illusory or else return to the confessional position in which we affirm the authenticity of our own stream of religious experience whilst dismissing as illusory those occurring within other traditions.[39]

While the plurality of religious traditions points to the necessity of a pluralistic approach to religions, it does not necessarily lead to the postulation of an ineffable divine Reality, i.e. the Real *an sich*.[40] Hick believes that there is a necessary correlation between the plurality of religions and the multiplicity of the objects of worship or contemplation. He argues that if we do not believe his postulation of Real *an sich* together with his hypothesis of religious pluralism, we are left with two options: either endorse the plurality of the objects of worship, i.e. polytheism, or return to traditional exclusivist language saying that mine is true while the rest is false.

There is no necessary correlation between the diversity of religions and the plurality of 'gods' and 'absolutes'. It is perfectly plausible to think that there would be one Absolute and many manifestations in many different traditions. In other words, the object of worship would be one reality with many names; all religions are speaking of the same reality in different languages. What is the difference between this and Hick's religious pluralism? The difference is that we need not deny, as Hick does, all the qualifications of God, attributed by different religions in order to reach an all-encompassing pluralistic position. On the contrary, one can accept the characteristics of God within his or her tradition without denying the existence of divine revelation in other traditions. In fact, from the Islamic point of view, one might claim that Hick is mistaken when he says that the Heavenly Father worshipped by Christians and Adonai worshipped by Jews and Allah worshipped by Muslims are different. As far as

Islam is concerned, Christians, Jews and Muslims are worshipping the same God. To name him differently through different languages does not change his personality. Hick's adoption of such an extreme position, i.e. to deny all the positive qualities of God in order to postulate a hypothesis of religious pluralism, is totally unnecessary. If we cannot accept the divine noumenon, we are not left with the plurality of 'gods', but we are left with the plurality of religious traditions.[41]

These are not, however, the only factors that make a 'trans-traditional' theory plausible. Besides all these external factors such as globalization, 'accidents of birth' and exclusive truth claims of religion, there are also some internal factors which are more decisive in forming a pluralistic approach. One is of course the overlapping characteristics of religions. Hick believes that there is not only one common objective that the major traditions want to achieve, such as creating a cosmic optimism, providing the ethical norms of the community and elevating religious people to a spiritually better state, but also a common ground for all religious experiences, that is the Real *an sich* which has been moulding the traditions of humankind towards a common unity, i.e. from 'self-centredness' to 'reality-centredness'.

Hick argues that while the task of pre-axial religions was to keep a society in a stable situation, the post-axial religions aimed at providing a cosmic optimism and soteriology. Every tradition in the post-axial age exhibits a soteriological structure recognising a human moral weakness and liability for suffering and also promising a limitlessly better state.[42] Hick sees that such a transformation of religions from one period, say pre-axial, to the other say, post-axial, together with a distinctive objective can be seen as the sign of the unitary act of the Real.

The question which should be asked here is this. How could we know that there is one global transformation from 'self-centredness' to 'reality-centredness' aimed at by the major traditions? Hick would reply to this question by asserting that there are many signs which show such a transformation is taking place. The most important of all is the capability of religions to produce saints.[43] Hick believes that this capability to produce saints – those in whom 'the transformation of human existence from self-centredness to Reality-centredness is so much more advanced than in the generality of us'[44] – is one of the valid criteria through which it is possible to identify the 'authenticity' of religious tradition as a salvific human response to the Real.[45]

Because of Hick's commitment to the empirical strand of philosophy, he is inclined to test religious traditions with something practical such as the 'saint productive' characteristics of the tradition in question. By doing so, Hick wants to cut short all doctrinal disputes and seek a common ground on which the fruits of religion can be harvested. On the other hand, only through such empirical methods, Hick believes, is one able to identify the transformative characteristics of the traditions. Although the saintly characters of a religion can be regarded as evidence for its capability to transform believers, they cannot be employed to test the truth of one great tradition against another. Therefore Hick thinks one cannot set up a comparative judgement in order to test tradition A against tradition B by considering that tradition A produces more and better saints per million of population than tradition B.[46] Here, one is tempted to ask why saintliness works as a criterion for the identification of a tradition's transformative character but not a criterion to understand whether or not a particular tradition offers a better or more genuine response to the Real than other traditions.

Another internal factor that leads to the possibility of a thesis of religious pluralism is the mostly-shared ethical codes of traditions. It is true that all the great traditions teach the moral ideal of generous goodwill, love and compassion which are contained in the Golden Rule. This universal ethical principle that can be defined as 'it is good to benefit others and it is evil to harm them',[47] is an indispensable principle of the great traditions which can be seen as a common objective of all religions.[48]

The Cultural Limits of Hick's Hypothesis of Religious Pluralism

Hick's hypothesis of religious pluralism has stemmed from a cultural context which is intrinsically incapable of accommodating the sacred traditions of humankind. This is simply because, the cultural context in which Hick has developed his views is principally a secular one. His hypothesis is ideological, while Nasr's is religious.

Firstly, Hick believes that religions come about through the encounter of human beings with the Real. More specifically, he points out that people are the main contributors to the formation of religion. In other words, he believes that creating the 'truth' is within the capacity of humans. Thus, he thinks he can offer his hypothesis of religious pluralism as the 'truth' for the post-axial religious world. His 'truth', i.e. his hypothesis of religious pluralism not only supersedes the 'truths' of religions but also regulates them within the context of a hypothesis of religious pluralism.[49] Consequently, Hick's pluralism is ideological because it depends upon his personal reasoning and commitment, and it superimposes its 'truth' on the 'truths' of religions.

Nasr, on the other hand, believes that truth, whether religious or otherwise is sacred and issues from God. What humans must do is to bow before this truth. We should not attempt to create a 'truth'. What we can do is to be a 'mirror' of that 'truth' and reflect it as it is. Consequently, Nasr's traditional point of view is intrinsically religious, because it aims to grant utmost value to the sacred qualities of a given religion, and it does not superimpose anything upon the truth of religions. It sees every sacred doctrine of a given religion as useful and true in the sense of 'relatively absolute' in the sacred context of that religion.

The second reason for arguing that Hick's hypothesis of religious pluralism is ideological is that it is *authoritative*. It presents itself in 'a truth dictating manner'. Some critics such as Donovan, Surin and Apczynski, who approach Hick from the post-modern point of view, have highlighted these aspects of his hypothesis. Nasr's traditional point of view is also authoritative, but in a different manner. It insists on the primacy of the traditional point of view. But the emphasis, in this context, is not put on the importance of the traditional point of view, but on the significance of the sacred principles of religion. It is authoritative because it aims to reflect the authority of religion. It does not aim to negotiate with external forces such as secularism, at the expense of relativising religion.

Thirdly, Hick's hypothesis of religious pluralism is meaningful within the context of a certain culture, i.e. the West. It is more culture-specific rather than 'trans-cultural'.[50] Nasr's approach to religion seems less culture-specific than Hick's in that it grants a vital role to the 'local culture', seeing it as something sacred. It does not want to impose the norms and values of one culture on other cultures.

Let me explore further some of the points that I have made above. Hick tends to over-generalize in the formation of his hypothesis of religious pluralism. This is the result of his commitment to modernity. As Surin points out, Hick and others like him, would like to state their thesis in rather general terms. By utilising general terms such as 'a common history', 'the world community' and 'global theology', they want to constitute a cosmos not only for themselves but also for everyone, making use of other cultures as secondary materials. In this context, for instance, Hick has primarily derived the core of his hypothesis from his own culture, that is, the Kantian notion of noumenon and phenomenon. Then he turns to Hindu, Islamic and Buddhist cultures in order to 'dress' up that core in order to make it 'attractive' to Hindus, Buddhists and Muslims. This is a 'Eurocentric' or 'First World' perspective and as such it is not proper for a 'trans-traditional' hypothesis.[51] Surin illustrates the point as follows:

> ... [T]he impoverished peasant from Kedah in Malaysia finds it well-nigh impossible to accept that (s)he and a wealthy landowner *from her own village* are situated in the same moral or social 'space', and yet we are urged by Cantwell Smith and Co. [including Hick] to believe that this Malay peasant, her/his landlord and even the Duke of Westminster or the Hunt brothers inhabit the same 'global city' or share a 'common human history'.[52]

Religious pluralism, according to Surin, is a discourse which does not differ substantially from the discourse of ethnography, anthropology and Orientalism. Orientalism is sectarian, coercive, and dominating. It eventually attempts to override the historical reality of that part of humanity. Hick's pluralistic hypothesis, he says, though it appears contrary, essentially functions in the same way and therefore is unable to subvert exclusiveness and discrimination and, in doing so to create cohesion and understanding among traditions. Surin, maintains that while in Orientalism the orient is perceived as the occident's 'silent other', in the same way, in the pluralistic vision, non-European and non-Christian religions are treated as something which can substantiate one of the main ends of the modern West such as religious pluralism.[53]

As Apczynski points out, Hick's commitment to a liberal intellectual heritage of Enlightenment – a tradition which speaks of universal rationality and neutrality of religion – has played an important part in his formation of a theory of religion. The signs of such an impact can be seen in his belief that the meanings of many religious traditions expressed in their appropriate languages and social contexts can be translated into contemporary English. That is to say, the meanings and values of other traditions can be made meaningful for those who live in totally different social and linguistic environments. Furthermore, Apczynski believes that Hick's neutral approach to other religions comes from his liberal background; it is his trust in contemporary liberalism that enables Hick to detach himself from all substantial truth claims of traditions.[54]

Another question which I would like to explore is whether Hick's pluralism promotes tolerance. As Donovan points out, it is an irony that Hick's hypothesis of religious pluralism, one of whose main aims is to advocate religious tolerance, has become the source of intolerance against religions. Donovan illustrates the point:

> On the contrary, pluralism is coercive. It does not allow others simply to be themselves. To play the pluralist game properly, parties are expected to countenance quite radical reinterpretations and amendments being made to their own positions as well as those of others. Pluralism presupposes liberalism, which involves compromise, accommodation, and the dismantling of distinctive traditional convictions. The common features and agreed truths it purports to arrive at, through embracing a wide range of viewpoints, are in fact simply reinforcements for the political and economic interests of a dominant ideology.[55]

Furthermore Donovan claims that a religious pluralism such as Hick's possesses a Western ideological attitude, rather than being based on the epistemic principle of 'recognition of human fallibility and responsibility to take account of all sides of an issue'.[56] He believes that such an attitude can not only prepare people for responsible judgement, but also provide a tolerant atmosphere in which competing ideas can be very well received.[57]

Although Donovan's criticism contains some good points, his overall conclusion regarding pluralism invokes a religious relativism which, I believe, stems from his commitment to the postmodernist outlook. The postmodern outlook is not able to accommodate the religious frame of mind, because it denies the possibility of an objective truth which is quite crucial in a religious point of view. Although a postmodernist outlook seems quite accommodating to some general pluralistic ideas, it is not helpful for constituting any forms of pluralistic theories that aim to offer a 'global' solution for a 'trans-traditional' problem, since it does not believe in the universality of truth. How can such an outlook, which ignores 'truth' which is intrinsically authoritative and universal, provide a context for an approach which aims to accommodate all religions? The postmodernist outlook can be useful for analysing a given social theory in order to *bring its merits and demerits to light*. It helps us to understand the nature and construction of certain attitudes. But, it cannot, ultimately generate an attitude which can be useful for the formation of a 'trans-traditional' approach.

The Traditional Conception of Religions

It is now time to introduce the traditional account of religions, i.e. the account of the perennial philosophy in general and Nasr's in particular. The value of such an account with regard to the problem in hand will be presented by highlighting some key concepts which are useful in dealing with the problem. Determining the merits and demerits of the perennial account entails a discussion of the difference between Hick's and Nasr's accounts of 'religious pluralism' as systems by which they attempt to solve the problem.

Before proceeding any further, we need to point out the fact that the issue of religious pluralism is a central and primary theme in Hick's philosophy of religion, while it is secondary in Nasr's. Nasr's main objective is to *revitalise* tradition and the traditional perspective through introducing the essentiality of sacred knowledge. The problem of the diversity of religions is one aspect among many aspects of the perennial philosophy. Hence, while dealing with Hick, I am compelled to address the issue of religious pluralism directly, and engage with it thoroughly, while in the case of Nasr, I have to introduce it within the context of his notion of tradition.[58]

Since, Nasr's account of 'religious pluralism is essentially different from Hick's. I believe it is crucial to explore the dissimilarities between those two visions. This can also provide a basis on which the traditional account can be studied. The difference between them is insurmountable for two interrelated reasons: their distinctive conceptions of reality and their understanding of religion serve as the crucial sources of difference between them.

For Nasr, God is reality; he is the source of all that exists and that will exist. The physical world, human beings and religions are the manifestations of God as Ultimate Reality. Nothing falls outside the domain of God. Everything that exists is interconnected with God.[59]

For Hick, there is no one 'holistic reality', in the sense that reality encompasses everything including God and the universe. Physical reality stands on its own. God interpenetrates into the physical and the human world as a regulating concept which makes religious interpretation possible. Religions are culturally defined systems through which humanity responds to the Transcendent. Such Ultimate Reality is the ground of religious experience and the cause of religious transformation. It is beyond human conceptualisation. It is ineffable, and therefore the religions' descriptions of it are not factual, but, rather mythological and are formulated to create an appropriate religious response to it.[60]

Their distinctive understanding of religion is the other major source of difference between Hick and Nasr, as far as the issue of religious pluralism is concerned. Nasr believes that the doctrines and sacred rites and sacred scriptures of a given religion are sacred and cannot be altered by the passing of time. Religion is the Divine response in respect to human needs. Religious statements made through revelations are factual statements about Reality in general and God in particular; their alternations and supposed disagreements in the description of this reality as such are 'formal', i.e, come from their forms, and are not essential. The unity of religions has to be sought in their esoteric dimensions.

According to Hick, however, religion is a human response to the transcendent. Religious doctrines can be modified according to requirements of the present time. Religious statements are essentially mythological and partially factual.

In addition to these basic and general differences, there are also more specific differences in their visions of religious pluralism. What are these differences?

a) Hick believes that his pluralism is a final goal. Through interactions and mutual convergence, religions are heading towards a unity which is likely to erase the boundaries of existing religions. Religious pluralism, in an ideological sense, is the final destiny of all religions; at that stage religions will come together and celebrate the peace between them by getting rid of doctrinal differences. In other words, religious pluralism can and must modify religion. Nasr, on the other hand, believes that 'religious pluralism' (tradition) is a vehicle through which the sacred qualities of other traditions can be realised. Such realisation, according to Nasr, does not initiate a process by which religions would merge together. Rather it highlights the boundaries between religions through promoting respect for every sacred tradition. Therefore, tradition does not attempt to modify the doctrines of any religion but to celebrate them as sacred articles.

b) Hick believes that his pluralism can convince any person, whether believer or non-believer, and can be understood by anyone. It is an intellectual (philosophical) analysis of the diversity of religions, as such; it aims at every intellectual who cares to think about the issue. Nasr, however, claims that the traditional vision of pluralism is 'elitist' and not meant for everyone, only for those who possess the capacity to acquaint themselves with the esoteric dimension of religions.

c) Hick believes that pluralism should guide religious people to create religious tolerance, peace and dialogue and therefore should have an impact on their existential life. Nasr, on the other hand, believes that ordinary religious people must not engage with such confusing ideas; they should remain existentially intact, observing their tradition fully. As for religious intellectuals, they can intellectually engage with the wisdom of other religions while remaining existentially committed to their own religion.

d) Hick believes that there is an urgent need to develop an approach that would accommodate the existing major traditions, thus enabling them to promote peace and tranquillity between them. The intellectuals from different traditions should come together in order to create a better religious world. Pluralistic ideas are useful for such purposes. Nasr, on the other hand, would argue that there is a need for the rediscovery of tradition which will provide a fresh outlook on the function and usefulness of religion. Hence, the intellectual activity in this century should be directed not to those engagements which help to *relativise* the 'truth' of religions, such as conventional religious pluralism, but to those, such as the perennial philosophy, which *revitalise* the 'truths' of religions.

Before proceeding any further, one has to point out that in general Nasr would endorse the view that factors such as 'globalization', the plurality of existing religious traditions and the absolute truth claims of religions make it necessary to adopt a pluralistic approach to religions. I would like to explore the factors that, according to Nasr, lead to the rediscovery of tradition. Now, let me briefly introduce the main principles of Nasr's account of 'pluralism'.

The problem of religious pluralism is to a certain extent the result of modernity, or, as one might call it, 'globalization'. As Nasr points out, in pre-traditional societies, people used to live in homogeneous religious worlds in which they treated the values of their religion in an absolute and binding manner. For them it was unnecessary or irrelevant to seek salvation or intellectual comfort in other traditions. Clearly, the phenomenon of the plurality of religions did not pose the same problem for a traditional Muslim living in Fez or Mashad, or a

Christian peasant living in the hills of Italy or Spain as it does for modern people. But, as Nasr maintains, now that the homogeneity of religious cultures has broken down, and the intellectual and existential contact with the authentic spirituality of other traditions has become increasingly available, it is no longer possible to ignore the religious and theological claims of other traditions.[61]

The solution to the problem lies neither in exclusivism, which destroys the very meaning of Divine justice and mercy, nor in 'universalism, which would destroy the precious elements of a religion that the faithful believe to have come from Heaven and which *are* of celestial origin'.[62] The solution lies in endorsing the traditional viewpoint which seeks the transcendental unity of religions at the level of the Absolute, endorsing the fact that 'all paths lead to the same summit'.

Nasr believes that the traditional point of view is preferable to other forms of pluralism because it has more in common with the essence of religion. It wants to give absolute value to anything that is sacred. Hence, it is able to create a sacred atmosphere in which the uniqueness as well as the diversity of all traditions can be acknowledged. However, currently active forms of religious pluralism are intrinsically negative with regard to the value of the sacred, and therefore cannot create a context in which religions would be both accommodated and reconciled. They seek to shift the direction of the argument concerning the problem of religious pluralism from the realm of theology to the realm of metaphysics. They claim that only at the metaphysical level can the unity of religion be realised.

Nasr also believes that the school of the *philosophia perennis* is vast enough to embrace all forms of traditional religions, whether primal or historical, Semitic or Indian. Such a traditional perspective aims to reflect a remarkable unanimity of views with regard to the meaning of life and the understanding of reality in all traditional worlds including those of the Eskimos and the Australian Aborigines, the Taoists and the Muslims,[63] whereas Hick's hypothesis of religious pluralism encompasses only the major traditions of the world, namely Judaism, Christianity, Islam, Hinduism and Buddhism.

There are two important key concepts which play a significant role in Nasr's engagement with the problem of religious pluralism. One is the concept of the 'relatively absolute', while the other is the concept of archetype. Nasr seems confident that he can surmount the problems caused by the absolute truth claims of religions by introducing the concept of the 'relatively absolute'. I shall explore the potential of this concept in the next chapter. Here, it will suffice to introduce it briefly. He states that only the Absolute is absolute, but each manifestation of the absolute in the form of revelation or religion, creates a world in which a certain determination of the Absolute, such as the Quran or Christ, appears to be absolute without being the Absolute in itself. He maintains that if Christians hold that Christ as the Logos determines absolute value and meaning for them, that is perfectly understandable from a religious point of view while, metaphysically speaking, the Logos as manifested in the Christian world is actually 'relatively absolute' with regard to the Godhead in Its Infinitude which is above all relativity. Hence, only the Absolute is absolute, and the manifestations that appear below the level of the Absolute are 'relatively absolute' although they may appear absolute in their particular universes.[64]

Nasr claims that the traditional point of view does not confine the reality of religions only to their historical unfolding. Each tradition possesses core principles and possibilities in its celestial archetype. When the right time comes for a particular tradition to emerge, those celestial principles or possibilities zoom onto the earth and start playing the role appointed for them by God. The historical unfolding of a particular tradition is determined by its celestial archetype. Religions decay or die (as was the case of Egyptian religion) in the sense that they exhaust all their earthly possibilities. But they can also be revived as long as the connection between their earthly manifestations and heavenly origin remains intact.[65]

What is the practical implication of the concept of the archetype of religion for the problem of religious pluralism? Firstly, it makes irrelevant the argument that one particular religion is better than others, since they are all generated from the same Origin. It should, therefore, be possible to create tolerance and understanding between traditional religions. Secondly, this concept make us able to understand the 'formal' differences and the essential convergence between religions. They are different, because they possess different possibilities in their celestial archetypes. Yet they are united in their essence since they have stemmed from the same origin and speak about the same reality in different languages.

Secularisation Process and the Eclipse of the Sacred

What is the relationship between the problem of religious pluralism and the secularisation process in the West? There is no an immediate link one could discover. One could say that the secularisation process has, to a certain extent, functioned indirectly as an incentive, to formulate a theory of 'ideological' religious pluralism such as that of Hick.[66] As far as Nasr's notion of tradition is concerned, the secularisation process is one of the main factors which has not only created the need for sacred knowledge, but has also underlined the crucial importance of tradition for the spiritual survival of the modern person.[67]

Nothing happens outside God's will. Religion, the cosmos and human beings, Nasr believes, are manifestations of Ultimate Reality. History, according to the traditional view is the collection or the disclosures of divinely determined 'truth-events'. Hence, it is a Divine Play *(lila)*. The existence of the modern and secularised world is accidental. God intentionally allowed such phenomena to appear in order to reassert the Truth that is available only through tradition.[68]

The secularisation process first began when a line was drawn between the realm of the sacred and the realm of the profane. Humans rebelled against Heaven and declared their independence of God. Hence, the sacred qualities of the human faculty of knowledge were ignored, thereby initiating the secularisation of knowledge. Then desacralised knowledge has had its impact not only upon whole segments of culture, including art, science and religion, but also upon human nature. When knowledge is divorced from the sacred, it becomes increasingly externalised and desacralized, especially in those cultures in which modernity is constantly at work.

Rationalism, which came into existence by the process that managed to reduce intellect to reason, says Nasr, is one of the causes of the secularisation process. Rationalism as such has eclipsed the sapiential perspective, making it almost impossible to attain sacred knowledge which is the essential means to acquiring spiritual perfection and deliverance. It turned against the foundations of religion so that 'many a religiously sensitive person in the West has been led to take refuge in faith alone, leaving belief and doctrinal creed to the mercy of ever-changing paradigms or theories caught in the process of relativization and constant transformation'.[69]

Secularisation is rooted in a particular history. Nasr claims that the Enlightenment, which is the source of rationalism, empiricism and mechanism, has not only played a major role in the secularisation of science and the cosmos, but has also given birth to several ideologies which have played an instrumental role in the eclipse of the sacred.[70]

Nasr maintains that one cannot speak of the secularisation process in Western thought without mentioning the role of Descartes, the father of modern philosophy, who is responsible more than anyone else for reducing the faculties of knowledge to mere individual reason divorced from intellect and revelation. Therefore, in seeking a new basis for a certain knowledge, says Nasr, Descartes neither appeals to the intellect, the root of reason, nor revelation, but to the individual consciousness of the thinking subject. He illustrates:

> But in saying 'I think, therefore I am' Descartes was not referring to the divine I who some seven centuries before Descartes had uttered through the mouth of Mansur al-Hallaj, 'I am the Truth' (*ana'l Haqq*), the Divine Self which alone *can* say I. It was Descartes' individual, and therefore from the gnosis point of view 'illusory' self, which was placing its experience and consciousness of thinking as the foundation of all epistemology and ontology and the source of certitude. Even being was subordinated to it and considered as a consequences of it, hence the *ergo*. Even if he did begin with the act of thinking, Descartes could have concluded with *est* rather than *sum*, asserting that my thinking and consciousness are themselves proofs that God is, not that 'I' as individual am.[71]

As Nasr observes, it was Descartes who put the thinking of the individual ego at the centre of reality as the criterion of all knowledge and therefore turned philosophy into pure rationalism. As a consequence of this, philosophy has shifted its main concern from ontology to epistemology. Knowledge, whether its object be human or divine was rooted in the ego of the thinking individual. Hence, the knowing subject and his or her faculty, i.e. reason is the only source from which a sound knowledge can be derived. Any other source of knowledge such as revelation and the intellect which transcends the human has no place in such an account. Knowledge that is emptied of its sacred content became a means to secularisation, extending its impact to all segments of modern culture.[72]

After Descartes, says Nasr, a further step was taken in the secularisation process by Kant, who denied the possibility of knowing the essence of things through denying the role of the intellect. Kant, says Nasr, is perhaps right in denying the knowledge of the noumena depending upon his rational faculties. But he is wrong when he endeavours to universalise his personal ability to know; as if to say 'since my reason is not illuminated by the Intellect, which would

permit me to know the noumena through intellectual intuition, no
one else can possess such an intellectual faculty either'.[73] The final
step toward secularisation was taken by Hegel and Marx who saw
reality as a dialectical becoming and change.[74] Nasr states:

> Since only the like can know the like, the secularized reason
> which became the sole instrument of knowing in the modern
> times could not but leave its mark and effect upon everything
> that it studied. All subjects studied by a secularized instrument
> of knowledge came out to be depleted and devoid of the quality
> of the sacred. The profane point of view could only observe a
> profane world in which the sacred did not play a role. The quest
> of the typically modern man has been in fact to 'kill the gods'
> wherever he has been able to find them and to banish the sacred
> from the world which has been rapidly woven into a new pattern
> drawn from the strands issuing from the secularized mentality.[75]

The secularisation of reason has caused, in a more practical sense, the
secularisation of the cosmos and time. But it was the secularisation of
language that played a more effective part in the process of the
desacralisation of knowledge. What is more surprising in fact, is that
the secularisation process has penetrated into religion,[76] the realm of
the sacred. Consequently:

> Theology ceases to have contact with either the world of nature
> or human history. The unifying vision which related knowledge
> to love and faith, religion to science, and theology to all the
> departments of intellectual concern is finally completely lost,
> leaving a world of compartmentalization where there is no
> wholeness because holiness has ceased to be of central concern,
> or is at best reduced to sentimentality.[77]

I believe that there is a correlation between secularisation and the
crises of the modern age, including environmental and social
problems. Such problems are generated not only by our perception
and therefore treatment of nature, but also by our perception of
ourselves. Hence, it is not enough to change our approach towards
nature. We have to reconsider our perception of humanity, which as a
concept has been subject to constant transformation by the effect of
secularisation. As Nasr observes, the real causes of the problems are
not only due to the destruction of the harmony between human
beings and nature but also due to the destruction of the harmony
between humanity and God.[78] The solution to such problems can be

realised by beginning to change the human image through the contribution of traditional wisdom.[79]

Human beings, Nasr claims, did not come into existence through evolution from animals.[80] They came to being through 'evolution' from the higher order of reality. First, the genesis of humans starts in the Divinity itself and they therefore possess a divine uncreated substance which was called by the traditional Islamic literature *ruh* (soul).[81] That must be the reason, says Nasr, why humans are able to achieve union with God. Then, says Nasr, humans are born through the Logos which is the prototype of all humanity, described by the Muslims as 'the Universal Man' (*al-insan al-kamil*).[82] Next, humans are created on the cosmic level, in the celestial paradise. From there, humans descend to the level of the terrestrial paradise in which they are dressed with the body of ethereal and incorruptible nature.[83] Finally humans are born in the physical world with bodies which perish, but which in essence embody the elements of the earlier stages of the elaboration of humans.[84]

In traditional cultures, human beings used to possess a god-like image; they were the vicegerent of God (*khalifat allah*) or the pontiff on earth. Secularisation has transformed this image, downgrading humanity from divinity to the state of animals. This process can be traced back to the Middle Ages. It was, says Nasr, initiated by the spread of rationalism which in fact resulted in the 'Aristotelianisation' of Western thought. Then in the seventeenth century, the secularisation of the science of the cosmos made the biggest impact on the 'naturalisation' of Christian people. The modern image of human beings was born in the atmosphere of positivism. Later in the context of the Hegelian notion of change and dialectical process, the image of humanity was to change leaving every element that is traditional, divorcing it from the sense of immutability.[85] Hence, maintains Nasr:

> Instead of man being seen as the image of God, the relation was now reversed and God came to be regarded as the image of man and the projection of his own consciousness. Promethean man not only sought to steal fire from Heaven but even kill the gods, little aware that man cannot destroy the image of the Divinity without destroying himself.[86]

Nevertheless, despite all these predicaments, and attempts to change human nature, a spiritual and contemplative aspect of human beings continues to appear. As Nasr observes, if humankind could maintain its earthly existence without spiritual 'experience', then the contemplative aspects of humankind would simply cease to exist. Nasr states:

> In reality, the needs of man, as far as the total nature of man is concerned, remain forever the same, precisely because of man's unchanging nature... The situation of man in the universal hierarchy of being, his standing between the two unknowns which comprise his state before terrestrial life, and his state of death, his need of a 'shelter' in the vast stretches of cosmic existence and his deep need for certainty (*yaqin* in the vocabulary of Sufism) remain unchanged.[87]

Nasr claims that traditional wisdom reminds human beings that the roots of their existence lead to a spiritual awakening by freeing them from the disturbance of everyday life. Tradition alone fulfils the real needs of human nature by creating harmony not only between the compartments of human beings, such as body and soul, but also between humanity and nature as well as humanity and God. The traditional point of view suggests that since the quest for spirituality has not ceased to exist and will not cease exist because of the existence of the 'heavenly' substance in human nature, then there will always be an urge or quest for a 'culture' which is able to provide a spiritually and physically healthy environment. This is none other than the *sophia perennis*. It is this quest for an authentic spirituality which originates from the divine aspects of humans that eventually will reverse the process of secularisation. The next phase to which human cultural history will be heading is the rediscovery of tradition.

The Rediscovery of Tradition

Both Hick and Nasr believe that eventually there will be a religious resurgence in the coming century. Although they agree on this point, they fundamentally differ about the features of this religious transformation. Hick believes that it will take place through a change in religions, through the convergence or interaction of religions with each other, and eventually the removal of the boundaries between them.[88] Hick would say that the Real will display its presence more effectively than before by highlighting the significance of religious transformation from 'self-centrednness' to 'Reality-centredness', rather than in the conflicting doctrines between religions. The realisation of this pluralistic hypothesis, is a possible future for religions. Nasr, however, believes that a religious transformation will take place through the re-discovery of tradition and traditional values for the survival of the individuals as well as societies. Unlike Hick, he thinks there will not be any radical change in the doctrinal patterns of the given religions. Rather there is going to be a revitalisation of the already existing doctrines. Hence, although religions would preserve their own identity, there is possibly going to be a mutual recognition of their 'essential' unity. This is a viable future for religion because God (who is at once Truth and Reality and the author of everything that occurs) would not simply allow religions to disappear from the surface of the earth leaving human beings in total darkness.[89]

The question that I am addressing here, is the issue of the occurrence of de-traditionalisation or re-traditionalisation as far as the current and future status of religion is concerned. We have realised that the positivist view on religion has proved to be wrong a century and half after Comte. Now, it has become almost a fashion in contemporary sociology of religion to argue that traditional religions are subject to constant change and transformation under the impact of new the 'norms' and new 'values' generated by science and the present social conditions. Hence, it is claimed that, we are witnessing a total collapse of tradition and traditional values which can be phrased as de-traditionalisation. From the traditional point of view, such a presentation is not an exact picture of what is taking place in the world's religious communities. Nor is this a plausible postulate as far as the future of religion is concerned.

There are several reasons that can make one suspicious of the verdict of social scientists. Firstly, they have formed their theories under the shadow of the legacy of the positivist outlook. Because of their existential condition, they are intrinsically biased against religion; how can the true sons of secularised culture be 'neutral' on the issue of religion?[90] Secondly, they have developed their theories through the observation of religious communities. It is generally the case that such observation often supports the pre-formed presumption of the social scientist in question. It is also the case that there are many different conclusions that can be drawn from observing a religious community. As far as the claim of 'de-traditionalisation' is concerned, if the current social and religious conditions of a religious community, such as Christians in Britain, indicate that such a 'transformation' is really at work, this does not mean that it is a phenomenon occurring globally. Thirdly, such findings are mostly dependent upon the observations of human conditions or the events that take place in a specific society. The social scientist's accounts of a social phenomenon are always the accounts of what has happened and never the accounts of what would probably happen. Therefore, one might even claim that they are unable to grasp the dynamics of what is shaping the events in a society.[91]

The traditional view, on the other hand, is 'intuitive'. It aims to identify the essential principles that govern the world of 'becoming'. With the aid of revelation, metaphysicians can be acquainted with the true nature of reality through an illuminated intellect. Through such sophisticated speculations, the traditional metaphysicians can picture a mechanism or order by which one can infer or predict a global social transformation.[92]

The traditional point of view sounds either illuminating or senseless according to one's standpoint. Nevertheless, Nasr seems certain about the future of tradition. 'The overall harmony and equilibrium of the cosmos', says Nasr requires a movement in the heart and soul of some distinguished metaphysicians to rediscover the sacred and its 'ground' as well as 'cover' i.e. tradition. 'The principle of cosmic compensation', an act of mercy from God, maintains Nasr, generates a quest for the rediscovery of the sacred at the precise moment when secularisation and modernism have endeavoured to root out the sacred from the present culture. Secularisation has proved to be counter-productive. The more it attempts to deplete the sacred contents of the human culture, the more it creates a quest for spiritual life. A sacred substance at the centre of human existence is the cause of an 'inner pull' which brings a person to the presence of the Sacred. It is the spiritual and material dissatisfaction and inner turmoil, which are the characteristics of the modern time, that would urge the rediscovery of the sacred as well as tradition.[93]

A revival of the traditional outlook, says Nasr cannot be possible without an authentic contact with the Oriental traditions which have preserved their sacred contents. The revival of tradition is already taking place in the Occident. It started with an interest in Oriental studies, which at least positively resulted in the translation of sacred scriptures and the works with sapiential nature. Goethe's romantic love for the Orient, Thomas Taylor's quest for Platonism and Neoplatonism, Emerson's reading of the Oriental sources and more importantly Corbin's and Massignon's[94] works on Sufism, have initially contributed to laying down a base on which the perennial philosophy has developed. Most of all it was the three remarkable thinkers, namely Gue'non, Coomaraswamy and Schuon who have become the prominent expositors of the *sophia perennis* thereby playing a major part in the rediscovery of tradition. There is no point in speculating about the future of religion. Whatever we say will not go beyond a lucky guess. Having said that, I still believe that rediscovery of tradition, or 're-traditionalisation' as it has been understood by the perennialists, is one of the highly plausible options for the future of religion. One of the reasons that leads one to maintain this view is the perennialists' confidence about the potential value of their outlook. They maintain their view for the following reasons:

a) They believe that the perennial philosophy is potentially capable of *creating an alternative culture* against modernity. Modernity has contributed to the creation of such problems including the fragmentation of community and community values, the collapse of the family, alienation and the environmental crisis. Traditional wisdom, however, can function as an antidote to every negative element of modernism. Firstly, while modernity emphasises reason and rationality, the traditional point of view, believes in reason plus wisdom; it claims that reason which is attached to the intellect, is more fruitful than the reason that is independent of it. Wisdom is the outcome of illumined reason. Secondly, while modernity seeks the knowledge that generates progress, growth and constant change, the perennial philosophy, on the other hand, aims to exhibit sacred knowledge which will halt the aimless growth and progress which threatens to destroy the mere existence of humanity on earth. While modernity has caused the fragmentation of communal or personal identity, the perennial philosophy, aims to achieve the integration of individuals into the community through underlying community values in a re-created 'sacred society'. While modernity promotes a totalitarian universality which destroys locality, the traditional view, on the other hand, propounds *unity within diversity* which underlies the importance of locality.[95]

b) They argue that the traditional point of view can *accommodate the diversity of religions* without upsetting the faithful. It is able to construct a framework in which a multi-cultural and multi-religious community could be united without dismissing local values. It is also able to sever the power of religious 'formalism', i.e. dogmatism, claiming that the Absolute alone is absolute and beyond that everything is relatively absolute. It can create a religious tolerance through dialogue and intellectual interchange between traditional religions since it sees all traditional religions as the different paths which lead to the same summit.

c) The perennial philosophy, *affirms morality and the virtuous life*. It intends to turn people inward by leading them to the richness of inner spirituality. It claims that the understanding and appreciation of the perennial philosophy is very much interconnected with a virtuous personal life; knowledge cannot be divorced from the moral life. It is interesting to note that the success of the traditional point of view presupposes a religious transformation which should make people morally sound. More importantly, there will not be so much room for religious fundamentalism in the pluralists view of the perennial philosophy.

d) The perennialists also claim that the *sophia perennis* can *open another cultural dimension* by making use of the past, i.e. traditions in the creation of art, literature, science and philosophy. It can bring traditional art, literature and science into focus. It can provide a source of inspiration for the present generations in the creation of an alternative culture.

e) They nevertheless are quite confident that the perennial philosophy is not only able to diagnose the real *causes of environmental problems* but can also show the way by which these problems can be solved. It is against the creation of unbridled technology which recognises no boundaries for its power. It is fundamentally opposed to consumerism and materialism, both of which play the biggest part in generating the current environmental crises. Instead of egoism, it encourages altruism; instead of aggressiveness, it advocate compassion and charity. Nasr himself summarises the perennialists' answer to environmental problems:

... [A]lthough science is legitimate in itself, the role and the function of science and its implication have become illegitimate and even dangerous because of the lack of a higher form of knowledge into which science could be integrated and the destruction of the sacred and spiritual value of nature. To remedy this situation the metaphysical knowledge pertaining to nature must be revived and the sacred quality of nature given back to it once again. In order to accomplish this end the history and the philosophy of science must be reinvestigated in relation to Christian theology and the traditional philosophy of nature which existed during most of European history.[96]

The Limits of the Traditional Outlook

The perennial philosophy is confronting a dilemma. On the one hand, it claims that it possesses a remedy for those who are affected by crises of modernity. On the other hand it presents itself in such a fashion that it does not seem attractive to the very people for whom the perennial philosophy would be an alternative in their quest for truth. That is to say, the remedy which the perennial philosophy claims to have, is bounded by such a condition that it would not be available to the very people who need it most.

Another obstacle that prevents the perennial philosophy from realising its full potential is that it addresses the issue by employing a style which sounds quite odd to the modern person. Those who are not familiar with such a 'symbolic', even perhaps poetic, style cannot really fully comprehend the message of the perennial philosophy. It uses a language that means more than it says.

The success of the traditional outlook is dependent upon the complete religious transformation of the culture. The perennial philosophy alone is not capable of achieving such a transformation. From the position that we are in, it seems quite unrealistic to reverse the process of secularisation in order to make the whole cultural enterprise sacred.

The perennialist's pluralism may accommodate all traditional religions in a sacred atmosphere, but it cannot offer any solution to the doctrinal and ethical conflicts of religions, since it wants to hold as true every sacred formulation of tradition. If every traditional doctrine of a given religion is venerated, how could the perennial philosophy possibly reconcile the resultant conflict? The Muslims will continue believe that Jesus is not the son of God and the Christians will continue believe that he is. The perennialist position does not provide a criterion that can determine the validity of either position or both. The problem of the perennial philosophy becomes more dramatic when such conflicts occur in the essential doctrines of religions. It would be quite interesting to see how the perennial philosophy could possibly reconcile the conflict between for example, Islam and Theravada Buddhism pertaining to the doctrine of God. It cannot really deny the doctrine of God if it really believes that the traditional Islamic, Christian and Judaic doctrine of God is true. Nor can it easily confirm this doctrine when it considers Theravada Buddhism and its traditional doctrine as true. Their doctrine of esoterism or the distinction between form and essence is not sufficient to surmount such a fundamental conflict. One cannot really say that God exists when one look at the forms or formal expression of religion whereas God does not exist when one looks beyond the formal expression of religion.[97]

In pre-modern societies there was a tradition or a religion for a community; in Islamic society, Islam was the religion, whereas in, let us say, Christian society, Christianity was the religion. In traditional societies, there were Islam, Christianity, Judaism and Hinduism. But there was no such philosophical system as the perennial philosophy which is intended to unite all religions. The attempt to see religions within a unified system is a modern innovation. In other words, one can even claim that the perennialists, under the cover of tradition, are offering something quite alien to the nature of traditions themselves. In this sense, the perennial philosophy is a modern discourse, to a certain extent an ideological attempt to discover the significance of traditions. For instance, according to the perennialists, the great metaphysicians such as Ibn 'Arabi and Eckhart are the main expositors of the *sophia perennis*. I would argue that they are traditional, but not perennialists in Nasr's sense of the word; they did not write about their religions in order to convince modern people. Instead, they presented their traditions from the mystical perspective of which they were a part. In other words, they presented a traditional view of their religion, but not the perennial philosophy in a modern sense, as Nasr and other perennialists understand it. Hence we are obliged to conclude that the traditional point of view is not traditional in the sense that traditional people understood it.

Chapter Five

The Ultimate and Pluralism

The Ineffable Deity

One immediate problem for such a 'supra religious' hypothesis is the problem of terminology. For this purpose, having identified some common terms among the major traditions, such as God, the Transcendent, Ultimate Reality, the Supreme Principle, the Divine, the One, the Eternal, the Real, Hick prefers the term 'the Real' to describe a putative transcendent reality. He argues that the term God is possible, but not preferable, for a number of reasons: firstly, it is not clear whether the term God signifies personal or non-personal or both characteristics of the Ultimate. Secondly, the theistic associations of the term are so strong that its usage might not be accommodating for those non-personal concepts of deity such as that of Buddhists, advaitic Hindus, Taoists and Confucians. The term 'the Real' is the most suitable, because it has the advantage of not being the exclusive property of any tradition, while being familiar to them all. Another reason why Hick is inclined to use it is that all major traditions have a specific term which more or less corresponds to the term the Real. For instance, in Christianity this term can be easily identified with God; the Real, *al-Haqq*, in Islam is one of the names of Allah. In the Hindu family of faith, the term *sat* or *satya* refers to Brahman as Ultimate Reality. In Mahayana Buddhism, the term *tattva*, the Real, signifies the Dharmakaya or *sunyata*; while in Chinese thought, the term *zhen*, the Real, signifies the Ultimate.[1]

Although the Real might be a suitable term for the task Hick has in mind, it seems that it is not fully capable of embodying the whole meaning of the terms used in other traditions, such as *al-haqq, sat, sunyata* and *zhen*. For instance, in Islamic tradition, *al-haqq*, though it is the name of God and literally means the Real, cannot embody the

130

meaning and the qualifications that Hick aims to embody when he employs the concept of the Real. In other words, I would argue that Hick extrapolates the Islamic term *al-haqq* and embodies it with such a meaning that no Muslim could possibly recognise in it anything to do with the God they believe in and worship.[2] Hence, my obvious conclusion is that the term the Real cannot carry the full weight of inter-religious discussion which Hick aims to promote. Nor can it deliver a cross cultural response, the task for which it is formed.

As Badham points out, the term embodies a secular and even naturalistic connotation which, though meaningful for intellectuals, sounds inauspicious for ordinary religious people. Badham suggests that it is more sensible to use mainstream religious words such as 'God', 'Allah', 'Brahman' or 'Dharmakaya', although the word God is preferable, since this term is widely recognised and found appropriate in both the personal and impersonal understanding of Ultimate Reality.[3]

Having pointed out the problem of terminology in constructing a 'trans-traditional' hypothesis, I would like to focus on Hick's formation of the concept of the Real and indicate some problems that it has produced. He explains how he has discovered the possibility of one all-encompassing concept for describing the object of worship in the major traditions. He suggests that even in a single theistic community of faith, the images of God vary extensively, differing from one person to another. If it were possible to inspect the images of God in the minds of in a typical congregation of worshippers in a Christian church, we should undoubtedly find wide variations. These images, would possibly range from the 'stern judge' to 'the gracious heavenly Father', from God as invisible person capable of observing our everyday thoughts and actions, to God who dwells in eternity. But the fact that there are these divergent images of God, does not entitle one to claim that individuals in Christian traditions are implicitly worshipping different gods. On the contrary, says Hick, Christians are worshipping the same God, but each focusing upon the aspect of the divine nature that is relevant to his or her spiritual needs at that time. If we enlarge our vision to include the distinctively different and still overlapping concepts of God envisaged by Jews, Muslims and Christians, we will naturally be able to understand the differences as well as the underlying common characteristics of their conception of God. One can go beyond this notion and go further by including the concepts of deities that exist in the Hindu traditions, such as Vishnu and Shiva, Kali and Durga.[4]

The principle of introducing a single concept of deity that can make sense of each different tradition is highly problematic. Firstly, whereas the realm in which the 'gods' of religions operate is religious, such a Hickian move reduces these 'living deities' to philosophical concepts. Secondly, the different images which individual Christians have of God cannot be deemed to be comparable to the different images of God, or gods, that are to be found in world religions. The differences between the gods of religions are greater than the differences between images of God among Christians. Thirdly, the main reason behind Hick's formation of the concept of the Real is the assumption that the figures of the 'gods' of religions with their qualities have been formed through religious experience within their distinctive religious histories. In other words, Hick would argue that since it is human beings who essentially form these images of 'gods', it always possible for anybody to form a concept of God.

Now, let me briefly state Hick's hypothesis of religious pluralism. He believes that we can certainly decrease, perhaps even obliterate, religious intolerance and conflicts by persuading religious people that the 'gods' they worship are manifestations of the One, i.e. the only Real. In other words, God figures like Allah of the Muslims, Adonai of the Jews, the Heavenly Father of the Christians, Shiva and Vishnu of the Hindus, are the ways through which the Real is worshipped and recognised.[5] These are what Hick calls *personae* and *impersonae* of the Real. Therefore, all religions have been brought about in response to the One and only Real. The doctrines and principles that cause religious conflicts and intolerance are accidental, not essential aspect of the major religions. Now, we can all come together under the umbrella of the Real through recognising other's spiritual ways as valid. Through this, Hick believes, we can eliminate religious conflicts and intolerance and promote peace and religious tolerance in the world.

The strength of his argument is based firstly on a religious justification for the distinction between the Real *an sich* and its manifestations, i.e. its *personae* and *impersonae,* and secondly the soundness of the supposed connection between the Real and the 'gods' of religions. I suggest that these two important points make Hick's hypothesis of religious pluralism seem vulnerable. Let me first address the problem of distinction.

Hick believes that he can reasonably justify such a distinction by arguing that the traditions themselves make a similar distinction. For instance, in the Christian tradition, God *a se* as infinite self-existent being is distinguished from God *pro nobis* as the creator and redeemer. In Islam, God as Ultimate Reality, *al-haqq*, the abyss of Godhead, is distinguished from God who revealed the Quran to humankind; in Judaism, *Eyn Soph*, the divine reality beyond human description is distinguished from the concrete God of the Bible; in Mahayana Buddhism, the Ultimate, Eternal *Dharmakaya* is distinguished from *Sambhogakaya*; in Hindu thought, *nirguna* Brahman, Brahman without attribute, is distinguished from *saguna* Brahman, Brahman with attributes known within human religious experience as *Ishvara*.[6]

My main objection to Hick's argument is that the distinction that religions make does not deny God's religious qualities, while Hick's distinction does. In order to elaborate this point further let us apply it to the Islamic tradition. Firstly, the distinction Hick has in mind is not recognised by mainstream Islamic theology. Nor is it freely used by Muslim scholars. Even if for the sake of argument, one accepts the distinction made between God as *al-haqq* and God who revealed the Quran in the Islamic tradition, this does not change the nature of the God of Islam. The Muslim believes that God is at once Godhead (*al-dhat*) and God with attributes; each attribute underlines one aspect of God. In other words, God as *al-haqq* is the same God who revealed the Quran, the One who is worthy of worship.

In Hick's hypothesis, however, the difference between the Real and its *personae* and *impersonae* is insurmountable; the Real is fundamentally different from its 'manifestations'. The distinction which is introduced to overcome religious disputes, has actually transformed God from a God who is worthy of worship to the God who is an unreachable and ineffable entity; from the God of the prophets to the God of the philosophers, if one uses the vocabulary of Pascal.[7]

Hick would claim that the distinction between the Real *an sich* and its *personae* and *impersonae* is proper and justifiable, not only because the major traditions have made such a distinction, but also because the Kantian epistemological model has introduced a suitable philosophical framework within which this distinction might make sense. We know that Kant's epistemological insight, namely that the mind actually interprets sensory information in terms of concepts, was his main source, when he identified faith as an interpretative element within the religious experience. Here, in Hick's formation of the concept of the Real, Kant yet again has played an important part; Kant's distinction between noumenon and phenomenon is identified as a suitable tool through which Hick is able to introduce a concept of the Real which aims to accommodate the 'gods' of traditions.[8]

Hick believes that Kant's distinction between noumenon and phenomenon, or between a *Ding an sich* and that thing as it appears to human consciousness, can be interpreted as the noumenal world existing independently of our perception of it and the phenomenal world as the appearance of the same world to our consciousness. But the world as it appears to us, according to Kant is thus entirely real. Hick starts where Kant stopped:

> The noumenal Real is experienced and thought by different human mentalities, forming and formed by different religious traditions, as the range of gods absolutes which the phenomenology of religion reports. And these divine *personae* and metaphysical *impersonae*, . . . are not illusory but are empirically, that is experientially, real as authentic manifestations of the Real.[9]

Hick is surely aware of the difficulties of applying this Kantian epistemological insight to the domain of God. The most obvious problem is that Kant never accepted the view that God as a reality can be experienced, but for him, God is an object postulated by practical reason in order to make sense of moral life. According to Kant, categorical moral obligation presupposes the reality of God. In other words, God is postulated not experienced. Hick elucidates how his concept of the Real becomes more meaningful when it is seen through Kant's epistemological insight:

> In practical agreement but also practical disagreement with him [Kant], I want to say that the Real *an sich* is postulated by us as a pre-supposition, not of the moral life, but of religious experience and the religious life, whilst the gods, as also the mystically known Brahman, Sunyata and so on, are phenomenal manifestations of the Real occurring within the realm of religious experience. Conflating these two theses one can say that the Real is experienced by human beings, but experienced in a manner analogous to that in which, according to Kant, we experience the world: namely by information input from external reality being interpreted by the mind in terms of its own categorical scheme and thus coming to consciousness as meaningful phenomenal experience.[10]

Through such an extrapolation of Kantian insight, Hick believes that the transcendent religious reality can be viewed as having two roles. The first is that it can function as the ground of religious experience, while in its second, it serves as an element within the cognitive structure of our consciousness through which we respond to the meaning and character of our environment including its religious meaning and character. In other words, a transcendent divine reality is brought into our consciousness through the awareness of the physical world, in terms of basic concepts and categories of the religious tradition in which we live. There are, Hick maintains two basic categories, God and the Absolute through which a range of particular gods and absolutes are 'schematised' or made concrete within actual religious experience.[11]

Hick's appeal to Kantian insight may have done more harm than good in his presentation of the Real as a common concept of religions.[12] Firstly, Hick's move from the 'gods' of religions to the noumenal Real is not justifiable in terms of his cognitive commitment. D'Costa, who dealt extensively with Hick's notion of the Copernican revolution in theology, sees Hick's move as confusing; instead of illuminating the religious perceptions of God, it actually mystifies by introducing a Kantian vocabulary.[13] Roth argues that even Kant was never able to satisfy fully those who kept asking how his epistemology enabled him to speak of 'things in themselves'. Roth points out that Hick's Kantian move is less persuasive than Kant's epistemology, since Hick affirms that the Real *an sich* is not even a necessary condition for religious experience.[14]

Why is Hick attracted by this Kantian model? The reason for this is that Hick wants to make the Real a necessary postulate – a postulate which can be thought but not known as envisaged in Kant's epistemology – of the phenomenal reality of various gods and ultimates. In this case my question would of course be: if the Real is a postulate, what content could Hick ascribe to the Real *an sich*, given that it is wholly beyond the realm of experience? Virtually none. Hick is in a dilemma. As J. Prabhu points out, Hick should accept the proposition that either the Real has no content, in which case its religious significance is at stake, or it has some content and in that case he cannot assert that the Real *an sich* is sheer mystery beyond the reach of our concepts.[15]

The postulation of the Real has caused more problems for Hick than it has solved. Another problem, one might add, is that since the Real cannot become the direct object of experience, it is difficult to envisage any model which could show that there is a correlation between the Real and its manifestations.[16] If Hick cannot secure such a connection how can he seriously claim that the *personae* and *impersonae* of the Real, thought and experienced by the major traditions, are images and manifestations of the Real *an sich*?[17]

Does the Real Possess any Qualities?

When one looks at Hick's early writings such as *Philosophy of Religion* (1963), *Existence of God* (1964), *Faith and Knowledge* (1957), *Evil and the God of Love* (1966) and *Christianity at the Centre* (1968), one can see that Hick's concept of God was mainly Christian; he perceived God in the same fashion as other Christian theologians and philosophers perceived God. In *Philosophy of Religion* (1963), having followed mainstream Christian tradition, Hick described God as a personal, infinite, self-existent, loving, being who created the world.[18] While in *Christianity at the Centre*, Hick described God as 'a cosmic brain millions of times larger and complex than the human brain'.[19] But in *God and the Universe of Faiths* and *God Has Many Names*, Hick began to take other religions' conceptions of God into account, including that of Islam, Hinduism and Buddhism. Ultimately, it was in *An Interpretation of Religion* that Hick's idea of God was transformed from the God of Christianity to the Real of the noumenal domain.

The postulation of the Real *an sich* is the bed-rock of Hick's pluralistic hypothesis without which his pluralism makes little sense. The efficacy of his pluralism is dependent upon his capability to justify the characteristics of his Real alongside the characteristics of the 'gods' of religions. But, unfortunately, he places the Real in a position that enables one to say little about it. All we know about the Real is what it is not, not what it is. For instance, according to Hick, we cannot attribute the characteristics of the 'gods' of religions to the Real *an sich* at all:

> But we cannot apply to the noumenal Real any of the distinctions with which we structure our phenomenal, including our religious, experience. We cannot say that it is personal or impersonal, one or many, active or passive, substance or process, good or evil, just or unjust, purposive or purposeless. No such categories can be applied, either positively or negatively, to the noumenal. Thus, whilst it is not correct to say, for example, that the Real is personal, it is also not correct to say that it is impersonal – nor that it is both personal and impersonal, or neither personal nor impersonal. All that one

can say is that these concepts, which have their use in relation to human experience, do not apply, even analogically, to the Real *an sich*.[20]

Why does Hick put himself into trouble by postulating such an unknown and unknowable Real *an sich*? The reasons which Hick would suggest for this problematic move can be stated as follows: Firstly, Hick would argue that God as the Eternal and Infinite One is by definition unknowable, because it is impossible to experience the infinite; we cannot say anything about something that is beyond our experience.[21]

Secondly, Hick believes that there is a framework, namely the Kantian distinction of noumenon and phenomenon, which enables him to introduce his conception of the Real to the culture in which Kantian philosophy is an important element. That is to say, the Western intellectual can be persuaded of the merits of his thesis when it is introduced within a Kantian framework.

Thirdly, to say that the Real is unknowable is not totally unintelligible because the major traditions have themselves affirmed the ineffability of God. I have addressed this issue at the beginning of the chapter.

These are some of the reasons which Hick would state to justify postulating the unknowable Real. But the main reason is that he is determined to eradicate the disputes between the different religious traditions over the description of God by removing the 'Real God' to the realm which no religion can reach. Hick places himself in a position in which he cannot accept a particular religion's depiction of God and deny the others', because he believes that they are equally valid in their transformative power. Nor can he afford to deny the qualities of God ascribed by the major traditions *altogether*, because he wants to remain a theist. Nor can he endorse the different attributes of God ascribed by the major traditions altogether, because they sometimes conflict in their descriptions of God. In this situation, he assumes that the only plausible solution that would satisfy his religious critics is to move the 'Real God' into undisputed and indisputable territory, that is the realm of the noumenon, while granting each god of religion a part to play in making the connection between the 'Real God' and the believers.

To say that the Real is unknown is not to say that it does not exist, and has no functions. We can, according to Hick, describe the Real *via negativa* saying what it is not rather than what it is. For instance, the Real is not one or many, good or evil, male or female, just or unjust, beautiful or ugly, personal or impersonal and so on. But *via positiva* we can make some purely formal statements such as Anselm's definition of God as that than which no greater can be conceived.[22] In the same way, Hick believes that he can say about the Real that 'it is the noumenal ground of the encountered gods and experienced absolutes witnessed by the religious traditions',[23] or 'the Real has the attribute of being referred to'.[24] In addition to these formal statements, one can at least affirm two significant qualities of the Real *via positiva*. These are: the Real is the ground of religious experience and it is also the cause of the religious transformation from self-centredness to Reality-centredness.

The identification of the Real as unknown and unknowable 'entity' is the most problematic aspect of Hick's hypothesis of religious pluralism which has attracted several criticisms. For instance, Keith Ward argues that Hick is mistaken when he assumes that the different traditions' statements about the ineffability of Ultimate Reality can be interpreted to mean that they all speak of the ineffability of the same Reality. He sees Hick's argument to be invalid. He maintains:

> If X is indescribable by me, and Y is indescribable by me, it does not follow that X is identical with Y. On the contrary, there is no way in which X could be identified with Y, since there are no criteria of identity to apply. It is rather like saying, 'I do not know what X is; and I do not know what Y is; therefore X must be the same as Y.' If I do not know what either is, I *ipso facto* do not know whether they are the same or different. To assert identity is thus to commit the quantifier-shift fallacy, of moving from 'Many religions believe in an ineffable Real' to 'There is an ineffable Real in which many religions believe'.[25]

More important than this, as Ward[26] and Davis[27] point out, is that Hick wants to hold two conflicting views at the same time. On the one hand, he says that the Real is beyond the scope of human thought and experience, while at the same time he applies many human concepts, such as *ground, real, one, cause,* to the Real. In reply to this point Hick argues that the postulated Real is not beyond the scope of these kinds of concepts. We can make a purely formal statement about the Real, such as the Real is the ultimate transcendent reality, which is experienced as the gods and the absolutes of religious traditions. But we cannot concretely describe it[28] saying for instance, it is living or not living, conscious or unconscious, good or evil.

I would like to approach this particular point from a slightly different perspective. Hick believes that the Real is beyond human apprehension, and yet humans are able to respond it. Through such a response, he assumes, we can envisage the Real not, of course, in itself but as it responds to us through one of its manifestations. In this respect whatever one says about the Real cannot be absolutely true, but relatively true, that is simply because any attribute that we intend to ascribe to the Real is generated out of our imaginations during our religious experience. By following the same argument, it seems that Hick, by depending upon his own intuition and religious experience, cannot state that the Real is the ultimate transcendent reality, which is experienced as the gods and the absolutes of religions, in a binding manner, since *whatever* he says about the Real must belong not to the Real in itself but to one of its manifestations, because we cannot experience the Real as it is but only through its manifestations. According to his own criteria when Hick says that the Real is the ultimate transcendent reality, he is not talking about the Absolute Real, but the relative Real which Hick himself has come to know through his own religious experience or intuition. Therefore, we cannot accept Hick's qualification of the Real as wholly true but perhaps as partly true.

The Real and the 'Gods' of Religions

Before proceeding any further let me briefly describe how Hick locates the 'gods' of religions in relation to the Real. The Real makes an impact upon the psyche of sensitive individuals not as itself but through masks (categories). There are two categories, namely, God and Absolute, by which the Real gets in touch with the believers. These are respectively *personae* (gods), namely, the Heavenly Father, Adonai, Allah, Shiva and Vishnu and also *impersonae* (absolutes), namely, Brahman, Sunyata, Nirvana, Being.[29]

Hick argues that as finite persons, we naturally envisage God as a divine Thou. From the archaic religions to the present great faiths of humanity throughout the centuries, God has always been thought of as a divine person. The Real is experienced as the divine Thou in the Semitic traditions, namely, Judaism, Christianity and Islam, while in oriental traditions the Real has mostly been experienced as absolutes.[30] But, the Semitic religions do endorse the absoluteness of the Real, while many of the oriental traditions approve the personal characteristics of the Real.

139

Having established that his pluralistic hypothesis of religion is based on the assumption that there is the ineffable Real which exhibits itself through the 'gods' of religions, the next thing Hick aims to do is to reformulate those aspects of the 'gods' of religions which conflict with the assumed nature of the Real. For instance, in the three Abrahamic traditions God is identified with omniattributes. These include infinite goodness and love, infinite wisdom and justice, omnipotence and omniscience and eternity. The ascription to God of such qualities clearly works against his theory. If the God of Christianity, Islam and Judaism is infinite, then it is not possible for him to postulate another infinite, i.e. the Real. In these circumstances the only possible solution for him is to limit the power of the God of Christianity, Judaism and Islam, thereby making the Real truly ultimate and infinite.[31] Hick's argument against such traditional claims is brief: the 'gods' of religions cannot be infinite because 'as finite observers we could never directly experience, observe, verify, the infinite dimensions of an infinite reality'.[32] In other words, since it is we who form the concepts of 'gods' of religions, then it naturally must be implausible for us as finite beings to constitute such concepts. My response to this argument is, as I discussed in chapter three, that ordinary believers do not constitute their concepts of God through their religious experience, and therefore Hick is mistaken in the first place, when he assumes that we do actually form our idea of God in this way.

One of the crucial questions which can test the coherence of Hick's hypothesis would be the inquiry that examines the ontological status of the Real in relation to the 'gods' of religion. It seems odd that Hick speaks of the ontological status of the 'gods' of religions, but never queries the ontological status of the Real. He may think that this is not a legitimate question to ask, since experience and the knowledge of the postulated Real is impossible. In my opinion, however, the Real deserves a proper ontological status, if Hick describes it as the ground of religious experience as well as the cause of the religious transformation from self-centredness to Reality-centredness. Otherwise, we would end up with the peculiar conclusion that the Real, while encountered by the mystics, and manifesting itself through the 'gods' of religions, does not, in fact, exist. Therefore, Hick must endorse the existence of the Real at least. My next question is this. If the Real truly possesses the only possible existence, i.e. if it occupies the only available ontic space, then what would happen to the 'gods' of religions? For instance, can a Muslim still believe that *there is* Allah who is the creator of the universe as well as the author of the Quran?

Hick's reply to my question would be that there are Allah, Adonai, Shiva, Vishnu and so on as well as the Real, all of which mysteriously share the available ontic space. In this context, there are two different issues that need to be addressed: one is the ontological status of the 'gods' of religions and the other the relation between the Real and its *personae* and *impersonae*. First let us see how Hick approaches the problem of the ontological status of the 'gods' of religions.

Hick argues that within the context of any one theistic religion, if one asks what is the nature of the divine person to whom prayer is addressed, the answer would be that in addition to many finite centres of consciousness, there is one Divine Self. In other words, in every theistic tradition, it is believed that there is only one divine person to be considered. As soon as we recognise, says Hick, other objects of religious worship such as Adonai, Allah, the heavenly Father, Shiva, Vishnu and many others, a more complex conception becomes necessary.[33]

Hick claims that to solve this problem we have several options. One is the polytheistic option. Since this model conflicts with the basic doctrines of each theistic tradition that there is one creator and source of existence, it cannot solve the issue. The second model is perhaps summarised as 'one-in-many which is also many in one'. This model supposes that the Godhead consists of Jahweh and the heavenly Father, and Allah and Vishnu and so on. This model, says Hick, also cannot settle the issue because each god, according to the tradition from which we learn about the particular god, is the sole creator and source of the universe. The third model can be summarised as 'there is one God but known differently through his different relations'. For instance, God is imaged as Jahweh through his acting in relation to the children of Israel; known as the Heavenly Father through his acting in relation to the disciples of Jesus; imaged as Allah through his acting in relation to Muslims and so on. Hick endorses that this model comes very close to his pluralistic hypothesis. The fourth model is that there is one God, but known with many names. Adonai, the Heavenly Father, Allah, Shiva, Vishnu and others are different names for the same divine person. Hick rejects this model too because he thinks that each name has its own different characteristics shaped through different history. If we accept this model, he points out, we will confront another problem, that is, how we can find the connection between these faces.[34] In addition to these models, Hick mentions a few other models from the Buddhist tradition which makes it possible to connect one eternal to its many manifestations. But he concludes that his pluralism 'could accommodate either of these models and does not require a decision between them'.[35]

Such a tentative statement, however, is not able to settle the problem. I still ask the same question. How does the Real who is devoid of any qualities become Allah, Adonai, the heavenly Father, Shiva, Vishnu, each of whom have their own different religious qualities? More specifically, when a Muslim, while praying, feels a 'spiritual' impact, does he or she feel the impact of the Real or the impact of Allah?

The gist of Hick's argument is this. The characteristics that we attribute to the 'gods' of religions, including their existence, are generated by us through the relationship with the Real. In other words, when we relate ourselves to the Real through worship, we are bound to relate ourselves through one of its phenomenal dimensions, that is, the concept of God given us by the culture in which we live. In other words, Hick claims, under no circumstances is one able to relate himself or herself directly to the Real.

Hick believes that his thesis stems from an insight that is able to perceive God properly insofar as it perceives the distinction between the Eternal God and the God which is subject to our religious experience. Moreover, Hick assumes that 'Arabi echoed the same insight long time before him:

> The Essence, as being beyond all these relationships, is not a divinity... it is we who make Him a divinity by being that through which He knows Himself as Divine. Thus, He is not known [as 'Allah'] until we are known.[36]

Although there seems to be a certain resemblance between 'Arabi's notion of *Dhat* (Essence) and *sifat* (attributes) of God, and Hick's notion of the Real *an sich* and its manifestations, they are completely different when one examines 'Arabi's passage within the context his entire thought. To illustrate the difference more clearly I would like, first, to quote the same passage in length and then, briefly, to present 'Arabi's account of the transcendent unity of being. 'Arabi explicates the relation between the Reality (*al-haqq*) and the creature (*al-khalq*):

> If, on the other hand, the Reality [*al-haqq*] is considered as being the Manifest and the creature [*al-khalq*] as being hidden

142

within Him, the creature will assume all the Names of the Reality, His hearing, sight, all His relationships [modes], and His knowledge. If, however, the creature is considered the manifest and the Reality the Unmanifest within him, then the Reality is in the hearing of the creature, as also in his sight, hand, foot, and all his faculties, as declared in the [well-known] Holy tradition of the Prophet.

The Essence, as being beyond all these relationships, is not a divinity. Since all these relationships originate in our eternally manifested essences, it is we [in our eternal latency] who make Him a divinity by being that through which He knows Himself as Divine. Thus, He is not known [as 'God'] until we are known.

Muhammad said, 'Who knows his [true] self, knows God'.[37]

'Arabi like Plotinus believes that the universe as a whole, including the worlds of 'spirits', has come into being through emanation from the Absolute. In this respect, 'Arabi speaks of a series of twenty-eight emanations manifested through a particular name of God which relate the whole of existence to the Absolute. For example, The First Intelligence which is the second in the order of emanation, is manifested through the name Innovator (al-Badi'), whereas water, which is thirteenth in the order of emanation, is emanated through the Reviver (al-Muhiyy); the sun, nineteenth in the order, through the Light (an-Nur); the angels twenty-third in the order, through the Strong (al-Qawi); the man which is the last in the order, through the Comprehensive (al-Jami'). From another perspective 'Arabi states that the Spirit which comprises both the Universal Spirit that contains the archetypes of all things and the individual spirits, that is the spirits of every material body such as the sun and the moon, is the first emanation from the Absolute. The angels and the individual spirits of the various physical bodies of the Universe, as well as human souls, are related to the Universal Spirit.[38]

When 'Arabi explains the relation between the universe and the Real, he obviously speaks of it in the context of his doctrine of 'transcendental unity of Being' (wahdat al-wujud). Let me briefly present this doctrine. 'Arabi believes that there is only one Reality in existence which is seen differently from different perspectives. One can name this Reality as Haqq, Allah (the Real) when one regards it as the Essence of phenomena; and as khalq (the creature) when one regards it as the phenomena manifesting that Essence. Haqq and

143

Khalq, the Reality and Appearance[39] are only names for two subjective aspects of one Reality which is none other than God. If one sees Him through Him, in other words, if one approaches God through the Essence of things, one can find only Unity. If one sees Him through the phenomenal world, the unity vanishes and therefore one can see only diversity.[40]

'Arabi essentially differs from Hick in many fundamental points. Firstly, according to 'Arabi, a distinction can be made between the manifest and the Essence although both are at once part and parcel of the same Reality. Hick's distinction between the Real and the 'gods' of religions as the phenomenal manifestations of the noumenal Real is meaningless as far as 'Arabi is concerned. One might say that according to 'Arabi, it is not the 'gods' of religions but the whole of existence that is the manifestation of Ultimate Reality. Secondly, although Hick's description of the Real resembles 'Arabi's qualification of the Absolute, they essentially differ in their function. While the Absolute in 'Arabi's thought is the source of the whole of existence, including the universe, the Real in Hick's hypothesis is a postulated ground of religious experience known through the god figures. Both, however, are united in their claim that the Real or the Absolute is ineffable; it is beyond human imagination. Thirdly, when 'Arabi says 'the Essence, as being beyond all these relationships is not a divinity . . . it is we who make him a divinity', he does not mean that the Essence becomes God through the application of our cultural concepts as Hick has in mind. What he means is that the essence as pure and unqualified being, or the Essence before emanations (if there is in fact a 'before'), is free from any characterisations, including divinity. What makes the Essence divine is his knowing himself through the emanated world, which includes us. One might even say that the Essence that is 'the unqualified divine' cannot be attributed with anything, including divinity, unless he manifests his qualities through the creature. That is to say God cannot be named as creator unless he displays these attributes by creating the Universe. God knows himself as divine through knowing himself through the manifested world. As 'Arabi maintains:

> Certain sages among them Abu Hamid al-Ghazzali, have asserted that God can be known without any reference to the created Cosmos, but this is mistaken. It is true that a primordial eternal essence can be known, but it cannot be known as a divinity unless knowledge of that to which it can be related is

assumed, for it is the dependent who confirm the independence of the Independent.[41]

However, a further spiritual intuition will reveal that that which was necessary to affirm His Divinity is none other than the Reality Himself, and that the Cosmos is nothing more than His Self-revelation in the forms [determined] by the eternally unmanifest essences, which could not possibly exist without Him.[42]

Having offered such a brief exploration of 'Arabi's account of Reality, my obvious conclusion is that Hick is not able to defend the ontological status of the 'gods' of religions together with the ontological status of the Real. This, obviously makes the 'gods' of religions devoid of any religious qualities.

Now let me return to the issue of the relation between the Real *an sich* and its *personae* and *impersonae*. For a moment, we have to assume that the Real occupies only ontic space and the 'gods' of religions can share this space while manifesting it within diverse religions.[43]

Hick identifies two thought-models through which he believes he can show the relationship between the Real in itself and its *personae* and *impersonae*. One is the Kantian distinction of the noumnenon and phenomenon. Hick seeks to draw in Kant's epistemology to explain how the noumenal Real can be experienced as a range of both theistic and non-theistic deities. In other words, Hick says, although the Real cannot manifest the characteristics displayed by its manifestations, such as love and justice, in the case of the Christian God, and consciousness and bliss, in the case of Hindu Brahman, nevertheless the Real is the noumenal ground of these characteristics. The other model is analogical predication, expounded by Aquinas. According to this model, for instance, we can say that God is good not in the sense that a human being is good but in the sense that God possesses a limitlessly superior goodness which, at the same time, is analogous to human goodness.[44] From this Hick wants to derive the conclusion that each characteristic displayed by one of the manifestations of the Real can be ascribed to the Real not in the sense displayed by that manifestation but in the sense in which the Real limitlessly is the source of that particular characteristic. According to Hick, for instance, the characteristics of Allah such as creator, sustainer, or merciful, can be related to the Real not in the sense that the Real is actually creator, sustainer and merciful, but in the sense that the Real is the ultimate ground of these qualities, which makes it possible for Allah to be creator, sustainer and merciful.[45]

The application of these two models to Hick's hypothesis is problematic. Firstly, both models – Aquinas' analogical predication and Kant's noumenon and phenomenon distinction – are formed for a specific purpose and are meaningful within the context of the philosophy of Kant and the theology of Aquinas. Hick's extrapolation of these models may not be justifiable. For instance, for Kant the phenomenon which comprises the things which are subject to our sense experience relies on the noumenon, things in themselves which are beyond our experience. In Hick's postulate, the 'gods' of religions are not things but figures and therefore cannot be the manifestations of the noumenal. In other words, how can the Real be related to the Universe apart from saying that it is a concept that helps us to interpret it religiously? In the major traditions, namely, Judaism, Christianity, Islam, Hinduism and Buddhism, God or the Ultimate is always related to the universe in which we live either as the creator or the source. Hick is almost silent on the issue of how the Real can be related to the material Universe. This is one of the issues which causes problems for Hick. In response to this inquiry, he cannot endorse the view that the Real is the source or the creator of the material universe, because according to him, the Real is beyond any such qualifications. Nor is he in a position to affirm that one of the manifestations of the Real is the source or the creator of the universe. This is simply because each of the 'gods' of religions is believed to be the creator or the source of the Universe. In these circumstances, the only option left for Hick is to believe that the material universe has nothing to do with the Real and with the 'gods' of religions. In that case, Hick's religious interpretation of religion is at stake; his hypothesis becomes less convincing for religious people for whom it was originally formulated.[46]

Secondly, the relationship between the Real and its manifestations cannot be easily established by these two models. That is because, the differences between the 'gods' of religions are too great for them to be united in a single domain. Hence, these two models are not able to secure the Real as the ground of such diverse and sometimes conflicting phenomena as of the 'gods' of religions. To say that the Real is ineffable should not be interpreted to mean that the Real can accommodate all diverse, and sometimes conflicting, concepts and ideas of deities. Furthermore, one might even suggest that if the Real is flexible enough to encompass the concepts of all different 'gods' and absolutes, why should it not also embrace the gods of archaic religions and the 'Focus' or the ultimate of humanism and Marxism?[47]

Salvation as Transformation

As has been pointed out, the Real has two significant functions. One is that it is the ground of religious experience or the 'source' of 'gods' and ultimates of religions. The other is that it is the cause of salvation/ liberation as a human transformation displayed in the religious traditions' soteriological structure. What is the fundamental feature of such transformation and how can one achieve it? Hick states:

> This may be by self-committing faith in Christ as one's lord and saviour; or by the total submission to God which is *islam*; or by faithful obedience to the Torah; or by transcendence of the ego, with its self-centred desires and cravings, to attain *moksa* or Nirvana. . . . [T]hese are variations within different conceptual schemes on a single fundamental theme: the sudden or gradual change of the individual from an absorbing self-concern to a new centring in the supposed unity-of-reality-and-value that is thought of as God, Brahman, the Dharma, Sunyata or the Tao. Thus the generic concept of salvation/liberation, which takes a different specific form in each of the great traditions, is that of the transformation of human existence from self-centredness to Reality-centredness.[48]

This transformation can be attained in the Hindu tradition by following the three paths, which are not mutually exclusive but rather represent different emphases which might be appropriate for different personalities. It can be attained through *jnana-marga*, the path of knowledge or spiritual insight, and also through the *karma-marga*, a way of action. The latter, which is generally for ordinary people, requires a service for society without concern about material benefit. The third way is the *bhakti*, self-giving devotion to the Real, which involves a radical recentering in the divine order.[49]

In Buddhism, Hick points out, salvation is generally understood as liberation from the powerful illusion of 'me' or 'self'. According to this tradition, experience of the world through the me-self lens is the distorted experience which is bound to reflect the world in a false character. To be liberated from this illusory me is to exchange this 'ego-infected' mystery for the glorious freedom of Nirvana.[50]

In Christianity, according to Hick, the transformation occurs, 'in a self-giving in faith to God's limitless sovereignty and grace, which engenders a new spirit of trust and joy that in turn frees the believer from anxious self-concern and makes him or her a channel of divine love to the world'.[51] Hick points out that the aim of Christian teaching is to break our ordinary self-enclosed existence in order to become part of God's present and future kingdom. In the teachings of Jesus and also in the practical consciousness of Christians, salvation is acknowledged as a transformation from ego-centredness to a radically God-centred life.[52] In Judaism, however, Hick believes that the expectation of an eventual messianic redemption or the hope for the Kingdom of God on a transformed earth can be interpreted from a perspective of the transformation from self-centredness to reality-centredness.

The concept of salvation as understood in Christianity is absent in Islam. In order to make sense of his notion of human transformation Hick claims that the Quran distinguishes radically between 'the state of *islam* – a self-surrender leading to peace with God – and the contrary state of those who have not yielded themselves to their Maker'.[53] The state of *islam*, according to Hick, is the Muslim form of his notion of transformation. Hick acknowledges that Islam aims to embrace all aspects of life by introducing not only five appointed times of prayer, alms giving, fasting, pilgrimage and confession of faith, which constitute the five pillars of Islam, but also the sacred formulas such as *Bismillah* (in the name of Allah), *Inshallah* (if God wills), which aim to 'sacralise' ordinary daily life. Hick claims that, the Sufi spiritual life, engaged with *dhikr* (God-consciousness), and which aims at achieving *fana* (annihilation in God) and *baqa* (union with divine life), can also be interpreted as a transformation from self-centredness to God-centredness.[54]

This notion of the 'state of *islam*' sounds odd from a Muslim perspective. By introducing this term, Hick wants to counter his idea of human transformation. In Islamic literature, however, there is no such thing as a 'state of *islam*', but there is a state of *taqwa* which I believe is the term which may correspond to Hick's notion of human transformation from self-centredness to Reality-centredness. The Quranic term *taqwa*, which means 'fear of Allah', signifies right-eousness, piety, good conduct as well as to restrain one's tongue, hand, and heart from evil. The Quran repeatedly praises those who are in state of *taqwa* (called *muttaqun*) and says that they will be rewarded in the Hereafter. This term is used specifically to characterise those Muslims who live and conduct their daily affairs in the consciousness of the presence of God. Hick's term 'state of *islam*' on the other hand, is unable to distinguish ordinary Muslims from those who live a saintly life.[55]

There are a number of possible objections to Hick's presentations of soteriology in religion as human transformation. The obvious one is that this term is arguably reductionist. It aims to reduce the distinctive soteriological structures of different religions into one human transformation. As Netland asks, can the Pauline theme of justification or the Hindu understanding of *moksa*, or the Zen notion of *satori* really be reduced to the human transformation from self centredness to Reality-centredness?[56]

Furthermore, Hick's notion of human transformation not only misrepresents a tradition's account of salvation, but also depletes its religious contents. It may possibly, be regarded as a philosophical account of the notion of religious salvation from a secular point of view. If Hick presents to the Muslim the Quranic idea of *falah* or *najat* (salvation) as human transformation from self-centredness to Reality-centredness, he or she not only fails to realise that Hick is talking about salvation but also would be disappointed by such a presentation, which *can make the Muslim lose the incentive to lead a saintly life.* In other words, Hick's notion of human transformation fails to offer something that could sustain the 'religious expectation' of a devout Muslim or Christian or Jew. Rather it aims to ignore the traditional account of a hereafter or Heaven and Hell which often functions as one of the most powerful incentives to lead a saintly life.

Such a human transformation, that which brings about a saintly life, is not the aim but the result of a pious life which can only be attained by the firm belief and commitment to the sacred principles of a particular tradition. As has been indicated the only reason that has led Hick to believe in the existence of a transcendent Reality, as well as the religious value of religions, is that religions produce saints. It is in fact, the production of saints that is considered as one of the valid criteria by which the authentic response to the Real can be distinguished from the non-authentic ones. As I have just said, saintliness is the result of a religious life conducted in the light of sacred principles including believing in the hereafter. It seems to be inconsistent, on the one hand, to grant a significant weight to saintliness as one of the important merits of a religious life and, on the other hand, to ignore the sacred principles that are themselves the causes of the production of saints. Let us consider Islam as a case in point. On the one hand, Hick holds that the emergence of saints within Islam is evidence of its valid response to the Ultimate. On the other hand, by introducing his notion of the Real and human transformation, he undermines the Muslim's religious commitment to the sacred principles or doctrines of Islam. In other words, Hick holds a position in which he cannot endorse the Muslim's belief in Heaven and Hell, but would praise the result of such belief, namely, their saintly life.[57]

Some Critical Remarks on Hick's Hypothesis

Hick's hypothesis of religious pluralism has received several criticisms from various thinkers. All of these criticisms can be gathered under two important headings. One is that the postulation of the Real and its *personae* and *impersonae* is philosophically indefensible and religiously unjustifiable. It is philosophically indefensible because it sounds incoherent when the ineffable Real is held as the ground of various conflicting concepts of gods, and also because Hick has failed to offer a working model which can secure the connection between the Real and Its manifestation. It is also religiously unjustifiable because the ineffable Real cancels out all the cognitive claims of religions. In this respect Hick is charged with 'transcendental agnosticism' by D'Costa. He claims that Hick can be considered as a transcendental agnostic because he affirms the transcendent divine Reality over and against the naturalistic position, while failing to affirm that the eschaton may eventually be theistic rather than non-theistic. D'Costa maintains that such agnosticism is consolidated when Hick says that 'we should tolerate and live with religious disagreement' and 'we cannot judge religions in their apprehension of the divine Reality' or believe in certain religious doctrine not essential for salvation or liberation.[58]

Hick's hypothesis of religious pluralism cannot be regarded as an adequate theory of religions since it requires a radical change in the traditional doctrines of religions. For instance, as John B. Cobb points out, what he calls the Real is what Hindus have called *Nirguna Brahman* and Mahayana Buddhists have called *Dharmakaya*. Like Hick's Real, *Dharmakaya* and *Brahman* manifest themselves in many ways. Hick cannot endorse this because to do so would be to adopt the view of some religious traditions against others. He seeks to be neutral. Instead of accepting *Nirguna Brahman* is the name of the Real, he sees it as one of the manifestations of the Real. Hick flatly contradicts the Vedantic idea of *Nirguna Brahman*. If the Vedantists tell Hick that what he calls the Real is what they name *Nirguna Brahman*, how can Hick insist that *Nirguna Brahman* is the name for one of the manifestations of the Real?[59] Apart from this, Hick's hypothesis of religious pluralism is also not able to accommodate even some major doctrines such as the Christian belief in the Incarnation and the Zen notion of *satori*. In order to fit these doctrines into his hypothesis he reinterprets them quite radically. Such reinterpreted doctrines bear little resemblance to the doctrines held in their respective traditions. Such radical interpretations of the sacred doctrines of the traditions can hardly be characterised as religious.[60]

God as Reality

The core of Nasr's argument that characterises God as the source of reality is based on the assumption that such a view is plainly exhibited by traditional metaphysics and thus it is an obvious truth for traditional people. We have lost this sense of reality because of the impact of modernity and its philosophical and psychological outlook, which have reduced reality to the world which is subject to sense perception and scientific observation, divorcing it from the Ultimate. Nasr contends that the sense of reality held by the modern sensualist and empirical epistemology is fortuitously brought about by certain cultural developments in the West. But, ultimately, he believes the traditional point of view will revive the traditional position that considers God as reality.

Historically, says Nasr, the major traditions always viewed reality as an aspect of Ultimate Reality developing different metaphysical doctrines in the context of their own specific culture. Traditional Christian metaphysics, for instance, has exhibited the doctrine which sees God as reality through the writings of such masters as Erigena, St. Bonaventure, St. Thomas and Eckhart. In Sufi Islamic tradition, reality has always been regarded as one of the aspects of the Divine Reality.[61]

There seem to be two main reasons that encourage Nasr to speak of God as reality. Firstly, the categories of modern epistemology by which the world of reality is constructed are not necessarily determinant and therefore they can be ruled out.[62] Secondly, the traditions themselves offer not only literature but also a context in which it is quite proper to speak of God as reality. I shall be later exploring the traditional background of Nasr's account of Reality.

Nasr's account of Reality is holistic: God as ultimate as well as immediate Reality is related to everything that exists. He is not only related to the world of matter and that of 'spirits' but also the world of ideas. God as Ultimate Reality, says Nasr is the source of all that is. God is the Supreme Person as well as Godhead or Infinite Essence of which Being is the first determination. God can be addressed as He or She or It and yet be beyond all pronominal categories. Ultimate Reality is both the Essence which is the origin of all forms and the Substance when he is compared to all that which is subject to change and transformation.[63] Nasr maintains:

> God as Reality is at once absolute, infinite and, good or perfect. In Himself He is the Absolute which partakes of no relativity in Itself or in Its Essence. The Divine Essence cannot but be absolute and one. All other considerations must belong to the order of relativity, to a level below that of the Essence. To assert that God is one is to assert His absoluteness and to envisage Him in Himself, as such. The Divine Order partakes of relativity in the sense that there is a Divine Relativity or Multiplicity which is included in the Divine Order, but this relativity does not reach the abode of the Divine Essence. God in His Essence cannot but be one, cannot but be the Absolute. To speak of God as reality is to speak of God as the Absolute.[64]

Nasr argues that God as Reality is also infinite not in the mathematical sense but in the metaphysical sense. He is the source of all cosmic possibilities. Metaphysically speaking it can be said that He is the All-Possibility.[65] He is also the Sacred that qualifies anything and everything which is sacred. According to Nasr, God can also be described as the Principle of Reality in contrast to all that appears as real not in the ultimate sense. The Principle can be described as Absolute compared to which all is relative. It is, says Nasr, One and Unique, while its manifestation is multiplicity. The Principle can be seen at once Beyond Being and Being in relation to the order of multiplicity which contains existents.[66] Nasr states:

> [The Principle] alone *is* while all else becomes, for It alone is eternal in the ultimate sense while all that is externalized partakes of change. It is the Origin but also the End, the alpha and the omega. It is Emptiness if the world is envisaged as fullness and Fullness if the relative is perceived in the light of its ontological poverty and essential nothingness.[67]

Moreover, Nasr argues that God as Reality can also be characterised as Being as well as Supra-Being. In this sense Ultimate Reality as Being is the ground of all that exists, it is like an entity which envelops the God as person and the world or multiplicity as manifestations of that the Divine Essence. Hence, it cannot, suggests Nasr, be defined because there is nothing outside it according to which one can define Being. The Divine Essence which contains all cosmic possibilities issues Being which is the first determination of the Absolute Reality.[68] God is not only the Transcendent but also the Immanent. He is the Supreme Self which manifests itself through the self. The Ultimate Self can be attained through the expansion of the awareness of the centre of consciousness. In this context, human self is the faint echo of the cosmic plane of the Self.[69]

There are three main sources from which Nasr has derived his notion of Reality: the Quran, Sufism and Islamic philosophy. The Quran describes God as one that alone has absolute being, totally independent and totally sufficient. Whatever exists and ever could exist does so by his will. He has no 'partner' in creating the universe or in maintaining it in existence. According to the Quran, God is not only 'the First Cause' but the only cause, and He is himself uncaused. It says: 'He is God, the One (*al-Ahad*), the eternal cause of all beings (*al-Samad*). He begetteth not nor was He begotten. And there is none like unto Him' (112:1–4).[70] The Quran often emphasises that there can be no power, force or agency in the heavens or on earth which is independent of God. Everything that exists and everything that happens is subject to his control.[71] The Quran describes God as *al-'Ala* (the Most High), totally transcendent in relation to his own creations. He is also *al-'Aziz*, (the Almighty) and *al-Jabbar* (the Irresistible). There is nothing that could possibly resist His power, which governs and regulates all existence.

One might even claim that the idea of God as Reality itself is derived from the Quran because it calls God *al-Haqq* (the Reality or the Real). He is *al-'Alim*, (the Omniscient) who knows everything in the heavens and the earth, and *al-Khabir* (the All-Aware) from whom nothing is hidden. He is *al-Shahid* (the Witness). He is also described as *al-Basir* (the Seer) and *al-Sami'* (the Hearer).

The verse (62:3) which is often quoted by Nasr describes God as *al-Awwal* (the First) before him there is nothing, and also *al-Akhir* (the Last), after whom there is nothing. In this respect, God is not the beginning and the end but also *al-Zahir* (the Outward), the appearance or manifest present in the world around us, *al-Batin* (the Inward), the unmanifest which is behind anything that appears. He is also described as *al-Khaliq* (the Creator) and *al-Musawwir* (the Shaper). This brief Quranic account of God is able to reveal that the sacred principles of the Quran, in fact, provide the main ingredients of Nasr's philosophy or 'metaphysics'.

From the Sufi tradition it is the writings of 'Arabi that have played a significant part in Nasr's attempt to relate God to the world of existence. 'Arabi's doctrine of the Transcendental Unity of Being (*wahdat al-wujud*) has remained an implicit central theme when Nasr speaks of God as reality.[72] Moreover, Nasr's account of the hierarchical levels of Being, which encompass both God as Godhead or as the Supreme Person and the subtle and physical world, is obviously derived from 'Arabi's metaphysics. The other significant influence of 'Arabi upon Nasr can be observed by Nasr's portrayal of the universe as theophany.[73] As has been pointed out, 'Arabi sees all existence as theophany (*tajalli*) or emanation from the Absolute. 'Arabi's impact on Nasr's view of reality is quite apparent. But what is new in Nasr is the presentation of his ideas in a context which integrates such ideas into the modern world. For instance, when Nasr speaks of Reality, he compares it with contemporary ways of thinking and defends and reshapes his view in the light of the views of such thinkers as Descartes, Hegel and Kant. One might even describe the *sophia perennis* as a philosophy which sees the modern world through the eyes of 'Arabi.[74]

In addition to the Quran and Sufism, Islamic Philosophy is another source from which Nasr has developed his account of Reality. His account of God as the necessary being who contains all cosmic possibilities reflects Ibn Sina's views on this issue. But it was Shihab al-Din al-Suhrawardi[75] and his philosophy of *Ishraq* (illumination) that has served as one of the important elements in Nasr's philosophy. For instance, Suhrawardi's view that the Divine Essence as the Light of lights (*nur al-anwar*) is the source of all existence has influenced Nasr. For instance, Suhrawardi sees the Universe and the planes of existence as the degrees of light and darkness. Nasr sounds like Suhrawardi when he says:

> Of the many worlds of Reality only the highest which is the world of the Divine Essence (*'alam al-dhat*) is absolutely Real. The other worlds are its multiple reflection in the mirror of non being. This is the only image that can convey to a certain extent this affable aspect of the Truth, for the transition from Unity to multiplicity is an ultimate mystery which no human language or thought can hope to express. From a negative point of view, each lower world can be said to be the shadow of the one above

it, each shadow being paler and farther away from the Absolute Reality as one descends from the world of the Essence through the intermediate realms to the world of earthly existence which is the lowest in this hierarchy. The world may thus be considered as the shadow of God.

If negatively this world is a shadow, positively it is a reflection and symbol of the worlds above it. In essence it has no reality outside of God – for there can – not be two completely independent orders of Reality.[76]

Having briefly presented Nasr's account of God as reality together with the background of the view as such, I would like to demonstrate the dissimilarities between Hick and Nasr in their account of Ultimate Reality.

Firstly, the fundamental difference between Hick and Nasr lies in their implicit intention when they approach the issue of Reality. For Hick, we make sense of our immediate and ultimate environment through our own effort; sense perception, philosophical reasoning and religious experience are ready and sufficient tools by which we perceive and make use of what we have encountered, including the universe, religions, and gods. While Hick is talking about reality or the Real, he aims to present a 'discovered truth' as a result of his own philosophical reasoning within a philosophical system. For Nasr, however, the question is not whether we are able to discover truth. Rather it is how we can make sense, i.e. philosophically explain, the revealed truth. For instance, the nature of God and his attributes and his relation with humanity and nature are described in the Quran. For Nasr, these are plain truths. As a Muslim his aim is not to question or cast doubt on the truth of these propositions, but to find a viable metaphysical system through which he could explain or interpret their meaning. In a sense Nasr does not aim to create 'truth' through his own philosophical reasoning, but to display what is already affirmed by revelation. This must be the reason why he picks up any metaphysical model he likes, whether that of 'Arabi or Suhrawardi or Eckhart and even those of the Neoplatonists.

Secondly, according to Hick, God is real in the sense that we can make use of it. The Real in Hick's philosophy of religion is postulated for practical purposes; God and religion are useful and real as long as we can derive benefit from them. Kant as well as James are the main sources of such ideas. For Nasr, on the other hand, God is real in the sense he is an actual entity occupying ontic space. He exists in the sense a person exists. He is the invisible and conscious agent behind everything that happens and that could happen.

Thirdly, for Hick the Real is beyond human categorisation and entirely ineffable. But it manifests itself through the 'gods' of religions. In this sense, the universe exists on its own. In Hick's view, God enters into the universe not as cause or creator but as a concept that is employed when a religious person interprets the physical world religiously. According to Nasr, however, the Divine Essence is beyond any human categories and is totally ineffable. But, Ultimate Reality manifests itself through the subtle and physical world, through religions[77], and humanity. The Divine Essence is ineffable, but God who is at once the Essence and the Supreme Person can be characterised through his attributes.

One of the striking differences between Hick and Nasr is that Hick considers the 'gods' of religion as different manifestations of the same Real, whereas Nasr believes that the 'gods' of religion are not different 'entities' but the different names of the same Reality which reveals itself in different ways within the context of a different religious universe. All traditional religions in this sense are speaking of the same reality but with different languages. Nasr states:

> The Ultimate Reality which is both Supra-Being and Being is at once transcendent and immanent. It is beyond everything and at the very heart and centre of man's soul. *Scientia sacra* can be expounded in the language of one as well as the other perspective. It can speak of God or the Godhead, Allah, the Tao, or even *nirvana* as being beyond the world, or forms or *samsara*, while asserting ultimately that *nirvana* is *samsara*, and *samsara*, *nirvana*. But it can also speak of the Supreme Self, of *Atman*, compared to which all objectivisation is *maya*. The Ultimate Reality can be seen as both the Supreme Object and the Innermost Subject, for God is both transcendent and immanent, but He can be experienced as immanent only after He has been experienced as transcendent.[78]

Fourthly, for Hick the Real is not personal or impersonal, good or bad, conscious or unconscious, and therefore revelation which speaks such a language does not issue from the Real *an sich* but from one of its manifestations.[79] 'God revealed himself through the Bible and the Quran' can only make sense if it is taken as mythological truth not literal truth. For Nasr, God can be characterised in the way he features himself in the sacred scriptures through revelations.

Therefore he is described as an omnipotent, omniscient and conscious person who is the author of all that exists. In this respect, Nasr believes that revelation in the sense of God revealing propositional truth in the sacred scriptures is viable and has occurred in the history of religions.

The Ultimate in the Manifested Order

The main problem for Nasr is not whether God exists nor whether one is able to discover the nature of God. These issues have been adequately elucidated by revelation. The crucial question for Nasr is to establish a sound metaphysics which must be able to explain sufficiently the relationship between the Absolute and the manifested world, including the physical and the subtle. He believes that he can achieve this task by employing any available traditional doctrines, whether Islamic, Christian or Hindu.

Nasr maintains that in traditional civilisation the cosmos is viewed as something which possesses spiritual meaning for peoples' life. It is regarded as the cosmic book containing a primordial revelation of utmost significance.[80] Some traditional cosmologies, such as that of the Native Americans, speak of a certain correspondence between certain Divine Qualities and the natural forms of the animals and plants. In those traditions based on the sacred scriptures the cosmos is regarded as a vast cosmic book whose pages display the words of the Author. Such a perspective can be found in Judaism and Islam[81] where the eternal Torah and the Quran are both seen as revealed books and where virgin nature is seen as grand book which reflects God's primordial revelation.[82] As Nasr puts it:

> To behold the cosmos with the eye of the intellect is to see it not as a pattern of externalized and brute facts, but as a theatre wherein are reflected aspects of the Divine Qualities, as a myriad of mirrors reflecting the face of the Beloved, as the theophany of that Reality which resides at the Centre of the being of man himself. To see the cosmos as theophany is to see the reflection of one-Self in the cosmos and its forms.[83]

Nasr argues that the world or multiplicity flows from the infinitude and goodness of the Real; to speak of the goodness is to speak of creation, multiplicity and effusion, whereas to speak of infinity is to speak of all possibilities. He maintains that the Divine qualities such as absolute, infinite and perfection or goodness are the hypostases of the Real which must also be reflected in the manifested order, including, the cosmos. Furthermore, he claims that the Ultimate gives rise to the world in such a way that the Divine Qualities can be realised. For instance, Nasr thinks that the world is principally good since it descends from the Divine Goodness. In this respect, however, the quality of absoluteness manifests itself in every aspect of existence.

Nasr argues that Divine Infinitude is reflected in space as indefinite extension, in time as endless duration, in form as unending diversity, in number as endless multiplicity and in matter as substance which is potentially capable of being formed in unbounded dimensions. As for Goodness, it is reflected in the cosmos through quality itself which is indispensable to existence; by virtue of the Divine Goodness space is qualified as that which preserves, time as that which changes and transforms, number as that which signifies indefinite quantity, matter as that which is characterised by limitless substantiality which is the condition of existence.

Nasr maintains that absoluteness as one of the Divine Hypostates is reflected in space as centre, in time as the present moment, in matter as ether, in form as the sphere and in number as unity which is the source and principle of all numbers. As for perfection, says Nasr, it is reflected in space as the content or objects in space reflecting Divine Qualities and also pure existence, in forms as beauty, in number as that qualitative aspect of number always related to geometric forms. Nasr claims the conditions of existence, matter, form, space and time reflect an aspect of the Divinity. For instance, matter and energy reflect the Divine Substance, form the Logos, number the Divine Unity which is inexhaustible, space the infinite extension of Divine Manifestation and time the rhythm of the universal cycle of existence.[84]

Nasr believes that the notion of necessity and possibility which was one of the most important subjects in Islamic Peripatetic philosophy is another model by which one can adequately establish the relation between God and the manifested order.[85]

Nasr points out that the possibility has two different meanings: the first is 'the quality or character of something that can exist or not exist' and the second is 'the quality or character of something which has the power and capability to perform or carry out an act'. In the first sense, 'possible', which is the opposite of 'necessary', means contingent. For instance, an object exists possibly, (not necessarily) in the sense that it can exist or not exist; there is no logical or metaphysical contradiction to affirm its existence or non-existence. In this sense, says Nasr, archetypes (*al-a'yan al-thabitah*) are also possible beings. God alone is necessary. Things which do not exist come into existence, and thus become necessary through the Necessary Being.[86]

In the second sense of the meaning, 'possibility' means power which is not opposed to necessity but complements it. As Nasr puts it:

> God is Absolute Necessity and Infinite Possibility, the omnipotence of God reflected in the Divine Attribute *al-Qadir* in the Quran, meaning exactly possibility in this second sense. Whatever happens in this world is according to the Will of God but also in conformity with a Divine Possibility. God could not will what is not possibility in this sense for He would then negate His own Nature. Whatever claims a blind type of religious voluntarism might make, God's omnipotence cannot contradict His Nature and when the Gospel claims, 'With God all things are possible,' it is referring precisely to this Infinite Possibility of God.[87]

As far as necessity is concerned, notes Nasr, God as the Beyond Being or Ultimate Reality is necessity, while Being can be regarded as necessity vis-à-vis the world. In other words, from the perspective of multiplicity or that of world, being can be seen as the Necessary Being. Things that exist are possibilities in the sense they are contingent; they may or may not exist. They are also necessary since they exist; they participate in the necessity of the Essence.[88] Nasr clarifies this point further:

> Objects in this world 'emerge' from what Islamic esoterism calls the 'treasury of the Unseen' (*khazanay-i ghayb*); nothing whatsoever can appear on the plane of physical reality without having its transcendent cause and the root of its being *in divinis*. There is, metaphysically speaking, no possibility of any temporal process adding something to the Divinity or to Reality as such. Whatever grows and develops is the actualization of a possibility which had preexisted in the Divine Order, this development or growth being always of an essence while total reality resides in the immutable world of the archetypes.[89]

Such a model is partly able to explain the relationship between the Absolute and the manifested order. But it cannot explain how the world as 'relative' or contingent stems from the Absolute or how the absolute Goodness of God can accommodate evil. Nasr believes that the Hindu doctrine of *maya* as a metaphysical model can establish such a relationship. Nasr argues that *maya* is illusion, only Atman, the Supreme Self being real from a nondualistic or Advaitist point of view. He claims that *maya* as creativity is relativity, which is the source of separateness, exteriorisation, and objectivisation. She is the divine creativity that brings manifestation into being. Infinitude could include the possibility of separation, division, externalisation which characterise everything other than the Absolute.[90] *Maya*, says Nasr, is 'the supreme veil and also supreme theophany which at once veils and reveals'.[91]

Moreover, Nasr argues that theology which envisages God and the world as separate entities cannot provide an answer for those kinds of questions that seek a means by which such duality can be surmounted. Nasr maintains that it is the doctrine of *maya* which introduces relativity into the principal plane without, however, reaching the level of the Absolute that can solve this perennial problem of duality. In other words, according to Nasr *maya* is the root of the relative world in the divine order.[92] He maintains:

> *Maya* acts through both radiation and reverberation or reflection, first preparing the ground or plane of manifestation and then manifesting both the radiation and reverberation which takes place on this plane... *Maya* is the source of all duality even on the principle level causing the distinction between the Essence and the Qualities. It is also the source of the dualism between the subject and the object even on the highest level beyond which there is but the One, in which knower and known, or subject and object are one. But *maya* does not remain bound to the principal level alone. She is self-projected through various levels of cosmic existence which a *hadith* calls the seventy thousand veils of light and darkness and which can be summarized as the three fundamental levels of angelic, animic, and physical existence.[93]

Nasr also assumes that the doctrine of *maya* can help us to understand the problem of evil, an issue which the various theistic theologies and philosophies have failed to solve. For Nasr evil is related not only to the omnipotence of God but also to the Divine Nature. Ultimate Reality or the Divine Nature is both infinite and good, and therefore radiates the multiple worlds and separation and elongation from the Source from which evil results. The will of God which separates the possibilities from the Source implies evil.[94] Nasr maintains that 'there are in reality two levels of operation of the Divine Will or even two Divine Wills, one related to the Absolute and Infinite Reality which cannot but manifest and create – hence, separation, elongation, and privation which appears as evil; and the second related to the Will of Being which opposes the presence of evil in accordance with the divine laws and norms which constitute the ethical structures of various traditional worlds'.[95] Nasr suggests there are two different aspects of one Divine Nature. One aspect is that which is Absolute and Infinite and therefore manifests an existence of which evil is a necessary ingredient. The other aspect of the Divine Nature manifests itself as divine will which forbids evil. But God, although he is good, cannot eradicate evil in the sense that he cannot contradict his own nature and cannot but manifest and create. The existence of evil, according to Nasr, can proceed until the plane of separation or moment of creation which is none other than the act of *maya*. Before separation, creation or beyond the level in which manifestation and multiplicity comes into being, there is no evil but only good.[96]

The Absolute in Diverse Religious Forms

One of the main problems of the discipline of the study of religion lies in the difficulties in finding an appropriate method by which one would be able not only to understand but also to appreciate religion. The products of secular culture which function as the source of the various methods in religious studies, such as scientism, historicism, ecumenism and phenomenological studies, are partly responsible for generating such problems, though they may be more tolerant towards religions than the polemical religious discourse of the past. Before modernity, the world was divided into different religious blocks. Exclusivism was the predominant discourse through which the 'other' was defined. Within the atmosphere of such a culture, the study of other religions was deemed not suitable to the cultural context, and therefore, it was only carried out for the purpose of proving the authenticity of one's own religion. Knowledge and information about other religions were often based not upon a true account of other religions but on a distortion of them.

Today's secular culture and its prevailing norm, liberalism, sound more tolerant in their study of 'other' if compared with 'religious studies' before modern times. They might be able to perceive religions from a neutral vantage-point. But ultimately, they are not able to create a spiritual atmosphere in which various traditions can be accommodated since they are intrinsically alien to religious values. The religious studies developed within such a culture can suggest to students of religion that they sympathise or even emphatise with other religions, but they cannot create a spiritual 'spontaneity' or 'rapport' between the subject (a student who may or may not belong to a religion) and the object (a religion other than that to which this student belongs). Nasr is confident that the study of religion within the context of the *sophia perennis* could create an esoteric ecumenism which can see in 'the multiplicity of sacred forms, not contradictions which relativise, but a confirmation of the universality of the Truth and the infinite creative power of the Real that unfolds Its inexhaustible possibilities in worlds of meaning which, although different, all reflect the unique Truth'.[97]

One of the impediments to a proper understanding of religion lies in the confusion between the expressions or forms and the meaning beyond those expressions and the essence beyond those forms. If, says Nasr, one contemplates the nature of the three grand theophanies of the Absolute as the cosmos, humanity and revelation, or religion, one can at least realise the fact that these three manifested universes must possess something that resembles or represents the root from which they are manifested. Since the concept of manifestation itself implies externalisation or 'formation', then it is reasonable to assume that there should be a method by which one would be able to penetrate the meaning of the external forms of these three manifested orders. This method, says Nasr, is esoterism. Such esoteric awareness is essential in order to go from the form to the essence, from the exterior to the interior, from the symbol to the reality symbolised, as far as the study of religion is concerned. Nasr maintains that to carry out the study of other religions in depth requires a penetration into one's own being through which one could attain the essence of religion.[98] In other words, since humans are also the manifestations of the Ultimate, they bear some elements which attach them to the Ultimate as well as to the cosmos. It is through this sacred substance inherent in humanity that human beings can properly engage with the other two grand theophanies of the Absolute, i.e. religion and the cosmos.[99]

Religion as the container of manifested 'truths' has two dimensions: the first, is the inner aspect of religion, esoterism which is the substance that provides the religious person with a profound spiritual awareness. The second, is the doctrines and dogmas of religion, that is, its exoteric aspect which is the forms that contain the rules and regulations sufficient for the salvation of ordinary religious people. Through this inner dimension of religion, one could realise fully the metaphysical truth of that particular religion, whereas one deals with the theological and philosophical aspects of a religion in its exoteric dimension.

Esoterism, claims Nasr, is hidden and thus accessible to only the few because in human history only a few people are gifted with the qualities that would enable them to reach such a stage. He states:

> The esoteric is the radius which provides the means of going from the circumference to the Centre, but it is not available to all because not everyone is willing or qualified to undertake the journey to the Centre in this life. To follow the exoteric dimension of religion, however, is to remain on the circumference and hence in a world which has a centre, and to remain qualified to carry out the journey to the Centre in the afterlife, the beatific vision being only a posthumous possibility from the exoteric point of view.[100]

From the traditional point of view, the exoteric expressions of a religion which often appear in the theological and doctrinal discourse of that particular religion are far from being irrelevant, but are necessary in order to convey the simple message of a religion to ordinary people. But what is wrong and perhaps dangerous is to confine the religious message within exoterism claiming that the theological discourse of one religion possesses the unique truth. Schuon elucidates the point:

> The exoteric claim to the exclusive possession of a unique truth, or of Truth without epithet, is therefore an error purely and simply; in reality, every expressed truth necessarily assumes a form, that of its expression, and it is metaphysically impossible that any form should possess a unique value to the exclusion of other forms; for a form, by definition, cannot be unique and exclusive, that is to say it cannot be the only possible expression of what is expresses. Form implies specification or distinction, and the specific is only conceivable as a modality of 'species', that is to say of a category which includes a combination of analogous modalities.[101]

The traditional view of esoterism can potentially be a base for a traditional account of religious pluralism if it is explored in the light of new developments. It sets a limit to the exclusive truth claims of religions made in their propositional and theological demonstrations. That must be the reason why Nasr bases his pluralistic ideas on Sufism, the discipline of Islamic esoterism. Great Sufi masters in the Islamic tradition such as 'Arabi, Rumi and Rabbani were able to go beyond the Islamic theology of religions and express some forms of pluralistic approaches, despite expected pressures from Islamic orthodoxy.[102]

Nasr claims that the diversity as well as the exclusive language of religions are intended and willed by God. God initiated various different religions in order to reveal the different aspects of the Divine Names and Qualities; each religion or tradition placed emphasis on one aspect of the Divinity. The multiplicity of religions is the direct result of the infinite richness of the Divine Being. For instance, 'Arabi considers the founder of each religion as an aspect of the universal logos.[103] In *Fusus al-Hikam* 'Arabi regards each prophet mentioned in the Quran as a vessel of divine Wisdom which takes on human nature and its limitations while remaining indivisible in itself. This principle, unity in diversity, is displayed on every level of existence whether macrocosm or microcosm, humanity, the cosmos and revelation.

To understand religions on this metaphysical level and go beyond the 'formal' expressions of religion is hard and not for everyone. In normal circumstances it is sufficient and sometimes necessary for ordinary religious people to adhere to the 'truth' of their own religions without paying as much notice to the others. Only those who are gifted or illuminated by the Intellect can attain a unifying vision and go beyond the plain meaning of the theological formulas and of religious rites. But the recent development in religious studies and concern with globalization have made us more aware of the presence of other religions and thus the need for a pluralistic approach. Nasr illustrates this point with a beautiful analogy:

> In fact, if there is one really new and significant dimension to the religious and spiritual life of man today, it is this presence of other worlds of sacred form and meaning not as archaeological or historical facts and phenomena but as religious reality. It is this necessity of living within one solar system and abiding by its laws yet knowing that there are other solar systems and even, by participation, coming to know something of their rhythms and

harmonies, thereby gaining a vision of the haunting beauty of each one as a planetary system which is *the* planetary system for those living within it. It is to be illuminated by the Sun of one's own planetary system and still to come to know through the remarkable power of intelligence, to know by anticipation and without 'being there,' that each solar system has its own sun, which again is both a sun and *the* Sun, for how can the sun which rises every morning and illuminates our world be other than *the* Sun itself?[104]

Nasr believes that these two concepts, namely 'relatively absolute' and the concept of 'archetype' can offer a useful insight to the solution of the problem of the multiplicity of religions. Although the term 'relatively absolute' (which originally goes back to Schuon) is potentially useful for a theory of religious pluralism, it has not developed in that fashion. Nasr assumes that to introduce this term would be sufficient without exploring its possibilities. In this respect, Nasr states that only the Absolute is absolute, but each manifestation of the Absolute in the form of revelation such as Christianity, Judaism and Islam creates a world in which certain determinations of the Absolute, like the Quran in the case of Islam and Jesus in the case of Christianity, appear absolute without being the Absolute in itself. They are 'relatively absolute' realities. For instance, maintains Nasr, if a Christian sees God as the Trinity, or Christ as the Logos, and holds this view in an absolute sense that is perfectly understandable from a religious point of view, while metaphysically speaking these are 'relatively absolute' since only Godhead in Its Infinitude and Oneness is above all relativity.[105]

Such a statement is not sufficient to overcome the problem of religious pluralism. This concept could be useful in acknowledging that there are similar aspects of different traditions. Through the term 'relatively absolute' we may come to understand and appreciate that there is a similarity between the Quran and Christ as both being the word of God, or between the Virgin Mary and the soul of the Prophet. It even may help us to see the rapport between the feminine Kwan-Yin and Krishna or Shiva.[106] But this term does not seem to be very helpful when it comes to the conflicting issues between the religions. It does not and cannot, for instance, settle the long disputed question between Christians and Muslims on the issue of the Trinity, the divine attributes and divine sonship of Christ. It cannot tell us for instance whether or not Christ is the son of God. In other words, such a key concept seems to be useless in the realm where it is needed most.

The implication of this term in the more practical sphere of a religion also seems ambiguous. Is there any difference at all between the claim that the Quran is 'relatively absolute' and the claim that the Quran is absolute? Furthermore, can such a statement permit Muslims to consider some of the rules of the Quran, such as capital punishment or the ban on alcohol, as relative, saying that particular rules are relevant in the historical context of that particular community?

As far as the metaphysical implication of this term is concerned, the dispute between Christians and Muslims on the issue of Trinity cannot be settled by the assertion of such a concept. If God is truly one and does not accept any other forms or associates as the Muslim claims, the Trinity is not true. To say that the term 'relatively absolute' helps us to acknowledge the Trinity and the unity at the same time is inaccurate. If one is correct, the other is wrong; it is difficult to find a meeting point between them.

Nasr believes that each religion possesses a celestial archetype which represents some aspect of the Divine Nature. Each religion manifests on earth the reflection of its celestial archetype. The total reality of a religion, let us say, Islam or Christianity, exists metahistorically and unfolds throughout its destined historical life what is contained in that archetype. Nasr maintains that it is even possible for a religion's archetypal reflection to be seen in another religion. Although Christianity and Islam have totally distinct archetypes, and yet Shi'ism in Islam reflects that type of archetypal religious reality that is similar to Christianity whereas Lutheranism represents an Islamic archetypal reality within Christianity without historically borrowing from each other.[107]

Although this concept can adequately illustrate the difference between religions and may shed light on the issue of the historical development of a religion and its possible end, it cannot settle the disputes between religions. In addition to this, one of the important questions related to this concept is that Nasr does not offer any rational argument or a detailed and convincing metaphysical exploration to persuade the reader that this is the case. One wonders how Nasr would respond if someone were to ask him: how do you know that religions have celestial archetypes?

In addition to these, argues Nasr, there are several other overlapping elements among religions that indicate a unity. In the major traditions, for example there are three basic ways that regulate the relation between God and humanity. These are fear, love and knowledge, which correspond to three mystical stations, namely, contraction, expansion and union. In each tradition, these elements manifest themselves according to the genius of the tradition in question. Although each tradition possesses these three elements, some emphasise one aspect more than others. For instance, Judaism places greater emphasis upon fear; Christianity upon love; and Islam upon knowledge.[108]

As for the common element among religions, Nasr also observes that in every religion there is a sense of the loss of perfection related to the Transcendent. And also in every religion there is an emphasis on the means of regaining that perfection. Hence, prayer is a very important means by which the faithful remoulds him or herself. In every religion, maintains Nasr, there is a sense of reality which is not confined within this world but goes Beyond.[109]

Nasr argues that another piece of evidence which supports the view that religions are manifestations of Ultimate Reality is that in every religion there is the element of truth and presence. Each traditional religion possesses a truth which delivers and saves and a presence which attracts and transforms. But these signs of divine elements are not found in the same manner in every religion. Some put more emphasis on the element of truth, others on presence. Within the Abrahamic family, for instance, Christianity stresses presence, whereas Islam stresses truth, although truth, of course, is as indispensable to Christianity as is presence to Islam. According to Nasr, such elements can also be observed in the different sects of a tradition. Within the Islamic tradition, Sunnism places considerable emphasis upon truth and Shi'ism upon presence. Nasr maintains that the same two elements can also be found in other great traditions including Hinduism and Buddhism.[110]

In order to clarify the issue let me point out some of the basic premises of Nasr's account of religion and the transcendental Reality. Firstly, Nasr like Hick believes that there is the Real, and that God and religions are related to that Reality. For Nasr, religions as a whole are one of the three grand theophanies of the Absolute, whereas for Hick religions were brought about by human response to the Transcendent. Both Nasr and Hick are pluralists but in a different manner. Hick believes that although religions are different they are united in their emphasis on a common purpose which can be summarised as a human transformation from self centredness to

167

Reality-centredness. To a certain extent, religions, Hick would claim, can be seen as one unitary system of ideas, since they all came about as a response to the same Ultimate Reality.

Nasr, on the other hand, believes that the unity of religions cannot be found at the level of external forms of religions; unity of religions is a transcendental unity which is above and beyond external manifestations.[111] Nasr writes:

> The unity of religions is to be found first and foremost in this Absolute which is at once Truth and Reality and the origin of revelations and of all truth. When the Sufis claim that the doctrine of Unity is unique (*al-tawhidu wahid*), they are asserting this fundamental but often forgotten principle. Only at the level of Absolute are the teachings of the religions the same. Below that level there are correspondences of the most profound order but not identity. The different religions are like so many languages speaking of that unique Truth as it manifests itself in different worlds according to its inner archetypal possibilities, but the syntax of these languages is not the same. Yet, because each religion comes from the Truth, everything in the religion in question which is revealed by the Logos is sacred and must be respected and cherished while being elucidated rather than being discarded and reduced to insignificance in the name of some kind of abstract universality.[112]

An Assessment of Nasr's Account of Reality

One of the fundamental claims that Nasr makes is that his account of Reality is *metaphysical*, whereas others' such as Hick's, he would describe as *philosophical*. His account is metaphysical, he would argue, in the sense that it is based not on reason and thus philosophical reasoning, but on *intellect* and therefore *'mystical'* *vision*. Metaphysics as science of the real can speak of Reality as it is, using a symbolic language. Therefore, it aims to reflect what is 'over there' in a manner which satisfies those advanced enough to understand the signs and symbols of such language. Philosophy, however, is creative and aims to create a theoretical system by using a discursive language. Nasr, furthermore, would argue that metaphysics speaks to the heart, while philosophy speaks to the mind. Philosophy is personal in the sense that is bound to the concept of a specific culture, whereas metaphysics transcends the personal realm of the individuals while it mirrors the Absolute through the esoteric teachings of tradition. In this context, Nasr naturally would regard his account of Reality as superior to any account that is philosophical, including Hick's.

Nasr claims that it is impossible to encompass Reality within the confines of a closed system of thought. Reality can be comprehended not through reasoning but only through intuition. In this respect, 'ratiocination', which belongs to the realm of relativity, cannot be fruitful in perceiving the Absolute. But intelligence can know the Absolute. Nasr maintains that, as a result of *maya*, human thought cannot become absolutely conformable to the Real. The existence of the innumerable schools of modern philosophy, which are far from agreeing with one another on even a single issue, can be regarded as evidence of the fact that the Real cannot be encompassed by mental activity alone.[113] In this context, one might even claim that Nasr would dismiss Hick's view with regard to the Real, having seen it as a philosophical attempt devoid of a 'mystical vision' which embodies the distortion of *maya*.

One of the problems of this idea is that it presents itself as if it is immune to criticism. To say 'metaphysical' is almost equal to saying that this is an objective truth. This is problematic. How can I know, for instance, that the Real manifests itself through the cosmos, humanity and religion? To such a question Nasr has no argument. He just asserts and expects to be confirmed as if he were stating the obvious; explication or philosophical discussion is irrelevant.

The second important criticism one can raise against Nasr is that his demand for esoterism legitimises élitism as far as the concept of Reality is concerned. To say that for instance, the unity of religions or other issues can only possibly be understood by a certain type of person is tantamount to saying that if you do not understand this proposition it is not because there might be something wrong with the proposition, but because there is something wrong with you. Nasr wants to counter such criticism by arguing that the perennial philosophy is élitist in the sense that modern physics is élitist.[114] In other words, Nasr claims, the traditional view is élitist in the way that only a few people have the capacity to attain sacred knowledge at such a level. This is not different from the principle that anyone can study physics but only a few scientists can reach a level at which that they can form new theories.

Another criticism made against Nasr is that he presents a particular metaphysical doctrine as the only true one, while in fact his school of the perennial philosophy is one among many. On this piont, Thomas Dean argues that, although Nasr seems to be oppose the ideologies and 'isms', he presents his ideas in a manner that 'absolutises' certain ideas and dismisses the others. In this sense, Nasr is as much in error as any other 'ism'.[115] Nasr refuses to admit that the perennial philosophy is an ideology. To Dean's charge that the perennial philosophy is an ideology Nasr asserts:

> To mistake even the traditional doctrine of the Absolute for the Absolute Itself would be to mistake traditional metaphysics for modern philosophy, which it is not. When I say the esoteric 'alone' I do not, in fact absolutize one particular metaphysical language but the esoterism as such. There is only one metaphysic but many traditional languages through which it is expressed and many religions with irreducible differences which nevertheless less contain in their heart that supreme science of the Real.[116]

Chapter Six

Christianity and Islam: Manifestations of the Ultimate

Christianity and Pluralism

Religions cannot be detached from their historical roots.[1] As compared to Islam, Christianity is a more 'historical' religion; some historical events such as the birth and the resurrection of Jesus have always played a crucial part in the formation of Christian tenets. To determine a Christian attitude to any subject would require a survey of Christian history. Therefore, we need to present a brief history of religious pluralism, i.e. a Christian approach to other religions in its history.

It is interesting to note that Hick makes no reference to the Judaic background of Jesus' teachings. Jesus did not live and teach in a cultural vacuum. As a person of Jewish origin, Jesus primarily addressed the Jewish folk of his time; and therefore his teachings in general related to Judaism. One might even say that hostile[2] as well as tolerant and, to some extent, merciful[3] Old Testament attitudes to other religions have certainly made some impact upon Christian teachings.

The Quran in Islam and the Gospels in Christianity are still prime sources which determine not only the doctrinal but also the 'historical' aspects of the religions in question. Jesus' reported attitude to Judaism as well as other religions in the Gospels may give us some hints with regard to a Christian approach to the other religions. Jesus, who was in intimate contact only with his ancestral Hebrew religion, more or less accepted the theology of the Old Testament. The God with whom he identified himself and about whom he preached is none other than 'the God of Abraham, Isaac, Ishmael and Jacob', if one were to use the phrase of the Quran as well as the Bible.[4] As the New Testament reports, he thought that he had

171

the right to 'judge' and care for the moral life of the community he lived in, and preached important moral principles such as 'Thou shalt love the Lord thy God . . . and neighbour.'[5] It is true that the New Testament's idea that Jesus came to fulfil the Old Testament, puts Christianity in an important relation to Judaism.[6]

As far as Jesus' attitude to non-Jewish religions is concerned, it is quite difficult to reach any conclusion. As St. John reports, Jesus was aware of the religion of the Samaritans, a religion regarded at that time as inferior to orthodox Judaism.[7] The parable of the good Samaritan[8] illustrates the duty of good neighbourliness between Jew and Samaritan. It is claimed that implicit in this parable is the moral principle that all branches of the human race should be treated as neighbours. However, as Dewick observes, it is extremely difficult to find any evidence in the Gospels or other historical materials that Jesus ever had any direct contact with Roman and Greek or Oriental religions.[9]

'No man knoweth the Son, but the Father; neither knoweth any man the Father, save the Son, and he to whomsoever the Son will reveal him'.[10] St. John states the same idea more clearly: 'I am the way, the truth and the life: no man cometh unto the Father, but by me.'[11] The same idea was also repeated in the Apostolic preaching in the Acts of the Apostles: 'Neither is there a salvation in any other: for there is none other name under heaven given among men, whereby we must be saved.'[12] Although there is another way of interpreting these passages,[13] historically they have always been seen as sacred principles that advocated Jesus and Christianity to provide the only way to salvation.[14]

I would like to examine how the Church has engaged with the issue of the theology of religions during its history through Hick's writings.[15] In the middle ages, the relationship of Christianity with other faiths was often in a hostile atmosphere; its conflict with Islam often ended on the battlefield. Christian theological argument with regard to the 'heathen world' and 'heretics' at that time was orchestrated by the Church. As Dewick observes there were a few Christian thinkers who endeavoured to set forth the fundamental principles that should govern the Christian attitude to other religions. For instance, St. Augustine of Hippo maintained a form of 'apologetic' line for Christianity against the old paganism of Greece and Rome. St. Thomas Aquinas, however, wrote *Summa Contra Gentiles* in order to assist missionaries in their attempt to convert the Muslims.[16] But such understandings separated not only Christians and non-Christians, but also Catholics and heretics. As a consequence, the motto *'Extra ecclesiam nulla salus'* (there is no salvation outside the Church) became a central principle of the Catholic Church.

In the middle ages, a Christian theology of religions was dominated by exclusivism, that is, all people (whatever race, colour or religion) must be Christian if they are to be saved. For instance the famous papal pronouncement of Boniface VIII in 1302 declared the following:

> We are required by faith to believe and hold that there is one holy, catholic and apostolic Church; we firmly believe it and unreservedly profess it; outside it there is neither salvation nor remission of sins... Further we declare, say, define and proclaim that to submit to the Roman pontiff is, for every human creature, an utter necessity of salvation.[17]

In the decree of the Council of Florence in 1438–45 it was stated:

> No one remaining outside the Catholic Church, not just pagans, but also Jews or heretics or schismatics, can become partakers of eternal life; but they will go to 'everlasting fire which was prepared for the devil and his angels', unless before the end of life they are joined to the Church.[18]

In the Protestant world, such an exclusive an attitude was also predominant. Luther in his *Large Catechism* asserted:

> Those who are outside Christianity, be they heathens, Turks, Jews or false Christians [i.e. Roman Catholics], although they may believe in only one true God, yet remain in eternal wrath and perdition.[19]

In the mediaeval period, the world was divided into different religious camps. The governing power in those days sought to justify itself through the way it displayed enmity towards the opposite religious camp. The polemical nature of writings aimed at the opponent reinforced an already existing exclusivist attitude. In those days, the Christian world's approach to Islam or Islam's attitude to the Christian world was dictated not by intellectual dialogue but by the power struggle of these two religions.[20]

In this century the attitude of the Church to other religions has not sufficiently changed to satisfy those, like Hick, who demand a pluralistic approach. For instance, the Frankfurt Declaration of 1970 addressed the non-Christian world stating that:

We therefore challenge all non-Christians, who belong to God on the basis of creation, to believe in him [Jesus Christ] and to be baptized to in his name, for in him alone is eternal salvation promised to them.[21]

In spite of the dominance of such an exclusivist attitude in the Christian world, there has appeared a notable shift from religious exclusivism to the religious inclusivism or even pluralism as a result of the impact of liberal values in the West. One might state that it would have been more fruitful if the Church had reached such a form of inclusive attitude through its own development rather than through the pressure of the dominant secular culture.[22] The Catholic Church's recent but significant paradigm shift made in the Second Vatican Council of 1963–1965 is arguably the result of such a cultural imperative. In its Dogmatic Constitution on the Church, promulgated in 1964, the Council declared:

> Those also can attain to everlasting salvation who through no fault of their own do not know the gospel of Christ or His Church, yet sincerely seek God and, moved by grace, strive by their deeds to do His will as it is known to them through the dictates of conscience. Nor does divine Providence deny the help necessary for salvation to those who, without blame on their part, have not yet arrived at an explicit knowledge of God, but who strive to live a good life, thanks to His grace. Whatever goodness and truth is found among them is looked upon by the Church as a preparation for the Gospel.[23]

A Declaration which aims to set the principles which would establish the relationship between the Church and non-Christian religions made at the end of the Council in 1965 decrees:

> The Catholic Church rejects nothing which is true and holy in these religions. She looks with sincere respect upon those ways of conduct and of life, those rules and teachings which, though differing in many particulars from what she holds and sets forth, nevertheless often reflect a ray of that Truth which enlightens all men.[24]

If one compares this passage with the statement of *'extra ecclesiam nulla salus'* one can surely realise the progress made towards a more tolerant and better understanding of other religions in the Catholic Church.[25] But Hick finds Vatican II inadequate, because it cannot

174

accommodate the form of pluralism that he has in mind. He explains his dissatisfaction in the following way:

> But still Vatican II has not made the Copernican revolution that is needed in the Christian attitude to other faiths. It still assumes without question that salvation is only in Christ and through incorporation into his mystical body, the church. Vatican II sees this incorporation as being possible on the basis of a sincere effort to follow the light available within other religious traditions. But the goodness and the truth that men of other faiths have is, the Dogmatic Constitution says, 'looked upon by the Church as a preparation for the gospel'. This suggests that faithful men in other religions are still required by God sooner or later to arrive at an explicit Christian faith. . .[26]

I shall be presenting a Muslim answer to the problem of religious pluralism in the next part of this chapter. Here, it will be sufficient to offer a brief consideration of the problem at hand.

From the traditional point of view, it would be a mistake to demand a change in religion simply to accommodate the requirements of secular culture: every revealed principle should be cherished within the realm of that particular religion. One of the drawbacks of modern culture is that it does not recognise any hierarchy in the field of knowledge. It assumes that there should be an answer for every problem for every individual. From the traditional point of view, there might be an answer for every question but not for everybody. Certain fields are only open to those who are chosen and prepared for that kind of task. According to this view, the problem of the plurality of religions is a metaphysical problem and should be approached by metaphysicians, i.e. 'mystics', only. On the level of theology or philosophy, it is simply not possible to find a satisfactory answer to a metaphysical problem. Therefore the problems inherent in the plurality of religions are not clarified, but rather confused and complicated when dealt with in the field of theology as well as philosophy.[27]

A New Christology for a New World

Hick is recognised as an eminent thinker not only because he is one of the leading advocates of religious pluralism, but also because he demands a new Christology, suggesting alternative interpretations for some of the traditional doctrines such as the Trinity, the Incarnation and the virgin birth. As his recent writings indicate,[28] Hick has put more emphasis on the criticism of traditional Christology than religious pluralism. Nevertheless, one also needs to state that Hick's demand for a new Christology is very much related to his account of religious pluralism; he aims to redefine those doctrines that grant a unique status to Christianity, precisely because he wants to make his hypothesis of religious pluralism more credible.

In *Christianity at the Centre* (1968), Hick describes his position as 'a middle way between a conservative cleaving to the traditional structure of belief, and a radical rejection of all traditional content including the transcendent'.[29] He further expounds his position with regard to some traditional doctrines of Christianity:

> As a middle way it has no exciting name or banner. It is radical in rejecting much of the orthodox system of belief. But it is conservative in affirming the transcendent – the reality of God, the divinity of Christ, and life after death. It is thus open to criticism from both sides – from the conservatives for denying the infallible inspiration of the scriptures, or the fall of man, or the virgin birth, or the bodily resurrection, or contra-natural miracles, or the sanctity of the church; and from the radicals for nevertheless stubbornly affirming a personal transcendent God whose love is directly manifest in the love of Christ and whose good purpose for mankind is ultimately to be fulfilled beyond bodily death. But in so far as this middle way is the way of truth it will make its own appeal to Christian minds, whether conservative or radical.[30]

It is interesting to note that having endorsed a Kantian framework for a 'religious' interpretation of religion, nothing much is left in those three articles of Christian faith that Hick affirmed in those days, namely, the reality of God, the divinity of Christ and life after death. In his new Kantian project the reality of God is transformed into the 'reality' of phenomenological manifestations of the noumenal Real, life after death into a human transformation from self-centredness to Reality-centredness, the divinity of Christ into a metaphor which describes the unique relation of Jesus to God.

As already stated, it was *The Myth of God Incarnate* that placed Hick at the centre of controversy as regards the doctrine of the incarnation.[31] In his recent writings on Christology, while more emphasis is put on the issue of the doctrine of incarnation, the doctrine of the virgin birth, on the other hand is marginalised.[32] For

Hick, the reinterpretation of the doctrine of the incarnation is crucial because it is used as the claim that 'Christianity is the only religion founded by God in person, and must as such be uniquely superior to all other religions'.[33] In addition to this, there are other reasons for him to consider that the doctrine at hand should be considered as a metaphorical truth rather than a literary truth.[34]

In such complicated issues one, says Hick, has to be aware of 'a distinction between the historical Jesus of Nazareth and the post-Easter development of the Church's mingled memories and interpretations of him'[35]; the fact that any access to the former is only possible through the latter, does not minimise the importance of such a distinction. Hick argues that it is also significant for any account of Christology to point out the fact that the earliest New Testament documents, some letters of St. Paul and the Gospel of Mark, were written about twenty years after Jesus' death and consequently none of these writers was an eye-witness of the life they depict.[36]

Hick starts his new Christology by offering a new interpretation of the doctrine of the resurrection. First of all, Hick draws our attention to the fact that people started to believe in Jesus' resurrection at the time when the gospels were written, that is almost two generations after Jesus death. He maintains that in the earliest strata of the New Testament there is not included any reference either to an empty tomb or to a visible body of the risen Jesus.[37] Therefore another interpretation is needed. He finds some similar elements between St. Paul's conversion experience of Jesus on the road to Damascus, and the resurrection stories. He maintains that the experience of a supernatural light within Christianity described as the 'being of light' with Christ was a common phenomenon. In other words, what Hick is trying to say is that the resurrection of Jesus did not occur in the manner believed by mainstream Christian theology, but perhaps 'the original resurrection 'appearances' may quite possibly have been waking versions of this type of experience'.[38]

Hick notes that the resurrection is not the only miracle story mentioned in the gospels. For instance there are also other stories such as the story of the empty tomb, the three hours darkness, the earthquake, the rising from death of the saints and their entering into Jerusalem, and so on. Hick seems to be puzzled as to why there has been such emphasis on the bodily resurrection while other stories such as the bodily resurrection of many saints were almost forgotten. In order to substantiate his interpretation, Hick argues that Mark's Gospel (which is between one and two decades nearer to the event in question than the other Gospels) does not mention appearances but only the empty tomb. Having reflected on the stories of St. Paul and its relation to the resurrection Hick concludes:

> There is thus reason to think that – as indeed we should expect on general psychological grounds – the tradition developed from the remembrance of a numinous and transforming experience into a story of miraculous physical events. This pattern suggests that the original happening is more likely to have been in the realm of inner spiritual experience than in that of outer sense experience. But we have to add that any unqualified assertions about what occurred in the days and weeks after Jesus' death, whether in terms of spiritual encounters or of physical miracles, can never be fully substantiated from an historical point of view.[39]

Another issue in Christology that Hick aims to interpret is the Christian belief that Jesus is the son of God or God the Son incarnate. He argues that the historical Jesus did not consider and understand himself as God or God the Son incarnate. Furthermore, he claims that if Jesus had been addressed in such terms during his life time, he would indeed have rejected the idea as blasphemous. He states that any statement with regard to Jesus' perception of himself cannot be made with certainty. But we can state that the available evidence has led 'the historians of the period to conclude, with an impressive degree of unanimity, that Jesus did not claim to be God incarnate'.[40] He argues that from the fifth until the late nineteenth century, Christians generally believed that Jesus had proclaimed himself to be God the Son, the second person of the divine Trinity. But the findings of twentieth century New Testament scholarship have claimed that this was not the case.

The deconstruction of the development of the doctrines with regard to Jesus' personality can indeed shed some light on the contemporary theological enterprise if accompanied with contextual analysis, comparing for instance modern society with the society in which Jesus lived. In this respect, having considered the impact of cultural circumstances upon the scriptures, Hick claims that the title divine and 'son of God' were frequently used for heroes, emperors and kings in the Roman and the New Testament period. Therefore, it is quite likely that Jesus should have come to be regarded as a person belonging to the class as such. Consequently, Jesus' prophetic mission and personality may have contributed to the creation of such metaphorical language. But, the important thing for Hick is that both, 'son of God' and other titles which ascribe to someone divine attributes, were widely used *metaphorically* in the world in which Jesus lived.[41]

But it was in the Council of Nicaea of 325, states Hick, that the church first officially adopted the non-biblical concept of *ousia*, declaring Jesus as God the Son Incarnate, *homoousios toi patri*, of the same substance as the Father, a term borrowed from Greek culture. As a consequence of this, maintains Hick, the original biblical metaphor which describes Jesus as 'son of God had became the metaphysical God the Son, second person of the Trinity'.[42] At the Council of Chalcedon in 451, this doctrine was consolidated declaring that Jesus is 'at once complete in Godhead and complete in manhood, truly God and truly man, consisting also of a reasonable soul and body; of one substance with the Father as regards his Godhead, and at the same time of one substance with us as regards his manhood'.[43]

Hick, however, believes that by affirming the doctrine of God incarnate, Christian theology jeopardises itself: on the one hand it claims that Jesus is a genuine human being, on the other hand it also claims that he possesses some divine qualities. The inevitable question emerged: Which divine qualities can be attributed to Jesus and which cannot? For instance, can we say that he is omnipotent and omniscient and at the same time, a human being? We certainly cannot say this. The gospels clearly suggest that the historical Jesus lacked divine attributes as such. On the other hand, it is believed that Jesus possesses some divine qualities. In other words, Hick argues, kenotic Christology ends up with a contradiction, namely, affirming 'a being who is God and yet lacks the attributes of God'.[44]

Having mentioned some historical as well as logical evidence which, he believes, makes a new interpretation of the doctrine of incarnation plausible, Hick moves on to the historical side-effects of such doctrines. He argues that the doctrine of the incarnation affirmed by the Church should be reinterpreted not only because the doctrine in question, is philosophically and theologically problematic, but because it has been used to justify 'great historical evils' such as anti-Semitism, the colonial exploitation of the Third World, Western patriarchism, and the Christian superiority complex.[45] In addition to these important side-effects, one further important consequence of this doctrine is that it is often used as a means to argue the superiority of Christianity over other religions.[46]

Hick believes that one of the ways in which Christology can escape from such an impasse lies in the modern analysis of the theological language of Christianity. Relying on this assumption, he suggests that it would be religiously sound if the traditional account of the incarnation is regarded not as a literal statement about God which aims to establish a precise theological formulation, but as an analogous or metaphorical statement which aims to invoke a religious dedication, ecstasy and devotion.

Hick notes that before the Council of Nicaea and Chalcedon, when Christians referred to Jesus through language that ascribed to him some divine attributes, they did not use such language for the theological articulation of the Christian faith. Rather, incarnational language as such in early Christianity is metaphorical. Even in modern English we use such a metaphor of incarnation. For instance, when we say: 'great men are the incarnation of the spirit of their age' or 'the qualities incarnated in a hero' or 'George Washington incarnated the spirit of American Independence in 1776', and so on, we are not speaking literally. Therefore, he asserts that the language of the divine incarnation in Christian theology must be interpreted not literally but metaphorically.[47] He explains:

> In the case of the metaphor of divine incarnation, what was lived out, made flesh, incarnated in the life of Jesus can be indicated in at least three ways, each of which is an aspect of the fact that Jesus was a human being exceptionally open and responsive to the divine presence: (1) In so far as Jesus was doing God's will, God was acting through him on earth and was in this respect 'incarnate' in Jesus' life; (2) In so far as Jesus was doing God's will he 'incarnated' the ideal of human life lived in openness and response to God; (3) In so far as Jesus lived a life of self-giving love, or *agape*, he 'incarnated' a love that is a finite reflection of the infinite divine love.[48]

Hick argues that the doctrine of the Trinity is derived from the doctrine of the incarnation. The idea of Jesus as literally God incarnate has, by implication, led to the idea of God as three persons in one. In other words, if Jesus was God on earth there must also have been God in heaven, and thus Christian theology required a binity. When the Holy Spirit was added as a distinct hypostasis of the Divine, the binity became a trinity.[49] As far as the history of the Trinitarian doctrine in Christianity is concerned, Hick states that virtually all New Testament scholars agree that the Trinity was not part of Jesus' own teaching about God. Jesus himself, says Hick, thought of God in Jewish monotheistic terms.[50]

Hick primarily notes that there is no Christian doctrine of *the* Trinity, but a range of Trinitarian theories which can be categorised into two main groups. In the first, the Trinity is thought of as containing three persons in a sense that has been called a 'social' conception of the Trinity; in this sense the divine Father, Son and Spirit share the same divine nature. In the second, God is understood as one, but is known to us in three roles or relationships. God is known as Creator (God the Father), Redeemer (God the Son) and Sanctifier (God the Spirit). In this sense, Hick notes, the Trinity does not in principle differ from the Quranic characterisation of God with ninety-nine names.[51]

In response to Hick, Muzammil H. Siddiqi proposes that Hick's paralleling of the Trinity with the Islamic account of the ninety-nine names of God is confusing. Muzammil argues that such an interpretation, which is intended to make the Trinity acceptable to Muslims, cannot work since it imposes a Christian pattern of deity upon the Islamic understating of God. In essence, he argues, ninety-nine names in Islam, do not suggest a limit but infinity.[52] In addition to these critical points, I would also state that in Islam the qualification of God with ninety-nine names is not a doctrine, or a theological tenet; it is not a part of Muslims' belief in God, whereas in Christianity, the Trinity is one of the essential parts of Christian theology.

Before concluding this section it has to be said that the main reason why Hick proposes a new theology is his commitment to the hypothesis of religious pluralism. For instance, Hick demands that the doctrine of the incarnation must be understood metaphorically not because the doctrine is totally unacceptable but because it functions as an incentive for a Christian superiority over other religions which contravenes the main aim of his version of pluralism. The reason why Hick is less critical of the doctrine of the Trinity than the Incarnation is because the doctrine of the Trinity has helped Hick to make sense of his hypothesis of pluralism. As in the doctrine of the Trinity one God can manifest himself in three ways or three distinct persons, in his hypothesis the Real *an sich* can manifest itself as the *personae* and *impersonae* of the phenomenal realm. In addition to this, there is also one other factor behind Hick's critical approach to Christology, that is, Hick's theological stand-point, which is based in the middle way. His stand-point between liberalism and conservatism enables him not only to offer a critical insight into traditional Christology but also to see those issues from a cross-religious perspective.

It is interesting to note that Hick's account of Christology is, to a certain extent, in accord with the Quranic account of Jesus. Hick's account as such is welcomed by some Muslim writers.[53] One can appreciate the motive behind their wholehearted appreciation of Hick's Christology. But what these Muslim writers do not realise is that Hick's Christology is an integral part of his entire philosophy of religion. Are they also prepared to accept Hick's theology of religion which describes Allah as a phenomenal manifestation of the Real *an sich*? Can they explain why they endorse Hick's account of the doctrine of the incarnation or the resurrection while rejecting his account of the virgin birth?

Hick's Perception of Islam

Hick places Islam among the five major traditions which are considered as authentic responses to the Ultimate and thus it is seen as one of the subjects of his hypothesis of pluralism.[54] Before proceeding any further one thing that has to be said is that Hick has come to know Islam through his encounter with Muslim people in the city of Birmingham, not through a formal study of Islam. This inevitably limited Hick's access to the treasures of Islamic civilisation. Nevertheless, his encounter with Muslims and his reading on Sufism was sufficient for him to consider Islam as one of the elements of his pluralistic model.

The Sufi strand of Islam has been more appealing to Hick than any others. That is because saintliness is important in Hick's interpretation of religion. In addition to this Hick also believes that Sufis, especially those such as 'Arabi and Rumi propagated a form of pluralism in Islam that is quite similar to his version.

Hick argues that when compared with Christianity and Judaism, Islam might have a better pluralistic attitude, but it cannot be fully integrated into a pluralistic framework for two reasons. Firstly, according to Hick, Islam has not yet developed in a manner that enables it to accommodate the norms of modern culture and ecumenical outlook, as Christianity has. Islam has not yet created a need for adopting secular norms to Muslim society. Nevertheless, one thing is certain: the unfolding or growth of Islam in the twenty first century will not produce the same Islam as we witnessed in the medieval period.

Secondly, the Quranic revelation portrays itself as the fulfilment of all previous revelations, and therefore demands a unique status.[55] This for Hick is one of the biggest obstacles that prevents Islam from being integrated into his pluralism. In the second part of this chapter, I shall be dealing with the problem of religious pluralism from a Quranic perspective. Hick might be wrong in assuming that there is a necessary correlation between the absolute truth claim of a religion and the possibility of establishing a pluralistic approach. In other words, he assumes that to endorse a religion as unique, necessarily rules out any scope for postulating a pluralistic attitude. But this is not necessarily so. As Nasr argues, is it possible to construe the absolute truth claim of a religion as evidence of its link with the Absolute.[56]

Hick approaches the Quran and the personality of the Prophet within the context of his hypothesis of pluralism. However, at a time of rampant criticisms levelled against Muslims and Islam, Hick's positive attitude towards the Prophet and the Quran, although fundamentally different from the Muslim's perception of them, is one significant step forward which can open the way to a genuine acknowledgement of Islam in the West.

One thing, however, that puzzles Hick is how Muhammad, as a prophet can behave as a political leader. In order to understand this phenomenon, Hick compares the socio-political condition of the society in which Jesus worked as a messenger with the socio-political condition by which Muhammad constructed his community. He argues that Jesus was born into the artisan class of a subject people, ruled by the Romans. Therefore, he was entirely without political power and influence. In fact, Hick maintains, any idea of reform and social criticism in the name of God was ruled out by his apocalyptic conviction of living at the end of the Age. Muhammad on the other hand, says Hick, was born into the dominant tribe of Arabia, into a society in which a new religious movement meant a new political entity and a new power among the Arabian tribes. Hick points out that one can even justify Muhammad's careful political calculation and effective use of force which he had to employ in order to protect his community under the circumstances in which he lived.[57] The logic behind Hick's argument is this. The political aspect of Islam is the result of the historical and therefore accidental socio-political condition of the community in which Islam originated. Hence, from the religious perspective, it is neither essential, nor significant. A Muslim would reply to Hick's analysis by arguing that although there

183

is a relationship between the contents of the message and the socio-political conditions of the society to which that message was delivered, it is ultimately God who decided what should be in the content of the Islamic message. In other words, Islam appeared in the course of history with such characteristics, not because it was so shaped by its socio-political context, but because God so willed and consequently prepared those conditions for the emergence of Islam in order to actualise what was already a possibility in its celestial archetype.

What is Hick's response to the question of whether Jews, Christians and Muslims worship the same God? The question and its religious implication for the three Abrahamic faiths are of crucial importance. Hick, argues that Jews, Christians and Muslims, must all have been worshipping the same God, because he is the only one. In addition to this, the scriptures of these three traditions encourage us to think that each successive holy book assumes that the God of whom it speaks is the God previously made known in earlier revelations. The Quran indeed speaks quite a lot about God's message to the children of Israel and later to Jesus and his community. According to Islam the God who revealed the Quran is the same God who sent the Torah to Moses, and ordained Jesus as a messenger.[58] The New Testament, however, is full of references to the Torah and assumes that the God about whom Jesus spoke is the God of Abraham, Isaac and Jacob. Hick maintains that although the Torah does not speak of Jahweh as being also the God of the New Testament and the Quran, with regard to Jesus' Jewishness and Islam's commitment to straight monotheism it is possible to assume that Christians and Muslims are, at least in their intention, worshipping the same God whom the Jews have always worshipped.[59]

Hick maintains that each tradition has presented God with two distinct qualities: universality and particularity. If one looks at the universal aspect of God, such as being creator of the universe, a moral agent demanding justice, or righteousness displayed within these three religions, one is bound to conclude that the adherents of these three traditions are worshipping the same God. But if one approaches the issue considering God's particular aspects displayed differently in different traditions, one cannot easily conclude that they worship the same God. For instance, the God of Judaism is presented in the Hebrew Bible, as distinctively God of the Jews standing in unique relationship to his chosen people. Again the God of Christianity, notes Hick, is presented as a triune Being related to humanity through Jesus, God the Son incarnate. And yet again the Allah of Islam, states Hick, with regard to his particular aspects is different from the Jahweh of Israel, and from the Holy Trinity of Christianity.[60] In short, Hick claims that If we consider the issue through focusing on those particular aspects of God which define the particularity of the traditions in question, we obviously cannot freely claim that Muslims, Christians and Jews worship the same God. Hick's answer to the question that he asks lies in his hypothesis of religious pluralism:

> ... [E]ach concrete historical divine personality – Jahweh, the heavenly Father, the Quranic Allah – is a joint product of the universal divine presence and a particular historically formed mode of constructive religious imagination. [T]here is an element of human imaginative projection in religion ...
>
> This means in turn that the biblical Jahweh was formed at the interface between the transcendent universal God and the particular mentality and circumstances of the people of Israel; later taking on a more universal character, whilst however retaining continuity with the tribal past, in the Judaism of the rabbis. With the birth of Christianity and its splitting away from Judaism, this divine personality can be said to have divided into two, one form developing into the Adonai of rabbinic Judaism and the other into the heavenly Father – later elaborated into the Holy Trinity – of Christianity, with both universal characteristics and a particular historical linkage to Jesus of Nazareth and the Christian church. Later again the divine presence that had formed in interaction with the Jewish people took yet another 'name and form' as the Allah of the Quran, again with both a particular historical linkage to the prophet Muhammad and the life of seventh-century CE Arabia, and universal characteristics which became increasingly prominent as Islam developed into a world faith.[61]

The frequent references to the prophets of the Old Testament and Jesus, the Torah and the gospels in the Quran are enough to convince Muslims that the God of the Quran is none other than the God of Abraham, Moses, Ishmael, Isaac and Jesus.[62]

I am also aware that such a conclusion, because of the historical stand-point of Islam in respect to Judaism and Christianity, can be appreciated by Muslims more freely than Christians and Jews. I also share Hick's concern that the first step forward towards mutual

185

constructive dialogue between these three great religions can only be taken after having accepted the proposition that they all worship the same God. Furthermore, as the Quran suggests,[63] I believe that the only ground on which the adherents of these three religions come together is a common religious ground which they all share, such as belief in God and upholding common sacred moral codes.

Islam and Pluralism

In contemporary Islam, there is no notable endeavour which would aim to explore the potential of Islamic culture in order to offer a comprehensive account that would deal with the problem of religious pluralism. It is interesting to note that in early and medieval Islam, Muslim scholars approached this issue within the context of Islamic jurisprudence, not that of *Kalam*, Islamic theology. They often thought that the issue of determining the status of those who live within the domain of Islam is a practical problem, i.e. it arises when a certain group of people or individuals are classified for administrative purposes. They did not consider it as an issue of faith. That is because ultimately only God can know who has a genuine faith in God, and therefore deserves salvation.

When one looks at the topics of classical Islamic disciplines such as *Kalam*, *Fiqh*, *Tafsir* and *Hadith*, one cannot find the issue of pluralism as an independent topic dealt with extensively. But this does not mean that Islam does not take the issue into consideration at all. On the contrary, Islam pays quite a lot of attention to the question of the plurality of religions. Therefore, we see that the basic principles exhibited by the Quran and the *sunnah* can offer a tangible account of a theology of religions. In addition to this we also see the historical implementation of those principles in Muslim societies throughout Islamic history. However, one thing that has to be made clear here is that while I deal with the problem of religious pluralism from the perspective of Islamic thought, I shall not look for an account of religious pluralism such as those of Hick and W. C. Smith. Nor shall I judge the value of the 'pluralistic' principles in Islam by applying the current norms of modern culture. Rather I shall try to propose an Islamic account of the question of religious pluralism through the Quran and other Islamic sources.[64]

Since I am going to present an account of 'Islamic pluralism', I first of all, have to say something about the way something is qualified as Islamic. What makes an opinion or a point of view Islamic is not well-defined and therefore it is always open to discussion. Compared to Christianity, it is difficult to establish an official view on an issue, since in Islamic tradition, there is no institution like a church or an official system of ideas like theology. Rather there is a sacred text, the Quran and the living tradition which includes the *sunnah* of the prophet which, as the prime sources of Islam, determine *a priori* what is Islamic. In addition to these two sources of religious authority, there are, of course, the secondary sources such as schools of thoughts like *Kalam*, Sufism and the *falasifa* and the individual scholars who established reputations as religious authorities such as Imam al-Shaf'i, al-Ghazzali, Ibn 'Arabi, Ibn Hazm and Ahmed Faruq al-Sirhindi, whose opinion can contribute to establishing an Islamic opinion.[65]

There is, however, a tradition or method by which an issue can be settled from an Islamic perspective. In this tradition, a subject is examined firstly with reference to primary religious authority, i.e. the Quran and the *sunnah* and secondly with reference secondary religious authority, i.e. certain schools of thought as well as individual scholars. Following this tradition, I will approach the issue from the perspective of the Quran thereby drawing a theoretical framework for an 'Islamic pluralism'. I shall also present a brief historical account of 'Islamic pluralism' as a concrete example of the implementation of such Quranic principles.

A Theoretical Framework for an 'Islamic Religious Pluralism'

In this section, I would like to enumerate the Quranic principles with regard to the issue of religious pluralism as propositions which aim to suggest an account of 'Islamic pluralism'. I will formulate these propositions by depending on the Quranic verses and arranging them in order, from those which suggest a pluralistic attitude to those which suggest an inclusivist attitude. At the end of the section I will offer an evaluation of these propositions and consider them the guide lines of an 'Islamic pluralistic' account.

Proposition I: *The universality as well as the diversity of God's revelation to humankind is affirmed.*

Islam explicitly endorses the universality of God's revelation, which plays a significant part in the Islamic understanding of other religions. The God of the Quran is not only the God of the Muslim people but the God of all humankind. The Quran illustrates this point by stating: 'Unto Allah belong the East and West, and whithersoever you turn, there is Allah's countenance. For Allah is All-Embracing, All-knowing' (2:115).

God of all humankind did not leave any nation in the dark, rather he illuminated them by sending messengers.[66] The logic of sending every nation a messenger is that people should not justify the rejection of faith in God by arguing that they did not receive any message.[67] A logical consequence of this line of thinking is that if a nation or community did not receive a messenger, they would not be responsible and therefore would have to be exempted from punishment.[68] Although God sent a messenger to every nation, he did not mention all of them in the Quran.[69] Therefore Muslims receive a Quranic sanction which enables them to expand an Islamic account of prophecy in such a manner that it could include those messengers who are not mentioned in the Quran, including Gautama the Buddha and the avatars of the Hindus. Although all the messengers spoke about the same reality and conveyed the same truth, the messages they delivered were not identical in their theological forms. That is simply because the message was expressed in the specific forms which would accord with and make sense for the culture it was sent to. Thus, a messenger is to speak within the cultural context of the community to which the message is revealed.[70]

The implication of seeing history as a ground upon which the heavenly messages are displayed is that all religions, in one way or another, are related and therefore share a common purpose. Islam in this respect is the name of the latest version of the message which has been displayed throughout history. That is to say, one heavenly religion cannot be a rival but only an ally of another heavenly religion. Therefore, in Islam the notion of the universality of God's revelations has always played a key role in constituting an Islamic theology of religions. As a result of adopting this belief, Muslims are able to participate in the essence and the 'religious proximity' of other traditions.

Proposition II: *Multiplicity of races, colours, communities and religions is regarded as the signs of God's mercy and glory exhibited through his creatures.*

Plurality in this sense is accepted as a natural phenomenon. The Quran states: 'O Humankind! Verily we have created you of a male and female; and we have distributed you in nations and tribes that

188

you might know one another and recognise that, in the sight of God the most honourable of you is the most pious. Verily God is wise and all knowing' (49:13). But what Islam aims to do is to integrate this diversity into unity through the sacred principles of the Quran; it explains the reason and purpose for racial and religious multiplicity. God created religious, racial and other forms of diversity in order to distinguish those who can appreciate the majesty of God and see his purpose from those who ignore the signs of God as such. Otherwise God could have created only one nation.[71]

One of the prime tasks of Islam is to eliminate discrimination based upon race or colour by proposing a single Islamic brotherhood which aims to unite all the different people under one faith. It has partly achieved this during its history. Beyond this, Islam even managed to establish a unity among all the subjects, including the Christians and Jews, that it governed. Furthermore, one might even claim that diversity, whether religious or racial, is considered in the Quran as the means to unity. In the Sufi strand of Islam, a unity in this sense has already been realised. Rumi illustrates a state of unity in which he saw himself:

> What is to be done, O Muslims? for I do not recognise myself.
> I am neither Christian, nor Jew, nor Gabr, nor Muslim.
> I am not of the East, nor of the West, not of the land, nor of the sea,
> I am not of Nature's mint, nor of the circling heavens.
> I am not of earth, nor of water, nor of air, nor of fire:
> I am not of the empyrean, nor of the dust, nor of existence, nor of entity.
> I am not of India, nor of China, nor of Bulgaria, nor of Saqsin:
> I am not of the Kingdom of Iraq, nor of the country of Khorasan.
> I am not of this world, nor of the next, nor of Paradise nor of Hell;
> I am not of Adam, nor of Eve, nor of Eden and nor of Rizwan,
> My place is Placeless, my trace is Traceless;
> It is neither body nor soul, for I belong to the soul of the Beloved.
> I have put duality away. I have seen that the two worlds are one;
> One I seek, One I know, One I see, One I call.
> He is the First, He is the Last, He is the Outward, He is the Inward.[72]

Proposition III: *Every revealed religion can be named as* islam, *when it is seen as 'a state of submission to God' (literally* islam*).*

Expanding the term *islam* in a manner that could envelope all other revealed religions is not an idea produced to counter the quest for a pluralistic approach. It is a Quranic endeavour which aims to show all revelations as part and parcel of God's plan. Muslims believe that *islam* is the name of the basic mission of all prophets throughout history. Hasan Askari illustrates the point:

> *Islam* now was the quality of all those, irrespective of the religion they practice, who are humble before God's Transcendence and submit to him as their Creator and Lord. While Muslims judged others, they came under their own judgement, for now the word *muslim* could be extended to any point in the past and any point in the future. This was the revolution which the Quran introduced into the religious history of humanity, and as such an universal revolution: now a *Noah* an *Abraham*, a *Moses*, a *Jesus*, a *Muhammed* are all *'muslims'*... [W]hoever among Jews and Christians and the people of other religions, surrenders to God, the One and only God, and does not explicitly and implicitly associate gods (race, religion and any other 'signs' and 'manifestations' of) with God, is a *'muslim'*.[73]

The Quran, itself promotes this notion by stating: 'Abraham was not a Jew nor yet a Christian; but he was true in faith (*hanif*) and bowed his will to Allah's, (*muslim*), and he joined not gods with Allah' (3:67); [Abraham in his prayer says] 'Our Lord! make us *muslims*, bowing to your (will) and of our progeny a people *muslim*, bowing to your (will)' (2:128).

According to the Quran, *islam* is not a name only given to a system of faith or religion, but it is also the name of an act of surrendering to the will of God. Anything which bows to God's will voluntarily or even involuntarily is qualified as *muslim*. Only human beings who have freedom of faith can go against God's will and reject *islam*, while all other creatures affirm it.[74]

Proposition IV: *There is no compulsion in religion.*

This is one of the unique principles of the Quran which was initiated in order to regulate freedom of religious belief in Islam. The Quran reads: 'Let there be no compulsion in religion: Truth stands out clear from Error: whoever rejects Evil and believes in Allah has grasped the most trustworthy handhold, that never, breaks. And God hears and knows all things' (2:256); 'Say "The Truth is from your Lord": let him who will, believe, let him who will, reject (it)' (18:29); 'If it had been the Lord's Will, they would all have believed – All who are on earth! Will you then compel mankind against their will to believe!' (10:99).

Many commentators cite some events in which the Prophet himself implemented the requirements of verse 2:256 and prohibited his companions from compelling people to accept Islam. For instance, Tabari mentions that when the two Jewish tribes of Qaynuqa and Nadr were expelled from Medina, they had in their charge children of the Ansar who had been placed with Jewish families. The biological parents asked the Prophet's permission to take their children back and raise them as a Muslims, but the Prophet said, 'There is no compulsion in religion'. Tabari mentions another event which indicates how this verse worked in practice. A Muslim named Al-Husayn had two sons, who having been influenced by Christian merchants, converted to Christianity and left Medina to go to Syria with these missionary merchants. Al-Husayn pleaded with the Prophet to pursue the convoy and bring his sons back to Islam. But the Prophet once against said, 'There is no compulsion in religion', that is let them follow the religion of their choice, even though it is not Islam.[75]

This verse itself has functioned as a law by safeguarding the freedom of religious belief throughout Islamic history.[76] It was such Quranic injunctions which have provided a rationale for the religious tolerance that has characterised Islamic history. As Lewis points out, religious persecution of the members of other faiths was almost absent; Jews and Christians under Muslim rule were not subject to exile, apostasy or death, which was the choice offered to Muslims and Jews in reconquered Spain. And Christian and Jews were not subject to any major territorial and occupational restrictions such as were the common lot of Jews in premodern Europe.[77]

It would, however, be wrong to say that Muslims consider Judaism and Christianity as authentic as Islam in leading to the truth. Like every religion and ideology, Islam considers itself superior to other religions when it presents truth. But what makes Islam different from other religions and ideologies is that it tolerates the existence of other religions *while it is in power*. As a result of this principle, although Islam has ruled for some thousand years over Christians and Jews, it did not encourage a systematic 'islamisation' of the adherents of these faiths.[78] Like any other religion, Islam aims to propagate its beliefs, but what makes it different from other religions is that it did not establish an organisation or institution for its propagation. In its history, Islam did not have missionary societies or any missionary institution. The work of *da'wa* is always left to individual effort.[79]

Proposition V: *The religion before God is Islam.*

Alongside those verses that indicate a form of 'Islamic pluralism' there are also some verses that indicate a form of Islamic exclusivism. In this context the Quran states: 'The religion before God is Islam (submission to His Will)' (3:19); 'If anyone desires a religion other than Islam (submission to Allah) never will it be accepted of him; in the hereafter he will be in the ranks of those who have lost (All spiritual good)' (3:85).

But the interesting thing here is that the verses that point to an exclusivist attitude in Islam are ambiguous and open to interpretation; they can be interpreted from the perspective of an 'Islamic pluralism' as well as that of an Islamic exclusivism. These verses can be interpreted as stating that Islam means *istislam*, i.e. submission to the Will of Allah; it is not meant to point to the specific Quranic revelation. For instance, Sheikh al-Maraghi interprets Islam in the first verse as *istislam* (surrender) or *ta'a* (obedience), hence equating Islam with *iman*, religious belief in general. He also goes on to say that a true 'Muslim' is anyone who is free from all traces of paganism and devoted in his deeds, regardless of the religious community to which he belongs or the period in which he lives.[80] Yusuf Ali, however, favours a pluralistic interpretation of these verses:

> The Muslim position is clear. The Muslim does not claim to have a religion peculiar to himself. Islam is not a sect or an ethnic religion. In its view all Religion is one, for the Truth is one. It was the religion preached by all the earlier prophets. It was the truth thought by all the inspired Books. In essence it amounts to a consciousness of the Will and Plan of Allah and a joyful submission to that Will and Plan. If anyone wants a religion other than that, he is false to his own nature, as he is false to Allah's Will and Plan. Such a one cannot expect guidance, for he has deliberately renounced guidance.[81]

Proposition VI: *Those who believe in God and the Last Day and work righteousness* (a'mila salihan) *will be saved.*

An Islamic notion of salvation cannot be equated with Buddhist or Enlightenment liberation or Christian salvation. Nor can it correspond to Hick's notion of human transformation from self-centredness to Reality-centredness. The Islamic notion of salvation is simple and uncomplicated. It believes that human beings were born into this world as a *tabula rasa*, sinless but with innate religiosity (*al-fitrah*). In addition to this, God made known his will through messengers. If one follows his or her innate religiosity and accepts the message, and works righteousness, he or she will be saved in the hereafter. Anyone who does good or evil, will be rewarded or punished accordingly.[82] Contrary to what is assumed, Islam affirms that Jews, Christians and Sabians can also attain salvation. The Quran simply states: 'Those who believe (in the Quran), and those who follow the Jewish (scriptures), and the Christians and the Sabians, – any who believe in Allah and the Last Day and work righteousness, shall have their reward with their Lord; on them shall be no fear, nor shall they grieve' (2:62); 'Those who believe (in the Quran), those who follow the Jewish (scriptures), and the Sabians and the Christians – any who believe in Allah and the Last Day, and work righteousness – on them shall be no fear nor shall they grieve' (5:69); 'Whoever works righteousness man and woman, and has Faith, verily, to him We give a new life and life that is good and pure, and We will bestow on such their reward according to the best of their actions' (16:97).

The question of the possibility of the salvation of non-Muslims according to Islamic belief is a matter of crucial importance, not only because the Quranic eschaton might well be the only possible destiny of humankind, but also because the answer to this question is the cause of the Muslim's attitude towards non-Muslims. As has become quite clear, Islam does not have a motto of *extra ecclesiam nulla salus*; exclusivism was not an official approach of Islam. It has always accepted the possibility of salvation outside its borders; it affirms the religious truth of Judaism and Christianity. Isma'il Raji al-Faruqi illustrates the point:

> The honour with which Islam regards Judaism and Christianity, their founders and scriptures, is not courtesy but acknowledgement of religious truth. Islam sees them in the world not as 'other views' that it has to tolerate, but as standing *de jure* as truly revealed religions from God. Moreover, their legitimate status is neither sociopolitical, nor cultural or civilizational, but religious. In this, Islam is unique. For no religion in the world has yet made belief in the truth of other religions a necessary condition of its own faith and witness.[83]

193

Although the Quran explicitly states that those Jews, Christians and Sabians who believe in God and the Last Day and work righteousness will attain salvation, Muslim scholars generally have related the salvation of non-Muslims to recognition of the Prophet by referring to the overall attitude of the Quran towards non-Muslims. Even if this might be the case, they still maintained that salvation has always remained possible outside the borders of Islam. Muhammed al-Ghazzali, a spokesman of Islamic orthodoxy in his *Faysal al-Tafriqa bayn al-Islam wa al-Zandaqa* states this:

> The above concerns the Community of Muhammad – God's blessing and peace be upon him – in a special way. But I go on to say: The divine mercy will embrace many of the bygone nations, even though most of them will be exposed to the Fire either slightly, even for a moment or for an hour, or for a period of time, so that one may apply to them the expression of 'the delegation of Fire'. Nay more I would say: Most of the Christians among the Byzantines [Greeks] and Turks in this time of ours will be embraced by the [same] mercy, If God the Most High wills. I mean those who are among the remote Byzantines and Turks whom the Call [to Islam] has not reached.[84]

From an Islamic point of view, what is crucial for one's salvation is not one's formal affiliation to a religion but the personal inner decision – which does not necessarily have to be formally declared – when one has been confronted with the call of the prophet Muhammad. But the question is this: In what circumstances can one be considered as a person who has received the call of Islam? Ghazzali argues that there are three conditions under which one can be considered as a person who *has* received the Call. He maintains one can only be regarded as an unbeliever and therefore exempted from salvation i) if one has heard the Prophet's name and description in a manner such as the Muslim has received it (al-Ghazzali says if someone is given inaccurate portrayal of the Prophet as being a liar and deceitful, and believes so, he or she is not obliged to believe in the Prophet, and therefore can be saved even though he or she did not believe him); ii) if one has also seen 'the miracle manifested in his regard' and yet has deliberately refuse to consider and reflect on the issue; iii) if one has suppressed a motive for inquiry that possibly could lead to truth in the matter, or the motive arose but was not pursued.[85]

One of the distinct qualities of the Quran is that it always refrains from making a general judgement about a particular group of people. For instance, it does not say that Muslims will be saved, Christians or Jews will not; rather it 'personalises' and directs its criticism or praise to specifically qualified people. For instance, it says those who believe in so and so and do so and so will be saved and those who do not believe so and so and do so and so will be punished. From a Quranic perspective, it is quite clear that being a Muslim by no means guaranties salvation. In addition to having faith, one not only has to be vigilant in performing good deeds, but also must seek the utmost to accomplish a perfect moral life. Even if a person has done his or her best to achieve salvation, he or she cannot and should not be certain about the end. The Prophet himself did not behave as if he was totally confident that he would be saved. The ideal position for a Muslim in this respect is to adopt an attitude of placing himself between *khawf* (fear) and *raja* (hope). In other words, a Muslim should be neither absolutely optimistic nor absolutely pessimistic about his or her own personal salvation. It is, I believe this ambiguous position with regard to salvation that has been a strong motive behind the desire to accomplish a sound moral life. It was this belief and commitment that functioned as an impulse for the desire for perfection (*kamal*).

In classical Islamic literature, faith is defined as 'confession by tongue and assent by heart' (*al-iman iqrarun bil-lisan wa tasdiqun bil-qalb*), though confessing by tongue is not the condition of faith. This is a very interesting definition. According to this definition, it is possible to think that although a person declares that he or she is a Muslim and performs five daily prayers and all the other Islamic duties, there is still a possibility that he or she might not be Muslim in fact.[86] The opposite to this is also the case. For instance, a person because of the circumstances in which he or she lives, who declares that he or she is not Muslim and lives accordingly still has the possibility that he or she might be Muslim in his or her inner being. Vahiduddin echoes what I have in mind:

> ... [W]hat counts at the deepest level in religion is the spirit of the faith not only formal affiliation. This means that even in Islam one may speak in a way of 'anonymous' Muslims in faiths other than the Islamic, of persons who breathe the spirit of Islam in truth, though officially belonging elsewhere.[87]

From an Islamic perspective, the resolution of the problem of salvation is easy and uncomplicated. Faith is an assent by the heart between God and the individual. It is *an inner act*; no one can have access to it except God. This means, at the end of the day, no one can really know who will be saved. This was the reason why the question of establishing an attitude towards other faiths has not arisen as a theological question, but only as a question of law, i.e. how Muslim authorities should deal with the affairs of non-Muslim subjects.

The argument I have offered so far supports the conclusion that from an Islamic point of view, it is possible to argue that those people who are outside the Islamic faith might possibly be saved if firstly they accomplish the ethical and religious requirements of their own traditions, and, secondly, if, when the truth is revealed to their inner being, they do not deliberately and consciously cover up[88] that truth, because of the social and economic pressure of their environment. I also believe that it is possible to maintain such a conclusion if one takes 'the spirit of the Quran' into account.

Historical Manifestation of the Principles of 'Islamic Pluralism'

Having drawn up a theoretical framework for a plausible 'Islamic pluralism', I would like to offer a brief historical survey in order to exhibit the practical implementation those theoretical propositions. Let me first start with the time of the Prophet himself. When the Prophet arrived in Medina, he demolished the current structure of that society and introduced a new structure. Instead of tribal relations and tribal values, he established a relation and value system which connects people through religion and citizenship. Immediately after he settled in Medina, the Prophet formed a constitution, a treaty which regulates the affairs of all the inhabitants of Medina, including the Jews.[89] As far as the overall conclusion of this thesis is concerned, the document itself is a concrete example of how the principles of 'Islamic pluralism' worked in practice. It begins with this introduction:

> In the name of God, the Merciful, the Compassionate!
> This is a writing of Muhammad, the prophet between the believers and Muslims of the Quraysh and Yathrib and those who follow them and are attached to them and who crusade (*jahadu*) along with them.[90]

The document itself contains 47 articles. I will only cite those related to our topics. They are as follows:

Article 1: They are a single community (*ummah*) distinct from (other) people.

Article 16: Whoever of the Jews follows us has the (same) help and support (*nasr, iswah*) (as the believers), so long as they are not wronged (by him) and he does not help (others) against them.

Article 25: The Jews of Banu 'Awf are a community (ummah) along with the believers. To the Jews their religion (*din*) and to the Muslims their religion. (This applies) both to their clients and to themselves, with the exception of anyone who has done wrong or acted treacherously; he brings evil on himself and on his household. [Articles 26 to 31 repeat this rule for six other Jewish tribes of Medina at that time.]

Article 37: It is for the Jews to bear their expenses and for the Muslims to bear their expenses. Between them (that is to one another) there is help (*nasr*) against whoever wars against the people of this document. *Between them is sincere friendship and honourable dealing, not treachery.* A man is not guilty of treachery through (the act of) his confederate. There is help for the person wronged[91] (my italics).

The Prophet extended the act of citizenship and co-operation to the Christians of Najran. His letter to the inhabitants of Najran can give us an idea about the relation between the Prophet of Islam and the Christians of that time. It reads as follows:

This is a letter from Muhammad the prophet, the Messenger of God, to the people of Najran. . . Najran and their followers have protection (*jiwar*) of God and the *dhimmah* of Muhammad the prophet, the Messenger of God, for themselves, their community, their land, and their goods, both those who are absent and those who are present, and for their churches and services (no bishop will be moved from his episcopate, and no monk from his monastic position, and no church-warden from his church-wardenship) and for all, great or little, that is under their hands.[92]

In Islamic culture, the term *al-dhimma* is formed to define the status of Jews and Christians who lived within the Islamic political domain. *Al-dhimma*, grants Christians and Jews an equal status with Muslims in religious, economic and administrative domains. In return they are asked to pay *jizya*, poll-tax. Although the *al-dhimma* status itself was initiated for Christians and Jews, it was also applied to Zoroastrians when Persia was conquered and to Hindus and Buddhists when India came under the rule of Islam.[93]

As Ahmad points out, the constitution of Medina, and other covenants of the Prophet with Jews and Christians, laid down the principles for building a multi-cultural and multi-religious community. These fundamental rules that the Prophet established have been practised throughout Islamic history. Islam has given *dhimmi*s of the Islamic community equal religious and cultural rights alongside Muslims. In other words their autonomy and their internal affairs and their freedom to practise their religion were guaranteed by Muslim authority.[94]

The term *ummah*, contrary to its conventional usage by Muslims so far, was historically used in a manner that includes *dhimmi*s who lived within the Islamic community. In the constitution of Medina, the Prophet defined the Jews as *ummah*, thereby integrating them into the already formed Muslim community. Later this term was applied to Christians. Now, it is possible that the term *ummah* can be applied to all the adherents of major traditions. One of the main aims of the constitution of Medina was to create a community spirit between different tribal and religious segments of the society. It was not only a formal treaty but also a code of practice which encourages sincere and honourable friendship between the various functions, as stated in article 37.[95]

After Muhammad, the four rightly guided caliphs and the rulers of Ummayyads and Abbasids always maintained the rules and regulations established by the Quran and the *sunnah* of the Prophet. For instance, when Jerusalem came under the rule of Islam, Omar the second caliph, signed a pact with the inhabitants of Jerusalem, which granted security for them and their property. It recognised rights of the Jews and Christians of Jerusalem freely to practise their religion; their churches and synagogues were respected and left intact.[96]

Under Islamic rule non-Muslims have always been encouraged to participate in and contribute to the intellectual and political life of the community. Christians and Jews were welcome to hold posts in public offices. Several of them became ministers, especially in the period of the Abbasids. For instance, most of the palace physicians in Baghdad were Christians, whereas the Jews were good at money exchanging, and they contributed to the welfare of society as tanners and gold- and silver-smiths. During the Mamluke era, a number of able Coptic Christians in Egypt were appointed as state secretary.[97]

Such religious tolerance was well observed by the Muslim rulers of Christian Spain. At that time, in Spanish cities like Cordova, Seville and Toledo (which was the ancient capital of the Goths) Christians, Jews and Muslims lived in peaceful coexistence.[98] Christian communities had their own judges who settled their disputes in accordance with Gothic law. Those 'arabised' Spanish Christians played a remarkable role in transmitting Christian culture in the Islamic world, and also the Islamic civilisation to the Christian world. There were many distinguished scholars and philosophers, the most famous of whom was Moses Maimonides.[99]

During the middle ages, the Ottoman Sultans fully observed the right of the sizeable numbers of Christians and Jews as well as other non-Muslims who lived within the Ottoman provinces. For instance, when Spain was reconqured by Christians, in 1492, Sultan Bayezid II permitted and even encouraged a great number of Jews from Spain and Portugal who were expelled from their own homelands to settle in the Ottoman realms to rebuild their lives.[100] Depending upon the Quranic and Prophetic injunction as well as the tradition which they received through their forefathers, the Ottomans developed a *millet* system through which the society was divided into estates, each of which was expected to function according to a given traditional position.[101]

Now, I would like to cite an Ottoman *ferman*, (decree) issued by Sultan Mehmed III, dated March 1602, which demonstrates an attitude typical of the Muslim ruler's towards non-Muslim subjects. It reads as follows:

> Since, in accordance with what Almighty God the Lord of the Universe commanded in His Manifest Book concerning the communities of Jews and Christians who are the people of the *dhimma*, their protection and preservation and the safeguarding of their lives and possessions are a perpetual and collective duty of the generality of Muslims and a necessary obligation incumbent on all the sovereigns of Islam and honourable rulers,
>
> Therefore it is necessary and important that my exalted and religiously inspired concern be directed to ensure that, in accordance with the noble Sharia, every one of these communities that pay tax to me, in the days of my imperial state and the period of my felicity-encompassed Caliphate, should live in

tranquillity and peace of mind and go about their business, that no one should prevent from this, nor anyone cause injury to their persons or their possessions, in violation of the command of God and in contravention of the Holy Law of the Prophet.[102]

My aim, however, here is not to enumerate the selected historical documents and practices, most of which support the argument which I am proposing, but to glance through Islamic history in order to identify a common official attitude of Muslim authority towards non-Muslim subjects. It is not, indeed, within the scope of our work to present a well-documented or meticulously surveyed historical account of 'Islamic pluralism'. Nor do I intend to demonstrate that Islam, both theoretically and practically, can match the norms of liberalism of modern times; concepts such as tolerance and equality, as understood by the liberals of our time were not known. In a Muslim's eyes, undefined and purposeless tolerance was not a virtue, and vague intolerance was not a crime.[103]

Islam and Modernity

As Nasr points out, Islam has responded to the cultural and political supremacy of the modern West through generating three different movements, namely, Islamic modernism, traditionalism, and Islamic revivalism or 'fundamentalism'. Islamic modernism, which appeared in the late nineteenth and early twentieth centuries, is an attitude that wants to modify or reformulate Islam in a manner that would accommodate the norms of modernity. It aims to highlight and put more stress on those aspects of Islam which are in accord with the norms of modernity, while attempting to moderate those Islamic issues that are in direct conflict with modernity, such as the *Shariah* laws and women's rights. As for Islamic revivalism or 'fundamentalism', although it is in accord with Islamic traditionalism in its acceptance of the authority of the Quran and the *sunnah* and its emphasis upon the *Shariah*, it is a religio-political movement which differs from traditionalism in its approach to the cultural heritage of traditional Islam. The 'fundamentalists' do not seek wisdom but 'truth'. For instance, they are not interested in the wisdom of revelation, the sacred scripture of Islam, but a plain formulated truth asserting a motto which they often use for their own goal. Therefore, they tend to ignore the traditional commentaries on the Quran. Nasr maintains that 'fundamentalists' basically differ from traditionalists in their approach to Sufism; they are quite dismissive of the value of the esoteric dimension of Islam. One of the criteria which distinguish the traditionalists from the 'fundamentalists' and the modernist is art, especially traditional art. They have no appreciation of traditional art at all, whereas traditional Islam believes that traditional art as 'crystallised truth' is one of the vehicles of wisdom. Like the modernists, the 'fundamentalists' accept with open arms modern science and technology without considering its negative impact upon the Muslim's spiritual life.

Nasr, as a traditionalist himself, believes that traditional Islam is rich enough to generate an alternative culture through which Muslims can confront the intellectual and material supremacy of the West.

He maintains that traditional Islam ignores nothing of the traditional character. It accepts the authority of the Quran, as the Word of God, and the traditional commentaries upon the Quran. It considers *hadith* as one of the important sources of tradition. It grants utmost value to the esoteric dimension of Islam, i.e. Sufism, without belittling its exoteric dimension.[104]

Throughout his career Nasr never lost hope in the revival of traditional Islam. He believes that God who has infinite mercy will eventually revitalise tradition in order to save humanity from the spiritual and intellectual impoverishment caused by modernity. Nasr maintains that tradition does not oppose modernity just for the sake of opposing. It wants to assimilate it within the higher dimension of spirituality. For Nasr, modernism stands for anything 'which is cut off from the Transcendent, from the immutable principles which in reality govern all things and which are made known to man through revelation in its most universal sense'.[105] He maintains that modernity stands for what is basically human; in this sense, it is anthropomorphic since it simply negates any principle that transcends the human, whereas, tradition stands for what is essentially sacred.[106]

As for the Islamic world today, Nasr argues that contemporary Muslims do not feel confident enough to make a thorough examination and careful criticism of the norms of modernity, because of the intellectual, technological and thus political superiority of the West. Most of them prefer to go along with the West and attempt to harmonise Islam with anything Western, including socialism, existentialism or liberalism. Such attempts, believes Nasr, are bound to fail, because Islam never allows 'itself to become reduced to a mere modifier or contingency *vis-à-vis* a system of thought which remains independent of it or even hostile to it'.[107] Nasr, therefore, believes that Islam still has a part to play in the modern era:

In reality nothing could be further from the truth. Despite serious encroachments upon the body of Islam by modernism and the confusion caused within the mind and soul of certain Muslims caught between the pull of their tradition and Western ideologies and values, Islam remains very much a living tradition on both the exoteric and the esoteric levels. Were this not so it would hardly be possible to speak of applying the teachings of Islam to the problems faced by modern man. If nothing had been left of Islam save some kind of sentimental or apologetic modern interpretation, one could hardly expect it to provide an antidote for the maladies caused by modernism itself. But authentic and traditional Islam continues to live. It is there to be studied and rediscovered in its totality by turning to both the oral and written sources of the tradition as it has been lived and transmitted since its revelation, and to its present-day manifestations in the souls and lives of the Muslim peoples in various parts of the Islamic world under the different historical, political and social conditions imposed upon the once unified *dar al-islam* during the most recent period of Islamic history.[108]

Christianity and Christ: A Muslim View

Nasr believes that since the unity of the human race and universality of the intellect permit the followers of one religion to think and evaluate the theological perspectives of another religion, as a Muslim he feels free to offer some comments of on Christian theology.[109] The main criticism Nasr makes of contemporary Christian theologians is that they are fundamentally mistaken in wanting to bind theology to the ever-changing norms of secular culture. Nasr argues that truth must always come before expediency. Theology, as a science of God, should explain 'the temporal with reference to the Eternal and not the Eternal in the light of temporality which is made to sound very *real*, central, and important by being baptized as the human condition, the modern world, or urgent human problems'.[110] Therefore, Nasr believes that it would be a grave mistake to permit secularised culture to determine the future of theology.[111] He argues that modern science cannot be a source for theology: it is not theology that should ask guidance and get inspiration from science, and surrender its findings.

Rather it is modern science and its findings which must be examined from the metaphysical and theological point of view. What theology, however, must do is to 'cast the light of the Eternal upon the experiences of mankind's terrestrial journey'.[112]

As for Christianity as a revealed religion, it manifests different aspects of the same reality, the Reality which is manifested in all religions and traditions. Nasr points out that Islam, Christianity and Judaism, as the Abrahamic traditions, should be examined together, if anyone who belongs to one of the three traditions wants to understand the other two. For instance because of its distinct celestial archetype, Christianity manifests truth in a manner that is different from both Islam and Judaism. For instance, there is a strong emphasis on miracles in Christianity; it manifests a mystery which 'veils the Divine from man'. Islam, however, looks quite plain. Miracles do not play a major part in it and therefore 'it is man who is veiled from God'.[113]

Within the Abrahamic tradition, Nasr argues, Judaism represents the law, the exoteric dimension, while Christianity represents the spiritual, esoteric, and Islam integrates law within spirituality and presents tradition with its original unity containing both law and 'the way'. From another point of view, Judaism is essentially based on the fear of God, Christianity on the love of God, and Islam is based on the knowledge of God, while all contain these three fundamental aspects which govern the relation between humankind and God.[114]

There is a basic difference between Islam and Christianity as far as the sacred law is concerned. The Christian view of law – which is summarised in a saying of Christ: 'Render therefore unto Caesar the things which are Ceasar's' – is an attitude which creates a dichotomy between human legislation and divine legislation which eventually played a significant part in the secularisation process. In Christian society, however, law did not enjoy Divine sanction as it did in both Jewish and Muslim societies. That is why people in the West, looking at Islam through Christianity, have often had difficulties in understanding the meaning and role of the *shariah* in Islam.[115]

In addition to many common characteristics, Islam and Christianity are in conflict with one another in some of the main theological issues such as the Trinity, the Incarnation and the crucifixion of Jesus. As Nasr points out, the Trinity is essentially alien to the Islamic perception of God since Islam is based on the Absolute in itself not its manifestations.[116] He, however, sees a meeting point between Christians and Muslims in these conflicting issues. He suggests that if the Trinity is interpreted as 'three hypostases which do not destroy the unity of God'[117] as some Sufis see it, and the Incarnation as the incarnation of the Logos through Christ, and then Christians and Muslims may have some common ground upon which to meet.

As has been discussed in the first section of this part, Islam strongly believes the universality of revelation. The Quran mentions the names of 27 prophets and indicates that many prophets were sent before the Prophet of Islam. The Quran pays special attention to Jesus, and his mother Mary.[118] The Quranic 'Christology', which is independent of the Christian understanding of Christ, has played an important role in the Islamic conception of sacred history.[119]

The Quran states that Jesus as a righteous prophet (6:85) was miraculously born from a virgin mother, Mary, without a father (3:45–47; 19:22–23). He was sent as a messenger to Israel (3:49–51). He is not more than a messenger (4:171; 5:75; 43:59, 63–64); neither God (5:17–72) nor son of God (9:30) but he is the Word of God (4:171) and was sent with the gospels (5:46). Contrary to Christian belief, the Quran also insists that he was not crucified (4:157).

Nasr believes that the way to settle the conflicting issues between Christians and Muslims such as the Trinity, the Incarnation, the divinity of Christ, is not to accept one party's version and reject the other's. Nor would it be the solution to suggest Muslims believe those doctrines which are in accord with Islam, such as the virgin birth, and reject those which conflict with it such as the crucifixion of Jesus or the Incarnation and the divine sonship of Christ. Such an attempt would not be successful at all, since Muslims 'can never accept the view that parts of the Quran are sort of indirectly inspired and very lofty while other parts are just accretions of the view prevalent in communities in Mecca'.[120] According to Nasr, the real solution for these problems between Muslims and Christians should be sought in a type of epistemology which allows a single reality to be seen in two different ways. He explains:

It is very important to bring out this issue, and I think in the future if there is to be serious Islamic-Christian dialogue on the question of Christology it will have to deal with this issue of whether modern epistemology and modern philosophy allow, in fact, *a single reality to be seen in two different ways* without causing what appears to the modern mind as logical contradictions.

From the traditional philosophical point of view it is possible for a single reality – especially of the order of Christ's final end – to be seen in two ways by two different worlds, or from two different religious perspectives, without there being an inner contradiction. It is modern Western philosophy that does not allow such a thing. By creating a one-to-one correspondence between a reality perceived and the knowledge thereof, while negating multiple levels or the hierarchy of being, this philosophy denies the possibility that God in his infinite power and wisdom could create two major world communities holding two different views concerning the earthly end of Christ. . . But when it comes to the question of the life of Christ, the historical life, on the level of fact it is either the Christian or Islamic version that can be held. But on the empirical level one cannot hold both simultaneously, at least not in the framework of modern epistemology[121] (my italics).

I am not sure whether the outcome of introducing such an epistemology would be useful in seeking a solution to the problems. There are a number of problematic points in the passage quoted. Firstly, although Nasr is implicitly suggesting another form of epistemology different from the modern one, he never spells out its basic characteristics. One wonders whether there really is a well-defined and well-established perennial epistemology which can cast light on the issues in question or whether this is an escape route from a plain logical contradiction.

Secondly, it is difficult to understand the suggestion that one single reality can be seen differently in two different worlds without falling into logical contradiction. It connotes Wittgenstein's 'seeing as' and Hick's 'experiencing as' notions. But I cannot understand how such a notion can be applied to the issue of Jesus' final end. If Jesus actually, i.e. historically, was crucified, how would it be possible to perceive that the event which we are talking about did and did not happen, i.e. Christ was and was not crucified? This is a plain contradiction. But if Nasr says that in spite of what happened in history with regard to Jesus' final end, God indeed is able to show one single reality in two different ways, this is something else. God is omnipotent and in his infinite power and wisdom can show one reality in two different ways. But does this involve telling a lie? What would be the purpose of telling different accounts to different communities? Let us accept that Jesus was crucified. If this is the truth, then the morally perfect Divine

Agent could not but report the event as it happened. There is no reason why he should report the event otherwise. So Nasr's suggestion of an alternative epistemology which could show one event in two different ways does not seem to be plausible.

Notes

Introduction

1 Approaches in religious studies, such as phenomenological and scientific studies, which claim a certain degree of neutrality have become popular during the last three decades. To adopt such an approach requires an identity which can feel comfortable in employing any of those approaches. Those people who have a strong religious identity and whose character is shaped through a devotional religious life often face difficulties in adopting such a so-called value-free approach. However, in defence of the religious perspective, one could argue that no position is absolutely value free. The claim that all truth should be considered from a value free perspective is, paradoxically, a value judgement of a kind.

2 Exclusivism was generally an official line and defended in the World Council Churches as well as most of the Vatican Councils. Some other writers who maintain the Kraemerian line are Stephen Neill, Lesslie Newbigin, Norman Anderson, Henricus van Straelen, Hans von Balthasar, Paul Hacker.

3 There is not of course one form of inclusivism. Apart from these writers, some others who maintain some forms of inclusivism are Gavin D'Costa who is a sound critic of Hick's version of pluralism, Rayumando Panikkar, Bede Griffiths, Hans Küng and Edward Schillebeeckx.

4 Some other writers who speak of pluralism are Alan Race, Paul Knitter, Rosemary Ruether and Gregory Baum. During the last two decades, the form of pluralism Hick advocates has become popular. There are a number of studies conducted on the topic. Recently, Kenneth Thomas Rose completed a Ph.D. thesis, *Knowing the Real: John Hick on the Cognitivity of Religions and Religious Pluralism* (1992) at Harvard University. Although he develops his criticisms against Hick in the direction that I will be pursuing in this dissertation, he does not fully explore the religious implication of Hick's hypothesis.

5 It is no accident that more than one hundred writers in the West have critically evaluated Hick's ideas in books and articles, whereas there are hardly any who have seriously considered Nasr's traditional views.

Chapter One – Intellectual Biographies

1 John Hick, *God Has Many Names* (London: Macmillan, 1980), 1.
2 Ibid., 2–3.
3 Ibid., 2.
4 Ibid.
5 G. D'Costa in 'the most comprehensive single guide to Hick's life' somehow misses out this very important point about Hick's confession with regard to his state of spiritual searching. *John Hick's Theology of Religion: A Critical Evaluation* (London: University Press of America, 1987), 5.
6 Hick, *God Has*, 2.
7 John Hick and Michael Goulder, *Why Believe in God?* (London: SCM Press Ltd., 1983), 40–41.
8 John Hick, *Disputed Questions in Theology and the Philosophy of Religion* (New Haven: Yale University Press, 1993), 139.
9 Hick, *God Has*, 2.
10 John Hick, *Problems of Religious Pluralism* (London: Macmillan, [1985] 1988), 1.
11 After the 1970s Hick devoted almost all his intellectual endeavour to the promotion of the hypothesis of religious pluralism and the reformulation of some of the traditional Christian doctrines.
12 At that time, Hick was an evangelical Christian, but was not yet completely successful in suppressing the questioning side of his personality. His preference to attend a degree course in philosophy, rather than theology or Biblical Studies, might indicate that he was, then, still seeking a rationally justifiable religious worldview rather than a faith which ignores reason.
13 John Hick, *Faith and Knowledge* (Glasgow: Collins Fount Paperback, [1957] 1978), V.
14 Hick, *God Has*, 3.
15 I believe that Hick's pacifist attitude – which functions as one of the main incentives in his formulation of a hypothesis of religious pluralism – was consolidated by his own experience during the Second World War.
16 For pacifist Hick, to decide to serve in a war was not easy and the decision was eventually reached through 'a guidance from Heaven': 'In the Second World War, I was a conscientious objector on Christian grounds to military service. It was a very difficult question whether to take the absolutist line of refusing any kind of alternative service or to volunteer for the army's medical corps or for some such organisations as the Friends' Ambulance Unit. Initially I was strongly inclined to the absolutist position, but was nevertheless in deep uncertainty, and prayed during a period of weeks for guidance. One morning I woke up with all my doubts completely resolved and with an absolute certainty that I must take the route of alternative service. It was utterly clear to me that I could not stand aside from the war, although I must not engage in its violence and destructiveness. And so I joined the Friends' Ambulance Unit and served in it for the duration of the war. The leading which I received was

as clear and as morally compelling as if I had heard a voice from heaven.'
Hick and Goulder, *Why Believe*, 76–77.

17 Hick, *Faith and Knowledge*, V.
18 Hick, *Disputed*, 139–140.
19 Hick, *God Has*, 3.
20 Ibid.
21 Hick, *Faith and Knowledge*, V.
22 D'Costa, *Hick's Theology*, 9–10.
23 Hick, *Faith and Knowledge*, VI.
24 This book was well-received in the United States, though hardly known in Britain until the second and revised Fontana edition came out in 1967. Hick, *Faith and Knowledge*, VI.
25 In the first part, Hick criticised the conception of faith as propositional belief, which includes the Thomist Catholic view of faith as representative of the traditional Christian notion of faith, and also some modern interpretations of faith such as those of William James, F. R. Tennant, Pascal and Cardinal Newman.
26 Terence Penelhum, comparing Hick with the Thomist account of faith, brings out the philosophical meat of Hick's view, characterising it as 'a remarkably balanced and resourceful combination of neo-orthodox theology and philosophical analysis'. See further details *Problems of Religious Knowledge* (London: Macmillan, 1971), 16–20.
27 Hick, *Faith and Knowledge*, VII.
28 For further explanation of this point see Terry Richard Mathis, *Against John Hick: An Examination of his Philosophy of Religion* (London: University Press of America, 1985), 6–7.
29 One might claim that there is a subtle relationship between a need for the focus on personal religion on the one hand, and the domination of ecclesiastical organisation in the history of Christianity on the other.
30 I shall later on argue that it is misleading to utilise a culture-specific term such as 'religious experience' in order to illustrate a hypothesis which attempts to embrace the major religions of humankind.
31 Amongst the writings of Oman, *The Natural and Supernatural* (Cambridge: Cambridge University Press, 1931) had a significant impact on Hick.
32 Hick, *Faith and Knowledge*, VIII.
33 Hick, *Problems*, 2.
34 Ibid., 3.
35 Hick, *God Has*, 4.
36 Paul Badham, 'Life and Work of John Hick' in *God Truth and Reality*, ed. Arvind Sharma. (London: Macmillan, 1993), 4.
37 Hick states: 'Even as a teacher at Cornell University, Princeton Theological Seminary and Cambridge University it did not occur to me that the subject which I taught, namely the philosophy of religion, should properly be just that and not simply the philosophy of Judeo-Christian tradition.' *Disputed*, 140.
38 John Hick, 'The Christology of D. M. Ballie', *Scottish Journal of Theology*, 11 (No. 1, 1958), 1–12.
39 Hick, *Disputed*, 139–140.

40 Ibid., 141.
41 Hick, *God Has*, 5.
42 For further information see Hick, *Problems*, 5–10.
43 Hick, *Disputed*, 141.
44 Another issue with which Hick has become increasingly engaged is the doctrine of the Incarnation. In this book, Hick argued that the doctrine of the Incarnation should be understood metaphorically or mythologically, not literally as had apparently been the case for most of Christian history. A literal understanding of the doctrine in question is implausible in the light of modern philosophical thought and recent developments in New Testament scholarship.
45 John Hick, *God and the Universe of Faiths* (London: Macmillan, [1973] 1988), 131.
46 When Hick says 'the major traditions' or 'great traditions of mankind' he means these five great religions, namely Christianity, Judaism, Hinduism, Buddhism and Islam. It appears that having studied Hinduism and Buddhism and having had first hand contact with adherents of these religions in India and Sri Lanka, Hick was moved by the transforming power of these religions and later decided to include them in his hypothesis of religious pluralism.
47 Hick, *Problems*, 11–12.
48 As Hick realises it was not the content of the book itself but its provocative title that caused controversy among ordinary church-goers. It is also due to its title that the book has succeeded in making a significant contribution to the growth of Christian understanding by communicating widely, selling over 30,000 copies in the first five months after its publication. Ibid., 13.
49 Ibid., 12.
50 Harold Hewitt, Jr., ed. *Problems in the Philosophy of Religion: Critical Studies of the Work of John Hick* (London: Macmillan, 1991), XI.
51 Several important books came out of these conferences. For instance, in 1986, Hick invited S. T. Davis, J. R. Cobb, D. R. Griffin, J. O'Connar and J. Prabhu to address the issue of the concept of God from various perspectives including feminism and process theology. In this conference, Hick also put forward his hypothesis of religious pluralism in order to receive constructive criticism from such respected scholars. In 1989, the proceedings of this conference were published as a book, *Concepts of Ultimate* edited by Linda J. Tessier. In 1989, having published *An Interpretation of Religion*, Hick offered his hypothesis of religious pluralism to the criticism of the eminent scholars of religious pluralism such as G. D'Costa, C. Gillis, C. R. Mesle, P. Badham and W. Rowe. Out of this conference yet another important book was published under the title of *Problems in the Philosophy of Religion: Critical Studies of the Work of John Hick*, edited by Harold Hewitt, Jr. (1991). At the ninth annual the Philosophy of Religion Conference, Hick invited the major representatives of religious realism and non-realism including D. Cupitt, S. T. Davis, B. R. Hebblethwaite, D. Z. Phillips to address the issue of the reality of God. The proceedings were published in a book *Is God Real?* by Joseph Runzo (1993).

52 Apart from Smith, one also has to mention the names of such thinkers as Masao Abe, John Bowker and Ninian Smart among those who have contributed to Hick's thought. John Hick, *An Interpretation of Religion: Human Response to the Transcendent* (London: Macmillan, 1989), XIV.

53 Hick, *God Has*, 5.

54 Smith believes that every positive theology is an idol, and to believe in the exclusive truth of a theology of one religion is idolatry. See Wilfred Cantwell Smith, 'Idolatry: In Comparative Perspective' in *The Myth of Christian Uniqueness*, ed. John Hick and Paul F. Knitter (London: SCM Press Ltd., 1987), 53–68.

55 A number of articles published in various journals which examined these two pluralistic views together indicates such similarity. See Dirk J. Louw, 'Theocentrism and Reality-centrism: a critique of John Hick and Wilfred Cantwell Smith's philosophy of religion', *South African Journal of Philosophy*, 13 (Part: 1, 1994), 1–8; and see also Kenneth Surin, 'Towards a "materialist" critique of "religious pluralism": An examination of the discourse of John Hick and Wilfred Cantwell Smith,' in *Religious Pluralism and Unbelief: Studies Critical and Comparative*, ed. Ian Hamnett (London: Routledge, 1990), 114–129; K. Surin, '"A Certain Politics of Speech": "Religious Pluralism" in the Age of the McDonald's Hamburger', *Modern Theology*, 7 (October 1990), 67–100.

56 Badham, 'Life and Work', 5.

57 This is the title of Hick's own autobiographical sketch. See Hick, *God Has*, 1.

58 Hick, *Disputed*, 144–145.

59 This is a title given to those who are, or are believed to be, the descendants of the Prophet Muhammad.

60 Seyyed Hossein Nasr, 'In Quest of the Eternal Sophia' in *Philosophers Critiques D'eux Memes – Philosophische Selbstbetrachtungen*, ed. Andre Mercier & Suilar Maja, Vol. 5–6, 1980, 113.

61 His father, Seyyed Valiollah Nasr occupied a position equivalent to that of today's Minister of Education during the late Qajar period and under Reza Shah. His mother was a member of the Kia family. Although Valiollah Nasr was a traditional man who educated Nasr in the traditional manner, and had never been abroad, he was well aware of the challenges of the modern world to traditional Islamic civilisation. This must be the reason why he decided to send Nasr to America for a Western education. See William C. Chittick, 'Preface' to *The Complete Bibliography of the Works of Seyyed Hossein Nasr from 1958 through April 1993*, ed. Mehdi Aminrazavi and Zailan Moris (Kuala Lumpur: Islamic Academy of Science of Malaysia, 1994), XIII.

62 Nasr, 'Quest of the Eternal', 113.

63 The main incentive that led Nasr, while he was in his late twenties to the rediscovery of Islamic tradition was, I believe, the effect of his early traditional education. Such a childhood experience, which involved many sentimental feelings, pulled him back to his roots, that is, traditional Islam, which had had a profound influence on his childhood. One can even claim that the rediscovery of traditional Islam meant for Nasr, reunion with his roots.

64 Nasr, 'Quest of the Eternal', 113.
65 Amy Aldrich, 'The Soul and Science of Islam,' *The George Washington University Magazine*, Spring 1992, 15.
66 Seyyed Hossein Nasr, 'Traditional Cosmology and Modern Science: An Interview with Seyyed Hossein Nasr' interview by Philip and Carol Zaleski, *Parabola*, VIII (No. 4, 1983), 20–21.
67 Chittick, 'Preface', XIV.
68 Nasr, 'Quest of the Eternal', 114.
69 Ibid.
70 It is interesting to note that in his youth John Hick, like Nasr, was interested in Oriental philosophy. But, unlike Nasr, he did not find it attractive enough to enter it.
71 As Chittick rightly observes Nasr's interest in the study of tradition finally caused him to change his field from geology and geophysics to history of science and philosophy. See 'Preface', XIV.
72 Nasr, 'Quest of the Eternal', 115.
73 Ibid.
74 Ibid.
75 Seyyed Hossein Nasr, *Knowledge and the Sacred* (Albany: State University of New York Press, [1981] 1989), 107.
76 Ibid., 180.
77 Although to a lesser degree, I myself, have also felt this 'existential' impact when reading the work of Nasr and Schuon.
78 Nasr, *Knowledge*, 108.
79 Nasr, 'Quest of the Eternal', 120.
80 Mehdi Aminrazavi, one of his students, illustrates this point: 'A major criticism that has been raised by the modernist school of Islam against Nasr has been his reluctance to venture beyond being an exponent of the teachings of the traditional masters. Being fully capable of doing so, he has refrained from becoming engaged in the critical assessment of the teachings of the traditional masters. It is as if he is in a flower garden but not desiring to destroy any one flower, he therefore chooses not to walk on them but remains still and observe the beauties before him.' M. Aminrazavi, 'The Intellectual Contribution of Seyyed Hossein Nasr' in *Complete Bibliography*, XXIV.
81 Nasr describes their experience at the tomb of Ibn 'Arabi as follows: 'We entered the sanctuary reverentially and, after offering prayers, sat down by the tomb of the great metaphysician and saint, which was surrounded by an atmosphere of contemplative tranquillity and calm. The peace and serenity of the atmosphere were accentuated by the fact that, at that moment, Burckhardt and I again happened to be alone in that sacred space, which, like every veritable sacred space, is the echo of the Centre and a reflection of Eternity upon the moving image of peripheral existence. While meditating upon the verities or the *Haqiqah* at the heart of Sufism, I occasionally glanced at the contemplative face of my companion, whose closed eyes seemed to gaze inwardly upon the heart and whose face reflected the light of the Intellect before which his mind and soul were transparent.' S. H. Nasr, *Traditional Islam in the Modern World* (London: Kegan Paul International, [1987] 1994), 293–294.

82 Ibid.

83 Ibid., 254.

84 Nasr, 'Quest of the Eternal', 116.

85 The first publication of The Iranian Academy of Philosophy was Nasr's first volume of *An Annotated Bibliography of Islamic Science*, in 1975. Nasr with the collaboration with William C. Chittick (and Peter Zirnis in the second volume 1978), published a brilliant and very important bibliography of Islamic science.

86 Aldrich, 'Soul and Science', 17.

87 Chittick, 'Preface', XIV.

88 Nasr, 'Quest of the Eternal', 116.

89 Ibid.

90 In 1970, Nasr delivered the Charles Strong Memorial Lecture on 'Sufism and the Perennity of Mystical Quest' in several Australian Universities.

91 W. Chittick characterises the book as follows: '... *Ideals and Realities of Islam*, perhaps the only book on the religion of Islam written by a devout born Muslim which will not offend a devout Christian.' See 'Preface', XV.

92 Nasr, 'Quest of the Eternal', 117–118.

93 In this book his affiliation to the perennial philosophy is noticeable. In the prologue, for instance, the term Revelation represents the *sophia perennis*, everlasting truth of all traditions. Although he presents a descriptive analysis of conceptions understood and methods used for study of Nature by the Ikhwan al-Safa, al-Biruni and Ibn Sina, he occasionally refers to the perennial philosophy in its relevant context.

94 In his *Exploration in Islamic Science*, (London: Mansell, 1989), Z. Sardar attempts to disparage Nasr's achievement in this field relating his ideas to Ismailism, Pythagoreanism and Hermeticism, by highlighting the non-Islamic characteristics of these schools. In the book, Nasr is not criticised due to the merits and demerits of his ideas through offering a sound argument, but due to his failure to fulfil Sardar's requirements of Islamic religious orthodoxy. Nasr is found 'guilty' because according Sardar under the cover of 'Islamic' he infiltrates non-Islamic ideas into the realm of Islam, as if there are clear definitions of Islamic and non-Islamic. Contrary to what Sardar assumes, using these Quranic principles (10:47; 11:118; 17:15), one can find a feasible relation between Islam and the ancient wisdom of past generations.

95 Seyyed Hossein Nasr, *Man and Nature: the Spiritual Crisis in Modern Man* (London: Mandala Unwin Paperbacks, [1968] 1990), 13.

96 Nasr, 'Quest of the Eternal', 118.

97 Nasr, *Knowledge*, VIII.

98 Ibid.

99 Muhammad Salman Raschid, in his review article 'Philosophia Perennis Universale Imperium', tries hard to find some inconsistencies in the book. He is quite dismissive about the achievements of Nasr, having evaluated him from 'a Muslim perspective'. For me, the reason why Raschid misses the message of this book should be sought in his experience of 'considerable difficulty in understanding the precise points and claims' which Nasr makes. See Muhammad Salman Raschid, 'Philosophia Perennis Universale Imperium,' *Religion*, 13 (April 1983), 158.

100 Huston Smith, review of *Knowledge and the Sacred*, by S. H. Nasr, in *Philosophy, East and West*, 34 (January 1984), 111.
101 Aldrich, 'Soul and Science', 15.
102 Mehdi Aminrazavi and Zailan Moris in *Complete Bibliography* listed 401 articles and 51 books by Nasr in 21 languages.
103 Chittick, 'Preface', XVII.
104 See Nasr, *Traditional Islam*, chap. 5.
105 The Library of Living Philosophers series edited by Lewis E. Hahn and published by Open Court Publishing Company is preparing a volume on Nasr's philosophy.
106 He himself describes how he writes: 'When I want to write something, the ideas begin to simmer in my mind, and I draw from two things. Either I'm writing a scholarly article, let's say on a particular philosopher, and I have to refer to his writings, to his books and the page numbers, etc., the scholarly underpinning of the writing. Or I'm writing a metaphysical or philosophical or mystical essay which does not need this scholarly apparatus. But in both cases, whether I draw from my own intellectual powers and memories or whether I have to go to the library and look up new footnotes and so forth, once that source is ready, then it begins to simmer within me. And whether I'm walking, or even sometimes talking, that essay or that book is being spun in my mind. And then I usually sit down and I pray. As a Muslim I pray five times a day, but besides that I do a kind of special contemplative prayer to cleanse myself, prepare myself, and then somehow what was prepared in my mind flows upon the page. I have very little trouble. All the work is done beforehand, and once I put the pen in my hand I always have trouble keeping up with my mind. I never type my writings; I always use an old-style pen with ink, not a ball-point pen. I still write with a traditional instrument, and I write very, very fast because everything is ready in my mind and it just flows through.' Nasr, 'Echoes of Infinity: An Interview with Seyyed Hossein Nasr,' interview by Jeffrey P. Zaleski, *Parabola*, 13 (1988), 32–33.
107 Chittick, 'Preface', XIV.
108 Jane I. Smith, 'Seyyed Hossein Nasr: Defender of the Sacred and Islamic Traditionalism' in *The Muslims of America*, ed. Yvonne Yazbeck Haddad, (New York: Oxford University Press, 1991), 91.
109 H. Smith, 'Review', 111.
110 This is the title of Nasr's own autobiographical sketch.
111 Nasr, 'Quest of the Eternal', 120.

Chapter Two – Religion and Tradition

1 Tomoko Masuzawa has made such an attempt. He believes that modern religious studies are ambivalent toward the question of origin. Historians of religion in the present time state that they have resigned from speculative quests for the origin of religion; at the same time, they claim that concepts of absolute beginnings are essential for religion itself. For further information see *In Search of Dreamtime: The Quest for the Origin of Religion* (Chicago & London: The University of Chicago Press, 1993).

Notes

2 Eric J. Sharpe, *Comparative Religion: A History* (London: Duckworth, 1975), 27.

3 Belief in the theory of evolution can function as a touchstone which is, in fact, clearly able to show the immense differences of opinion between Hick and Nasr with regard to science and religion in their distinctive world view. However, Hick believes that, although there are some mysteries and missing links within the evolutionary theory, 'it is abundantly evident, and agreed by virtually everyone who has confronted the evidence, that life has indeed gradually developed on earth from the simplest unicellular organisms to the most complex mammals.' *Interpretation*, 82. On the other hand, for Nasr, the modern evolutionary theory 'is a desperate attempt to substitute a set of horizontal, material causes in a unidimentional world to explain effects whose causes belong to other levels of reality, to the vertical dimensions of existence.' *Knowledge*, 169–170. He also notes that the theory of evolution is the result of 'the deification of the historical process' which has taken the place of religion by metamorphosing from a scientific truth to a 'faith'. *Knowledge*, 234–235.

4 Friedrich Max Müller, Natural Religion (Collected Works I, 1899), 188, quoted in Eric Sharpe, *Comparative*, 39.

5 Sharpe, *Comparative*, 39.

6 Emile Durkheim, *The Elementary Forms of the Religious Life*, trans. Joseph Ward Swain (London: George Allen & Unvin Ltd [1915] 1971), 47.

7 Rudolf Otto, *The Idea of the Holy* (London: Oxford University Press, [1923] 1952), Cf. Chap. IV.

8 It is interesting to note that Hick's characterisation of the Real as the noumenal ground of phenomenal religious experience bears some resemblance to Otto's idea of *numen*. Like Otto's *numen*, Hick's Real is also ineffable and experienced in very mysterious ways.

9 Brill Ed, *The Basic Writings of Sigmund Freud*, 930, quoted in Eric Shape, *Comparative*, 201.

10 William James, *The Varieties of Religious Experience: A Study of Human Nature*, (London: Collier-Macmillan [1961] 1968), 42.

11 It is equally true that in the Islamic world the concept of religion sounds entirely Islamic. In Islamic literature, the word *din*, which signifies a broader sense than religion, to include senses such as judgement and retribution, custom and law, can, nevertheless, be regarded as the Arabic equivalent of the term religion. To illustrate the point, it is just sufficient to mention two distinctive yet similar Islamic definitions of religion. Sayyid Sharif al-Jurjani in his *Ta'rifat* defines religion (*din*) as 'a divine institution (*wad'*) which creatures endowed with reason receive from the Apostle'. Bajuri in his elementary manual defines religion (*din*) as 'the corpus of prescriptions (*ahkam*) which God has promulgated through the voice of His Apostle' See *Encyclopaedia of Islam*, new ed., s.v. 'Din' by L. Gardet.

12 It is interesting to note that Peter B. Clarke and Peter Byrne think that there are certain resemblances between Hick's religious interpretations and the old-age secular theories of religion such as that of Max Müller and others. See *Religion Defined and Explained* (London: St. Martin's Press, 1993), 80.

215

13 John Hick, *Philosophy of Religion*, (London: Prentice-Hall, 1963), 3.
14 Hick, *Interpretation*, 3.
15 Hick illustrates that a secular phenomenological definition of religion can best be observed in Ferre's definition, that is 'One's religion ... is one's way of valuing most intensively and comprehensively', whereas a secular psychological definition of religion can be observed in Gallowey's definition of religion as 'man's faith in a power beyond himself whereby he seeks to satisfy emotional needs and gains stability of life which he expresses in act of worship and service'. *Interpretation*, 16.
16 John Hick, *God and the Universe*, 133.
17 Hick, *Interpretation*, 3.
18 Hick, *God and the Universe*, 141.
19 He states: 'What however of the lesser traditions, and the new religious movements which have sprung up within, say, the last hundred and fifty years – including Bahai, Christian Science, Rissho Koseikaki, Soka Gakkai, Tendiko, the Church of Jesus Christ of Latter Day Saints, Spiritualism, Theosophy, the Kimbanguist movement, Johrei, the Unification Church...? To what extent are these also contexts of salvation/liberation? The same soteriological criterion and the same index of saintliness are valid, but are harder to apply to the much slighter data-base presented by such relatively recent phenomena. Our pluralistic hypothesis does not entail any *a priori* judgement concerning the salvific value of these new movements.' *Interpretation*, 307–308.
20 Wittgenstein applies the family resemblance model to the concept of 'game', but not to religion. See *Philosophical Investigations*, (Oxford: Basil Blackwell, [1953]1968), Para. 66–67.
21 As Clark and Byrne point out there are some obvious disadvantages to this family resemblance model. In particular, if the class of 'religions' do not have essential unity, then how can Hick form a feasible hypothesis of religious pluralism which attempts to encompass the major traditions? See *Religion Defined*, 89.
22 Ibid., Hick, *Interpretation*.
23 Another reason one might think of is that the question of the origin is intrinsic in human nature. When one starts to investigate the nature of anything, the process of investigation naturally leads to the question of origin. Hick could not form a grand hypothesis if he had not taken the issue of the origin of religion into account.
24 As will be explicated in the fifth chapter, the Real of Hick is utterly unknowable and ineffable. Hence, we cannot apply any concrete qualities which we have received through our traditions to the Real. But the question here is how this ineffable Real (even the oneness cannot be applicable) is able to affect the human psyche. Hick would argue that since Real *an sich* is neither conscious nor unconscious, it is able to affect the human psyche as the way that the sun provides light and heat for organic life on the earth.
25 Hick, *Interpretation*, 169.
26 Ibid.
27 Ibid., 154.
28 Ibid., 165.

understandings are con
developed, and therefore
productions there are im
divine truth. In other w
specific cultural interpret
49 Hick, *God and The Unive*
50 Ibid.
51 By this term it is meant
and ends in the first mill
52 Hick, *Interpretation*, 23.
53 Ibid., 28.
54 Ibid., 31.
55 Ibid., 30.
56 See John V. Apczynski,
Implicitly Exclusivist?' M
57 Wilfred Cantwell Smith,
New American Library, |
58 Smith observes that *Isla*
Muslims' religion, poses
59 Historically people were
understanding of specific
concept or overt system
Philosophers on Religion: A
1987) sufficiently illustra
case, were more intereste
of God, immortality, mira
system.
60 Northbourne, *Religion*, vi
61 Seyyed Hossein Nasr, *T*
Press, 1993), 62.
62 I mean Christianity as sp
Randall.
63 Hick, *Interpretation*, 378.
64 Smith, *End of Religion*, 14
65 Ibid.
66 Ibid., 148.
67 Ibid., 148–149.
68 It is rather odd that W. C
into consideration as far
69 Seyyed Hossein Nasr, 'R
Muslim Dialogue', *Musli*
70 Islam's unwavering and
including homosexuality,
the norms of modernity a
71 The book itself has soug
content of everlasting per
drawn from various trac
relevance and importance
opinion, it lacks a certai

29 Ibid., 295.
30 Furthermore, Hick claims that a religion functions as a cognitive filter making sense of the presence of the Real, 'functioning as a system for filtering out the infinite divine reality and reducing it to forms that could be coped with.' Ibid., 163.
31 The relationship between the content of the Quran and the culture of seventh century Arabia is a modern issue which has caused some controversies among Muslim intellectuals. The traditional view, represented notably by Nasr, would argue that the Quran is a verbatim revelation of God through Muhammad who was nothing but the vehicle, and who did not add anything to the content of the Quran whether ideas or words. The embodiment in the Quran of the cultural concepts of that time and the values of that community should be considered together with the fact that the sole aim of the Quran is to communicate with and transform the people it addresses. Hence, traditionalists believe that the aim of revelation is not to give specific cultural details of Arabia but to convey the sacred principles; that culture is nothing but the vehicle of the divine word. On the other hand, the modernists, represented notably by Fazlur Rahman, claim that 'the Quran is the divine response, through the Prophet's mind, to the moral-social situation of the Prophet's Arabia, particularly to the problems of the commercial Maccan society of his day'. Fazlur Rahman, *Islam and Modernity: Transformation of an Intellectual Tradition* (Chicago & London: The University of Chicago Press, 1982), 5. From this argument they want to conclude that the contents and the principles contributed by the culture of that day, such as the *Shariah* law, were meant for the people of the Prophet's Arabia. What is of little relevance to our time, does not bind contemporary Muslims, whereas the ethical and theological content of the Quran is universal and therefore binding on Muslims.
32 Shabbir Akhtar, *A Faith for All Seasons: Islam and Western Modernity* (London: Bellew Publishing, 1990), 74.
33 According to Hick, religions were born through human responses to the Transcendent. Such an idea implies that human openness to a divine reality is vital in the emergence of a new religion. In other words, religions were invented through human responses. The traditional view in this respect argues that it is not a human but God alone who can 'invent' religions. 'Religion is founded on the belief – or on the certainty – that God has shown his love as well as His justice and His wisdom, to the world in the first place and most directly in His Revelation of Himself through the founder (or founders) of the Religion in question. This implies that the founder did not invent that Religion, his part being entirely receptive, in so far as a distinction can be made between his divine and human nature.' Lord Northbourne, *Religion in the Modern World* (London: J. M. Dent & Sons Ltd., 1963), 2–3.
34 John Hick, 'On Grading Religions', *Religious Studies* (17 December 1981), 457–458.
35 Ibid., 459.
36 Ibid., 460.

37 In her book, *A Histo*
   Armstrong defends thi:
   geographical circumsta
   created. In my opinion,
   and suffers from over-
   over-stretches the avai
   credible.
38 Hick, *God and the Univ*
39 Ibid., 134–135.
40 Ibid., 135.
41 One wonders how H:
   convincing evidence th
   that was more suitable :
   such a thesis sounds
   religion is the product c
   This theory of religior
   secular and naturalist:
   phenomenon of religio
   such theories is that the
   question and are intenc
   them in a manner th:
   theories would have b
   predict correctly the co
   data with regard to e
   certain places. That is t
   what really occurred in
   indicate that it is plaus
   emergence of a new re
   work.
42 Mircea Eliade, 'The (
   Religion 4, (Part. 1, 196
43 Ibid., 156.
44 He concludes: 'To kno
   that he is equally a creat
   of the cosmic, psycholc
   we no longer accept the
   religions. To give only a
   not – and as a matter c
   the time of Max Mül
   naturalistic cults and o
   natural objects. But the
   is not the tree, the spri
   which is manifested throu
45 Ibid., 166.
46 Ibid., 168.
47 Ibid., 168–169.
48 It is true that no theo
   relativity. Hence, there :
   one. The traditional re

traditional point of view. In this context, W. N. Perry's remarkable but neglected work, *A Treasury of Traditional Wisdom* (Cambridge: Quinta Essentia, 1971) is a key work for the understanding of what traditional authors mean by the perennial philosophy.

72 See Huston Smith, *Beyond the Post-Modern Mind* (London: Quest Books, [1982] 1989) chap. 3 for a comprehensive analysis of this definition.

73 Aldous Huxley, *The Perennial Philosophy* (London: Fontana Books, [1946] 1958), 9.

74 Ibid.

75 Sheldon R. Isenberg and Gene R. Thursby, 'Esoteric Anthropology: "Devolutionary" and "Evolutionary" Orientations in Perennial Philosophy', *Religious Traditions: A Journal in the Study of Religion*, 79 (1984–1986), 177.

76 Ibid., 178.

77 Ibid., 195–196.

78 Religious unity is one of the reflections of such an all-encompassing unity. In this context, N. Smart believes that the perennial philosophy is defective since it presupposes a religious unity in the diverse teachings of religions. See *The Religious Experience of Mankind* (Glasgow: Collins Fount Paperbacks, [1969] 1981), 675. But, contrary to what Smart thinks, the perennial philosophy does not seek unity in the formal expression of religions but in their esoteric essence.

79 It is of interest to note that Hick's theory of faith and his notion of 'experiencing as' say more or less the same thing from a different perspective.

80 Peter Brierley, *'Christian' England: What the 1989 English Church Census Reveals* (London: Marc Europe, 1991), 30.

81 In the 1992 general election in Britain over forty percent of people under the age of 25 did not vote.

82 See Roger Finke, 'An Unsecular America' in *Religion and Modernization: Sociologist and Historian Debate the Secularization Thesis*, ed. Steve Bruce (Oxford: Clarendon Press, 1992), 145–169.

83 Ibid., 163–164.

84 It is estimated that there are already more Muslims than Methodist in the UK. And towards the end of the '90s, it is estimated that there may be more Muslims than Reformed Christians. See John Clayton, *Thomas Jefferson and the Study of Religion*, (Inaugural Lecture delivered at Lancaster University, 1992), 21.

85 For further information see Jørgen Nielsen, *Muslims in Western Europe* (Edinburgh: Edinburgh University Press, 1992).

86 Mauriac has said that the coming millennium 'will either be the century of religion or it will be nothing'. See Juan Arias 'Hans Kung: Seeking a Religious Dialogue In a World that Lacks Values' in *Leonardo: the Age of Discoveries*, 1992, 163–165.

87 Nasr, *Knowledge*, 65.

88 Ibid., 66.

89 *Encyclopaedia of Religion*, 1987 ed., s. v. 'Tradition'.

90 Nasr, *Knowledge*, 67.

91 Ibid., 68.

92 'I am Alpha and Omega' (Rev. I. 8). 'He is the Beginning and the End' (Quran, 57:3).

93 Northbourne, *Religion*, 4–5.

94 Here, Nasr is not aware of the danger which the consequences of such thinking may produce. To say, in order to be aware of the sense of tradition, there necessarily should be a secularised world, is to say that the secularisation process which he wants passionately to reverse was necessary to be able to formulate the concept of tradition. In other words, those writers who oppose and therefore want to reverse the secularisation process are not aware of the fact that it is the secularised world itself which constitutes the basis for their existence.

95 Nasr, *Knowledge*, 68.

96 Ibid., 80–81.

97 This idea is not very alien to the Islamic tradition. For instance, the Quranic term *al-lawh al-makhfudh* (a Guarded Tablet) is treated as the archetype of the Quranic revelation.

98 Nasr, Knowledge, 74.

99 Ibid., 74–75.

100 Ibid., 76–77.

101 Ibid., 72–73.

102 There are various ways of classifying religious traditions by focusing on particular aspects. One of the common approaches to religion in its classification is to distinguish the theological tenets i.e. the doctrinal features of a religion, from its application or manifestation in its community. In this respect, Robert Redfield's characterisation of religions as great and little tradition is worth mentioning. For Redfield, 'great tradition' is the tradition of the philosophers, theologians, and the literary people, cultivated and handed down as a body of well-thought beliefs and principles, whereas little tradition is the tradition of illiterate people in their village communities. As far as Islam is concerned, one would say the 'officially' recognised beliefs and doctrines can be seen as the great tradition, whereas the manifestation of its beliefs and principles in local cultures can be regarded as the 'little tradition'. See for further information, *The Little Community and Peasant Society and Culture* (Chicago & London: Phoenix Books, The University of Chicago Press, [1956] 1963).

103 Ibid., 73.

104 Seyyed Hossein Nasr, *Ideals and Realities of Islam*, (London: Aquarian, [1966], 1994.), 16–17.

105 Nasr, *Sacred Science*, 56–57.

106 This term was coined by Frithjof Schuon. See *Light on the Ancient Worlds* (London: Perennial Books, 1965) trans. Lord Northbourne: 138–143.

107 Nasr, *Sacred Science*, 60.

108 Nasr, *Knowledge*, 84.

109 The best example to illustrate the point is the state of the family in both traditional and modern societies. In every traditional society the principles that maintain the family and family values are very well established. Tradition in this context not only functions as the source of family values but is also the source of a mechanism that preserves its

integrity. Modernism, although it does not deny the relevance of family values, creates norms and an environment in which it is hard to maintain such values.

110 Eric Hobsbawm, 'Introduction: Inventing Traditions' in *The Invention of Tradition*, ed. Eric Hobsbawm and Terence Ranger (Cambridge: Cambridge University Press, [1983] 1987), 1–14.

111 Thomas Dean, review of *Knowledge and the Sacred*, by Seyyed Hossein Nasr, in *Philosophy East and West*, 34 (April 1984), 217–226.

112 Seyyed Hossein Nasr, 'Response to Thomas Dean's review of *Knowledge and Sacred*', *Philosophy East and West*, 39 (January 1985), 87.

113 Ibid.

Chapter Three – Knowledge and the Ultimate

1 William L. Rowe identifies the most interesting aspects of Hick's scholarly works as being (a) his thesis that the world is religiously ambiguous, (b) his efforts to show that his soul-making theodicy can justify the existence of evils and (c) his comprehensive theory of religious pluralism. See 'John Hick's Contribution to the Philosophy of Religion' in *God Truth and Reality: Essays in Honour of John Hick*, ed. Arvind Sharma (London: M. St. Martin's Press, 1993), 18. Although Rowe's findings on this point are similar to mine, I am more inclined to favour Hick's theory of faith over his theodicy.

2 If one analyses the content and implication of this interesting proposition, one could see that there is a subtle relationship between the notion of the religious ambiguity of the universe and the following passage from Pascal's *Pensées*, which has been quoted on more than ten accounts by Hick: 'It was not then right that He should appear in a manner manifestly divine, and completely capable of convincing all men; but it was also not right that He should come in so hidden a manner that He could not be known by those who should sincerely seek Him. He has willed to make Himself quite recognisable by those; and thus, willing to appear openly to those who seek Him with all their heart... He so regulates the knowledge of Himself that He has given signs of Himself, visible to those who seek Him, and not to those who seek Him not. There is enough light for those who only desire to see, and enough obscurity for those who have a contrary disposition.' Pascal Blaise, *Pensées* (London: J. M. Dent & Sons Ltd., 1931), 118.

3 Hick, *Faith and Knowledge*, 139; see also 'Sceptics and Believers' in *Faith and the Philosophers*, ed. John Hick (London: Macmillan, 1964), 247–248.

4 In Islamic tradition in general, the proofs (not arguments) for the existence of God have been mostly employed as a kind of intellectual exercise not for producing a faith, but for confirming an already existent belief. What generally happens is that people, in the majority of cases, adopt the faith of their families or communities. At the stage of the formation of faith, the arguments for the existence of God may influence the person one way or other. The *kalam* scholars in Islamic tradition say

222

that there are two forms of faith (*iman*): one is the faith through imitation (*al-iman al-taqlidi*) and the second, the faith through reasoning (*al-iman al-tahqiqi*). The majority of the scholars of *kalam* consider that the faith acquired by imitation is not a sound one. For further discussion of the issue see Toshihiko Izutsu, *The Concept of Belief in Islamic Theology – A Semantic Analysis of Iman and Islam* (Yokohama: Yurindo Publishing Co. Ltd., 1965), chap. VI. In this respect it is said that proofs for the existence of God can be useful for elevating the individual from faith through imitation to faith through reasoning.

5   Hick clearly illustrates this point: 'God was known to them [the man of faith] as a dynamic will interacting with their own wills, a sheer given reality, as inescapable to be reckoned with as destructive storm and the life-giving sunshine, or the hatred of their enemies and the friendship of their neighbours. They did not think of God as an inferred entity but as an experienced reality... It would be as sensible for a husband to desire a philosophical proof of the existence of the wife and family who contribute so much of the meaning and value of life for him as for the man of faith to seek a proof of the existence of the God within whose purpose he believes that he lives and moves and has his being.' *The Existence of God* (London and New York: Macmillan, 1964), 13–14.

6   Hick has contributed to the prevailing criticisms of the ontological arguments by tackling the concept of necessity. He scrutinises the idea that God is a necessary being, a very wide-spread notion among medieval Christian and Islamic philosophers, including Thomas Aquinas, Ibn Sina, al-Ghazzali and Ibn Rushd. Hick maintains that the term 'logical necessity' or 'logically necessary' is only applicable to propositions, not to things. Therefore, the idea of necessary being is not only unintelligible but also meaningless. That is to say, for Hick God can be a factually or ontologically, but not logically necessary being if he exists eternally and independently. See 'Necessary Being', *Scottish Journal of Theology*, 14 (December 1961), 353–369; *The Universe of Faiths*, 75–91. On the other hand, Charles Hartshorne argues that Hick's division between logical and ontological necessity is meaningless. See 'John Hick on Ontological and Logical Necessity', *Religious Studies*, 13 (June 1977), 155–165. For further discussion of Hick's notion of necessary being see Kai Nielsen, 'Truth Conditions and Necessary Existence', *Scottish Journal of Theology*, 27 (August 1974), 257–267; D. R. Duff-Forbes, 'Hick, Necessary Being, and the Cosmological Argument' *Canadian Journal of Philosophy*, 1 (June 1972), 473–483.

7   Hick, *Interpretation*, 75–79.

8   Ibid., 80.

9   For Hick's evaluation of the design argument from the perspective of the religious ambiguity of the Universe see Ibid., 81–91.

10 Ibid., 123.

11 Gavin D'Costa, 'John Hick and Religious Pluralism: Yet Another Revolution' in *Problems in the Philosophy of Religion: Critical Studies of the Work of John Hick*, ed. Harold Hewitt, Jr. (London: Macmillan, 1991), 7–8.

12 Hick, *Interpretation*, 74.

13 Empiricism has gained its high credibility through the European Enlightenment. Science and its benevolent result, technology, are amongst the outcomes of empiricism. Scientific observation and experiment are regarded as the most reliable methods not only in science but also in the humanities. Now it is not surprising to see that recently there has been a growing tendency among the students of religious studies to undertake researches which are empirical in nature, i.e. carried out through questionnaires, interviews, fieldwork, etc. From the traditional point of view, such a methodology is futile since it is not able to deduct something substantial as regards the knowledge of Ultimate Reality. What counts in attaining the knowledge of the Ultimate is the 'flash' of intuition or revelation together with the divinely illuminated intellect. The twin sources of knowledge, intuition and the intellect are able to go beyond the temporal norms of a culture and can reveal the Real.

14 See the passage quoted in fn. 2.

15 To say that sense perception is coercive is to say that we cannot doubt its veracity. Such a statement brings Descartes' *cogito* in to mind. It implies that Descartes' doubt with regard to the testimony of the senses is not only unwarranted but also implausible.

16 Hick, *Faith and Knowledge*, 135.

17 Donald F. Henze 'Faith, Evidence and Coercion', *Philosophy*, XLII (January 1967), 78–85.

18 John Hick 'Discussions: Faith and Coercion', *Philosophy*, XLII (July 1967), 272–273.

19 For further discussion of this point see Barry Miller, 'The No-Evidence Defence', *International Journal for Philosophy of Religion*, 3 (Spring 1972), 44–50.

20 As far as Islamic thought is concerned, this problem can be stated in the following manner. In Islam, it is affirmed God is entirely sovereign and the author of everything. Then the question naturally arises: if God is considered to be the creator of everything including human action, how can humans be free to act? In other words, how does God's total control of the universe affect my freedom? Do I have the capacity to act against God's will? To what extent can I be free given that God is the agent of everything that occurs?.

In the Quran regarded as a unitary whole are to be found those verses which affirm the ideas both of Divine sovereignty and of human responsibility. For instance, verses such as 18:28–30; 21:48; 36:54 affirm human responsibility whereas verses such as 18:16; 42:48; 16:95; 10:99 affirm divine omnipotence. That is why the advocates of predestination, as well as those of free will, could claim a spiritual basis for their views. In the Islamic tradition, perhaps for the first time, it was the Kharijites who made this issue the principle of their sects. They, or at least the majority of their subdivisions, acknowledged pre-destination. A minority known as Qadariyya declared a human being to be the author of his or her own acts. Later this view functioned as the basis of the movement of the Mu'tazila. The Mu'tazila, which is considered as by far the most representative of Islamic rationalism, argued that individuals have control over their acts.

God does not create human acts. What God does is to create in the individual the power (*qudra*) corresponding to this act. On the other hand, Ash'ari insisted on God's omnipotence; everything good and evil is willed by God. He creates the acts of individuals by creating in them the power to do each act. Maturidi school of thought, however, affirmed that human acts are created by God, subject to his will and decree. They are, on the one hand, acts of God in one respect (*wajha*), on the other hand, they are in another respect really (not metaphorically) individuals' acts. For instance, Ma'turidi insisted that God will lead astray only those who, He knows, will choose the wrong way, and will guide those who, He knows, will choose the straight path. For further information see A. J. Wensick, *The Muslim Creed: Its Genesis and Historical Development* (London: Frank Cass & Co. Ltd., 1965); W. Montgomery Watt, *Free Will and Human Destination in Early Islam* (London: Luzac & Company Ltd., 1948).

In Christian tradition throughout the centuries, however, it is believed that faith is voluntary. Such a view is affirmed by the Catholic Church by decrees of the First and the Second Vatican Councils. On the other hand those who are influenced by the classical Protestantism of Luther and Calvin believe that faith is involuntary. It is interesting to note that by affirming the belief that faith is voluntary, Hick goes against his own Calvinist tradition. For a Christian account of this issue see Richard Swinburne, *Faith and Reason* (Oxford: The Clarendon Press, 1981), esp. epilogue. Cardinal Newman defended the thesis that faith is voluntary in his *An Essay in Aid of a Grammer of Assent* (Westminster: Christian Classics Inc. 1973).

21 Roy W. Perret, 'John Hick on Faith: A Critique', *International Journal for Philosophy of Religion*, 15 (No. 12, 1984), 57–66.

22 Hick's indiscriminate use of the terms or concepts produced in the secular cultural ambience of the West is one of the signs of that he has adopted a Eurocentric attitude in his approach to other traditions. Such an approach is apparent in his application of Kantian vocabulary in his 'supra-traditional' theory of the major traditions, as if such vocabulary is as relevant to Buddhist, Hindu and Islamic cultures as it has been to Western cultures.

23 Wayne Proudfoot, *Religious Experience* (Berkley & London: University of California Press, 1985), XIII.

24 Ibid., 156.

25 Ibid., 184–185.

26 Hick, *Interpretation*, 153.

27 Ibid., 154.

28 Ibid., 165.

29 Ibid.

30 Ibid., 166.

31 Hick states: 'There is, I suggest, an analogy between mystical visions and the "crisis apparitions" that were recorded so abundantly in the early period of psychical research before radio had been invented and when news could still take days or weeks to be transmitted. A typical case would be one in which, say, a man travelling in India is suddenly killed in an

accident, and that night his wife in England sees an apparition of him that includes some element suggesting death... Then, several weeks later, a letter arrives informing the family of his death. What would seem to have happened in such a case is that the man's sudden crisis experience makes a telepathic impact upon the wife's unconscious mind, and the information thus received is then presented to her consciousness (often at night, when the mind is relatively designated from the world) in the form of an apparition. The apparition – whose content is derived from the percipient's memory and imagination – is hallucinatory in that there is no physical body present where she sees one; but the hallucination is nevertheless veridical, embodying true information.' Ibid., 167.

32 One might even state that since most of the great mystical moments, such as Buddha's, Moses', Jesus' and Muhammad's, occurred before the rise of science, and since the record of such moments might not be accurate (there were no tape recorders at that time), the application of scientific methods in order to explain them does not seem to be plausible.

33 There are two theses considering the studies of mystical experience: the essentialist and constructivist view (using Katz's terms). Those who consider that mystical experiences are essentially the same are classified as essentialists, those who claim that mystical experiences are essentially and characteristically different and generally constructed by the mystics according to the concepts of their culture, are classified as constructivists. Hick can be regarded as constructivist in this sense. I shall deal with this issue in the first section of the second part of this chapter.

34 For a comprehensive analysis of the notion of revelation from perspectives of major traditions see Keith Ward, *Religion and Revelation: A Theology of Revelation in the World Religions* (Oxford: Clarendon Press, 1994).

35 Caroline Franks Davis, *The Evidential Force of Religious Experience* (Oxford: Clarendon Press, 1989), esp. chap. II.

36 Ibid., 19.

37 As I shall discuss in the fifth chapter, one of the main reasons why Hick denies the concrete characteristics of the Real is that he believes these infinite qualities such as infinite love, wisdom, knowledge, power and goodness, are not applicable to the Real because the finite observer intrinsically cannot experience the Infinite Being.

38 The Quran explicitly states that God is transcendent and inexperienceable in the ordinary sense of experience. For instance, it states that 'Nothing is like a likeness of Him', (*Laysa ka mithlihi shay'un*), 42:11; 'Vision comprehends Him not, and He comprehends (all) vision' (*La tudriku al-absar wa huwa yudriku al-absar*): 'And when Moses came at our appointed time and his Lord spoke to him, he said show me (Thyself) so that I may look upon Thee. He said you cannot see me...', 7:143. In Islam, the Divine Being is purely transcendent and above all material conceptions. A likeness of him cannot be imagined, even metaphorically. That is to say, He is not only above all material limitations, but even above the limitation of metaphor.

39 One of the most prominent champions of Islamic orthodoxy, Ibn Taymiyya, reflects a common Muslim belief with regard to the Islamic

doctrine of God. He states that God is not something to be merely perceived, or admired and cherished, but must be recognised as the only One to whom our allegiance is due. For further discussion Fazlur Rahman, *Prophecy in Islam* (London: George Allen & Unwin Ltd., 1957), 101.

40 Muhammad Iqbal in his *The Reconstruction of Religious Thought in Islam* (Lahore: Sh. Muhammad Ashraf, 1982) outlines the main characteristics of mystical experience. But strangely enough, he completely ignores the fundamental differences between mystical experience and prophetic revelation, which we consider as crucial in order to understand *wahy* adequately.

41 That is why I am able to number a hundred thousand mystics in Islamic tradition while I can name only one prophet.

42 Shabbir Akhtar illustrates this point very well: 'The content of the Quran is wholly divine; it constitutes formulations of exclusively divine beliefs about man, the Creator and the created order. The Qur'an's Arabic segments 'descend' on one particular individual, an Arab called Muhammad Ibn 'Abdullah, but he has no role to play in the production of the Qur'anic materials. The prophet of Islam passively receives the sacred text; he repeats it verbatim to his amanuensis for recording. The Qur'an, then, is not in any way co-authored... Muhammad is an instrument of the divine will, a medium through which God's literary endeavours in Arabic reach the human world.' 'An Islamic Model of Revelation', *Islam and Christian-Muslim Relations*, 2 (No. 1, 1991), 96. This fact is also endorsed by the Quran itself: 'I follow naught but what is revealed unto me: If I were to disobey my Lord, I should myself fear the Penalty of the Great Day (to come)' (10:15); 'Say: "I am no bringer of new-fangled doctrine among the messengers, nor do I know what will be done with me or with you. I follow but that which is revealed to me"' (46:9) and also see 11:12–14.

43 Ibn Khaldun, *The Muqaddimah: An Introduction to History*, trans. Franz Rosental; abridged and ed. N. J. Dawood (London: Routledge and Kegan Paul, [1967] 1987), 70.

44 Hick, *Faith and Knowledge*, 27–28.

45 For further analysis of the point that the knowledge issued through mystical experience is generally tradition-specific knowledge and does not exceed the tradition in which the mystic brought up, see Steven T. Katz, 'The "conservative" Character of Mystical Experience' in *Mysticism and Religious Traditions*, ed. Steven T. Katz (Oxford: Oxford University Press, 1983), 3–60.

46 It is interesting to note that the mystics themselves often do not name the occurrences which they encounter as mystical experiences.

47 This must be one of the reasons why the Islamic orthodoxy felt quite irritated by the emergence of *kalam* and *falsafa*.

48 Shabbir Akhtar, 'An Islamic Model of Revelation', 103.

49 Hick, *Faith and Knowledge*, 95.

50 This statement is more accurate than Hick's, because, I believe, it properly corresponds with the feelings of religious people. If one asks religious believers themselves, I think that the majority of them would

attribute their knowledge of God to the information they receive through various channels rather then their own 'experience'.

51 Even those scientists who have made great scientific discoveries often confess that it was generally by a flash of intuition that they were able to reach a result worthy of a life-time reasoning and investigation.

52 For the difference between Christian revelation and the Islamic notion of *wahy* see Ward, *Religion and Revelation*, 173–192.

53 Ibn Khaldun, *The Muqaddimah*, 70.

54 Rahman, *Prophecy*, 30.

55 Ibid., 31.

56 Ibid., 35.

57 Ibid., 39.

58 Ibid., 96.

59 Ibid., 103.

60 Ibn Khaldun, *The Muqaddimah*, 75–76.

61 Ibid., 76.

62 Ibid., 77.

63 Ibid.

64 Ibid.

65 Ibid, 77–78.

66 Rahman, *Prophecy*, 107.

67 William A. Graham devotes his entire work to the analysis of the relation between the categories of *wahy* in the Islamic tradition. He pays special attention to the category of *al-hadith al-qudsi*. Unfortunately, in this work he totally neglects to examine the nature of *wahy* as I indicate ii here. See *Divine Word and Prophetic Word in Early Islam* (Paris: Mouton & The Hague, 1977).

68 It is important to note that in Islam the articles of faith must depend upon the Quran not the *hadith*, since it is believed that the *hadith* is historically contingent and thus contains human elements. Consequently Muslim theologians have claimed that any Muslim who rejects an article of faith that originates from the Quran, such as believing in life after death, excludes himself or herself from the boundaries of Islam. A Muslim who rejects an article of faith that comes from the *hadith*, such as believing in the second coming of Christ, cannot, however, be excluded from Islam.

69 Yaqub Zaki, 'The Quran and Revelation' in *Islam in a World of Diverse Faiths*, ed. Dan Cohn-Sherbok (London: Macmillan, 1991), 47.

70 Ibn Khaldun, *The Muqaddimah*, 78.

71 Ibid., 78.

72 Bukhari states: 'Narrated 'Aisha, the mother of the faithful believers: Al-Harith bin Hisham asked Allah's Apostle, "O Allah's Apostle! How does *wahy* come (*ya'ti ka*) to you?" Allah's Apostle replied, "Sometimes it comes like a ringing of the bell, this form of *wahy* is the hardest of all and then this state passes off after I have grasped what is revealed. Sometimes the angel comes in the form of a man and talks to me and I grasp whatever he says." 'Aisha added: "Verily I saw the Prophet while *wahy* was descending on him on a very cold day and noticed the sweat dropping from his forehead."' Muhammad bin Ismail bin Ibrahim al-Mughra al-Bukhari, *Sahih al-Bukhari*, The Book of Revelation, Hadith No. 2.

73 Hick, *Interpretation*, 173.
74 Hick, once again, defended his critical realism in 1991 at the ninth annual Philosophy of Religion Conference at Claremont Graduate School against D. Z. Phillips, Don Cupitt and Jack Verheyden. The proceedings of this conference are published in *Is God Real?* ed. Joseph Runzo (London: Macmillan, 1993). At this conference Hick re-stated his critical realist position by claiming that non-realism is élitist and pessimistic, while religious realism is optimistic.
75 Recently, Rev. Antony Freeman in his controversial book, *God in Us: A Case for Christian Humanism*, (London: SCM Press, 1993) has reopened the debate between realism and religious non-realism and defended a religious non-realism by stating flatly that 'there is nothing out there'. Hick participated in this debate by writing a letter to *The Independent* (9 August 1994). In his letter Hick argued that his own critical realism is the most viable stand-point between naive religious realism and non-realism.
76 Interpretation, 173–174.
77 Ibid., 175.
78 Dawi Z. Phillips, *Death and Immortality* (London: Macmillan, 1970), 48.
79 Ibid.
80 Don Cupitt, *Taking Leave of God* (London: SCM Press, 1980), 1.
81 Hick, *Interpretation*, 199–205.
82 Ibid., 177.
83 Ibid., 205–206.
84 Ibid., 348.
85 Ibid., 348–349.
86 Ibid., 248.
87 So far as I have understood Hick's exposition of this 'infallibilist theory of knowledge', I would say that Nasr's notion of sacred knowledge falls within the scope of such a theory. Hence, Hick's critique of the infallibilist theory can be seen as a critique of Nasr's theory of knowledge.
88 Hick, *Faith and Knowledge*, 200–201.
89 Ibid., 202.
90 Ibid., 204.
91 As a believer I have never assumed that I am, according to my own capacity and experience, forming my own concept of God.
92 It appears from the perennialist perspective that Hick is open to the charge of being confused about the hierarchical structure of being which can be attained by a hierarchical means of knowledge. In the perennial philosophy, and to a certain extent in Neoplatonism, it is claimed that the realm of metaphysics, which includes the metaphysical aspects of God, can only be attainable through the intellect. In such a hierarchical structure of being it is assumed that the physical world is situated at the bottom. This realm can be perceived by sense perception, that is, scientific observation and the senses. One can say that Hick is mistaken in insisting that the infallibilist theory of knowledge is self-defeating because it cuts off all contact with common experience by elevating knowledge to a metaphysical status.
93 Nasr is well aware of this predicament: 'Since the traditionalist school encompasses so much and has dealt with so many aspects of religion in

depth and in such a unique fashion, it might be asked why it is not better
known in academic circles. Why is it that in France where the books of
Gue'non are still reprinted regularly fifty or sixty years after their
appearance, he is passed over nearly completely in silence in university
circles, and why in other countries where there is not the same planned
conspiracy of silence the situation is not much better? The reason must
be sought in the nature of the *philosophia perennis* itself. To accept to
follow it demands not only the dedication of the mind of the scholar but
his whole being. It needs a total *engagement* which is more than many
scholars are willing to give except those who speak as committed
Christians, Jews, Muslims, etc. from the vantage point of their own
particular religion.' *Sacred Science*, 64.
94 A. C. Lloyd, *The Anatomy of Neoplatonism* (Oxford: Clarendon Press,
1990), chap. V–VI; and also see Philip Merlan, *From Platonism to
Neoplatonism* (Netherlands: The Hague, 1975); Richard Tyrell Wallis,
Neoplatonism (London: Duckworth, 1972).
95 Nasr, *Knowledge*, 288.
96 W. T. Stace, *Philosophy and Mysticism* (London: Macmillan, 1960),
chap. 2.
97 Robert Charles Zaehner, *Mysticism: Sacred and Profane* (Oxford: Oxford
University Press, [1957] 1961), chap. 8–9.
98 Here I prefer Katz's classification of the mysticism that is categorised
according the relation between the mystics and the nature of his or her
experience. For a detailed analysis of such a classification see Steven T.
Katz, 'Language Epistemology and Mysticism' in *Mysticism and
Philosophical Analysis*, ed. S. T. Katz (London: Sheldon Press, 1978),
22–74; and also 'The "Conservative" Character of Mystical Experience'
in *Mysticism and Religious Traditions*, ed. S. T. Katz: 3–60; 'Mystical
Speech and Mystical Meaning' in *Mysticism and Language*, ed. S. T.
Katz (Oxford: Oxford University Press, 1992), 2–41.
99 See Robert M. Gimello, 'Mysticism in Its Contexts' in *Mysticism and
Religious Tradition*, 61–88.
100 See Micheal Stoeber, 'Constructivist Epistemologies of Mysticism: A
Critique and a Revision', *Religious Studies*, 28 (March 1992), 107–116.
101 Hick himself admits that he is in agreement with Steven Katz on this
issue. *Interpretation*, 169.
102 The difference between the traditional point of view and other
essentialist views is significant. In this context, Nasr observes that the
proponents of essentialist views, with the exception of those who
represent the sapiential perspective, are mistaken in their 'oversenti-
mentalized' and intellectually impoverished approaches, confusing 'the
unity which transforms forms with a unity which disregards forms'.
They are, he claims, unable to acknowledge the unity which,
metaphysically speaking, lies at the opposite pole of uniformity.
Knowledge, 288.
    In considering the constructivist theories – including Hick's theory –
Nasr acknowledges that such approaches play an essential role in
establishing the importance and significance of sacred forms by
emphasising the role of sacred languages and sacred scriptures, but he

feels they fall short in their lack of awareness of the fact that 'sacred form is not only form as particularity and limitation but also that it opens unto the Infinite and the formless'. 'The Kabbalists', says Nasr, 'do begin with the text of the Hebrew Bible and not with the Sanskrit Upanishads, but when they speak of the *En Sof* they are dealing with that Reality, which one can recognise as the same Reality with which the Advaitist school of the Vedanta is concerned'. *Knowledge*, 289.

103 See Rudolf Otto, *Mysticism East and West: A Comparative Analysis of the Nature of Mysticism* (London: Macmillan, 1932).

104 See Evelyn Underhill, *Mysticism: A Study in the Nature and Development of Man's Spiritual Consciousness* (London: Methuen & Co. Ltd., [1911] 1930); *The Life of the Spirit and the Life of To-day* (London: Methuen and Co. Ltd., [1922] 1928); *The Essentials of Mysticism and Other Essays* (London & Toronto: J. M. Dent & Sons Ltd., 1920); *Practical Mysticism: A Little Book for Normal People* (London & Toronto: J. M. Dent & Sons Ltd., [1914] 1931).

105 Ninian Smart, 'Interpretation and Mystical Experience', *Religious Studies*, 1 (1965), 75–87.

106 Ibid., 86.

107 Katz, 'Language, Epistemology', 23–24.

108 However, this very idea of the necessity of knowing something that is strictly transcendent indicates that such knowledge has to be 'given' knowledge not 'gained'.

109 Antony Flew, *A Dictionary of Philosophy*, s.v. 'Metaphysics'.

110 Nasr, *Knowledge*, 133.

111 I am aware of the fact that from a Kantian point of view such a claim is an unwarranted innovation, since it upholds the possibility of a science of pure reason which was the very target of Kant's critical philosophy. Nevertheless, Nasr would assume that apart from the revealed principles, no philosophy can possess a binding power over one's understanding of reality.

112 Nasr, *Knowledge*, 133.

113 William C. Chittick points out how incongruent Nasr's ideas appear in the contemporary context: 'For others inclined toward a more rationalistic world-view, such as that which prevailed in the West until a few years ago and is now so much on the upsurge in the East, Nasr's writings are annoying precisely because they present articulately and coherently a supposedly "outmoded" religious view of reality without the slightest sign of any inferiority complex toward the modern world or any attempt to "apologize" (in the common sense of the word) for the point of view represented.' Chittick, 'Preface', XIII.

114 Ibid., 130–131.

115 Ibid., 131.

116 Donald Evans, in his paper entitled 'Can Philosophers Limit What Mystics Can Do? A Critique of Steven Katz', considers the difficulties in grasping the nature of mystical experience and concludes, in agreement with my views, that one could only understand the nature of mystical experience by becoming a mystic. *Religious Studies*, 25 (No. 1, 1989), 53–60.

117 Nasr, *Knowledge*, 147.
118 Ibid., 147.
119 Ibid., 148.
120 Ibid., 149.
121 Ibid., 152.
122 Hick has argued that the infallibilist theory of knowledge is misguided because 'instead of scrutinising human knowledge in the sense in which we actually possess it', it has 'sought to view human knowledge from a vantage point outside human nature.' (*Faith and Knowledge*, 202). If one considers this criticism from the perspective of the perennial philosophy, one could respond that the perennialist does not deny the validity of sense perception and reasoning within their own legitimate domain. What the perennialist objects to is the detachment of reason from the intellect in order to give the former absolute authority.
123 In an interview, Nasr tried to counter this kind of criticism. He believes that tradition has always had its own criteria for distinguishing genuine sacred knowledge from the fake. He proposes, for instance, that orthodoxy has functioned as a criterion for genuine spirituality. In traditional civilisations, Nasr adds, the intellectual elite established the criteria for genuine sacred knowledge. Just as in the modern scientific age ordinary people trust the scientific élite, so in traditional civilisation ordinary people used to trust the spiritual élite within their community. Seyyed Hossein Nasr 'Religious Pluralism from the Perspective of the Traditional View' (unpublished interview with S. H. Nasr, by Adnan Aslan, 1992), 13–14.
124 See Richard Swinburne, *The Existence of God* (Oxford: Clarendon Press, 1979).
125 Alvin Plantinga, *The Nature of Necessity*; *God and Other Minds: A Study of the Rational Justification of Belief in God* (Ithaca and London: Cornell University Press, 1976).
126 Aldous Huxley illustrates this point from the perspective of the perennial philosophy. He states: 'The Perennial Philosophy is primarily concerned with the one, divine Reality substantial to the manifold world of things and lives and minds. But the nature of this one Reality is such that it cannot be directly and immediately apprehended except by those who have chosen to fulfil certain conditions, making themselves loving, pure in heart, poor in spirit. Why should this be so? We do not know. It is just one of those facts which we have to accept, whether we like them or not and however implausible and unlikely they may seem. Nothing in our everyday experience gives us any reason for supposing that water is made up of hydrogen and oxygen; and yet when we subject water to certain rather drastic treatments, the nature of its constituent elements becomes manifest. Similarly, nothing in our everyday experience gives us much reason for supposing that the mind of average sensual man has, as one of its constituents, something resembling, or identical with, the Reality substantial to the manifold world; and yet, when that mind is subjected to certain rather drastic treatments, the divine element, of which it is in part at least composed, becomes manifest, not only to the mind itself, but also, by its reflection in external behaviour, to other minds.' *The Perennial Philosophy*, 10–11.

127 Nasr, *Knowledge*, 1–2.
128 Ibid., 2–3.
129 Ibid., 138.
130 Len Bowmen made such an implicit presupposition explicit and raised some question about the metaphysical nature of the hierarchical levels of existence. See 'The Status of Conceptual Schemata: A Dilemma for Perennialists' *A. R. I. E. S.*, 11 (1990), 9–19.
131 Seyyed Hossein Nasr, *The Plight of Modern Man* (London: Longman, 1975), 10.
132 S. R. Isenberg and G. R. Thursby's evaluation of the perennial perspective is worth mentioning. 'All manifestations, of macrocosm and microcosm, are understood as energy/spirit enformed as different levels of "density". And since all existents are on a continuum of hierarchically ordered levels, no dualism – psychological or cosmological – is final. Thus a perennial anthropology acknowledges a hierarchy of levels within which the human being moves toward sustained awareness of internal unity, unity with all humans (since we are all identically constituted by the same laws), and unity with all creation or manifested being. But this very recognition of the unity of all creation opens us to the question of the origin of being – in *what* is our soul-level embedded? This leads us to consider what is beyond Being. For perennial philosophy, what takes us beyond soul to spirit is the continuum of Intellect, from which emerges our experiencing as soul and mind.' 'Esoteric Anthropology: "Devolutionary" and "Evolutionary" Orientations in Perennial Philosophy', *Religious Traditions: A Journal in the Study of Religion*, 79 (1984–1986), 199.
133 Nasr, *Knowledge*, 11.
134 John Hick, *The Centre of Christianity* (London: SCM Press Ltd., [1968] 1977), 9.
135 Hick, *Interpretation*, 327.
136 Nasr, *Knowledge*, 205.
137 Ibid., 205–206.
138 Ibid., 309–310.
139 Isenberg and Thursby clearly illustrate the difference between the perennial philosophy and modern epistemology as far as the nature of such knowledge is concerned: '... Perennial philosophy is in profound disagreement with virtually all Enlightenment and post-Enlightenment assumptions about the nature of knowing. A crucial difference is that knowledge, for perennial philosophy, is not *produced* by either a hypothetico-deductive system or by induction; knowledge is revealed or recollected. Obviously there is knowledge of the material world, and the effectiveness of modern science in utilising knowledge to manipulate matter is hardly to be ignored. But mind – which comprehends reason, imagination and memory – functions as a particular, individualized, formalized manifestation of Intellect. In the vertical sense of causality characteristic of traditional metaphysics, Intellect "causes" mind. To attribute mental functioning to any collection and organisation of physical properties – as is common in contemporary neuro-sciences and attendant philosophies – is regarded by perennialists as a category error

which proceeds from an inadequate ontology'. ('Esoteric Anthropology', 200–201).
140 Nasr, *Knowledge*, 311.
141 Ibid., 311–313.
142 Ibid., 314.
143 Ibid., 317.
144 Ibid., 325.
145 Seyyed Hossein Nasr, *Man and Nature* (London: Mandala Unwin Paperbacks, [1968] 1990), 18.
146 Ibid., 20.
147 Nasr, *Sacred Science*, 83.
148 Nasr, *Man and Nature*, 135.

Chapter Four – The Need for a Pluralistic Approach in Religion

1 For a further analysis of the subject see Peter Bayer, *Religion and Globalization* (London: Sage Publications, 1994); Ronald Robertson, 'Globalization, Politics and Religion' in *The Changing Face of Religion*, ed. James A Beckford and Thomas Luckmann (London: Sage Publication, 1989); 'Globalization, Modernization, and Postmodernization: The Ambiguous Position of Religion' in *Religion and Global Order*, ed. Ronald Robertson and William R. Garret (New York: Paragon House Publishers, 1991); John H. Simpson, 'Globalization and Religion: Themes and Prospects' in *Religion and Global Order*. See also Akbar S. Ahmed and Hastings Donnan, 'Islam in the Age of Postmodernity' in *Islam, Globalization and Postmodernity*, ed. Akbar S. Ahmed and Hastings Donnan, (London and New York, Routledge, 1994).
2 It is interesting to note that the emergence of so-called Islamic fundamentalism, oddly coincides with the rise of the domination of the world by a global system. Hence, one might argue that 'Islamic fundamentalism' is the instantaneous and undigested response of traditional Muslims to the impact of globalization.
3 Beyer, *Religion and Globalization*, 3.
4 I have briefly examined this issue under the section of 'Religion and Change' in chapter two.
5 Hick, *God and the Universe*, 103.
6 Ibid., 106.
7 As we shall see in chapter six, Islam not only possesses a theoretical framework which enable one to postulate such a 'pluralistic' approach, but also has a rich history in which those theoretical principles have been actualised.
8 Surin, 'A Certain "Politics of Speech"', 70.
9 Ibid., 72.
10 Any working solution for the plurality of religions must be religiously convincing. That is so, because only a consensus among the religious communities would possibly reduce religious conflicts and intolerance, which is the one of the main objectives of constituting a theory of religious pluralism.

Notes

11 Hick, *God Has*, 44.
12 It is interesting to note that the frequent use of this passage demonstrates that it is indicative of Hick's formulation of religious pluralism.
13 One might object to Hick by stating that the determination of the religious identity of an individual by the parents is a phenomenon that mostly occurs in traditional societies. In today's global world, individuals have a choice; the parent's religion is not the only option; it is one option among many. In this context, Phillip E. Hammond argues that in today's America personal autonomy plays a more important part in the formation of one's religious identity than one's religious heritage inherited through the parents. See *Religion and Personal Autonomy: The Third Disestablishment in America* (Columbia, South Carolina: University of South Carolina Press, 1992). On behalf of Hick, one can counter such a criticism suggesting that our main concern here is the major traditions such as Christianity, Islam, Judaism, Buddhism and Hinduism. Transference of these religions from one generation to another has still been primarily through the parents; plurality of options is not the case, as is the case for non-traditional religions such as the New Age movement.
14 Hick, *Faith and Knowledge*, 136.
15 Ibid., 137.
16 As Nasr points out, Islam sees itself as the reassertion of the primordial religiosity which might be called 'innate religious tendency' in this context. Seyyed Hossein Nasr, *Sufi Essays* (Albany: State University of New York Press, 1991, 2nd ed.), 132.
17 Bukhari, The Book of Tafsir, Hadith No. 298.
18 Relying on this verse one could speculate that Islam considers that human beings inherit a religious propensity by birth. This primordial religiosity is pure and well-rooted in one's being. There is no alteration in God's creation: he does not contradict himself by primarily creating humankind in a nature which is alien to religion and then inviting him or her to acknowledge religion. Rather, humankind is naturally endowed with a religion which is pure and simple. What humankind needs is to recollect what is already there through the aid of a particular revelation. This also indicates that *islam* is the name of the primordial religion which manifests itself through all revealed religions.
19 I identify Nasr's traditional solution as a religious one, although my suggestion in chapter six differs from his insofar as it seeks a solution within the boundaries of one particular religion, i.e. Islam, rather than seeking a trans-traditional solution i.e. the perennial philosophy.
20 In chapter six, I argue that the exclusive truth claim of Islam differs to a considerable degree from the Christian one.
21 John Hick, 'Religious Pluralism' in *The World's Religious Traditions: Current Perspectives in Religious Studies* (Edinburgh: T & T Clark Ltd., 1984), 147.
22 Hick, *God and the Universe*, 175.
23 Islam, I would suggest, does not consider itself as the only religion that holds truth, but sees itself rather as one member of many divinely revealed religions. In other words, the Muslim does not claim that God revealed the truth through Muhammad only, rather that God revealed the

truth through many prophets before Muhammad. When one reads the Quran, bearing this specific point in mind, one can find a considerable amount of evidence which indicates that *islam* is a name for all revealed religions. This point in itself will be explored in chapter six. Here suffice it to cite one of the verses which indicates such a conclusion:

'Say: "we believe in Allah, and in what has been revealed to us and what was revealed to Abraham, Ismail, Isaac, Jacob and the Tribes and in (the Books) given to Moses, Jesus and the Prophets from their Lord: we make no distinction between one and another among them, and to Allah do we bow our will."' (3:84).

24 Hick, *God and the Universe*, 122.

25 This issue will be examined in detail in chapter six.

26 Hick, *God and the Universe*, 130–131.

27 J. J. Lipner in the article 'Does Copernicus Help? Reflection for A Christian Theology of Religions' *Religious Studies*, 13 (June 1977), 243–258 considers its theological implication from a Christian point of view. For further analysis of Hick's thesis of the Copernican Revolution in theology see Philip Almond, 'John Hick's Copernican Theology', *Theology*, 86 (January 1983), 36–41 and for Hick's response to this article see 'The Theology of Religious Pluralism', *Theology*, 86 (September 1983), 335–340; Gavin D'Costa, 'John Hick's Copernican Revolution: Ten Years After', *New Blackfriars*, 65 (July-August 1984), 323–331; Harold W. Turner, 'Historical Support for Pluralism? The 'The Copernican Revolution' Re-visited', *Mission Studies*, 8 (Part.1 1991), 72–92.

28 D'Costa is one of the prominent critics of Hick. He devoted his entire Ph.D. thesis to the criticism of Hick's 'Copernican revolution'. Although his work possesses many philosophically valid points, as a whole, it is theological in tone. In this work, *John Hick's Theology of Religions* (New York: University Press of America, 1987) D'Costa, through Hick's works, identifies seven arguments in favour of the Copernican revolution. Each argument is thoroughly examined and criticised to show that it should point to a thesis of Christian inclusivism rather than a thesis of religious pluralism. In addition to this work he has written several articles most of which are devoted to criticism of Hick's philosophy of religion. For further information D'Costa's general criticism of Hick see 'The New Missionary: John Hick and Religious Plurality', *International Bulletin of Missionary Research*, 15 (April 1991), 66–69; 'Elephants, Ropes and a Christian Theology of Religions', *Theology*, 88 (July 1985), 259–268.

29 D'Costa, *Theology and Pluralism*, 31.

30 Ibid., 32.

31 In all the major traditions, whether theistic or non-theistic, it is believed that God or the Absolute possess the absolute goodness. Although some primal traditions envisaged evil deities, they remained marginal.

32 As a Muslim I believe that Hick's argument is equally applicable for the God of Islam, who is good and wills the goodness of all people, though I am aware that this view is not the view of mainstream Islamic orthodoxy.

33 Hick, *God and the Universe*, 92.

34 Frithjof Schuon, *Understanding Islam*, trans. D. M. Matheson (London: George Allen & Unwin Ltd., [1963] 1972), 41.

236

Notes

35 John 14:9.
36 John 14:6.
37 See the appendix.
38 Hick states: 'If there were only one tradition, so that all religious experience and belief had the same intentional object, an epistemology of religion could come to rest at this point. But in fact there are a number of different traditions and families of traditions witnessing to many different personal deities and non-personal ultimates.' *Interpretation*, 233.
39 Ibid., 249.
40 This is, I believe one of the loose points which weakens the coherence of Hick's hypothesis of religious pluralism.
41 I shall be discussing this issue in detail in the next chapter.
42 Hick, *Interpretation*, 56–57.
43 In his book, *Spirit, Saints and Immortality* (London: Macmillan, 1984), Patrick Sherry explores the religious significance of saintliness. He sees the existence of saintly people as a 'truth-condition' of Christianity and many other theistic religions. He maintains that the existence of saints, while not verifying theism, is evidence for its truth. In a sense, theism provides a plausible explanation of the existence of saintliness.
44 Hick, *Interpretation*, 301.
45 Ibid., 307.
46 Ibid., 307.
47 Ibid., 313.
48 In various traditions the Golden Rule is affirmed as an ethical principle. In Hindu scripture, in the *Mahabharata*, it is stated that: 'one should never do that to another which one regards as injurious to one's own self'. In the Jain *Kritoga* Sutra it is said that: 'one should go about treating all creatures in the world as himself would be treated'. In the Taoist *Thai Shang* we read that: 'the good man will regard others' gains as if they were his own, and their losses in the same way'. The Zoroastrian *Dadistan-i dinik* declares that 'nature only is good when it shall not do unto another whatever is not good for its own self'. Jesus said: 'As ye would that men should do to you, do ye also to them likewise'. In the Jewish Talmud it is said: 'what is hateful to yourself do not do to your fellow man'. In a Hadith the prophet Muhammad said: 'No man is a true believer unless he desires for his brother that which he desires for himself'. Quoted in *Interpretation*, 313.
49 For instance, in the context of Christianity, Hick's pluralism not only aims to obliterate some doctrines such as the Incarnation and the virgin birth, in order to promote tolerance among religions, but also to regulate some of the doctrines such as the creation, the atonement and deity of Jesus. For further information on these issues see *The Metaphor of God Incarnate* (London: SCM Press, 1993).
50 This is one of the important defects in Hick's hypothesis of religious pluralism. Hick should have seen that such a 'trans-traditional' approach is not possible given the fact that an individual is always compelled to operate with the norms of his or her culture. Or he should have sought a way of overcoming such difficulties by perhaps presenting a method which is common in every religion, such as esoterism.

51 The perspective that finds a significant connection between the Western history of colonialism and the images of 'other' was principally initiated by Edward W. Said. His book *Orientalism: Western Conception of the Orient* (London: Penguin Books, [1978], 1991) has introduced a method through which it has become possible to realise the limits of a cultural perspective.

52 Kenneth Surin, 'A Certain Politics of Speech', 71.

53 Kenneth Surin, 'Towards a "materialist" critique of religious pluralism', 119–120.

54 John V. Apczynski, 'John Hick's Theocentrism' 47.

55 Peter Donovan, 'The Intolerance of Religious Pluralism', *Religious Studies*, 29 (June 1993), 218.

56 Ibid., 229.

57 Ibid.

58 The difficulty in maintaining the balance between the two thinkers as far as the subject is concerned is the natural result of this fact.

59 Nasr says, 'God as Ultimate Reality is not only the Supreme Person but also the source of all that is, hence at once Supra-Being and Being, God as Person and the Godhead or Infinite Essence of which Being is the first determination. Both He or She and It and yet beyond all pronominal categories, God as Ultimate Reality is the Essence which is the origin of all forms, the Substance compared with which all else is accident, the One who alone is and who stands even above the category of being as usually understood.' *Sacred Science*, 8.

60 There is a danger here. Hick appears to endorse the idea that God is a useful concept which must be assumed in order to make sense of our religious and ethical life. He does not seem to fully endorse that God is a 'living' being. Rather he leaves such ways of talking about God to the domains of religions in which, he thinks, reality is confused with mythology.

61 Nasr, *Sufi Essays*, 125–126.

62 Nasr, *Knowledge*, 291.

63 Nasr, *Sacred Science*, 57–58.

64 Nasr, *Knowledge*, 294.

65 Nasr, *Sacred Science*, 62.

66 Hick's hypothesis of religious pluralism is, he claims, religious as opposed to 'naturalistic' or non-realist accounts of religion. From the point of view of the perennial philosophy, Hick's hypothesis of religious pluralism owes its existence as well as its popularity to the prevailing secularisation process. The secularisation process, firstly has created a context for such a hypothesis which aims to modify some aspects of Christology, such as the doctrine of the Incarnation. Secondly, the secularisation process has severed the power of orthodoxy, thereby generating an atmosphere in which one can more freely consider, even acknowledge, the value of other religions.

67 The implication of this statement is that the secularisation process is instrumental in the rediscovery of tradition. Like a fish in water, traditional people do not understand the value of tradition while they are in the traditional world. When they experience secularisation they realise the

vitality of tradition for themselves. This is an interesting phenomenon. If the secularisation process is something unfavourable, how is it able to play such a crucial role in the discovery of the traditional outlook?

68 Nasr writes: 'This truth has to be stated anew and reformulated in the name of tradition precisely because of the nearly total eclipse and loss of that reality which has constituted the matrix of life of normal humanity over the ages. The usage of the term and recourse to the concept of tradition as found in the contemporary world are themselves, in a sense, an anomaly made necessary by the anomaly which constitutes the modern world as such.' *Knowledge*, 66.

69 Nasr, *Knowledge*, 6.

70 Ibid., 31.

71 Ibid., 41.

72 Ibid., 42.

73 Ibid.

74 Ibid., 43.

75 Ibid., 43–44.

76 There is a significant connection between modernity and secularisation. Secularisation is more apparent in those religions which have more interaction with modernity. The impact of secularisation on Christianity is greater than on Islam. Ernest Gellner illustrates the point: 'Apparent exceptions to the trend towards secularization turn out on examination to be special cases, explicable by special circumstances, as when a church is used as a counter-organization against an oppressive state committed to a secular belief-system. It is possible to disagree about the extent, homogeneity or irreversibility of this trend, and, unquestionably, secularization does assume many quite different forms; but, by and large, it would seem reasonable to say that it is real.

But there is one very real, dramatic and conspicuous exception to all this: Islam. To say that secularization prevails in Islam is not contentious. It is simply false. Islam is as strong now as it was a century ago. In some ways it is much stronger'. *Postmodernism Reason and Religion* (London: Routledge, 1992), 5.

77 Nasr, *Knowledge*, 48.

78 Nasr, *Man and Nature*, 20.

79 Nasr argues that it is not enough to ask people to discipline their passions, to be rational, and to be kind and thoughtful to one's neighbours, human and non-human. What we need is to adhere to a firm commitment to the sacred principles and responsibility which cannot be carried out unless one believes in a spiritual power. See Nasr, *The Plight*, 13.

80 Nasr rejects the Darwinian theory of evolution and offers a 'metaphysical' critique of it. For further information see. *Man and Nature*, 124–129; *Knowledge*, 234–242.

81 The Quran supports this idea by stating: 'When I have fashioned him (human) and breathed in to him from my soul (*ruhi*)' (15:29).

82 In this sense, prophets and great sages display the possible perfection which an earthly creature can achieve. Thus, humans can participate in those divine qualities which make people perfect and holy but not in those which are the source of the power of the Divine.

83 From the contemporary scientific and cultural point of view, this notion
of human origin sounds not only superstitious but also ludicrous. That
is because the modern person accepts science and reason as the only
criteria by which one can establish the truth, whereas, the traditional
point of view gives a certain priority to the wisdom of traditions which
comes from revelations. In my opinion the existence of various forms of
this notion in several traditions and scriptures can be regarded as
evidence for the viability this doctrine. In this context, the Quran
speaks of pre-eternal (*azali*) covenant between God and humanity.
(7:172).

84 Nasr, *Knowledge*, 170.

85 Ibid., 163–164.

86 Ibid., 165.

87 Nasr, *The Plight* , 49–50.

88 Hick, *God and the Universe*, 146.

89 Nasr, *Knowledge*, 66.

90 In this context one might claim that the traditional point of view and
other religious approaches are also biased in favour of religion. They
naturally tend to over-exaggerate the fruit and importance of religion for
the individual as well as the community. They do not want to see the
defects and deficiencies of tradition. Even if one assumes that these exist,
the traditional point of view still insists that it is in a better position than
the others in the description of religion, because it possesses an ability to
empathise with religion better than any other scientific and religious
approaches.

91 The social scientists are accused of being impotent in picturing the course
of social events adequately. For instance, no social scientist was able to
predict the collapse of socialism in the old Soviet Union and Eastern
European.

92 In the major traditional cosmology, history is conceived as cyclic and
qualitative. Every major step is made by the coming of *mahdis*, *avatars*
and Christ(s). This notion is not at all alien to Islam.

93 Nasr, *Knowledge*, 93.

94 See for Nasr's remarks on the works and the life of these two outstanding
scholars of Sufism, *Traditional Islam* , Chap. 15–16.

95 For the relationship between modernity and religion see James A.
Beckford, 'Religion, Modernity and Post-modernity' in *Religion: Contemporary Issues*, ed. Bryan Wilson (London: Bellew Publishing, 1992),
11–27.

96 Nasr, *Man and Nature*, 14.

97 An Islamic answer to this question is straightforward. Islam claims that
every tradition is in essence monotheistic. But historical and social
changes sometimes transformed some doctrines in a given tradition.
Hence, not every traditional doctrinal formula of traditions is true. It
would maintain that Theravada Buddhism was originally monotheistic, but because of certain cultural and human conditions it has
changed.

Notes

Chapter Five – The Ultimate and Pluralism

1 Hick, *Interpretation*, 9–11.
2 The problem that I am trying to indicate becomes more evident when one attempts to translate *An Interpretation of Religion* into non-European languages. For instance, if I translate this book into Turkish or Arabic, I could not find a suitable term which would represent Hick's notion of the Real. If I were to translate this word as *al-haqq* it would be misleading and also confusing.
3 Paul Badham, 'John Hick's *An Interpretation of Religion*' in *Problems in the Philosophy of Religion: Critical Studies of the Work of John Hick*, ed. Harold Hewitt, Jr. (London: Macmillan, 1991), 90–91.
   In reply to Paul Badham, Hick says that although the word 'God' has been widely used, it is basically understood as the divine person and cannot accommodate the Buddhist and Hindu conception of Ultimate Reality. Therefore, Hick insists on employing a neutral term such as Ultimate reality, the Ultimate, or the Real. Hick, 'Reply' in *Problems in the Philosophy*, 104.
4 Hick, *Disputed Questions*, 166–168.
5 One of the apparent problems appears to be that Hick considers the various names of God in the different languages and cultures as totally distinct concepts of different gods. This might be true if Hinduism is taken into consideration together with Christianity. It would seem that such an account is problematic when concepts of God in the three Abrahamic faiths are considered as different 'gods'. After all the contention of the book which he edited, *Three Faiths – One God*, goes against the argument that he is putting forward here. It is interesting to note that Arab Christians do not have any name other than Allah to describe what Hick names the Heavenly Father. That is to say, if Hick were an Arab Christian and reading the Bible in Arabic, he would not have held a view that sees the Heavenly Father as different from Allah.
6 Hick, *Interpretation*, 236–237.
7 Hick pays considerable attention to the significance of religious devotion, but seems in conflict with himself when he introduces God in such a manner that he becomes unrecognisable to the devotees of the major traditions.
8 To make his concept of the Real more religiously sound, Hick claims that the same epistemological principle was asserted by St. Thomas Aquinas' in his well-known proposition: 'Things known are in the knower according to the modes of the knower.' Even Hick goes on to say that his distinction between the Real and 'gods' of religions was vaguely affirmed by Aquinas, when he said God, although *a se* and simple, can only be known by human beings through complex propositions. It is also the same factor, i.e. the difficulty of a religious justification of his formation of the concept of the Real, that led Hick to point out a Muslim Sufi, al-Junayd, who asserted the same epistemological insight in a metaphor which he applied to the plurality of the forms of awareness of God: 'The colour of the water is the same as that of its container.'

241

Interpretation, 240–241. My objection to Hick's presentation is the same as before. A Sufi Muslim thinker such as al-Junayd, or a Catholic theologian like Thomas Aquinas, may agree with Hick's distinction, but they will not agree with Hick's conclusion that we experience the Real as a god of our culture through the concepts which are presented to us by that culture.

9   Ibid., 242.

10 Ibid., 243.

11 Ibid., 244–245.

12 For an evaluation of Hick's hypothesis of religious pluralism from a Kantian perspective see Bernard J. Verkamp 'Hick's Interpretation of Religious Pluralism', *International Journal for Philosophy of Religion*, 30 (October 1991), 103–124.

13 D'Costa introduces Hick's hypothesis of religious pluralism as 'Kantian revolution'. D'Costa believes that Hick made such an unnecessary move in order to counter his charge, that is, Hick's Copernican revolution is not successful since it places the Christian God at the centre of the universe of faiths, thereby excluding the other forms of deities. Gavin D'Costa, 'John Hick and Religious Pluralism: Yet Another Revolution' in *Problems in the Philosophy*, 4–5.

14 John K. Roth, 'Reply: Can John Hick Say What He Said?' in *Concept of the Ultimate*, ed. Linda J. Tessier (London: Macmillan, 1989), 160–161.

15 Prabhu expands this point by maintaining that Hick cannot secure the transformative power of the Real unless he offers some independent characterisation of the Real. Joseph Prabhu, 'Response to Hick' in *Concepts*, 169–170.

16 Kenneth Surin draws attention to the same question and asserts that Hick's hypothesis is not convincing unless he suggests the modalities whereby the phenomenal domain yields noumenal truth. See 'Towards a "Materialist" Critique of "Religious Pluralism": An Examination of the Discourse of John Hick and Wilfred Cantwell Smith', *in Religious Pluralism and Unbelief*, 124.

17 Harold A. Netland, 'Professor Hick on Religious Pluralism', *Religious Studies*, 22 (1986), 249–261.

18 Hick, *Philosophy of Religion*, 4–14.

19 Hick, *Christianity at the Centre*, 24.

20 Hick, *Disputed Questions*, 177.

21 One can easily turn this argument against Hick by asking the source of the sense of infinitude, if we are never able to experience infinitude. My reply is, however, different than the concern above. As I argued in chapter three, I do not accept that religious people constitute their ideas of God through their own religious experiences. Therefore, Hick's argument, that is, the Real as infinite must be unknowable because we cannot experience infinitude, does not register in the first place. That is simply because we do not form our concept of God through our religious experience.

22 Keith Ward, however, argues that Anselm's formula is far from being purely formal. Rather it captures the element of absolute value which is essential for any religious qualification of the Real. See *Religion and Revelation*, 312.

23 Hick, *Interpretation*, 246.
24 Hick, *Disputed Questions*, 172.
25 Keith Ward, 'Truth and the Diversity of Religions', *Religious Studies*, 26 (March 1990), 5.
26 Ibid., 6.
27 Davis, 'Comment on John Hick' in *Concepts of the Ultimate*, 163.
28 Hick, 'Response', in *Concepts of the Ultimate*, 172.
29 Hick, *Interpretation*, 245.
30 Ibid., 252.
31 Hick believes that the omniattributes of God are produced by later philosophical speculation rather than in the 'actual first-order business of the religious life'. (*Interpretation*, 259) Hick obviously, favours religious experience over philosophical reasoning. And yet, if one analyses Hick's hypothesis of pluralism, one can see that he himself has not constituted his theory of religious pluralism through religious experience but through philosophical reasoning.
32 Ibid., 259.
33 Ibid., 269.
34 Ibid., 169–171.
35 Ibid., 275.
36 Quoted in Ibid., 274.
37 Ibn al-'Arabi, *The Bezels of Wisdom*, trans. R. W. J. Austin (London: SPCK, 1980), 92.
38 For further information see S. A. Q. Husaini, *The Pantheistic Monism of Ibn 'Arabi* (Lahore: Sh. Muhammad Ashraf, 1970).
39 A speculative interpretation of 'Arabi's doctrine of unity of being through using Kantian vocabulary would cast light on the difference between Hick and 'Arabi. For 'Arabi the world of 'Appearances' emanates from the Absolute, from the Essence. In other words, using a Kantian vocabulary one can say that the phenomenal world corresponds to the world of appearance, and the noumenal, to the Essence. Extrapolating Kantian epistemological insight one can say that the things themselves 'reside' in the realm of Essence which is not accessible to experience, but nevertheless gives existence to everything that appears. This can feasibly explain the doctrine of creation. This interpretation of Kantian insight is more appropriate than Hick's application of it to the Real and the 'gods' of religions.
40 A. E. Affifi, *The Mystical Philosophy of Muhyid Din-Ibnul Arabi* (Lahore: Sh. Muhammad Ashraf, 1971), 10–11. For further readings with regard to 'Arabi's doctrine of unity of being see Henri Corbin, *Creative Imagination in the Sufism of Ibn 'Arabi*, trans. Ralph Manheim, (Princeton: Princeton University Press, 1969); William Chittick, *Ibn al-'Arabi's Metphysics of Imagination: the Sufi Path of Knowledge* (Albany: State University of New York Press, 1989); Toshihiko Izutsu, *A Comparative Study of the Key Philosophical Concepts in Sufism and Lao-tzu, Chuang-tzu* (Tokyo: The Keio Institude of Cultural and Linguistic Studies, 1966); Rom Landau, *The Philosophy of Ibn 'Arabi* (London: George Allen & Unwin Ltd, 1959).
41 'The dependent' here is the universe or existence. The universe's dependence is the conformity of the existence of the Independent, i.e.

God. In other words, if the universe is actually dependent, this proves two things: Firstly, there must be something on which the universe is dependent and secondly, this must necessarily be independent of anything.

42 'Arabi, *The Bezels of Wisdom*, 92–93.

43 For the analysis of this point see Summer B. Twiss, 'The Philosophy of Religious Pluralism: A Critical Appraisal of Hick and His Critics', *The Journal of Religion*, 70 (October 1990), 533–568; Gerard Loughlin, 'Prefacing Pluralism: John Hick and the Mastery of Religion', *Modern Theology*, 7 (October, 1990), 29–55; for the reply to this article see John Hick, 'A Response to Gerard Loughlin', *Modern Theology*, 7 (October, 1990), 57–65.

44 Hick, *Interpretation*, 246–247.

45 The obvious Muslim objection to such an account is that God by definition must be great, absolutely independent of anybody or anything. A notion of Allah displayed in Hick's hypothesis is a god which owes its existence to the Real, i.e. it is dependent and therefore cannot be a god Muslims can worship.

46 Hick's main aim is surely to convince those religious people who are the main source of religious intolerance. But he constitutes his pluralism in such a fashion that only philosophically minded liberal intellectuals can acknowledge it, not devoted Christians, Muslims, Jews, Buddhists and Hindus.

47 For an 'ideological' implication of religion see Ninian Smart, *Beyond Ideology: Religion and the Future of Western Civilization* (London: Collins, 1981).

48 Hick, *Interpretation*, 36.

49 Ibid., 37–41.

50 Ibid., 41–43.

51 Ibid., 44.

52 Ibid., 45.

53 Ibid., 48.

54 Ibid., 49.

55 As will be explored in chapter six, *islam* as used in the Quran, signifies not only the Quranic revelation as religion but also all the messages sent through prophets. In the Quran, Abraham and the apostles of Jesus are also named as *muslims*. It is even used in a broader sense to signify anything which submits to the will of God. In this sense the sun and moon are regarded also as *muslims*.

56 Netland, 'On Religious Pluralsim', 156.

57 For the evaluation of Hick's notion of a human transformation from self-centredness to Reality-centredness and its impact on 'religious salvation' see Mark Heim, 'The Pluralistic Hypothesis, Realism, and Post-eschatology', *Religious Studies*, (June 1992), 207–219.

58 For an extended discussion of this point see D'Costa, 'John Hick and Religious Pluralism: Yet Another Revolution'; James Kellenberger, 'Critical Response' and Hick, 'Reply' in *Problems in the Philosophy*, 24–27.

59 John B. Cobb, Jr. 'Comment on John Hick' in *Concepts of Ultimate.*

60 For further analysis of Hick's hypothesis of religious pluralism see Joseph Runzo, 'God, Commitment, and Other Faiths: Pluralism vs. Relativism', *Faith and Philosophy*, 5 (October 1988), 343–364; Robert McKim, 'Could God Have More Than One Nature?', *Faith and Philosophy*, 5 (October 1988), 378–398; David Basinger, 'Hick's Religious Pluralism and "Reformed Epistemology": A Middle Ground', *Faith and Philosophy*, 5 (October 1988), 421–432; Julius Lipner, 'At the Bend in the Road: A Story about Religious Pluralism,' and for critical response to this article see Joseph Prabhu, 'The Road not Taken: A Story about Religious Pluralism, Part 2,' in *Problems in the Philosophy*; Patrick Shaw, 'On Worshipping the Same God', *Religious Studies*, 28 (December 1992), 511–532; Hendrik M. Vroom, 'Do All Religious Traditions Worship the Same God?' *Religious Studies*, 26 (March 1990), 73–90; J. Kellenberger, 'The Slippery Slope of Religious Relativism', *Religious Studies*, 21 (March 1985), 39–52; Anne Hunt, 'No Other Name? A Critique of Religious Pluralism', *Pacifica*, 3 (February 1990), 45–60; Peter Byrne, 'John Hick's Philosophy of World Religions', *Scottish Journal of Theology*, 35 (August 1982), 289–301; Dan Cohn-Sherbok, 'Ranking Religions', *Religious Studies*, 22 (1986), 377–386; Rebecca Petz, 'Hick and Saints: Is Saint-Production a Valid Test?' *Faith and Philosophy*, 8 (January 1991), 96–103.
61 Nasr, *Sacred Science*, 8.
62 Nasr believes that it would be extremely difficult for him to demonstrate his ideas in the context of modern philosophy. In other words, it would be a troublesome task to demonstrate Reality as such starting with the modern paradigms. The best way forward for Nasr is to ignore the norms of modern philosophy with regard to this issue and undertake to introduce his traditional account without exploring its implications for modern epistemology.
63 Nasr, *Sacred Science*, 8.
64 Ibid.
65 Ibid., 9.
66 Nasr, *Knowledge*, 133–134.
67 Ibid., 134.
68 Nasr, *Islamic Studies* (Beirut: Systeco Press, 1967), 136–139.
69 Nasr, *Sacred Science*, 16.
70 In *The Need for Sacred Science*, Nasr quotes this *sura* and offers an interpretation of it as support of his account of Reality. This alone is sufficient to point out that the Quran has always been one of the significant sources of Nasr's ideas.
71 It says: 'He knows all that goes into the earth, and all that comes out thereof: all that comes down from the sky and all that ascends thereto, and He is the most Merciful, the Oft-Forgiving' (34–2).
72 Nasr strongly opposes the idea that sees 'Arabi's transcendental unity of Being as a form of pantheism or panentheism. He claims that 'Arabi cannot be accused of being pantheist because, firstly pantheism is a philosophical system, whereas 'Arabi and other Sufis never claimed that they were intended to create philosophical systems, and secondly pantheism implies a continuity between God and the universe, whereas

'Arabi strongly emphasises God's absolute transcendence over every category. Seyyed Hossein Nasr, *Three Muslim Sages: Avicenna – Suhrawardi – Ibn 'Arabi* (Massachusetts: Harvard University Press, 1964), 105.

73 In fact this idea is the main theme of chapter six of his *Knowledge and the Sacred*.

74 Nasr's own writings bear evidence of his interest in Ibn al-'Arabi. For instance, in *Three Muslim Sages*, 'Arabi's is one of the three sages who deserves Nasr attention. In *Sufi Essays* his frequent reference to 'Arabi proves this point.

75 Nasr's own writings about Suhrawardi reveal his interest in the philosophy of this Persian thinker. He wrote an entry on Suhrawardi entitled 'Shihab al-Din Suhrawardi Maqtul' in *A History of Muslim Philosophy* (Wiesbaden: Otto Harrassowitz, 1963), 372–398. In *Three Muslim Sages* he also devoted one of the chapters to Suhrawardi.

76 Nasr, *Islamic Studies*, 142–143.

77 Since Nasr endorses the view that religion is one of the manifestations of the Ultimate, he comes close to Hick's idea that the god figures are the manifestations of the Real.

78 Nasr, *Knowledge*, 137.

79 From a Muslim perspective, it seems that Hick confuses the Divine Essence (*al-dhat*) with the divine attributes. Therefore, he cannot make sense of how the eternal and infinite and yet indescribable God can be related to the world and worldly affairs. How can such a God talk to Moses, reveal himself through Jesus and reveal the Quran to Muhammad? Hence, the business of ascribing such actions to God is more a human affair and therefore must come not from direct revelation but from human imaginations. Traditional Islamic theology affirms that although the divine attributes of God such as hearing, knowing, seeing, willing and speaking cannot be identified with God, they are not totally detached from God. This theme was one of the main controversies between Mu'tazila and al-Ash'ariyya. For instance, al-Shahrastani in his *Kitab Nihayat al-Iqdam fi 'Ilm al-Kalam* states: 'Al-Ashari [states that] [t]here are no changes or novelties in God's perception, state or quality. His knowledge is one eternal knowledge, embracing all that is and will be knowable... There is no difference between its relation to things in eternity and things that happen at different times. His essence is not affected by the advent of the knowable, as it is not affected by changes in time. The nature of knowledge is to follow the knowable, without acquiring a quality from it nor acquiring it as quality; and though knowables differ and multiply they are one in being knowable. The way in which they differ is nothing to do with the knowledge about them, but it is peculiar to themselves. They are known because knowledge comes into contact with them but that does not alter. The same argument applies to all the eternal attributes... We do not say that God knows the existent and non-existent simultaneously for that is absurd; but He knows each in its own time, and knowledge that a thing will be is precisely knowledge of its being in the time that it actually comes into being... ' *Kitab Nihayet*

al-Iqdam fi 'Ilm al-Kalam, ed. and trans. Alfred Guillaume (London: Oxford University Press, 1934), 79.

80 In the Western tradition, Simone Weil, also considers the cosmos as one way of realising God's existence and his love. See *Gravity and Grace*, trans. Emma Craufurd (London: Routledge and Kegan Paul, 1952); *Waiting on God*, trans. Emma Craufurd (London: Collins Fontana Books, [1951] 1959); *On Science Necessity and Love of God*, trans. and ed. Richard Rees (London: Oxford University Press, 1968).

81 In the Islamic tradition for instance, it is stated that there is a correspondence between humans, the cosmos and the sacred book. In this respect the Quran is referred to as the written Quran or composed Quran (*al-Quran al-Tadwini*) as well as the cosmic Quran (*al-Quran al-Takwini*). Its verses are called *ayat* which also means the symbols and signs which exhibit the presence and beauty of God. The Quran confirms that the *ayat* manifest themselves in the Holy Book in the heavens and earth as well as in the soul of humans (*anfus*) (41:53).

82 Nasr, *Knowledge*, 190–191.
83 Ibid., 191.
84 Ibid., 135–136.
85 Nasr claims that the notion of necessity and possibility held in the philosophy of Ibn Sina should not be considered as ideas which aim to speculate over the nature of reality through philosophical reasoning. Rather, the notion is principally metaphysical tries to expose a metaphysical structure of reality which includes God as well as the physical world. Ibid., 139.
86 Ibid.
87 Ibid., 139–140.
88 Ibid., 140.
89 Ibid., 235.
90 Ibid, 141.
91 Ibid.
92 Ibid., 142.
93 Ibid.
94 Ibid., 143–144.
95 Ibid., 144.
96 Such an account with regard to the problem of evil does not seem to be convincing since it cannot answer the question, Why does the Omnipotent and Good God still permit the existence of evil even in the lower level of reality?.
97 Nasr, *Knowledge*, 281.
98 Ibid., 282.
99 From the traditional perspective, one might claim that the ecological problem that today's humanity is facing is the result of ignorance of the divine substance in humans as well as in nature which is the source of the equilibrium between humanity and nature.
100 Nasr, *Knowledge*, 77.
101 Frithjof Schuon, *The Transcendent Unity of Religions*, trans. Peter Townsend (London: Faber and Faber Limited, 1953), 34.

102 This verse from Rumi which is often quoted by Nasr can illustrate his view on religious pluralism. He says:
The difference among creatures comes from the outward form (*nam*); When one penetrates into the inner meaning (*ma'na*) there is peace. Oh marrow of existence! It is because of the point of view in question. That there have come into being differences among the Muslim, Zoroastrian and Jew. Nasr, *Sufi Essays*, 123.

103 Ibid., 148.

104 Nasr, Knowledge, 292.

105 Ibid., 294.

106 Ibid., 297.

107 Ibid., 294–295.

108 Ibid., 299–300.

109 Ibid., 298–299.

110 Ibid., 300.

111 Nasr, *Sacred Science*, 60.

112 Nasr, *Knowledge*, 293.

113 Ibid., 143.

114 Nasr, *Sacred Science*, 59.

115 Thomas Dean, 'Primordial Traditional or Post-Modern Hermeneutics?' review of *Knowledge and Sacred*, by Seyyed Hossein Nasr, *Philosophy East and West*, 34 (April 1984), 223.

116 Seyyed Hossein Nasr, 'Response to Thomas Dean's Review of *Knowledge and the Sacred*', *Philosophy East and West*, 39 (January 1985), 88–89.

Chapter Six – Christianity and Islam: Manifestations of the Ultimate

1 I also object to the identification of religions with their historical manifestations. I believe that the core of a religion is determined by revelation, which is often embodied in the sacred scriptures. But what we see in a specific history of a religion is the 'actualisation' of its sacred principles on earth.

2 Numb. 10: 35; Exod. 12: 12; Deut. 7: 2–5.

3 Amos. 1: 3; 2: 5; Is. 56: 6.

4 Mark. 12: 26: Quran 2: 136.

5 Deut. 6: 5; Lev. 19: 17.

6 Mark 1: 15; Matt. 5: 17–18; Luke 21: 22; 24: 44.

7 John 8: 48; 4: 9.

8 Luke 10: 25–37.

9 E. C. Dewick, *The Christian Attitude to Other Religions* (Cambridge: Cambridge University Press, 1953), 84.

10 Matt. 11: 27; cf. Luke 10: 22.

11 John 14: 6.

12 Acts 4: 12.

13 As indicated in chapter four, in the Gospels the emphasis is placed on the uniqueness of Jesus not in order to exclude the other religions as a means

of salvation but to exclude any personal attempt which aims to reach God without taking Jesus as a messenger into consideration.

14 One of the ways of developing a pluralistic attitude within Christianity can be achieved by making a distinction between the historic personality of Jesus and his identification as the Word of God, Logos (if one were to use the phrase of the Quran: 4; 171, and the Gospels: John I, 1–3). In this sense, one might be able to distinguish a Christianity, that is a historical manifestation of the Eternal Word, actualised by Jesus in a particular time and place from a Christianity that goes beyond its historical manifestations. In this respect it might be possible to envisage a Muslim-Christian dialogue through Jesus' 'meta-historical' personality as the Word of God which was one of the vehicles of God's revelation.

15 I am aware that such a topic cannot possibly be explored in a section of a book of this kind. I aim to present this topic through my reading of Hick in order to expose, firstly, Hick's perception of Christianity as pluralist, and, secondly, a Christian theology of religions.

16 Dewick, *Christian Attitude*, 103–104.

17 Denzinger, 468–9 *The Church Teaches: Documents of the Church in English Translation* (St. Louis and London: B. Herder Book Co., 1955), 153–154, quoted in Hick, *God and the Universe*, 120.

18 Ibid., 165 quoted in Hick, *God and the Universe*, 120.

19 Martin Luther, *Large Catechism*, II. iii, tans. H. Wace and C. A. Buchheim in *Luther's Primary Works* (London, 1896), 106, quoted in Dewick, *Christian Attitude*, 116.

20 Philip C. Almond in his *Heretic and Hero: Muhammad and the Victorians*, (Wiesbaden: Otto Harrassowitz, 1989) gives an interesting account of the Victorians' image of the Prophet of Islam.

21 Para. 3. *Christianity Today*, 19 June 1970, quoted in Hick, *God and the Universe*, 121.

22 From the traditional point of view, the marriage between secular culture and religion, although possibly having some good and useful outcome, eventually aims to establish the authority of secularism at the expense of downgrading sacred principles.

23 Ch. ii, para. 16, quoted in Hick, *God and the Universe*, 125–126.

24 Para. 2, quoted in Hick, *God and the Universe*, 126.

25 As far as the attitude of the Catholic Church toward Islam is concerned, The Vatican Council II has not yet produced a meeting point between Muslims and Christians. What Muslims expect to see from the Christian world is a fair understanding with regard to both the nature of the Quran and the personality of the Prophet. Such an understanding seems quite crucial if there is to be any hope of a Muslim-Christian dialogue.

26 Hick, *God and the Universe*, 126.

27 In this context, Nasr would claim that Hick is mistaken when he naively assumes that there is and should be an answer to the issue of diversity of religion within the realm of theology or philosophy.

28 Hick's two most recent books, *The Metaphor of God Incarnate* and *Disputed Questions in Theology and the Philosophy of Religion* are devoted to the issue of Christology.

29 John Hick, *Christianity at the Centre* (London: Macmillan, 1968), 16.

30 Ibid.
31 One of the positive results of publishing *The Myth of God Incarnate* was that it triggered a notable publication on the subject. For instance, in 1977, Michael Green edited *The Truth of God Incarnate* (London: Hodder & Stoughton), George Carey, *God Incarnate* (Leicester: Inter-Varsity Press). In 1979 Durston R. MacDonald wrote *The Myth/Truth of God Incarnate* (Wilton, Connecticut: Barlow). And later Michael Goulder edited *Incarnation and Myth; The Debate Continued* (London: SCM Press, 1979). In 1981, A. E. Harvey edited *God Incarnate : Story and Belief* (London: SPCK) and in 1986, Thomas V. Morris wrote *The Logic of God Incarnate* (New York: Cornell University Press). Hick replied to this book with an article 'Logic of God Incarnate' published in *Religious Studies* in 1989 which was later reprinted in his book *Disputed Questions*. In 1988 G. Robert Crawford published *The Saga of God Incarnate* (Pretoria: University of South Africa).
32 The main reason for this is not only that the virgin birth is less important with regard to the incarnation, but also that criticism of the virgin birth does not contribute to the propagation of the hypothesis of religious pluralism, since Muslims, as Hick is aware (Hick, *Problems*, 89), oddly affirm the doctrine in question.
33 John Hick, *The Metaphor of God Incarnate*, (London: SCM Press, 1993), IX.
34 The other reasons that Hick has in mind are: firstly, Hick believes that the doctrine of the Incarnation was not among the teachings of Jesus; secondly, he believes that it would be quite difficult to make sense of it, if it is compared with the other fundamental doctrines of Christianity; thirdly, the idea of Divine Incarnation makes more sense if it is understood as metaphorical rather than literal; fourthly, if Jesus is introduced without reference to God Incarnate, he would be in a better position to serve the purpose of the Christian religious community. Hick, Ibid.
35 Ibid., 15.
36 Ibid., 16.
37 Ibid., 23–24.
38 Ibid., 24.
39 Ibid., 25.
40 Ibid., 27.
41 Ibid., 41–42.
42 Ibid., 44–45.
43 Ibid., 47.
44 Ibid., 62.
45 Ibid., 80.
46 Hick explains: 'If Jesus was God incarnate, the Christian religion is unique in having been founded by God in person. The Christian story is that in Jesus God came down to earth and inaugurated a new and redeemed community, the church; and it seems self-evident that God must wish all human creatures to become part of this community; so the church is called to convert the human race to the Christian faith.' Ibid., 87.

47 Ibid., 104–105.
48 Ibid., 105.
49 Ibid., 152.
50 John Hick, 'Trinity and Incarnation in the Light of Religious Pluralism' in *Three Faiths – One God: A Jewish Christian and Muslim Encounter*, ed. John Hick and Edmund S. Meltzer (London: Macmillan, 1989), 202.
51 Ibid., 199–201.
52 Muzammil H. Siddiqi, 'A Muslim Response to John Hick: Trinity and Incarnation in the Light of Religious Pluralism' in *Three Faiths*, 212–213.
53 For instance, as Siddiqi notes, Hick's *The Myth of God Incarnate* is very well received by Muslims (Ibid., 213). Dan Cohn-Sherbok mentions that Abdus-Samad Sharafuddin from King Abdul-Aziz University comme-morated *The Myth* by writing a short book entitled, *About the Myth of God Incarnate – An Impartial Survey of its Main Topics*, in which he praised *The Myth* with such words as 'it shatters agelong darkness like a bolt from the blue; like a rational, godsent lightening it strikes the London horizon to explode an agelong blunder in Christian thought' quoted in Dan Cohn-Sherbok, 'Incarnation and Trialogue' in *Islam in Diverse Faiths*, 18.
54 Some of the other reasons which led Hick to include Islam into his hypothesis might be: firstly, Islam is one of the largest religions; according to Hick, it will become numerically the largest one in the twenty first century (*Metaphor*, 87). Secondly, Islam is a sister religion of Judaism and Christianity and shares a common history with them. Thirdly, compared to Christianity and Judaism, Islam possesses a more pluralistic attitude which recognises Jews and Christians as People of the Book.
55 Hick, *Problems*, 48.
56 Nasr illustrates the point: 'Within each religious universe the laws revealed, the symbols sanctified, the doctrines hallowed by traditional authorities, the grace which vivifies the religion in question are absolute within the religious world for which they were meant without being absolute as such. At the heart of every religion is to be found the echo of God exclaiming "I". There is only one Supreme Self who can utter "I", but there are many cosmic and even metacosmic reverberations of the Word which is at once one and many and which each religion identifies with its founder. As Jalal al-Din Rumi, speaking as a Muslim saint, says: When the number hundred has arrived, ninety is also present. The name of Ahmad (the Prophet of Islam) is the name of all prophets.' Nasr, *Sacred Science*, 62.
57 John Hick, 'Jesus and Mohammad' in *Islam in a World of Diverse Faiths*, 115–116.
58 The Quran states: 'We sent revelation to you as we sent revelation to Noah and the prophets (who came) after him; and we sent revelation to Abraham and Ishmael and Isaac and Jacob and their offspring, and to Jesus and Job... and to Moses God spoke directly' (4:163–4; see also 3:73, 84; 6:85–86; 2:46, 51; 32:23–24; 40:53–54; 3:33, 55).
59 Hick, *Questions*, 146–147.
60 Ibid., 148–149.
61 Ibid., 159–161.

62 The main Islamic objections to the present day Jews and Christians is not that the God whom they worship is a false God, but that the way they acknowledge and worship him is not the way that God himself wants to be acknowledged or worshipped as he informed us in his last revelation. In other words, Muslims claim that the Quran came down not to deny and ignore but to reaffirm the messages of Moses and Jesus which, they believe, have been subject to a human transformation.

63 The Quran states: 'Say: "O people of the Book! come to common terms as between us and you: that we worship none but Allah; that we associate no partners with Him; that we erect not, from among ourselves, lords and patrons other than Allah." If then they turn back say ye: "Bear witness that we (at least) are muslims (bowing to Allah's will)".' (3:64).

64 One might object to this undertaking on the ground that Islamic principles do not promote pluralism but Islamic inclusivism. This objection has some merit. It is true that the Quran expands the term *islam* in a manner that can embrace those individuals who belong to other traditions but submit to the will of God (*muslims*). Ultimately, Christians and Jews as a whole are not considered as anonymous Muslims, but are identified as the People of the Book, a category which distinguishes them from Muslims. I maintain that one can speak of an 'Islamic pluralism' since the Quran not only identifies Jews and Christians as the People of the Book distinct from Muslims but also issues the rules which regulate Muslims' attitude towards Christians and Jews.

65 In certain circumstances, the opinions of such scholars are *the* Islamic opinion *per se* for certain Muslims.

66 The Quran states: 'To every nation (was sent) a messenger' (10:47); 'and verily we have raised in every nation a messenger, (proclaiming) serve Allah and shun false gods' (16:36); 'there is not a nation but a warner had passed among them' (35:24).

67 Again it is stated: '(We sent) messengers of good cheer and warning, in order to that mankind might have no arguments against Allah after the messengers' (4:165).

68 The Quran says: 'We never punish until we sent a messenger' (17:15).

69 It says: 'Verily we sent messengers before you, among them those of whom we have told you, and some of whom we have not told you' (40:78).

70 The Quran endorses this view: 'We sent not a messenger except in the language of his own people in order to make things clear to them' (14:4).

71 The Quran simply states this point: 'If your Lord had so willed, he could have made mankind one nation: but they will not cease to dispute' (11:118).

72 Jalalu'ddin Rumi, *Divan-i Shamsi Tabriz*, trans. R. A. Nicholson (Cambridge: Cambridge University Press, 1898), 125.

73 Hasan Askari, 'Within and Beyond the Experience of Religious Diversity' in *The Experience of Religious Diversity*, ed. John Hick and Hasan Askari (Aldershot and Brookfield: Gower, 1985), 199.

74 The Quran simply states this point: 'Do they seek for other than the Religion of Allah? while all creatures in the heavens and on earth have,

willingly and unwillingly bowed to his will (accepted *islam*) and to Him shall they all brought back' (3:83).

75 Muhammad bin Jarir al-Tabari, *Jami' al-Bayan an Ta'wil al-Quran*, (Cairo: Dar al-Ma'arif, 1954), Vol. 5, 407–416.

76 Vardit Rispler-Chaim compares verse 2:256 with the other verses in the Quran that speak of the regulation of war and concludes that the verse that propagates religious tolerance was not intended in the first place. It was a *taqiyya* and initiated for a strategic purposes in order to establish the Islamic community. When the community was established it was not tolerance but military campaigns that decided the destiny of Islam. See 'There is no compulsion in Religion (Quran 2, 256), Freedom of Religious Belief in the Qur'an', *The Bulletin of Henry Martyn Institute of Islamic Studies*, 11 (July-December, 1992), 19–32. In response to Rispler-Chaim, I argue that the mere existence of such a sacred injunction is sufficient to show the intention of the Quran. If Risper-Chaim really wants to bring out the actual position of Islam with regard religious tolerance, he must compare it with historical Christianity and Judaism. No Muslim claims that Islam can satisfy the requirements of the liberal values of the secular culture, but, its own history proves that Islamic power has tolerated the existence of other religions within its own realm.

77 Bernard Lewis, *The Jews of Islam* (Princeton: Princeton University Press, 1984), 8.

78 In *The Preaching of Islam: A History of Propagation of the Muslim Faith* (Lahore: Sh. Muhammad Ashraf, 1961) T. W. Arnold presents a historical account of the spread of Islam and concludes that Islam has expanded through persuasion and preaching rather than force and compulsion.

79 For instance, the Quran lays down the principles of propagating Islam: 'Invite to the way of your Lord with wisdom and beautiful preaching; argue with them in ways that are best and most gracious: for your Lord knows best, who strayed from His Path, and who received guidance' (16:125).

80 Sheikh al-Maraghi, *Tafsir al-Maraghi* (Cairo: 1962), 119, quoted in Vardit Rispler-Chaim, 'Freedom of Religious Belief', 24.

81 Abdullah Yusuf Ali, *The Qur'an: Text, Translation and Commentary* (Maryland: Amana Corporation, 1989), 150.

82 The Quran says: 'Then shall anyone who has done an atom's (*zarra*) weight of good see it. And anyone who has done an atom's weight of evil, shall see it' (99:7–8).

83 Ismail Raji al-Faruqi, 'Towards a Critical World Theology' in *Towards Islamization of Disciplines*, ed. The International Institute of Islamic Thought, (Heindon: The International Institute of Islamic Thought, 1989), 435–436.

84 Muhammad Abu Hamid al-Ghazzali, *Freedom and Fulfilment*, trans. Richard Joseph McCarthy (Boston: Twayne Publishers, 1980), 170.

85 Ibid., 172.

86 In Islamic literature there is another category, called *munafiqun*. These people, although they were not Muslim in their heart, pretended to be Muslim in their daily affairs. In his time, the Prophet himself was

informed about these people by revelation. He did not publicly identify them, but made them known to some of his close friends.

87 Syed Vahiduddin, 'Islam and Diversity of Religions' *Islam and Christian and Muslim Relations*, 1 (No. 1, 1990), 9.

88 It is interesting to note that *kafir*, which is generally translated in English as infidel in Islamic literature, literally means the person who covers. *Kafir* means also farmer or peasant because he or she plants the seed and covers it with soil. In a sense it indicates that an infidel is a person who knows the truth but consciously covers it up.

89 This document as a whole is cited in Ibn Ishaq's *Sira al-Nabi* and translated by Muhammad Hamidullah into English. He published this document together with the Arabic text under the provocative title 'The First Written Constitution in the World' (Lahore: Sh Muhammad Ashraf, 1968).

90 W. Montgomery Watt, *Muhammad at Medina* (Oxford: Clarendon Press, [1956], 1977), 221.

91 Ibid., 121–124.

92 Abu Yusuf, *Kitab al-Kharaj*, 44 (tr. 108), quoted in Watt, *Muhammad at Medina*, 359–360.

93 Al-Faruqi states: 'Following the conquest of India by Muhammad bin Qasim in 91/711, the Muslims faced new religions which they had never known before, Buddhism and Hinduism... Muhammad bin Qasim sought instruction from the caliph in Damascus on how to treat Hindus and Buddhists... The judgement was that as long as Hindus and Buddhists did not fight the Islamic state, as long as they paid the *jizya* or tax due, they must be free to worship their gods as they please, to maintain their temples, and to determine their lives by the precepts of their faith. Thus the same status as that of the Jews and Christians was accorded to them.' Al-Faruqi, 'World Theology', 447.

94 Barakat Ahmad, *Muhammad and the Jews: A Re-examination* (New Delhi: Vikas Publishing House Pvt Ltd, 1979), 47.

95 Al-Faruqi explains the importance and impact of this constitution to Jewish life: 'For the first time in history since the Babylonian invasion of 586 BC, and as citizens of the Islamic state, the Jew could model his life after the Torah, and so legitimately, supported by the public laws of the state where he resided. For the first time, a non-Jewish state put its executive power at the service of rabbinic court. For the first time, the state-institution assumed responsibility for the maintenance of Jewishness, and declared itself ready to use its power to defend the Jewishness of Jews against the enemies of Jewishness, be they Jews or non-Jews.' Al-Faruqi, 'World Theology', 445.

96 Historically this document played a very important role in safeguarding the rights of *dhimmis* throughout Islamic history. It reads as follows: 'This is what has been given by the servant of God, Omar ibn Al-Khattab to the people of Aelia. He gave them security for themselves, their property, churches and crosses, the invalid and health and other co-religionists: that their churches shall not be inhabited nor destroyed nor damaged, nor their confines be encroached upon, nor their cross be molested, nor their property be infringed, nor shall they be forced to abandon their religion,

nor shall anyone of them be hurt, nor shall Jews live with them in Aelia.' Abu Ja'far Muhammad Ibn Jarir al-Tabari, *Tarikh al-Rusul wal-Muluk*, Vol. 3, 609, quoted in Sheikh Izz al-Din al-Khatib al-Tameemi, 'Pluralism and Its Limits in the Holy Quran' in Proceedings of the 6th Muslim – Christian Consultation, held in Istanbul, 11–13 September, 1989, 40.

97 Ahmad Sidqi al-Dajani, 'Religious Pluralism and its Limits Through History' in Proceedings of the 6th Muslim – Christian Consultation, held in Istanbul, 11–13 September, 1989, 105.

98 The principles of 'Islamic pluralism' have played a vital role in maintaining Jewish identity in history. Al-Faruqi explains the importance of such Islamic rules for Jewish survival: 'After centuries of Greek, Roman, and Byzantine (Christian) oppression and persecution, the Jews of the Near East, of North Africa, of Spain, and Persia, looked upon the Islamic state as a liberator. Many of them readily helped its armies in their conquest and co-operated enthusiastically with the Islamic state administration. This co-operation was followed by acculturation into Arabic and Islamic culture, which produced a dazzling blossoming of Jewish arts, letters, sciences, and medicine. It brought affluence and prestige to the Jews, some of whom became ministers and advisors to the caliphs. Indeed, Judaism and its Hebrew language developed their "golden age" under the aegis of Islam. Hebrew acquired its first grammar, the Torah its most highly developed jurisprudence, Hebrew letters their lyrical poetry; and Hebrew philosophy found its first Aristotelian, Musa ibn Meymun (Maimonides), whose thirteen precepts, couched in Arabic first, defined the Jewish creed and identity. Judaism developed its first mystical thinker as well, Ibn Gabirol, whose 'Sufi' thought brought reconciliation and inner peace to Jews throughout Europe. Under 'Abd al-Rahman III in Cordoba, the Jewish prime minister, Hasdai ben Shapirut, managed to effect reconciliation between Christian monarchs whom even the Catholic Church could not bring together. All this was possible because of one Islamic principle on which it all rested, namely, the recognition of the Torah as revelation and of Judaism as God's religion, which the Quran attested and proclaimed.' Al-Faruqi, 'World Theology', 445–446.

99 Al-Dajani, 'Religious Pluralism', 103.

100 Lewis, *Jews of Islam*, 50.

101 Niyazi Berkes points out how unity was realised between different ethnic and religious groups during the Ottoman era: 'Through the application of certain principles implied in this concept of society, a great degree of unity was realized over a long period of time. Disorder broke out only when the principles ceased to be applied or to be applicable and the various groups began to develop tendencies that were incompatible with these principles... Each [estate of the society] was recognized by the ruler and possessed privileges granted by his favour. In each there was some authority recognized as partial delegate of the supreme holder of power. For example, heads of the guilds or of Christian and Jewish *millets* had administrative and juridical rights and duties. (The Turkish system found a place for non-Muslim communities in its medieval

structure, without segregating them into ghettos or resorting to expulsion or extermination, by according to right of jurisdiction to their respective ecclesiastical authorities, a method which invited praise from Arnold J. Toynbee).' Niyazi Berkes, *The Development of Secularism in Turkey* (Montreal: McGill University Press, 1964), 11–12.

102 Quoted in Lewis, *Jews of Islam*, 43–44.

103 Concepts such as tolerance, intolerance are extremely ambiguous and culture specific. One action or state of affairs can be seen as quite intolerant according to the norms of one culture, whereas appropriate according to others. The objective of Muslim rulers throughout Islamic history was not to achieve tolerance, religious or otherwise, but to establish order and unity among subjects from different religions and races. They believed that, like laws of God in nature (*sunnatu-llah*), i.e. laws of nature in the modern sense, there are the sacred laws issued by God to establish unity in society. They saw themselves as rulers appointed by God to achieve this unity.

104 Nasr, *Traditional Islam*, 11–22.

105 Ibid., 98.

106 Ibid.

107 Nasr, *The Plight*, 132.

108 Ibid., 86–87.

109 For instance, Nasr offered a critical response to Hans Kung's article, entitled 'Toward a New Consensus in Catholic (and Ecumenical) Theology' in *Journal of Ecumenical Studies*, 17 (1980), 1–17, in an article 'A Muslim Reflection on Religion and Theology' (112–120). In this article Nasr extended his comments on each of Kung's ten guiding principles for contemporary theology.

110 Nasr, *Sacred Science*, 160.

111 He asserts: '. . . [A]s a result of the rampant secularism of the Western world, the water is first charted by nonreligious forces and then religion is asked to take the map of a secularized cosmos and navigate through it. From the traditional point of view, however, it is religion itself which must lead the way and charter the course. Theology as the intellectual expression of religion must be able to make the future and not simply follow the secularized disciplines with the hope of guaranteeing some kind of survival for itself by placating the "enemy" or even ceasing to call a spade a spade.' Ibid., 162.

112 Ibid., 163.

113 Nasr, *Ideals and Realities*, 21.

114 Ibid., 35.

115 Ibid, 95.

116 Ibid., 34.

117 Seyyed Hossein Nasr, 'Response to Hans Kung's Paper on Christian Muslim Dialogue', *Muslim World*, 77 (Ap. 1987), 102.

118 One of the chapters of the Quran was given the name of Mary.

119 Nasr, *Sufi Essays*, 134.

120 Nasr, 'Christian Muslim Dialogue', 100.

121 Ibid.

Appendix

Religions and the Concept of the Ultimate

While Seyyed Hossein Nasr was delivering the Cadbury Lectures at Birmingham University during October 1994, I had the opportunity to interview him together with John Hick and ask their opinions about the concept of the ultimate and religions. This conversation took place at John Hick's house in Birmingham on 25th October 1994. Hick started the conversation by explaining the difference between himself and Nasr.

Hick: I think that I am basically in agreement with your position, though differing at one fairly important point. There is a difference of approach. What you are saying comes out of a particular tradition, the perennial philosophy, whereas what I am saying comes out of an inductive approach. Starting within my own Christian tradition I am committed to the faith that Christian religious experience is not purely imaginative projection but is also a response to a transcendent Reality. Because the other great world religions report their own forms of experience of the Transcendent, and show the same kind of moral and spiritual fruits in human life, I have to believe that they also are responding to the Transcendent. And so I affirm an ultimate divine Reality which is beyond our network of human concepts, and which is differently conceived, and therefore differently experienced, and therefore differently responded to in life from within the great religious traditions. The religions are totalities with many dimensions – forms of religious experience, beliefs, scriptures, rituals, life-styles and so on. But they are all formed under the impact on human life of the Ultimate. Just as a matter of verbal preference I tend to use the term 'the Real' which roughly corresponds to '*al-Haqq*'.

Nasr: I myself use that word, sometimes with a capital 'R'.

Hick: Yes, with a capital 'R'. This term also roughly corresponds to the Sanskrit *sat* and Chinese *zhen*. But in discussing with Christians I felt that I needed to get away from the word 'God', because it has such strong theistic and Trinitarian associations. So, I prefer to use the term 'the Real'. This Reality is humanly responded to in different ways. Such differences, which all arise from human and historical factors, give the religions their distinctive and unique characters. I differ from you when you said that we must not (so to speak) tamper with the specific teachings of a given religion. I would have agreed with you if we had all lived within our separate universes of faith and did not interact with one another. But today we are all mixed up together, and listen to one another's distinctive religious language. My adoption of this broad picture (which is essentially the same as your broad picture) does have repercussions on my own Christian form of belief, because any traditionally orthodox Christian would hold that Jesus was God, God the Son, the second person of a divine Trinity. From this it follows that Christianity alone among the religions of the world has been founded by God in person, who came down from Heaven to earth to save humanity. Traditionally orthodox Christians believe that this is not only true within the Christian universe of faith, but that it is true universally. If other people don't believe it, they are wrong. It is at this point that I feel that the absolute claims of religion do have to be modified. Whereas I understand you to be saying: 'No. They must all be left untouched.'

Nasr: Two points are brought out in this discussion: one on which we differ, one on which we agree. I think one of the points on which we differ is that you consider the various 'crystallisations' of religious truth in each universe as more a human response to the Divine presence, whereas I consider them to be a Divine formulation within the light of various human situations. There is a difference between us although there is, no doubt, an intermediate domain where we meet. Just as you have said with regard to Christian theology, I would not say every formulation of Islamic theology is divinely revealed. So on that point I would agree with you. But, I believe that the sacred rites, the sacred scriptures, and also certain fundamental formulations of theology are divinely ordained within each religion by God. I do not say they are simply human responses to the Ultimate. But this divine ordaining occurs always in the light of a human receptacle. This, I think is an element of difference between our perspectives. But I do, indeed, agree with you on one point, that the sense of absoluteness which each religion feels within itself – which historically has led each religion to claim to be alone true, or the best of all truths – has to be modified in the light of the doctrine which I have expressed from one point of view and you have expressed from another. That is, the Absolute is always absolute, the Real alone is absolutely real, everything else is a manifestation within a particular spiritual universe. I believe such a modification of views can be made by theologians, sages and saints of various religions. To live in more than one religious universe for ordinary human beings, even in an anticipatory way is not humanly possible. An ordinary Christian cannot say this: 'Since Christianity is relative, therefore I accept in an anticipatory way the truth of Buddhism'. This could only be done by someone who has climbed to the top of the mountain. Otherwise what such an approach does is in fact to destroy the expressions of truth within the particular religious world (in which they themselves are, what I would call 'relatively absolute') and eventually to lead to the destruction of religion itself. That is what I emphasise very much.

Hick: I do see the danger there. I think it is a real danger. To live as a Christian with the consciousness that Christianity is not the one and only truth is, I agree, very difficult. But I think that something else comes into this. I do not see any of the religions, as a matter of actual historical fact, as unchanging. Certainly, in the case of Christianity, the development, proliferation and variation has been, as you know, immense. Therefore, you cannot really easily say that such and such is *the* Christian belief.

A. A: That brings us to the question of religious language. Now, how do you understand the traditional religious language which speaks of God who is the One, the creator, omnipotent and omniscient?

Hick: It seems to me that the situation is that we intend to talk about the Ultimate, but we can only talk about the Ultimate as manifested to us in a particular form, not the Ultimate in itself. The language of each form is peculiar to that form. Some elements of religious language really apply to the Ultimate. For instance, I say the Ultimate is infinite, whereas the form is not. So, it would not be correct to say that the specifically Christian form, which is a limited form of awareness of the Ultimate, is itself infinite, ultimate and eternal, etc., So we have a mixture, we are talking about one thing in terms of another.

259

A. A: Are you saying that such language is not applicable to the Ultimate?

Hick: Well, I was saying that some of it is, some of it is not. Infinity, I would say yes.

A. A: But omnipotence and omniscience are not.

Hick: These, the notion of power and also the moral notion of goodness and love, and intentionality, are human concepts. They do not strictly speaking apply to the Ultimate in itself.

A. A: Professor Nasr, how do you understand the traditional religious language for referring to God?

Nasr: I would say that although the Real in itself is of course beyond all language, all categories, those qualities which the Real has given to itself in order to reveal itself in each religion are gates to It. And therefore they remain always meaningful, even though they might be contradicted by other qualities and by other manifestations in other religious universes. For example, in the Quran God is called *al-Qadir*, all powerful. Now, I believe that cannot be abrogated by us, because of the fact that we live in a period of history in which we don't like to look at God as being powerful and because human civilisations have waves of various fashions of thoughts that come and go. In my view, such qualities of the Ultimate cannot be changed simply by human whim. Our participation is an understanding of what it means to say that God is *al-Qadir*, what it means to say that God is omnipotent. It does not mean, therefore, that my understanding and Ghazzali's understanding are necessarily the same. But the way that God has manifested himself, (especially in the theophany, in the Divine Names in Islam, and in other ways in Christianity or Judaism or other places) I believe is part of the sacred universe of that religion and cannot be tampered with or changed according to human social conditions. They can always be reinterpreted.

That bring us to a very important point which (here we differ) is the question of the elements of change, the transformation within religion. I do not deny that each religion changes. But I see this change like the growing of this oak tree. Now, this oak tree was not the same fifty years ago, and will not be like this fifty years from now. But it always is an oak tree. Its form and its later development are depending upon (you could say, philosophically) the Platonic idea of oak tree, the idea and the reality as it manifests itself into space, or upon the genetic code according to modern science. But this oak tree in order to survive and live as a living being always remains an oak tree growing in different countries to different sizes and does not look identical in different climates. But it still looks always like an oak tree. So I see the changes and transformations within religions in the light of this example, like the changes and transformation in an oak tree. For example, an oak tree could also catch a disease and it could lose some of its branches and you could graft another branch to it; sometimes it catches on, sometimes it does not.

Religion is like this. One religion is forced to become part of another religion, becomes integrated into another religion. Sometimes it does not work and it dies out. But there is always the living reality of religion. So I do not deny that all these religions have had elements of change in them. For example, in Christianity, by virtue of the fact that Christ said 'my kingdom is not of this world', there is no body of legal opinion or legal matters which are considered to be immutable law. So, Christianity had no trouble incorporating Roman law, later English law, German common law and American law, and so on. Whereas in both Judaism and Islam, law is considered as a participation in divine immutability. Jews believe that since God wrote on the Tablet: 'Thou shall not kill', there is an immutable divine law. This law cannot evolve. A Christian understanding of how human law governs over human society is not identical with that of Islam and Judaism. But even that can be understood in the light of different ways in which that Real manifested itself in these different worlds.

A. A: Professor Hick, how would you comment on this notion of immutability?

Hick: I think there is a difference between Islam and Judaism on the one hand, and Christianity on the other, because Islam centres (does it not?) on the Quran which is unchanging, although there will be interpretations of it which change. Christianity centres on the figure of a historical person, Jesus of Nazareth. Now this is the question to you: Supposing it is true, as many New Testament scholars say (this is the development of the last hundred years roughly) that Jesus himself, the historical individual, did not think of himself as God, or the second person of the divine Trinity, incarnate. On the other hand, Christianity has come to think of him in that way. Well, is it an immutable truth that he was God, even though he himself did not think so, or is it perhaps an accretion that has to be eventually filtered out? How does one decide this?

Nasr: I would not have the audacity to decide this theological question for Christians. Since you ask me as a Muslim scholar, I would say that this recent discovery confirms what the Quran says explicitly about Christ, that he is in fact a prophet and not the son of God. But, putting that question aside, the question that comes out is this: If this was simply a mistake, how could God allow, with his infinite wisdom and justice, one of the major religions of the world within which millions of people have sought their salvation, to be misguided for two thousand years. Was this simply a mistake? That is a very important theological question to consider.

Hick: Yes, it is.

Nasr: So I believe that even if this doctrine is not historically borne out by existing documents, it was divinely willed for Christians and of course not Muslims. But what happens is that the possibility of interpretation of that particular revelation allows, in fact, this revelation to flower as it did. According to this infinite possibility, I believe, the creation of Durham Cathedral as sacred art was related to some truth which is manifested by it. So I would, as a Muslim, defend the traditional Christian understanding of that doctrine within the context of Christianity, while considering it not to be an absolute understanding of Christ, since Christ is also a figure for Muslims independent of Christianity. If all Christians (God forbid) ceased to believe in the traditional doctrines of Christianity, Muslims will still have to believe in Christ and the Virgin Mary. But the being Christ is not exhausted by the interpretation which considers him as the son of God. That interpretation must have corresponded to some aspect of the Will of God, some aspect of manifestations of the Real, in order to allow the possibility of this doctrine to flower. If one says that this was all a horrendous mistake for this thousand years, I cannot accept this.

Hick: In actual practice, the God who is worshipped in almost all the churches is God the Father, the Heavenly Father of whom Jesus spoke. The doctrine of the Trinity is something theologians have later developed. But in actual religious reality the enormous majority of Christians have always been worshipping God the Father.

Nasr: Which means in actual practice Christians are very close to Muslims.

Hick: Yes.

Nasr: I always say to Muslim friends when they say that Christians worship three Gods, look (I attended the Church many times while I was going to school in America) once you are sitting in the Church, you feel you are before God the One, and you are worshipping God the One.

Hick: Yes, that is right. To think of the idea of Divine incarnation as a metaphor would not be doing anything more than bringing out what is already there in Christian consciousness. In the ancient world, in the world of Jesus' time, the phrase 'son of God' was very common, and it was meant metaphorically. What I have in my mind is a clarification of Christian language rather than a change of much actual Christian belief. But nevertheless for many people, to say that it is not to be taken literally that Jesus was God, is unacceptable. There will be a lot of people, doctrinal fundamentalists, who insist that is literally true.

A. A: That brings us to the issue of religious language. Now, my question is this: how far are the descriptions of God in religious language authentic?

Nasr: Let me say a word about this. You use the word 'religious language' here. You know, my writings make a clear distinction between what I call sacred language, liturgical language, and common language. Now, I believe that in sacred languages such as Arabic, Sanskrit and Hebrew through which it is claimed that God has spoken directly, everything that is said within those languages as revelation is the language of God. God has said 'I' in those languages. Hence this question does not even pertain to them. If you say, 'How far is it authentic?' once you doubt this authenticity, you doubt God's revelation. However, your question pertains to the religions in which language does not have such a central role, as is the case with Christianity and Buddhism. The language that Christ spoke was Aramaic, which, although historically very important was not even significant in the Gospels, which were written in Greek. But later, Greek and Latin became the two great languages of Western Christianity, though they were not used by the founder of the religion, and certainly not used by God through him. No Christian claims that God spoke Latin and Greek. I think your question really has meaning in the context of those religions in which human language speaks about God's revelation.

A. A: Are you saying that in the sacred language the expressions and the descriptions of the Ultimate as they are, are authentic?

Nasr: Yes, although there are many levels of meaning. How you interpret it, that is quite something else. In classical Islamic sources it is said that a verse in the Quran has several different levels of meaning and is not bounded by only the literal. So again, as far as the language of the Quran is concerned, it is possible to talk about metaphorical meaning (I would rather use the word symbolic) without destroying the context. God is called *al-Qadir* in the Quran. Even the question of the authenticity of that is meaningless in the context of Islam.

A. A: From this perspective how do you see the Bible?

Nasr: The question of the Bible is different. Jews believe that the Old Testament was revealed to different prophets over thousands years, over a long period of history. The New Testament is really a set of compilations of the sayings of Christ in a time some forty to fifty years after his death by the apostles who were men of great spiritual perfection. It is not that they were making things up. If you ask the question how much the verses of the New Testament are the direct revelations of God, technically speaking, that is a different kind of question. I also believe that the words which were uttered by Christ were divinely inspired, since he was a manifestation of the Logos. That is why the Quran speaks of *al-Injil*, the Gospel, as one of the books of God. Therefore, four different versions of the New Testament, Luke and Matthew and so forth, cannot be seen as four 'qurans' or four 'torahs'. They are four different versions of this incredible life which was that of the Logos.

A. A: Professor Hick, would you like to make some comment on the idea of revelation and sacred language?

Hick: That 'God reveals divine words that takes account of human circumstances' entails God being a person with intentions, operating in different times in history. But does such language properly apply to the Ultimate?

Nasr: The Ultimate is not exhausted by what this language means. But it cannot be deprived of it. For example, the Ultimate can also be conceived as the Sun which shines, as Tao which manifests itself, or as laws and principles which constitute the nature of things and which emanate from the Divine Principle. But that does not mean that on some level of understanding even in a religion such as Taoism, there is not an awareness of the Divine Principle as to what is being manifested as the forms of the physical world of time and space.

Hick: But is it strictly correct to say that the Ultimate is a personal, self revealing, intentional, and historically acting divine person?

Nasr: No. Not always. There are two different things. I do not believe that the Real manifests itself always in the terms you have just mentioned. But I also do not believe that these terms are simply man made, to cover the face (you might say) of the Real. But the Real is infinite and therefore does possess the possibility of manifesting itself in different forms including those which are not personal. But it can also manifest itself in those categories which you have just mentioned.

Hick: These categories apply to manifestations of the Real rather than to the Real in itself?

Nasr: You are right, the Ultimately Real is beyond all these categories.

Hick: This is what I also want to say. But there may here may be a major difference. I am not sure. I would say that each different manifestation of the Real is partly contributed to by human thought and circumstances.

Nasr: Yes, here is our major difference!.. I believe that this is contributed only to the extent that. the Divine Itself takes into consideration the various receptacles for the revelation, the various forms of the cup into which He is going to pour the divine nectar.

Hick: The phrase 'takes into consideration' suggest to me, not the Ultimate in itself but a personal self-revealing God.

Nasr: Even if this is not personal, as in certain other worlds such as the Buddhist it occurs on a lower level of manifestation from the Supreme Reality. It is on the level of manifestation that these elements come to being!..

Hick: But can you elevate the language of personal intentionality into the Real? Is the Real personal? If this is the case, that means you are using the language of personal intentionality of the Ultimate in itself rather than only of certain manifestations of the Ultimate.

Nasr: Not always. I make it very clear, when I use the term 'Word of God' and 'Divine Will' and so forth, I always say that only in certain worlds, types of language and parts of the globe in which this type of exposition has meaning, not because we human beings have made it up but because the Divine Order, the Real has manifested itself in that world in such a way that these categories have meaning.

A. A: One of the important issues in contemporary religious thought is the issue of the conflicting truth claims of the religions. How can you reconcile such conflicting claims, for instance, Muslims believe that Christ is not the son of God while Christians believe the contrary?

Nasr: The discussion so far partly answers your question. Each religion has a truth claim which is based upon the way in which the Real has manifested itself in that world, which is not identical with the way in which It manifested itself in other worlds. There is no reason whatsoever why the truth claims should be the same. But the problems come when two different universes refer to a single divine reality. For example, this kind of problem does not ever exist between Buddhism and Judaism. The problems come when Islam and Judaism or Islam and Christianity claim to refer to the same reality. How did Moses get down from mount Sinai? Or the question of the personality of Christ, which is the most important question!.. I believe that to understand this question is very difficult from a rationalistic point of view. It is very crucial to understand that the reality of Christ (the historical, not trans-historical, reality of Christ) in the world cannot be exhausted by a single description of it. And therefore both Christian and Islamic descriptions of that Reality are true.

A. A: Even though they may appear as contradictory?

Nasr: Yes, although contradictory, that is right. This can be understood even on a more simple human plane. In modern thought it is said that let us say you have an object A at the table, and the subject B who is also at the table. The line which links A and B is only a single line. Or there is only one kind of knowledge which B can have of A. But this is not necessarily true. You can understand that by applying the same principle to certain modes of human experience such as music. If someone comes here, plays let us say a Bach Partita our understanding of it can be different although we are hearing one single phenomenon, a sound system. So there is the possibility that the historical reality or series of historical realities of such exceptional amplitude as the life of Christ are described in two different revelations in different ways and they both be true.

A. A: Are you suggesting another epistemology in which the doctrines of two different revelations can make sense?

Nasr: Definitely, both another epistemology and another metaphysics. I believe, for instance, that an object, let us say a tree out there is not only a physical tree that is described in botany and physics, it also itself participates in higher levels of Reality. And the knowing subject also has levels of knowledge, modes of knowing. Therefore, there are correspondences of several modes of knowing within the knower and of several levels of existence of the being in question. This does not usually manifest itself in everyday life, but sometimes it does. For example, the way you know your wife is different from the way the neighbour knows your wife. This is not a question of more knowledge on a horizontal level. But there is vertical, deeper knowledge which is not simply expansion of the neighbour's non-knowing of her age, where she went to school, or what is the name of her uncle. I mean another kind of knowledge in depth. This usually does not occur in everyday life. But when you come to a major event like revelation, especially with figures like Christ, who is a manifestation of God and the Logos, a very special manifestation of the Real in the world (using Hick's language), there is every possibility that this phenomenon be seen differently in two different religious universes. So I have no trouble whatsoever, intellectually and even rationally, in accepting the Christian account of the crucifixion and the Islamic account which rejects the crucifixion.

A. A: But if such an understanding is possible, there must be very limited access to it. Only a few people would go beyond the everyday understanding.

Nasr: Yes, that is my claim. Serious ecumenism and authentic esoterism is meant for only a few. In fact, this is also the case with the lower levels of reality. For example, on the simple level of astronomy, any one of us, getting up in the morning walking in the street, could hardly consciously and concretely believe that we are floating through the air at thousands of miles a second. Only a few astronomers could actually live in this kind of world, working on astronomical problems during the day and thinking about them during the night. So you are right, only few people can comprehend esoteric ecumenism. But those few could make it clear for many.

A. A: On the other hand, there seems to be another problem. One might ask: Why God revealed, for instance, the personality of Christ in two very different and even contradictory manners so that Christians and Muslims believe differently?

Hick: ... They have even gone to war over it.

Nasr: This question expands why there is more than one religion. Yes, once you have a plurality of religions, such a plurality can only exist as a result of distinctions among them. If everything were to be identical, there would of course be no plurality. There must be some kind of distinction that makes one religion different from another and which results in plurality. When this is applied to Christianity and Islam, one of the points that becomes clear is that, Christianity had a very different role to perform than Islam. Christianity had to save a world which was dying from rationalism and naturalism. Therefore it had to present itself as the way of love and sacrifice, which provided an answer to several hundred years of sophistic, sceptical philosophy based on excessively cerebral development which was cut off from the imperious Presence of the Divine, as it had existed in the Greek and Roman religions. But they both died and left people in a spiritual desert. As for Islam, it came into a very different world. It did not have to confront solipsists, sophists and rationalist in Mecca. It came to reassert, in fact, the idea of Abrahamic revelation in which Christ also played an important role. That means Christ plays two roles in these different religious worlds. One is the role in Islam in which he comes as the last in the chain of the prophets of the Abrahamic family before the Prophet of Islam and the other is the role of the single saviour of a world which could not be saved in other way.

Hick: Do you not think that if we have that picture of the Ultimate manifesting itself in these different ways these manifestations will not include as absolute truths the elements that cause people to go to war with one another? Do you think they could?

Nasr: They could. And that is something which sages, wise men, try to prevent through their own understanding of other religions. But this fact of going to war has not been so much caused by the religions as by the divisiveness within human nature in which religion has been until now a strong element, and therefore it has taken a religious colour. That is why we observe complicated wars without a religious element in the twentieth century. For example, Hitler did not bomb Birmingham because of Christianity. Nor did the Russians fight with the Chinese for religious reasons. We had so many secular wars during these centuries. The case of Ireland, and of the Arabs and Palestinians, are exceptions. And again, President Bush did not order a war which resulted in deaths of the hundreds of thousand Iraqis for religious reasons. All these emanate from the rebellious and divisive element within human nature.

Hick: I agree. But this divisiveness is very often validated by the absolute claims of religions, is it not?

Nasr: It is a basic reality that the idea of saving human beings is the central concern of various religions. If there had been only one humanity, there would have not been a need for more than one religion. Religions express themselves using different languages. The very existence of different languages in fact confirms the fact that there must be different humanities. There are Chinese, Indian and Icelandic people who are different from the Mediterranean people. I accept that you might say why God was not powerful enough just to create one single humanity and that has its own answer into which I cannot go here. The different religions, I believe, are to confirm the separate existence of various human collectivities. So some Hindus think that they are basing themselves in Hinduism when they kill off Muslims. The attempt to create a Hindu *raj* and destroy Islamic sites and Muslim lives is a tragic consequence, not of Hinduism or Islam but discord that results from the nature of human's belonging to different human collectivities. These differences have also been confirmed by different religions although the universal message of peace is also always present. In any case that is why in our world it is so essential to create a bridge by those who can.

A. A: Professor Hick, are you saying that the religions should get rid of their absolute truth claims?

Hick: No, not their absolute truth claims, but the claims to be the one and the only truth.

Nasr: Yes, I agree on this point one hundred percent.

Hick: You see, in the fourth Gospel Jesus says, 'No man comes to the Father but by me.' And in the Acts of the Apostles St. Peter says, 'There is no other name given under the Heaven whereby man may be saved except the name of Jesus.' Now modern scholarship has shown (you cannot say proved because nothing in this area is strictly provable) it to be overwhelmingly probable that Jesus, the historical Jesus, did not say that. This is the work of a writer about sixty or seventy years later, towards the end of the first century expressing the theology of the Church at that time. Now, if we insist that what Jesus is reported to have said he really did say, and if we say this is the direct manifestation of the Real, then Christianity is the only perfect religion.

Nasr: No. We would also say that the prophet said: *man ra'ani fa qad ra'a al-haqq* (he who sees me alone sees the Lord). Now what do you do with such truth claims? In fact, both of these are really addressed to a particular humanity which is the humanity for that religion. That is how I see it. Christ's saying this is for Christians. It is meant to prevent somebody in the Christian world trying to reach God by circumventing Christ as some are now inventing their own religions in the modern World and trying to reach the Divine without the aid of Jesus. The same is true for Islam. No one can reach God in Islam except through the Blessed Prophet Muhammed.

A. A: How do you see religious pluralism in today's 'global village'?

Nasr: In the global village!.. I don't believe in this metaphor but in any case, I would say, each of these manifestations of the Absolute came into being within a human collectivity which was, for its members, humanity as such. For Confucians, China was the world, it was *the* humanity. When the *maharashis* of India spoke, for them India was the world. I, as a Muslim would accept that no Christians can come to God except through the Son, through Christ – no matter who wrote that sentence. I am not going to get into the debate of the authenticity of this and similar statements since I am not a scholar of the New Testament. But I hope that Christians would also accept the *hadith* of the Prophet which I just quoted for Muslims. You cannot, in the Islamic world, say, 'I do not care about the Prophet. I am reaching God directly' as some modernised Muslims try to talk. Such blasphemy will never work.

Hick: But when I speak of the change or modification of theology I, as a Christian, only have responsibility for Christian thought. The modification I want to make, is to say that 'No one comes to the Father but by me', is true for Christians but it is not true universally.

Nasr: I would do exactly the same thing for Islam.

Hick: Yes, but for many Muslims this would be a modification would it not?

Nasr: In the case of Islam, this is interesting. Throughout history (like these verses which I read from Jala al-Din Rumi in the lecture yesterday) there have been those who asserted that!.. That is why Islam has an easier situation than Christianity.

Hick: Yes, the Sufi element of Islam has always been pluralistic.

Nasr: Islam accepts all the prophets before it. The question of salvation, I mean is universal among Muslims. It is true that if I go to the mosque in Birmingham and say Jews and Christians are also saved like Muslims, some people are going to be unhappy. But throughout history many theologians and Sufis have asserted the view which I uphold. Some people are bigoted and limited in perspective. They cannot understand it. In the case of Christianity, however there is a bigger step that must be taken, as I understand it.

A. A: Professor Hick, how do you understand religious salvation?

Hick: In a word. I understand it as being empty of self and open to the Divine, the Ultimate.

A. A: Is it an 'earthly salvation'?

Hick: It starts on earth, but it is not confined to earth. It leads to the life to come.

A. A: Professor Nasr, how do you understand religious salvation?

Nasr: In the classical Islamic understanding of it, it is said that we have a soul, a substance within us which is immortal and does not perish with death. Experience here in life is very important for it but it is not accidental. It also affects its ultimate destiny. Salvation means to live in such a way, both towards God and towards human beings, and towards the world of nature that at the moment of death, the soul goes to a felicitous state, to a pardisial state, rather than to be tortured in an infernal state. It is in this sense that I understand salvation, not only for Muslims, but also for the followers of other religions.

A. A: In this case, which religion's depiction of salvation is more acceptable?

Nasr: That is a very good question. I believe that what happens to the soul after death is part and parcel of the religious universe of the particular religion which we are speaking about. And that all the traditions concerning eschatology are meaningful within that universe. For example, in the case of the Christian and Islamic paradise, once you reach paradise, you have been saved. In Hinduism you fall out from Paradise when your good *Karma* comes to an end. I would not say that ours is correct and theirs is false or that theirs is correct and ours is false. It is interesting again that in this supreme state of union with God which they well call *moskha*, deliverance, all the religious believers meet. As for what happens in between, in this intermediate world, I think all of the religions are true, it depends upon the rites, the way of burial and sacred rites and practices, some of which are extremely complicated. So I would not say that some of these traditional depictions of eschatological states are correct and some are not. I would say that they are all correct in their own spiritual universe.

A. A: Do you accept such an account of salvation?

Hick: Essentially, yes. I think that what we expect to happen will happen in the intermediate stage, but beyond that is beyond our imaginations.

A. A: If I can put it quite frankly: do you believe in Heaven and Hell?

Hick: Well, it depends what you mean by this. I think the ultimate state may possibly be beyond individual personality altogether. I do not believe that there is eternal torture, but there may conceivably be non-existence.

A. A: Do you believe in Heaven and Hell?

Nasr: Yes, I believe in Heaven and Hell. But all descriptions must be treated symbolically without destroying the literal interpretation and the power it has upon the soul of human beings and through which the vast majority of human beings have been prevented from committing many sins. The power in the vision of Heaven and Hell is described so majestically in the Quran. Working with John Hick, many other Muslim theologians want to decrease the power of the fire of hell! . . For my part, I believe this sort of suffering to be not eternal, but perpetual. These are very different things and can be forgiven by God's grace and by Him alone. As far as Heaven is concerned, it also has many levels; the highest level, which is called *Jannat al-Dhat*, the paradise of Divine Essence, is really beyond all possible conceptualisations and even imagination. But I take the descriptions of Heaven and Hell in the Quran, as well as in other sacred scriptures, very seriously.

A. A: According to you, in what sense can science be a guide to theology?

Nasr: I believe that science teaches nothing about the nature of God and the nature of the Real. During the last few centuries, there has been a remarkable development of modern science. This is certainly the case. In a discussion a short time ago in the US to a number of great scientists and theologians this question was posed. But nobody came out with a positive answer to the question how any discovery of modern science would tell us anything about the nature of God and the nature of the Real. However, modern science has posed very important challenges to theology in the sense that it challenges our view of the universe, and of the world and of human beings. Secondly, it sets part of an agenda for much of theological thought, as it has done throughout the ages and not only in modern times. Both Muslim and Christian theology were often developed in response to the agenda set for them by the science and philosophy of the day, such as Aristotelian cosmology, Pythagoreanism, and all other kinds of different sciences: natural, cosmological and mathematical. But I do not believe that science can guide theology.

Hick: I can agree with that.

Selected Bibliography

A. Primary Sources

i) BOOKS

Akhtar, Shabbir. *A Faith for All Seasons: Islam and Western Modernity.* London: Bellew Publishing, 1990.

Askari, Hasan. *Spiritual Quest: An Inter-Religious Dimension.* Pudsey, West Yorkshire, 1991.

al-'Arabi, Ibn. *The Bezels of Wisdom.* Translated by R. W. J. Austin. London: SPCK, 1980.

Chittick, William. *Ibn al-'Arabi's Metaphysics of Imagination: the Sufi Path of Knowledge.* Albany: State University of New York Press, 1989.

Davis, Caroline Franks. *The Evidential Force of Religious Experience.* Oxford: Clarendon Press, 1989.

D'Costa, Gavin. *John Hick's Theology of Religion: A Critical Evaluation.* London: University Press of America, 1987.

——. *Theology and Religious Pluralism*: Signpost in Theology. Oxford: Basil Blackwell, 1986.

Dewick, E. C. *The Christian Attitude to Other Religions.* Cambridge: Cambridge University Press, 1953.

Gellner, Ernest. *Postmodernism Reason and Religion.* London: Routledge, 1992.

al-Ghazzali, Muhammad Abu Hamid. *Freedom and Fulfilment.* Translated by Richard Joseph McCarty. Boston: Twayne Publishers, 1980.

Hamidullah, Muhammad. *The First Written Constitution in the World.* Lahore: Sh. Muhammad Ashraf, 1968.

Hamnett, Ian, ed. *Religious Pluralism and Unbelief: Studies Critical and Comparative.* London: Routledge, 1990.

Hewitt, Harold Jr. ed. *Problems In the Philosophy of Religion: Critical Studies of the Work of John Hick.* London: Macmillan, 1991.

Hick, John. *The Metaphor of God Incarnate.* London: SCM Press, 1993.

——. *Disputed Questions in Theology and the Philosophy of Religion.* New Haven: Yale University Press, 1993.

——. *An Interpretation of Religion: Human Response to the Transcendent.* London: Macmillan, 1989.

—— and Edmund S. Meltzer, ed. *Three Faiths – One God.* London: Macmillan, 1989.

—— and Paul F. Knitter, ed. *The Myth of Christian Uniqueness.* London: SCM, 1987.

——. *Problems of Religious Pluralism.* London: Macmillan, [1985] 1988.

—— and Hasan Askari. *The Experience of Religious Diversity.* Aldershot and Brookfield: Gower, 1985.

—— and Michael Goulder. *Why Believe in God?* London: SCM Press Ltd., 1983.

——. *God Has Many Names.* London: Macmillan, 1980.

—— and Brain Hebblethwaite, ed, *Christianity and Other Religions.* London: Collins, 1980.

——. ed. *The Myth of God Incarnate.* London: SCM Press, 1977.

——. *Death and Eternal Life.* London: Collins, 1976.

——. ed. *Truth and Dialogue.* London: Sheldon Press, 1974.

——. *God and the Universe of Faiths.* London: Macmillan, [1973] 1988.

——. *Christianity at the Centre.* London: Macmillan, 1968.

——. *The Centre of Christianity.* London: SCM Press Ltd., [1968] 1977.

——. ed. *Faith and the Philosophers.* London: Macmillan, 1964.

——. ed. *The Existence of God.* London and New York: Macmillan, 1964.

——. *Philosophy of Religion.* London: Prentice-Hall, 1963.

——. *Faith and Knowledge.* Glasgow: Collins Fount Paperback, [1957] 1978.

Huxley, Aldous. *The Perennial Philosophy.* London: Fontana Books, [1946] 1958.

Ibn Khaldun, Abu Zayd ibn Muhammad ibn Muhammad. *The Muqaddimah: An Introduction to History.* Translated by Franz Rosental and abridged and edited by N. J. Dawood. London: Routledge and Kegan Paul, [1967] 1987.

Iqbal, Muhammad. *The Reconstruction of Religious Thought in Islam.* Lahore: Sh. Muhammad Ashraf, 1982.

James, William. *The Varieties of Religious Experience: A Study of Human Nature.* London: Collier-Macmillan [1961] 1968.

Lewis, Bernard. *The Jews of Islam.* Princeton: Princeton University Press, 1984.

Mathis, Terry Richard. *Against John Hick: An Examination of his Philosophy of Religion.* London: University Press of America, 1985.

Nasr, Seyyed Hossein. *The Need for a Sacred Science.* London: Curzon Press, 1993.

——. *The Young Muslim's Guide to the Modern World.* Cambridge: Islamic Text Society, [1993] 1994.

——. ed. *Islamic Spirituality: Manifestations.* Vol. 20 of World Spirituality. London: Routledge and Kegan Paul, [1991] 1992.

—— and W. Stoddart. *Religion of the Heart: Essays Presented to Frithjof Schuon on his Eightieth Birthday.* Washington: Foundation for Traditional Studies, 1991.

——. *Muhammad Man of Allah.* London: Muhammadi Trust, 1988.

——. ed. *Islamic Spirituality: Foundations,* Vol. 19 of World Spirituality. London: Routledge and Kegan Paul, [1987] 1992.

275

——. *Traditional Islam in the Modern World.* London: Kegan Paul International, [1987] 1994.

——. *Islamic Art and Spirituality.* London: Golgonooza Press, 1987.

——. ed. *The Essential Writings of Frithjof Schuon.* Rockport: Element Books, [1986] 1991.

——. ed. *Philosophy Literature and Fine Arts: Islamic Education Series.* Kent: Hodder and Stoughton, 1982.

——. *Knowledge and the Sacred.* Albany: State University of New York Press, [1981] 1989.

——. *Islamic Life and Thought.* London: George Allen & Unwin, 1981. William C. Chittick and Peter Zirnis. Vol. II. Tehran: Imperial Iranian Academy of Philosophy, 1978.

——. *Islam and The Plight of Modern Man.* London: Longman, 1975.

——. *An Annotated Bibliography of Islamic Science,* 1975. With the collaboration of William C. Chittick. Vol. I. Tehran: Imperial Iranian Academy of Philosophy, 1975

——. *Sufi Essays.* Albany: State University of New York Press, [1971] 1991.

——. *Man and Nature: the Spiritual Crisis in Modern Man.* London: Mandala Unwin Paperbacks, [1968] 1990.

——. *Science and Civilization in Islam.* Cambridge: Harvard University Press, 1968.

——. *Islamic Studies.* Beirut: Systeco Press, 1967.

——. *Ideals and Realities of Islam.* London: Aquarian, [1966], 1994.

——. *Three Muslim Sages: Avicenna – Suhrawardi – Ibn 'Arabi.* Massachusetts: Harvard University Press, 1964.

——. *An Introduction to Islamic Cosmological Doctrines.* Albany: State University of New York Press, [1964], 1993.

Northbourne, Lord. *Religion in the Modern World.* London: J. M. Dent & Sons Ltd., 1963.

Oman, John. *The Natural and Supernatural.* Cambridge: Cambridge University Press, 1931.

Penelhum, Terence. *Problems of Religious Knowledge.* London: Macmillan, 1971.

Perry, W. N. *A Treasury of Traditional Wisdom.* Cambridge: Quinta Essentia, 1971.

Proudfoot, Wayne. *Religious Experience.* Berkley & London: University of California Press, 1985.

Rahman, Fazlur. *Islam and Modernity: Transformation of an Intellectual Tradition.* Chicago & London: The University of Chicago Press, 1982.

——. *Prophecy in Islam.* London: George Allen & Unwin Ltd., 1957.

Runzo, Joseph, ed. *Is God Real?* London: Macmillan, 1993.

Said, Edward W. *Orientalism: Western Conception of the Orient.* London: Penguin Books, [1978] 1991.

Schuon, Frithjof. *Light on the Ancient Worlds.* London: Perennial Books, 1965.

——. *Understanding Islam.* Translated by D. M. Matheson. London: George Allen & Unvin Ltd., [1963] 1972.

——. *The Transcendent Unity of Religions.* Translated by Peter Townsend. London: Faber and Faber Limited, 1953.

Sharpe, Eric. J. *Comparative Religion: A History.* London: Duckworth, 1975.
Smart, Ninian. *The Religious Experience of Mankind.* Glasgow: Collins Fount Paperbacks, [1969] 1981).
Smith, Huston. *Beyond the Post-Modern Mind.* London: Quest Books, [1982] 1989.
Smith, Wilfred Cantwell. *Towards A World Theology: Faith and the Comparative History of Religion.* London: Macmillan, 1981.
——. *The Meaning and End of Religion.* London: The New American Library, [1961] 1964.
Tessier, Linda J., ed. *Concepts of Ultimate.* London: Macmillan, 1989.
Ward, Keith. *Religion and Revelation: A Theology of Revelation in the World Religions.* Oxford: Clarendon Press, 1994.
Watt, Montgomery W. *Muhammad at Medina.* Oxford: Clarendon Press, [1956] 1977.

ii) ARTICLES

Ahmed, Akbar S. and Hastings Donnan. 'Islam in the Age of Postmodernity,' in *Islam Globalization and Postmodernity,* ed. Akbar S. Ahmed and Hastings Donan, London and New York, Routledge, 1994, 1–20.
Akhtar, Shabbir. 'An Islamic Model of Revelation.' *Islam and Christian-Muslim Relations,* 2 (No. 1, 1991), 95–105.
Aldrich, Amy. 'The Soul and Science of Islam.' *The George Washington University Magazine,* Spring 1992, 15–17.
Aminrazavi, M. 'The Intellectual Contribution of Seyyed Hossein Nasr,' in *Complete Bibliography of the Works of Seyyed Hossein Nasr from 1958 through April 1993,* ed. Mehdi Aminrazavi and Zailan Moris. Kuala Lumpur: Islamic Academy of Science of Malasia, 1994, XIX–XXV.
Apczynski, John. V. 'John Hick's Theocentricism: Revolution or Implicitly Exclusivist?' *Modern Theology,* 8 (No. 1, 1992), 39–52.
Askari, Hasan. 'Within and Beyond the Experience of Religious Diversity,' in *The Experience of Religious Diversity,* ed. John Hick and Hasan Askari. Aldershot and Brookfield: Gower, 1985.
Badham, Paul. 'Life and Work of John Hick,' in *God Truth and Reality: Essays in Honour of John Hick,* ed. Arvind Sharma. London: Macmillan, 1993, 3–5.
——. 'John Hick's *An Interpretation of Religion,*' in *Problems in the Philosophy of Religion: Critical Studies of the Work of John Hick,* ed. Harold Hewitt, Jr. London: Macmillan, 1991, 86–97.
Beckford, James A. 'Religion, Modernity and Post-modernity,' in *Religion: Contemporary Issues,* ed. Bryan Wilson. London: Bellew Publishing, 1992, 11–23.
Bowmen, Len. 'The Status of Conceptual Schemata: A Dilemma for Prennialists.' *A. R. I. E. S.,* 11 (1990), 9–19.
Chittick, William, C. 'Preface' to *The Complete Bibliography of the Works of Seyyed Hossein Nasr from 1958 through April 1993,* ed. Mehdi Aminrazavi and Zailan Moris. Kuala Lumpur: Islamic Academy of Science of Malasia, 1994, XIII–XVIII.

al-Dajani, Ahmad Sidqi. 'Religious Pluralism and its Limits Through History,' in *Religious Pluralism*: Proceedings of the 6th Muslim – Christian Consultation, held in Istanbul (September, 1989), 93–116.

D'Costa, Gavin. 'John Hick and Religious Pluralism: Yet Another Revolution,' in *Problems in the Philosophy of Religion: Critical Studies of the Work of John Hick*, ed. Harold Hewitt, Jr. London: Macmillan, 1991, 3–18.

Dean, Thomas. Review of *Knowledge and the Sacred*, by Seyyed Hossein Nasr. In *Philosophy East and West*, 34 (April 1984), 211–226.

Donovan, Peter. 'The Intolerance of Religious Pluralism.' *Religious Studies*, 29 (June 1993), 217–229.

Eliade, Mircea. 'The Quest for the 'Origin' of Religion.' *History of Religion*, 4 (Part. 1, 1964), 154–169.

Evans, Donald. 'Can Philosophers Limit What Mystics Can Do? A Critique of Steven Katz.' *Religious Studies*, 25 (No. 1, 1989), 53–60.

al-Faruqi, Ismail Raji. 'Towards a Critical World Theology,' in *Towards Islamization of Disciplines*, ed. The International Institute of Islamic Thought. Heindon: The International Institute of Islamic Thought, 1989, 409–453.

Hick, John. 'Trinity and Incarnation in the Light of Religious Pluralism,' in *Three Faiths – One God: A Jewish Christian and Muslim Encounter*, ed. John Hick and Edmund S. Meltzer. London: Macmillan, 1989, 197–210.

——. 'Religious Pluralism,' in *The World's Religious Traditions: Current Perspectives in Religious Studies*, ed. Frank Whaling. Edinburgh: T & T Clark Ltd., 1984, 147–164.

——. 'The Theology of Religious Pluralism.' *Theology*, 86 (September 1983), 335–340.

——. 'Jesus and Mohammad,' in *Islam in a World of Diverse Faiths*, ed. Dan Cohn-Sherbok. London: Macmillan, 1991, 114–118.

——. 'On Grading Religions.' *Religious Studies*, 17 (December 1981), 451–467.

——. 'Discussions: Faith and Coercion.' *Philosophy*, 42 (July 1967), 272–273.

——. 'Sceptics and Believers,' in *Faith and the Philosophers*, ed. John Hick. London: Macmillan, 1964, 235–250.

——'Necessary Being.' *Scottish Journal of Theology*, 14 (December 1961), 353–369.

Isenberg, Sheldon. R. and Gene R. Thursby. 'Esoteric Anthropology: "Devolutionary" and "Evolutionary" Orientations in Perennial Philosophy.' *Religious Traditions: A Journal in the Study of Religion*, 79 (1984–1986), 177–226.

Katz, Steven T. 'Mystical Speech and Mystical Meaning,' in *Mysticism and Language*, ed. S. T. Katz. Oxford: Oxford University Press, 1992, 3–41.

——. 'The 'Conservative' Character of Mystical Experience,' in *Mysticism and Religious Traditions*, ed. Steven T. Katz. Oxford: Oxford University Press, 1983, 3–60.

——. 'Language Epistemology and Mysticism,' in *Mysticism and Philosophical Analysis*, ed. S. T. Katz. London: Sheldon Press, 1978, 22–74.

Kung, Hans. 'Toward a New Consensus in Catholic (and Ecumenical) Theology.' *Journal of Ecumenical Studies*, 17 (1980), 1–17.

Lipner, Julius. 'At the Bend in the Road: A Story about Religious Pluralism,' in *Problems in the Philosophy of Religion: Critical Studies of the Work of John Hick*, ed.Harold Hewitt, Jr. London: Macmillan, 1991, 213–234.

Nasr, Seyyed Hossein. 'Echoes of Infinity: An Interview with Seyyed Hossein Nasr.' Interview by Jeffrey P. Zaleski, *Parabola*, 13 (1988), 24–35.

———. 'Response to Hans Kung's Paper on Christian Muslim Dialogue.' *Muslim World*, 77 (April 1987), 96–105.

———. 'Response to Thomas Dean's review of *Knowledge and Sacred*.' *Philosophy East and West*, 39 (January 1985), 87–90.

———. 'Traditional Cosmology and Modern Science: An Interview with Seyyed Hossein Nasr.' Interview by Philip and Carol Zaleski, *Parabola*, 8 (No. 4, 1983), 20–31.

———. 'A Muslim Reflection on Religion and Theology.' *Journal of Ecumenical Studies*, 17 (1980), 112–120.

———. 'In Quest of the Eternal Sophia,' in *Philosophers Critiques D'eux Memes – Philosophische Selhstbetrachtungen*, ed. Andre Mercier & Suilar Maja. Vol. 6, Bern: Peter Lang, 1980, 109–131.

Netland, Harold A. 'Professor Hick on Religious Pluralism.' *Religious Studies*, 22 (1986), 249–261.

Perret, W. 'John Hick on Faith: A Critique.' *International Journal for Philosophy of Religion*, 15 (No. 12, 1984), 57–66.

Petz, Rebecca. 'Hick and Saints: Is Saint-Production a Valid Test?' *Faith and Philosophy*, 8 (January 1991), 96–103.

Prabhu, Joseph. 'The Road not Taken: A Story about Religious Pluralism, Part 2,' in *Problems in the Philosophy of Religion: Critical Studies of the Work of John Hick*, ed.Harold Hewitt, Jr. (London: Macmillan, 1991), 235–241.

Rispler-Chaim, Vardit. 'There is no Compulsion in Religion (Quran 2,256), Freedom of Religious Belief in the Qur'an.' *The Bulletin of Henry Martyn Institute of Islamic Studies*, 11 (July–December, 1992), 19–32.

Rowe, William L. 'John Hick's Contribution to the Philosophy of Religion,' in *God Truth and Reality*, ed. by Arvind Sharma. London: M. St. Martin's Press, 1993, 18–23.

Runzo, Joseph. 'God, Commitment, and Other Faiths: Pluralism vs. Relativism.' *Faith and Philosophy*, 5 (October 1988), 343–364.

Siddiqi, Muzammil H. 'A Muslim Response to John Hick: Trinity and Incarnation in the Light of Religious Pluralism.' in *Three Faiths – One God: A Jewish Christian and Muslim Encounter*, ed. John Hick and Edmund S. Meltzer. London: Macmillan, 1989, 211–213.

Smart, Ninian. 'Interpretation and Mystical Experience.' *Religious Studies*, 1 (1965), 75–87.

Smith, Huston. Review of *Knowledge and the Sacred*, by S. H. Nasr. *Philosophy, East and West*, 34 (January 1984), 111–113.

Smith, Jane. I. 'Seyyed Hossein Nasr: Defender of the Sacred and Islamic Traditionalism,' in *The Muslims of America*, ed. Yzonne Yazbeck Haddad. Oxford: Oxford University Press, 1991, 80–95.

Smith, Wilfred Cantwell, 'Idolatry: in Comparative Perspective,' in *The Myth of Christian Uniqueness*, ed. John Hick and Paul F. Knitter. London: SCM Press Ltd., 1987, 53–68.

Stoeber, Michael. 'Constructivist Epistemologies of Mysticism: A Critique and A Revision.' *Religious Studies*, 28 (March 1992), 107–116.

Surin, Kenneth. '"A Certain Politics of Speech": "Religious Pluralism" in the Age of the McDonald's Hamburger.' *Modern Theology*, 7 (October 1990), 67–100.

——. 'Towards a "Materialist" Critique of "Religious Pluralism": An Examination of the Discourse of John Hick and Wilfred Cantwell Smith,' in *Religious Pluralism and Unbelief: Studies Critical and Comparative*, ed. Ian Hamnett. London: Routledge, 1990, 114–129.

Vahiduddin, Syed. 'Islam and Diversity of Religions.' *Islam and Christian Muslim Relations*, 1 (No. 1 1990), 3–11.

Ward, Keith. 'Truth and the Diversity of Religions.' *Religious Studies*, 26 (March 1990), 1–18.

Zaki, Yaqub, 'The Quran and Revelation,' in *Islam in a World of Diverse Faiths*, ed. Dan Cohn-Sherbok. London: Macmillan, 1991, 41–54.

B. Secondary Sources

i) BOOKS

Affifi, A. E. *The Mystical Philosophy of Muhyid Din-Ibnul Arabi*. Lahore: Sh. Muhammad Ashraf, 1971.

Ali, Abdullah Yusuf. *The Qur'an: Text, Translation and Commentary*. Maryland: Amana Corporation, 1989.

Almond, Philip C. *Heretic and Hero: Muhammad and the Victorians*. Wiesbeden: Otto Harrassowitz, 1989.

Arnold, T. W. *The Preaching of Islam: A History of Propagation of the Muslim Faith*. Lahore: Sh. Muhammad Ashraf, 1961.

Armstrong, Karen. *A History of God*. London: Mandarin, 1993.

Ahmad, Barakat. *Muhammad and the Jews: A Re-examination*. New Delhi: Vikas Publishing House Pvt Ltd, 1979.

Bayer, Peter. *Religion and Globalization*. London: Sage Publications, 1994.

Berkes, Niyazi. *The Development of Secularism in Turkey*. Montreal: McGill University Press, 1964.

Blaise, Pascal. *Pensées*. London: J. M. Dent & Sons Ltd., 1931.

al-Bukhari, Muhammad bin Ismail bin Ibrahim al-Mughra, *Sahih al-Bukhari*. Beirut: Dar al-Arabia, 1985.

Brierley, Peter. *'Christian' England: What the 1989 English Church Census Reveals*. London: March Europe, 1991.

Carey, George. *God Incarnate*. Leicester: Inter-Varsity Press, 1977.

Clarke, Peter. B. and Peter Byrne, *Religion Defined and Explained*. London: St. Martin's Press, 1993.

Clayton, John. *Thomas Jefferson and the Study of Religion*. Inaugural Lecture delivered at Lancaster University, 1992.

Cobb, John. *Beyond Dialogue: Towards a Mutual Transformation of Christianity and Buddhism*. Philadelphia, Fortress Press, 1982.

Corbin, Henri. *Creative Imagination in the Sufism of Ibn 'Arabi*. Translated by Ralph Manheim. Princeton: Princeton University Press, 1969.

Crawford, Robert. *The Saga of God Incarnate*. Pretoria: University of South Africa, 1988.

Cupitt, Don. *Taking Leave of God*. London: SCM Press, 1980.

Durkheim, Emile. *The Elementary Forms of the Religious Life*. Translated by Joseph Ward Swain. London: George Allen & Unwin Ltd [1915] 1971.

Farquhar, John N. *The Crown of Hinduism*. Oxford: Oxford University Press, 1930.

Freeman, Anthony. *God in Us: A Case for Christian Humanism*, (London: SCM Press, 1993.

Goulder, Michael, ed. *Incarnation and Myth: The Debate Continued*. London: SCM Press, 1979.

Graham, William A. *Divine Word and Prophetic Word in Early Islam*. Paris: Mouton & The Hague, 1977.

Green, Michael, ed. *The Truth of God Incarnate*. London: Hodder & Stoughton, 1977.

Hammond, Phillip. *Religion and Personal Autonomy: The Third Disestablishment in America*. Columbia, South Carolina: University of South Carolina Press, 1992.

Hartshorne, Charles. *Anselm's Discovery*. La Salle, Illinois: Open Court, 1965.

Harvey, A. E., ed. *God Incarnate: Story and Belief*. London: SPCK, 1981.

Hocking, William. *Re-thinking Missions*. New York: Harper & Row, 1932.

Izutsu, Toshihiko. *The Concept of Belief in Islamic Theology: A Semantic Analysis of Iman and Islam*. Yokohama: Yurindo Publishing Co. Ltd., 1965.

———. *A Comparative Study of the Key Philosophical Concepts in Sufism and Lao-tzu, Chuang-tzu*. Tokyo: The Keio Institude of Cultural and Linguistic Studies, 1966.

Knitter, Paul F. *No Other Name? A Critical Survey of Christian Attitudes Toward the World Religions*. London: SCM Press, 1985.

Kraemer, Hendrick. *Religion and Christian Faith*. London: Lutterworth Press, 1956.

———. *The Christian Message in a Non-Christian World*. London: Edinburgh House Press, 1938.

Landau, Rom. *The Philosophy of Ibn 'Arabi*. London: George Allen & Unwin Ltd, 1959.

Lloyd, A. C. *The Anatomy of Neoplatonism*. Oxford: Clarendon Press, 1990.

MacDonald, Durston R. *The Myth/Truth of God Incarnate*. Wilton, Connecticut: Barlow, 1979.

Masuzawa, Tomoko. *In Search of Dreamtime: The Quest for the Origin of Religion*. Chicago & London: The University of Chicago Press, 1993.

Merlan, Philip. *From Platonism to Neoplatonism*. Netherlands: The Hague, 1975.

Morris, Thomas V. *The Logic of God Incarnate*. New York: Cornell University Press, 1986.

Nielsen, Jorgen. *Muslims in Western Europe*. Edinburgh: Edinburgh University Press, 1992.

Otto, Rudolf. *The Idea of the Holy*. London: Oxford University Press, [1923] 1952.

———. *Mysticism East and West: A Comparative Analysis of the Nature of Mysticism.* London: Macmillan, 1932.

Phillips, Dawi Z. *Death and Immortality.* London: Macmillan, 1970.

Plantinga, Alvin. *The Nature of Necessity; God and Other Minds: A Study of the Rational Justification of Belief in God.* Ithaca and London: Cornell University Press, 1976.

———. *The Nature of Necessity.* Oxford: Clarendon Press, 1974.

———. *God, Freedom and Evil.* Michigan: Wiliam B. Werdmans, [1974] 1977.

Redfield, Robert. *The Little Community and Peasant Society and Culture.* Chicago & London: Phoenix Books, The University of Chicago Press, [1956] 1963.

Rumi, Jalalu'ddin. *Divan-i Shamsi Tabriz.* Translated by R. A. Nicholson. Cambridge: Cambridge University Press, 1898.

Sardar, Z. *Exploration in Islamic Science.* London: Mansel, 1989.

Shahrastani, Abd al-Karim. *Kitab Nihayet al-Iqdam fi 'Ilm al-Kalam.* Edited and translated by Alfred Guillaume. London: Oxford University Press, 1934.

Sherry, Patrick. *Philosophers on Religion: A Historical Reader.* London: Geoffrey Chapman, 1987.

———. *Spirit, Saints and Immortality.* London: Macmillan, 1984.

Smart, Ninian. *Beyond Ideology: Religion and the Future of Western Civilization.* London: Collins, 1981.

———. *The Phenomenon of Religion.* London & Oxford: Mowbrays, [1973] 1978.

Stace, W. T. *Philosophy and Mysticism.* London: Macmillan, 1960.

Swinburne, Richard. *Faith and Reason.* Oxford: The Clarendon Press, 1981.

———. *The Existence of God.* Oxford: Clarendon Press, 1979.

al-Tabari, Muhammad bin Jarir. *Jami' al-Bayan an Ta'wil al-Quran.* Cairo: Dar al-Ma'arif, 1954.

Toynbee, Arnold. *Christianity Among the Religions of the World.* New York: Scribners, 1957.

Underhill, Evelyn. *The Life of the Spirit and the Life of To-day.* London: Methuen and Co. Ltd., [1922] 1928.

———. *The Essentials of Mysticism and Other Essays.* London & Toronto: J. M. Dent & Sons Ltd., 1920.

———. *Practical Mysticism: A Little Book for Normal People.* London & Toronto: J. M. Dent & Sons Ltd., [1914] 1931.

———. *Mysticism: A Study in the Nature and Development of Man's Spiritual Consciousness.* London: Methuen & Co. Ltd., [1911] 1930.

Waines, David. *An Introduction to Islam.* Cambridge: Cambridge University Press, 1995.

Wallis, Richard Tyrell. *Neoplatonism.* London: Duckworth, 1972.

Watt, W. Montgomery. *Free Will and Human Destination in Early Islam.* London: Luzac & Company Ltd., 1948.

Weil, Simone. *Gravity and Grace.* Translated by Emma Craufurd. London: Routledge and Kegan Paul, 1952.

———. *On Science, Necessity, and Love of God.* Translated and Edited by Richard Rees. London: Oxford University Press, 1968.

———. *Waiting on God.* Translated by Emma Craufurd. London: Collins Fontana Books, [1951] 1959.

Wensick, A. J. *The Muslim Creed: Its Genesis and Historical Development.* London: Frank Cass & Co. Ltd., 1965.

Wittgenstein, Ludwig. *Philosophical Investigations.* Oxford: Basil Blackwell, [1953] 1968.

Zaehner, Robert Charles. *Mysticism: Sacred and Profane.* Oxford: Oxford University Press, [1957] 1961.

ii) ARTICLES

Almond, Philip. 'John Hick's Copernican Theology.' *Theology*, 86 (January 1983), 36–41.

Arias, Juan. 'Hans Kung: Seeking A Religious Dialogue in a World That Lacks Values,' in *Leonardo the Age of Discoveries*, 1992.

Basinger, David 'Hick's Religious Pluralism and 'Reformed Epistemology': A Middle Ground.' *Faith and Philosophy*, 5 (October 1988), 421–432.

Byrne, Peter. 'John Hick's Philosophy of World Religions.' *Scottish Journal of Theology*, 35 (August 1982) 289–301.

Cohn-Sherbok, Dan. 'Ranking Religions.' *Religious Studies*, 22 (1986), 377–386.

——. 'Incarnation and Trialogue,' in *Islam in a World of Diverse Faiths*, ed. Dan Cohn-Sherbok. London: Macmillan, 1991, 18–32.

D'Costa, Gavin. 'The New Missionary: John Hick and Religious Plurality.' *International Bulletin of Missionary Research*, 15 (April 1991), 66–69.

——. 'Elephants, Ropes and a Christian Theology of Religions.' *Theology*, 88 (July 1985), 259–268.

——. 'John Hick's Copernican Revolution: Ten Years After.' *New Blackfriars*, 65 (July-August 1984), 323–331.

Duff-Forbes, D. R. 'Hick, Necessary Being, and the Cosmological Argument.' *Canadian Journal of Philosophy*, 1 (June 1972), 473–483.

Finke, Roger. 'An Unsecular America,' in *Religion and Modernization: Sociologist and Historian Debate the Secularization Thesis*, ed. Steve Bruce. Oxford: Clarendon Press, 1992, 145–169.

Gimello, Robert M. 'Mysticism in Its Contexts,' in *Mysticism and Religious Traditions*, ed. Steven T. Katz. Oxford: Oxford University Press, 1983, 61–88.

Hartshorne, Charles. 'John Hick on Ontological and Logical Necessity.' *Religious Studies*, 13 (June 1977), 155–165.

——. 'The Formal Validity and the Real Significance of the Ontological Argument.' *Philosophical Review*, 53 (May 1944), 225–245.

Heim, Mark. 'The Pluralistic Hypothesis, Realism, and Post-eschatology.' *Religious Studies*, (June 1992), 207–219.

Henze, Donald F. 'Faith, Evidence and Coercion.' *Philosophy*, 42 (January 1967), 78–85.

Hick, John 'A Response to Gerard Loughlin.' *Modern Theology*, 7 (October, 1990), 57–66.

——. 'The Christology of D. M. Ballie.' *Scottish Journal of Theology*, 11 (No. 1, 1958), 1–12.

Hobsbawm, Eric. 'Introduction: Inventing Traditions,' in *The Invention of Tradition*, ed. Eric Hobsbawm and Terence Ranger. Cambridge: Cambridge University Press, [1983] 1987, 1–14.

Hunt, Anne. 'No Other Name? A Critique of Religious Pluralism.' *Pacifica*, 3 (February 1990), 45–60.

Kellenberger, J. 'The Slippery Slope of Religious Relativism.' *Religious Studies*, 21 (March 1985), 39–52.

Lipner, J. J. 'Does Copernicus Help? Reflection for A Christian Theology of Religions.' *Religious Studies*, 13 (June 1977), 243–258.

Loughlin, Gerard. 'Prefacing Pluralism: John Hick and the Mastery of Religion.' *Modern Theology*, 7 (October, 1990), 29–66.

Louw, Dirk J. 'Theocentrism and Reality-centrism: a Critique of John Hick and Wilfred Cantwell Smith's Philosophy of Religion.' *South African Journal of Philosophy*, 13 (Part:1, 1994), 1–8.

Malcolm, N. 'Anselm's Ontological Arguments' *Philosophical Review*, 69 (January 1960), 41–62.

McKim, Robert. 'Could God Have More Than One Nature?' *Faith and Philosophy*, 5 (October 1988), 378–398.

Miller, Barry. 'The No-Evidence Defence.' *International Journal for Philosophy of Religion*, 3 (Spring 1972), 44–50.

Nasr, Seyyed Hossein. 'Islam and Environmental Crises.' *The Islamic Quarterly*, 34 (No. 4, 1990), 217–234.

——. 'The Prayer of the Heart in Hesychasm and Sufism.' *Greek Orthodox Theological Review* (Sp-Summer 1986), 195–203.

——. 'The Role of the Traditional Science in the Encounter of Religion and Science: An Oriental Perspective.' *Religious Studies*, 20 (December 1984), 519–541.

——. 'Ibn Sina's Fourth Ontological Argument for God's Existence.' *The Muslim World*, 74 (July 1984), 161–171.

——. 'Reflection on Islam and Modern Thought.' *Studies in Comparative Religion*, 15 (Part. 3-4, 1983), 164–176.

——. 'The Relation Between Sufism and Philosophy in Persian Culture.' *Hamdard Islamicus*, 6 (Winter 1883), 33–47.

——. 'Progress and Evolution: A Reappraisal from Traditional Perspective.' *Parabola*, 6 (Part 2, 1981), 44–51.

——. 'Metaphysics Poetry and Logic in Oriental Traditions.' *Sophia Perennis*, 3 (Autumn 1977), 119–128.

——. 'The Complementarity of Contemplation and Action in Islam.' *Main Currents in Modern Thought*, 30 (November-December 1973), 64–68.

——. 'Mulla Sadra and the Doctrine of the Unity of Being.' *Philosophical Forum*, (Fall, 1973), 153–161.

——. 'Conditions for Meaningful Comparative Philosophy.' *Philosophy East and West* (January 1972), 53–61.

——. 'Post-Avicennan Islamic Philosophy and Study of Being.' *International Philosophical Quarterly*, 17 (September 1972), 265–271.

——. 'Who is Man? The Perennial Answer of Islam.' *Studies in Comparative Religion*, 2 (1968), 45–56.

——. 'Shihab al-Din Suhrawardi Maqtul,' in *A History of Muslim Philosophy*. Wiesbaden: Otto Harrassowitz, 1963.

Nielsen, Kai. 'Truth Conditions and Necessary Existence.' *Scottish Journal of Theology*, 27 (August 1974), 257–267.

Robertson, Ronald. 'Globalization, Politics and Religion,' in *The Changing Face of Religion*, ed. James A. Beckford and Thomas Luckmann. London: Sage Publication, 1989, 10–23.

——. 'Globalization, Modernization, and Postmodernization: The Ambiguous Position of Religion,' in *Religion and Global Order*, ed. Ronald Robertson and William R. Garret. New York: Paragon House Publishers, 1991, 281–291.

Raschid, Muhammad Saman. 'Philosophia Perennis Universale Imperium.' *Religion*, 13 (April 1983), 155–171.

Roth, John K. 'Reply: Can John Hick Say What He Said?' in *Concept of the Ultimate*, ed. Linda J. Tessier. London: Macmillan, 1989, 159–162.

Shaw, Patrick. 'On Worshipping the Same God.' *Religious Studies*, 28 (December 1992), 511–532.

Simpson, John H. 'Globalization and Religion: Themes and Prospects,' in *Religion and Global Order*, ed. Ronald Robertson and William R. Garret. New York: Paragon House Publishers, 1991, 1–17.

Turner, Harold W. 'Historical Support for Pluralism? The 'The Copernican Revolution' Re-visited.' *Mission Studies*, 8 (Part. 1 1991), 72–92.

Twiss, Summer B. 'The Philosophy of Religious Pluralism: A Critical Appraisal of Hick and His Critics.' *The Journal of Religion*, 70 (October 1990), 533–568.

Verkamp, Bernard J. 'Hick's Interpretation of Religious Pluralism' *International Journal for Philosophy of Religion*, 30 (October 1991), 103–124.

Vroom, Hendrik M. 'Do All Religious Traditions Worship the Same God?' *Religious Studies*, 26 (March 1990), 73–90.

Index

Index

Husaini, S. A. Q. 243
Huxley, Aldous 43, 83, 220, 232

Ibn 'Arabi xiii, 18, 65, 66, 89, 129,
   142, 143, 144, 154, 155, 164,
   182, 187, 212, 243, 245, 246
Ibn Hazm 187
Ibn Khaldun 66, 68, 70, 71, 73, 227,
   228
Ibn Rushd 223
Ibn Sina 18, 41, 42, 69, 154, 223,
   247
Ibn Taymiyya 69, 71, 226
Inclusivism, xi
Iqbal, Muhammad 227
Isaac 171, 184, 185
Isenberg, S. R. 44, 220, 233
Islam, ix, xiv, 4, 5, 7, 11, 33, 51, 52,
   53, 65, 71, 99, 100, 101, 102,
   106, 117, 128, 129, 130, 133,
   146, 148, 150, 157, 165, 167,
   171, 172, 173, 183, 184, 185,
   186, 187, 188, 189, 190, 191,
   201, 202, 203, 228, 251
Islamic Cosmology, 19
Islamic Science, 19
Ishmael, 171
Izutsu, Toshihiko 223, 243

Jacob 171, 184
James, William 5, 6, 29, 61, 62, 155,
   209, 21
jazba 64
Jesus 3, 4, 107, 165, 171, 172, 177,
   180, 183, 184, 185, 190, 203,
   205, 226, 249, 250
Judaism 4, 7, 50, 65, 91, 92, 98, 104,
   117, 129, 133, 139, 140, 146,
   148, 157, 165, 171, 172, 185,
   191, 193, 203, 210
al-Jurjani, S. S. 215

Kabbalah 50
Kant, Immanuel xiii, 3, 5, 6, 56, 61,
   120, 134, 136, 137
kashf 64
Katz, Steven T. 82, 83, 227, 230,
   231
Kellenberger, James 224, 245

Knitter, Paul xi, 207, 211
Küng, Hans 207, 256

Landau, R. 243
Laughlin, G. 244
Lewis, Bernard 191, 253
Lings, Martin 17
Lipner, Julius J. 236, 245
Lloyd, A. C. 230
Louw, D. J. 211
Luckmann, T. 234
Luther, Martin 249

MacDonald, D. R. 250
MacLaine, S. 73
MacKim, R. 245
al-Maraghi, S. 253
Marsiglio, F. 22
Marx, Karl 121
Massignon, Louis 17
Masuzawa, Tomoko 214
Mathis, Terry Richard 209
maya 160, 169
Meltzer, E. S. 251
Mesle, C. R. 210
Merlan, P. 230
Meyerson, E. 14
Miller, Barry 224
Moerbeke, W. 22
Moris, Zeylan 211
Morris, T. V. 250
Moses 36, 185, 190, 226
Muhammed, 33, 34, 38, 66, 73,
   143, 183, 184, 190, 194, 196,
   198, 211, 217, 226
Mulla Sadra 21
Mu'tazila 59
Müller, F. M. 28, 29, 31, 36, 215,
   218

Nasr, Seyyed Hossein passim; on
   Christianity 202–6; on God as
   Reality 151–7, as Ultimate 157–8;
   on knowledge 77–88, 90–7; on
   religion and change 40, religious
   pluralism 164–70 on tradition
   48–54
Nasr, Seyyed Valiollah 211
National Front 8